The Castle Chapel

THE

CASTLE CHAPEL.

A Romantic Tale.

—◆—

IN THREE VOLUMES.

BY

REGINA MARIA ROCHE,

AUTHOR OF THE

CHILDREN OF THE ABBEY; BRIDAL OF DUNAMORE; CLERMONT; DISCARDED
SON; HOUSES OF OSMA AND ALMERIA; MUNSTER COTTAGE BOY;
TRADITION OF THE CASTLE; TRECOTHICK BOWER; MAID
OF THE HAMLET; VICAR OF LANSDOWNE, &c.

VOL. I.

>>>●◀◀◀

LONDON:

PRINTED FOR
A. K. NEWMAN AND CO. LEADENHALL-STREET.

1825.

223

THE
CASTLE CHAPEL.

CHAPTER I.

" With awe-struck thought and pitying tears,
  I view that noble, stately dome,
Where *Ulster's* kings of other years,
  Fam'd heroes! had their royal home:
Alas! how chang'd the times to come!
  Their royal name low in the dust—
Their hapless race wild, wand'ring roam—
  Though rigid law cries out—'twas just!"

IN the province of Ulster, on a commanding eminence, stands the ancient castle of St. Doulagh's: at some distance it appears only a shapeless mass, but on a nearer approach, assumes a more distinct

form, and presents an assemblage highly
grand and picturesque. We shall not attempt a particular description of its numerous outworks, or fortifications, but content ourselves with simply stating, that
these majestic ruins cover a considerable
space of ground, the walls enclosing two
spacious courts, to which a Gothic portal
forms the entrance, flanked by two mas-
sive towers, and secured by a portcullis.

The great extent of the building, the
grandeur and size of the apartments, give
strong proof of kingly magnificence and
hospitality, such as, according to tradition,
in former days it was famed for, when
the residence of its just and regal posses-
sors. The state hall alone would have
been sufficient to bear evidence to this,
from the grandeur of its dimensions, and
the vestiges of ancient hospitality it still
retained.

From the summit of the hill on which
the castle of St. Doulagh's stands, falls
a noble torrent, because mighty in force,
which, dashing in its course over project-

ing rocks, stumps of old oaks, and ash-
trees, which grow out of clefts in the side
of the hill, causes a thick spray to spread
around, to a great height and distance, as
the water dashes from precipice to precipice, down a descent of several hundred
feet, when, forming a basin of great extent at the foot of the eminence, after reposing therein for some time, it takes its
course to the left, through a rich, luxuri-
ant vale, winding and serpentining through
flowery meadows, corn-fields, and clumps
of trees, in a deep, smooth channel, or
foaming and tossing amongst a bed of
broken rocks, as the vale rises or sinks in
gentle elevation, until it is lost amongst
hills, dotted with rural dwellings, monas-
tic ruins, and lofty woods, behind which
rise, in grand succession, yet more lofty
hills and gigantic mountains, which, com-
bining the varieties of light and shade, vie
in contrast and singularity of romantic
beauty, in colour and form: whilst to the
right the vale is closed in by hills, man-

tled with wood, some swelling in elegant
modulation, backed by others which rise
more wildly, until the eye is lost amidst
the gloom and irregularities of gigantic
mountains that bound the horizon. At
the rear of the hill on which stands the
castle, ranges of mountains rise in succession, until lost in the clouds, sprinkled
with trees, and traversed by torrents.

No general description can give an adequate idea of such scenery, because so
great a similarity must appear; but this is
by no means the case when viewed in
reality, Nature still presenting us with a
different aspect, and from rocks, woods,
and water, forming endless combinations.
In short, from its mountainous situation,
the depth and profound gloom of its scattered woods, the noise of its waterfalls,
and the thinness of the neighbourhood, nothing could be more romantic or impressive than the scenery about St. Doulagh's.

In this interesting because ancient fortress, the only descendant of the royal
house of O'Neil had taken shelter from

" the storms of wintry time," and awaited
the coming of that " unbounded spring
that shall encircle all." O'Neil, from whom
lieutenant O'Shaughnessy O'Neil was a
lineal descendant, in defiance of the whole
force of the English, kept his station as
king of Ulster, in his ancient castle of St.
Doulagh's, down to the sixteenth century,
as his coins, dated fifteen hundred and
thirty-five, make plainly to appear; but
as all human things must have an end,
this great Irish monarch lost his power
about the time that his holiness the pope
lost his over Henry the Eighth, at which
period this defender of the faith ravished
the castle of St. Doulagh's, and its rich domains, from the rightful possessor, and bestowed them on a creature of his own.

Thus stripped unjustly of their birth-
right, O'Neil's descendants became scattered about the country: one, however,
still contrived, amongst his vassals and retainers, to keep up a rank in society suitable to the royal house from which he
sprung: but this branch was finally des-

tined to experience again the oppression of England, through the medium of Oliver Cromwell, who, seizing on what had been retained by them of the original property of the family, banished them, with many others, into the comparatively wild and uncivilized province of Connaught, where, in place of their goodly lands, they were assigned waste, sterile spots, on the sides of bleak and rugged mountains; but this was the policy of Oliver, to break and crush down the spirit of all whom he thought capable of resisting his usurpation; he was jealous of all who seemed likely to oppose him; and thus driving them into this district, had square castles built about it, for the purpose of hemming in these unfortunate *Milesians.*

There is particularly blended in the human composition a consoling aptitude to hope, capable of supporting us under almost all afflictions: for this none perhaps are more remarked than the Irish; no sooner is one door shut against them, than their lively imaginations open another. This was the case in the present instance; these oppressed people fully calculated on the retrieval of all they had lost, the moment Cromwell left the kingdom; but his unremitting vigilance defeated this expectation; and when, on the restoration of monarchy, they applied for the recovery of what he had robbed them of, to their utter confusion and disappointment, they were informed that the *law* considered his grants too firmly established to be shaken.

Barren and bare as their *new* possessions were, still, in course of time, the descendants of the original Irish managed not only to involve themselves in debt, but to part with most part of their lands to strangers. Of this number was the father of lieutenant O'Shaughnessy O'Neil—so that when the poor boy, on the death of his parents, came to look about him, all he found himself actual heir to, was about twenty acres of bog, on the top of one of the Cunnamara Mountains; and to heighten the melancholy circumstance, without.

his being able to discover, either to the right or the left, any friend to serve him; not certainly from there not being many who had the inclination to do so, but from all with whom he was either connected or acquainted being left in no better plight than he was himself. An attentive observer might indeed fairly have thought that there was a competition amongst the families here, to see which would be the soonest ruined, so wild and inconsiderate in general was their conduct; but to close the door against any one, was a meanness which none could permit themselves to be guilty of, how inconvenient so ever it might be to keep a *caravansary*, as in those days a gentleman's house in this quarter might be considered, a traveller having only to look about him, to consider where he should like to stop, to immediately quarter himself according to his fancy.

How O'Shaughnessy O'Neil managed to get on we know not, except through the immediate assistance of *Him* " who tempers the wind to the shorn lamb," and has especially declared himself the friend of the orphan; that he did so, however, in some way or other, was evident, from his attaining the rank of lieutenant in the navy, on the half-pay of which, soon after the termination of the war, he returned to his native country, after many years of hard service. Two children, a boy and a girl, accompanied him, his offspring by an English lady, who lost her life in bringing the latter into the world, and who, had she lived, would have proved an invincible obstacle to his seeing his native land again, from the terror with which she had been inspired by the exploits of captain Rock's men.

He returned to it, with an intention of settling, if possible, near the seat of his renowned ancestors; this being the case, with what delight did he find that he might obtain a residence in the castle itself! It had for some time been untenanted; and the person into whose hands it had fallen evidently proving he set no value on the venerable pile, from not only grudging, though immensely rich, to expend a sixpence to keep it in repair, but allowing depredations to be committed on it, to save expence about other places, it was suggested to the lieutenant, that for a comparative trifle he might obtain possession of it—a suggestion which he accordingly lost no time in acting upon; and, to his unutterable satisfaction, shortly found himself its purchaser, with about ten acres of land, immediately adjoining the building.

This business was no sooner accomplished, than his only sister, Miss Agnes Flora Judith, came to take up her abode with him, as had been previously agreed on whenever he should be settled, for the purpose of managing his establishment, and educating his children. For this *latter* office she was infinitely better calculated than the former, neither her education, habits, or pursuits, having been of a feminine description. She was now up-

wards of forty, and almost from her infancy to this period, had resided solely
with a maternal uncle, a minister of the
dissenting church, who, either from conceiving her possessed of extraordinary abilities, or else to gratify a whim, had given
her an education more suitable to the opposite sex than hers, to the utter neglect
of those acquirements absolutely indispensable to a female, at least of a middling
rank in life. Hence poor Miss Agnes
Flora Judith (for having been called after
three great-aunts, all equally great and
distinguished in her estimation, she would
not, for the world, have had one of her
names omitted) often found herself exposed to very serious inconveniences; but
for all which she still conceived she was
fully compensated by the admiration her
extraordinary attainments for a female inspired; but whether this was not quite so
great as she persuaded herself, or that she
possessed nothing else to be admired for,
she found herself advancing in life, to her

equal wonder and disappointment, without a change of name.

This disappointment, however, had not that effect upon her which it has been sometimes known to produce upon the female temper; hasty, and even obstinate, she might be termed, but to any thing like peevishness or ill-will, she was an utter stranger. Her disposition was, if possible, still more excellent than her temper; through her overweening opinion of herself, however, and ignorance of life, she often did mischief where she wished and intended to render a service; and notwithstanding her amiable qualities, was the laugh and ridicule of many, from her eccentric habits, and the oddity of her manner.

If her brother did not regard her as a superior being, he certainly did as a wonderful creature from her learning, his own being confined to what he had acquired on board ship: in his way, however, he was equally satisfied with himself; he was aware that no one knew their profession

better than he did—that he was a loyal
subject, and a true friend to the established church—and conceived, that there was
no one who could say all this, but what
had a right to think well of themselves.

In disposition alone this brother and
sister resembled each other, being equally
generous and compassionate; but in every
other respect they differed, often acting as
antipodes to each other—she frequently
only going to bed when he was rising,
and he often thinking of repose when she
was only getting up. She declaimed a-
gainst church and state, being a Whig in
politics, and a Methodist in religion;
while he would have considered it high
treason to speak against either one or the
other. He was fond of old systems—she
delighted in new ones; a new plan, or
idea, no matter how extravagant it seemed, had her immediate sanction, from the
additional opportunities, as she said, it afforded the human mind of evincing its
comprehensiveness, and the encouragement she conceived due to whatever ex-

ercised the faculties: he was fond of quiet
discussions, she of argument—particularly
if she met with an opponent she thought
worthy of contending with. Her chief
pleasure, however, was derived from study,
and her highest pride and ambition, now
that personal vanity had a little subsided,
of which, notwithstanding her alleged su-
periority to the generality of her sex, she
had not been without her share, to be considered a woman of uncommon attainments.

But much as they differed with regard
to education, habits, and opinions, they
were still most sincerely attached to each
other. On one point, however, they perfectly agreed—that of their attachment to
the children. This, however, as might
naturally be supposed, from their different
way of thinking, was displayed in rather
a different manner by them. To inspire
them with a thirst for knowledge, render
them virtuous and religious, and cultivate
a taste for polite literature, were the proofs
of affection offered by the aunt; while the

father's consisted in furnishing them with opportunities for play, and contriving a musement for them.

The interruption this occasioned to their studies, and the romping habits it gave her niece, frequently gave rise to no slight disputations between the brother and sister. She could not deny, however, that he had a right to some interference about Eugene, and accordingly particular hours in the day were at length settled for his being given up to him.

In consequence of this arrangement, he had him out at an early hour in the morning in the fields, for the purpose of instructing him in all exercises calculated to improve muscular strength, and render the lad bold, active, and enterprising; and by which Eugene so much profited, that, while yet a mere child, he could clamber, with all the dexterity and fearlessness of a squirrel, to the top of the tallest tree, and swim, play ball, and hurl, with almost any one in the parish. Thus, while his mind was improved and enlightened by his aunt, his body was strengthened, his nerves braced, and manly habits acquired, through means of his father.

The methods pursued for this purpose were not such, however, as by any means to meet the approbation of Miss Agnes Flora Judith, from the danger with which she conceived they were attended to the boy.

"Now, Eugene," the father was in the habit of saying, on getting him to a particular spot, " we must commence the business of the day ; still remembering, that what I have taught you, and am still intent on teaching you, will be of more real service to you, than all the outlandish lingo your aunt is cramming your head with ; not but that, in its way, it may, at some time or other, be serviceable, for in the navy," the profession to which he had destined him, from conceiving it the first in the world, " there is no knowing the out of the way coast on which we may be tossed ; so clap this here pistol in your belt, and mount to the topmost head of yonder oak, whence, if you can discern Nell Tierney's cabin in the distance, you are immediately to discharge it, in signal of an enemy's vessel being in sight, and then hasten down, to prepare for the attack."

On these orders being obeyed, and Eugene's return to what his father chose to call the deck, he was commanded to load a swivel, and fire away without intermission, at the opposite side of the lake, on which these supposed engagements always took place, till the signal was given of the vessel having struck, when with loud huzzas at their imagined victory, he was paraded back to the castle, to be resigned, for a few hours, to the more serious instructions of his aunt.

It so happened, however, that, in the order of attack, or hurry to commence it, he more than once fell into the lake, and had a tumble from the tree; which accidents so alarmed his aunt, that she at length began a serious remonstrance with the lieutenant, on the subject of the dan-

ger to which he was exposing him by his
conduct, protesting, if he continued to encourage him in such exploits, she had not
a doubt he would be the means of his losing an eye, or getting a fever, or breaking his neck.

But the amusement derived by the lieutenant from his plan was too great to
permit her arguments to be of any avail.
—" Pooh, pooh! it is a sign you are a woman," he said, " or you would not speak
in such a manner; lose an eye, indeed! no
great danger of that—and if he did, what
then? why there was more than twenty
sailors on board the Royal George, that had
but one apiece, and they were the very
best hands on board: then as to falling
from the mast-head, in the field, and breaking his neck, that is morally impossible,
except the ship heeled too greatly in a
storm, seeing I have taught him to hold
both by legs and arms; and as to being
drowned, why, with all your learning,
Agnes, I am sure you should know that
all animals learn how, from nature, to

swim; and this being the case, how the deuce is there any danger of any one's sinking."

The kind of education he received early gave something of peculiarity to the character of Eugene: from his father he acquired a thirst for enterprise, that rendered exploits of danger, of all others, the most pleasing to him; from his aunt a sovereign contempt for trade, and an enthusiastic love of liberty, that rendered him ready to start forward, as the champion of the oppressed, at the slightest mention of tyranny or injustice.

On giving up Eugene to his studies with his aunt, the lieutenant generally betook himself to loitering about the neighbourhood, amongst the old retainers of his kingly house, whose stories and traditions concerning it were a never-failing source of delight to him.

A path led to the summit of a mountain, behind the castle, overlooking a torrent below, where, crossing a rude bridge, formed of trunks of trees, cast across a deep glen, you arrived at a neat cabin, or cottage, embosomed in alder trees, where a sod seat invited the passenger to rest, and view the surrounding scenery, hence beheld to the greatest advantage, and abounding in all that could charm the eye or fix the attention.

This was the lieutenant's favourite walk —here he loved to rest upon the turf seat, for he had a limp in his gait, from a severe wound, that rendered the ascent of the eminence rather a work of fatigue to him, and listen to the funny anecdotes or wild stories of Nell Tierney, the owner of the cabin. Among these was one that made a particular impression on the mind of the lieutenant, a little inclined, like most of his profession, to credulity and superstition.

At the period of the Reformation, Nell related, that commissioners being sent over to Ireland, to take account of, and value the church lands, one amongst them, a man of most abandoned character, was so charmed with the castle of St. Doulagh's, and its rich dependencies, as to form a plan for the destruction of its owner, in order to get himself possessed of his valuable property. For this end he artfully represented to the jealous tyrant, that the king of Ulster aimed at sovereign sway, to the destruction of course of the English power in Ireland; in corroboration of which many circumstances were stated, any one of which was sufficient of itself to have excited the jealousy of such a tyrant as Henry, but all of which were the fabrication of the commissioner's own fertile brain.

Having sufficiently worked upon the gloomy mind of Henry, he asserted that he had the power of putting the suspected monarch's loyalty to a decisive test, if he had but his majesty's permission so to do, and promise of pardon for whatever might be the result. Both being obtained, he proceeded to state, that there was a particular species of dogs, possessed of the extraordinary sagacity of discovering a traitor, even though amongst thousands of other men, one of which he had then in his possession, and would make use of in the way he wished, now that he was permitted.

Prior to entering upon this plan, the Englishman shut up a bloodhound in a room by itself, and having kept it for some days without food, brought it out to a garden, in which was placed a figure, fashioned so as to represent the king of Ulster, and in the belly of which was deposited the entrails of a sheep; at this the hound was set, and, infuriated by hunger, quickly succeeded in tearing it to pieces. This was repeated, till his treacherous owner conceived there could be but little doubt of his performing the part he intended: accordingly, on an appointed day, the destined victim was brought forth, and, as foreseen, no sooner recognised by the dog, than he flew at him, and literally tore him to atoms.

The place in which this tragedy was acted was a field adjoining the castle; and there was a tradition, that whenever this (from that period named the king's field of blood) should be planted with English hops, the castle, with all its rich domains, would be restored to his descendants.

Whenever the poor lieutenant's spirits sunk beneath the pressure of worldly circumstances, for he was neither rich, nor passing rich, his thoughts would revert to this tradition, and rekindle courage to bear up a little longer against what might ensue.

CHAPTER II.

" 'Tis granted, and no plainer truth appears,
Our most important are our earliest years.

The heart, surrender'd to the ruling power,
Finds by degrees the truths that once bore sway,
And all their deep impressions wear away."

BUT if Miss Agnes Flora Judith was annoyed by the frequent interruptions the studies of her nephew met, through his

own volatility, and the restless disposition
of his father, as she termed it, how much
more was she by those her niece received
through her propensity to play! in vain
she tried to check or correct this—she
might as well have attempted to arrest the
fugitive butterfly in its flight, or the sportive kid in its gambols, as hinder Grace
from a bout of romps, when intent on one.
The more she descanted against hoydenish
manners, the wilder the other seemed to
become, apparently delighting in all manner of mischievous tricks—setting the
dogs and cats by the ears, the birds scream-
ing, and the maids squalling, with the unusual noises she made.

At length, just as her aunt, in despair,
was on the very point of giving her up as
an incorrigible creature, she took a studious
turn, and from not knowing what it was
before to be at rest for a moment, could
now hardly be got from her book.

In delight at this sudden change, or reformation, as she called it, which she imputed, with no little degree of exultation, to

her own perseverance, Miss Agnes Flora Judith would not allow herself to disturb her, by calling her attention to the mechanical parts of education.—" No," she said, " she is now imbibing such a passion for knowledge, as will reconcile her to all that is tiresome and tedious in the attainment; I will not, therefore, for a little while longer, resume my part of instructress."

At length, one day that she was sitting absorbed in the perusal of the Iliad, suddenly observing a tear stealing down her cheek, Miss Agnes Flora Judith demanded, in the softest accents, what part of it it was that so deeply interested her feelings—" But I dare say the parting scene between Hector and Andromache," she added; " for I know nothing in the book so affecting—is it so, my love?"

" Oh no, ma'am!" replied the sobbing Grace, " it is the heart-rending cruelty of the inflexible aunt, not to permit a parting interview between the unhappy lovers."

" Aunt !" exclaimed Miss Agnes ; " why how is this, my dear? I don't recollect any relation in the book mentioned by that title."

" Oh yes, ma'am, there is—there is Mrs. Wilson—she who educated poor Emily, and——"

" Why what nonsense is this you are speaking about, child ?" said Miss Agnes Flora Judith, impatiently interrupting her : " let me see what it is you are really reading."

" The Iliad, ma'am," said Grace, but in a very timid tone, and making rather a retrograde movement as she spoke.

" No, that I am convinced it is not," said her aunt, and starting from her chair, she made a sudden snatch at the book, and discovered, snugly concealed within it, the novel of " Precaution."—" So, so !" she exclaimed, as soon as indignation would permit her to speak, " this is the kind of study you have been pursuing all the time I conceived you were storing your mind with classical knowledge, and qualifying yourself to become a second prodigy in the family! Fie, fie! aint you ashamed of yourself for being so artful?"

"I am sure, ma'am," in a whimpering tone, said Grace, "I thought there was no harm in reading things of the kind; if you only look over that book, you'll find it as good as it is beautiful."

"Oh yes, very likely indeed! but we shall soon have proof of that by its effect upon you. By this time, I dare say, your head is running on nothing but love adventures. Come, confess—is it not so?—should you not like to have a lover?"

Grace blushed, and hid her face in her handkerchief.

"Ay, I see how it is; we shall have you running off some night with a strolling Romeo, or attempting it, I mean; for now that I understand you, Miss, I shall take care, I promise you, to keep you under proper restraint."

"I hope, ma'am," a little spiritedly re-

plied Grace, " I sha'n't need any restrain
on the score you allude to; if I did ven
ture to make choice of any one withou
the consent of my family, I trust it woul
not be any one that would disparag
them."

" Indeed! and pray, if you were at l
berty to make a choice for yourself, wh;
are the qualities that you would deem ii
dispensable in a lover?"

" Why, a tall, slight, elegant figure
replied Grace, in the interesting subje
recovering all her animation, " with vei
dark, thick, curling hair; eyes still darke
and so eloquent, as to render any oth
vehicle for the glowing sentiments of h
soul unnecessary; and then a heart!
heart capable of loving even to adoratior

" Oh, a perfect Lydia Languish! We
Miss, and supposing you did meet wi
such a captivating being, as in the la
guage of romance I suppose you wou
style such an one as you have describe
do you think it is by an ignorant, unt
tored mind, you would captivate hin

No, believe me. I speak from experience. To excite more than a transitory passion, the union of internal with external graces is requisite. I believe none could boast of a more numerous set of lovers than I had; but do you imagine I acquired them merely by my personal charms? no; though without vanity (a weakness indeed I have always despised), I believe I could boast of some in my day;" and applying her hand to the adjustment of her flaxen tresses, she cast her eyes upon a glass: " are you attending to me, Miss?"

" Yes, ma'am," was the almost smothered reply of Grace, as, nearly convulsed with laughter, she buried her face in her handkerchief.

" This, perhaps," resumed Miss Agnes Flora Judith, " may be doubted—that is, my having had many admirers, I mean, from the circumstance of my having remained single—a circumstance that drew upon me, for years, the imputation of being cruel and cold hearted; but what

then?—I had early determined on neve
giving my hand but where I discovered
kindred mind, and, in consequence, re
mained as I am; which, let me tell you
Miss, you may have reason to congratu
late yourself on; since, had I had a famil
of my own, it is not probable I shoul
have been able to have taken the pain
with you I am anxious to do, as a proc
of which, my anxiety on every point t
enlighten you. I will now, since we hav
so prematurely entered upon the subjec
of love and matrimony, inform you, tha
in so serious a matter as that of enterin
the marriage state, the consideration shoul
be—is the object of our attachment th
being Providence would approve of?
depend on our own judgment is entire
out of the question, for on such occasio
the passions are generally under a wroi
bias, more particularly so when the lo
of beauty is that which governs. W
that knew what happiness really is, wou
seek it in that bloom that every brea
can blast, and which time will certair

efface? Something, Grace, tickles your
fancy just now; but be assured, if you
are silly enough to imagine *outward* appearances will fix the heart of a man of
worth, you'll find yourself wofully mistaken. It may catch the eye at first
glance; but without the strong auxiliary
of a well-cultivated mind, can never hold
fast the affections of the heart. The finest
set of features, the very blush of the da-
mask rose itself, will only cause a woman
to be regarded as a beautiful picture; except there be sentiment and sensibility
within her soul, to give expression to
these features, and vary the hue of this
complexion; for instance, my countenance," Miss Agnes Flora Judith was
still before the glass, " fixed in the still,
or rather dead calm of insensibility, is
viewed by the other sex without emotion;
but restored to all its wonted animation,
kindness, and sense, and spirit, thrown
into it, as thus—and see the effect it produces!"

This was too much for poor Grace; the

the grimaces made by her aunt at the m
ment were so truly grotesque, that sl
absolutely fell on the carpet, convulse
with laughter.

Miss Agnes Flora Judith immediatel
seated herself, with an air of offended m
jesty, and continued calmly viewing h
niece during this attack of mirth. On i
a little subsiding, Grace endeavoured
apologize for it, by laying the blan
of it entirely on the cat and dog, the
whilst her aunt was lecturing her, ha
been quarrelling, in a manner that rende
ed it impossible for her to control her ri
bility.

" I am sorry to hear you say so," sa
Miss Agnes Flora Judith, gravely, " sin
a person who cannot command themselv
in this way, must appear as a fool; ho
ever, that is not the question at presen
I now demand, who the person was th
supplied you with these books, to t
prejudice of the studies I thought y
pursuing?"

Grace hesitated to confess; but t

question was repeated in a manner that
proved evasion would be unavailing; and
Grace accordingly, with reluctance, acknowledged it was William Delamere, a
lad in the neighbourhood.

"Ay, it was the act of a boy," said
Miss Agnes Flora Judith; "however, I
shall take care that Mr. William gives no
further proofs of his mistaken kindness
towards you at present. I would be understood, however, not to intend by this
restricting you from the perusal of such
works hereafter—I only wish to do so till
your mind is sufficiently strengthened and
enlightened to permit you to indulge yourself in it without injury, or, in other
words, to allow you to discriminate the
wheat from the chaff; then you shall have
my free permission to range at will through
the delightful regions of romance—weep
over the sorrows of the exalted Clemen-
tina—sympathize with the lovely Harriet
—and sigh to think that, in these degenerate days, no such men as the all-elegant

c 3

and accomplished Grandison, he who kne
how to pay such proper homage to o
sex, and raise woman to the altitude
which Nature intended to place her, are
be found."

Miss Agnes Flora Judith was as go
as her word—novels were absolutely
booed at the castle of St. Doulagh's; a
Grace, suddenly deprived of the wo
that, from the excitement they had giv
to her curiosity, and the new world of
joyment they had opened to her liv
sensibilities, had had a taming effect up
the exuberance of her spirits, relapsed
to her wonted ones, to the utter desp
of her aunt, who began to think it v
to hope she should ever be able to br
her in, in such a manner as to render
capable of receiving the instructions
wished to impart to her.

Just at this period, the sublime syst
of Gall and Spurzheim, on Phrenolo
began to make a noise in the world, o
least to reach the loophole of retreat
which Miss Agnes Flora Judith loo

out upon what was passing amongst mankind. With the eagerness with which whatever was new caught her fancy, she immediately set about endeavouring to make herself mistress of it; but in vain, till by chance some volumes of Blackwood's Magazine fell into her hands, fully explaining it to her, to her great satisfaction and delight.

"It is a well-known fact," says sir Toby Tickletoby, in the work just mentioned, "that the human cranium may be moulded, in early infancy, into any conceivable shape, from the elastic nature of the bones of which it is formed; and it is equally well ascertained, that several tribes of savages take their distinctive mark from the form of the skull. It is fashionable, for instance, among one tribe, to wear their brain in a case shaped like a sugar-loaf, while others prefer to have their terminating prominence moulded in imitation of a cocoa-nut. And I have little doubt, when the interior of the African continent is better known, that nations will

be found, with their craniums compresse
into forms still more unaccountable.—
Othello says, ' Men whose heads do gro
beneath their shoulders,' and he was a na
tive of Africa. The mere mention o
these undoubted facts, when coupled wit
the knowledge of the functions of th
brain, derived from the writings of Ga
and Spurzheim, must awaken in the mind
of philosophical observers, ideas of th
perfectibility of the human race, and th
concentration and expansion of the powe
of the human mind, which may make th
golden age of the old world, or the miller
nium of the present, an event within th
reach of ordinary life, and perfectly pra
ticable in the next generation.

" As all the organs of thought and vol
tion are as distinctly laid down," he go
on, " in the *cranial* map of Gall and Spur
heim, as the position of the isle of May
or the Bell-rock, in the charts of the coa
of Scotland, and as I have already de
monstrated the practicability of compres
ing the cranial bones, at an early age, in

to any conceivable form, nothing more is
required to give a new and definite direction to the thoughts and feelings of the
next generation, than to mould the infant
head to a given form, by the simple application of an unyielding metal headdress,
formed so as only to permit the developement of the required organs."

" Oh Heavens, what a glorious discovery !" exclaimed Miss Agnes Flora Judith, in an absolute transport; " what
trouble is it not calculated to save parents,
and tutors, and governesses—in short, all
concerned in the instruction of youth, in
future! had I been sooner acquainted with
it, what moments of labour and anxiety
should I have been spared about Eugene
and Grace! but it is not yet too late to
profit by it—much yet remains to be done
for them, and I shall immediately therefore proceed to act upon it; that is," and
she turned pale with dismay at the
thoughts of the opposition she might meet
with in the effort from them, " if their un-

suppressed bump, or organ of obstinacy
will permit me."

Suspense on such a subject was not en
durable—they were immediately sum
moned to her; and after a good deal o
coaxing, in order to wheedle them into
complying humour with her intention o
having their heads immediately prepare
for the adoption of the metal cap, she thu
began:—" By this time, my dear childrei
I must hope you are so well assured o
my affection for you, that you must be cor
vinced I can propose nothing that is no
for your advantage. That there are bi
two kingdoms in this world, the kingdoi
of light and the kingdom of darkness,
early endeavoured to impress upon yoi
infant minds; now to one or other v
must belong; but how difficult it is to a
tain to the one we must all naturally pr
fer, let the constant struggles we are e
during between our good and bad pr
pensities tell. To conquer the latter
course must be our aim, as the only mea
of enabling us to aspire to ultima

happiness. But how is this to be done? in what way are we to accomplish so desirable, so essential a matter? I pronounce, with a heart overflowing with gratitude to the Giver of all Good, the Enlightener of the human understanding, by availing ourselves of the glorious suggestion or discovery of sir Toby Tickletoby, the greatest, the most renowned of our modern philosophers. Before I read the sublime system of Gall and Spurzheim," she proceeded—" that which you were poring over the other day, Eugene— like other ignorant creatures, I fancied man born a free agent, endued with powers to discriminate between good and evil, but left entirely to his own choice, with a knowledge of the penalty or rewards attached to it. The contrary I find, however, from these great men, Gall and Spurzheim, to be the case; from them I find, that man is sent into the world with organs of thought and volition, that propel him as they please, either to evil or to good, according to the organs that prepon-

derate, so that he can have no will of hi
own, but must, like an automaton, whe
wound up, perform certain evolution
whether he will or no. But how wretcl
ed must the knowledge of this have mad
us, by the constant apprehension it woul
have caused us to live in, of renderin
others wretched, in spite of our best wishe
and intentions, but for the discovery
have alluded to—a discovery that prove
there is a way by which we can re-organiz
ourselves, if I may use such an expressior
so as to render ourselves what creature
we please, or others wish to have us! fc
infancy, or early youth, is the time fc
new modelling our construction, or sup
pressing whatever from it might be likel
to lead us astray. Happily you are nc
past the latter period; all that therefor
remains to be done, ere I give orders fc
the metal caps I mean you to wear, is t
examine your craniums, in order to ascer
tain what bumps most require to be press
ed on; to permit this, the cutting off you
hair, or, in other words, close shaving c

your heads, will be necessary; but, against this, I must flatter myself, my dear chil- dren, that the good sense you both pos- sess, as well as the wish I must conclude you experience to be good and amiable, will prevent your offering any objection."

To describe the astonishment of her au- ditors, when they found she was real- ly serious in this proposition, would be impossible. They were, however, very differently affected by it; there appeared in it something so extremely ludicrous to Eugene, that he was nearly suffocated with laughter by it, whilst rage absolute- ly sparkled in the eyes of Grace at the thought.

She was just on the point of vehement- ly protesting that she would die sooner than consent to a thing of the kind, when Caty, one of the helps, according to the American phrase, rushed into the parlour, to say that her master had just been *kilt dead* by captain Rock's men, and was coming in at the gate—a proof that, in

Ireland, to a certainty, they consider k
ing no murder.

All was now confusion and dismay,
the voice of the lieutenant was heard,
claiming—" Don't be alarmed! don't
alarmed! 'tis a mere trifle—nothing m
than a scratch!" wiping, as he advan
into the room, his forehead, from whicl
little blood was slowly flowing.

"Good Heavens!" exclaimed Miss Ag
Flora Judith, whilst Eugene flew off
Mr. Barney O'Rooke, the village s
geon, or barber, or both in one, for si
was actually the case, " I never co
have apprehended a thing of this kii
never could have thought that the
scendants of the O'Neils would, here
least, have met with injury! that
their own neighbourhood, at least, tl
did not bear a charmed life about then

" Pooh, pooh! I suppose you mean
a charming life," said the lieutena
" however, that's as it may be—when
tide runs smooth, and the breeze bl
fair, why they are well enough off th

but when it sets in contrary, and there's a stiff gale, they are no more over comfortable here than they would be elsewhere."

" Ah! you don't understand me," said Miss Agnes Flora Judith; " but that's nothing new, or at present of any consequence : but, in the name of Heaven, tell me, I conjure you, how it is we have provoked the enmity of captain Rock, or any of his banditti ?"

" The pirate! what the devil has put him in your noddle, Agnes ?"

" Noddle! what an extraordinary manner you have of expressing yourself, brother! but is not that wound in your forehead owing to him, or some of his men ?"

" No, how the deuce should it, when I never yet came alongside of them! though 'tis a sign you were never on board a seventy-four during an engagement, to call this scratch a wound."

" Well, as the poet says, ' a rose by any other name would smell as sweet,' so call that hurt in your forehead by what name

you please, 'tis still a wound; so pray
plain how you came by it?"

"Pooh, what signifies! but since y
must know—by the flashing of a pistol
my face, that I was endeavouring to te
Martin to fire at a mark with, in or
that Eugene and I might have him as
assistant in our engagements, when we
hard pressed."

The uplifting of Miss Agnes Flora
dith's eyes evinced she was on the po
of exclaiming—" What folly!" when
entrance of the surgeon, or barber-s
geon, as he should more properly be
nominated, prevented her. His exa
nation of the lieutenant's forehead quic
dissipated the alarm the accident he
with had occasioned.

Order restored, and Miss Agnes F
Judith again collected, it suddenly oc
red to her, as O'Rooke and her brol
sat regaling themselves with some
meat and a glass of grog, to make a c
dant of the former, in the project she
in view, should she find that, without

sistance, she could not carry it into effect,
and of which indeed, from the manner in
which it had been received by Grace, she
had very little hope. From the aid she
was aware he could give her, she could
not help considering what had just happened, since it had ended in the manner
it had done, as a lucky circumstance, as,
but for seeing O'Rooke at the moment,
she might not have thought of him, and
there was not a person in the place that
could be of such service to her in the affair.

Whilst she was thus making up her
mind to let nothing prevent her from
pursuing the plan of the immortalized sir
Toby Tickletoby, Grace, all indignation
at the barbarous idea it had suggested,
had flown off, to make her complaint to
Nell Tierney, the repository of most of
her girlish grievances.

In giving utterance to her anger, however, it evaporated, and seating herself on
the turf bank at the door of the cabin, she
began gaily singing, whilst she amused herself with re-stringing an old necklace of

beads she had coaxed her aunt out of
preceding day, with a prospect before
on which the eye could never be t
expatiating—of hills, separated by
gles, mantled with thickets of oak,
watered by torrents, which heightened
effect of the most romantic scenery,
their incessant roar and glittering f
while a beautiful valley lay stretche
their feet, through which rapidly flo
another mountain stream, now obsc
by tufted trees and hillocks, then a
bursting on the view, sparkling in
beams of a meridian sun, mellowing
the softest tints the verdure of the di
mountains.

CHAPTER III.

" Beneath th' umbrageous grove,
By kindly acts he often found
To recommend his love."

. . . .

" The breach, though small at first, soon op'ning wide,
In rushes folly with a full-moon tide."

IN this romantic spot Grace was surprised, or rather joined, by her friend William, for she could not well be said to be surprised by the appearance of a person who was always on the watch to converse with her.

William Delamere was an orphan lad, who had been brought up in the neighbourhood, at the expence of an uncle in the East Indies, who had always signified his intention of sending for him, as soon as he was qualified by age and education to join him there. He had now nearly

completed his seventeenth year, and v
in consequence daily looking to be cal'
away, a circumstance that would h
caused him but little regret, but for
pang he felt at the thought of being t
from Grace, for whose pretty face he 1
early conceived a boyish fancy, as he
clared in the rhymes with which he 1
wounded the barks of the trees in
praise.   She was indeed his inspi1
muse, and had had her charms celebr;
in all manner of ways by him, in sonr
odes, and acrosticks, while he was cc
nually making her some little presen'
other, and ready on all occasions to c
lenge any one to mortal combat who se
ed inclined to rival him.

   All this was very gratifying to
youthful vanity of Grace; but vanity
the only feeling that William, for ;
time, succeeded in interesting. At le
his unceasing kindness and attention ;
ed her right good will, and without k
absolutely in love with him, she cert
became very fond of him.

Poor William was not altogether indeed a kind of being to inspire this romantic passion in the breast of a young
girl: his appearance was against him—he
was stunted in his growth, through the
studious life perhaps he had been compelled to lead, to be ready for the summons
of his uncle, and the anxieties inseparable
from a dependent state, and was of a bi-
lious complexion, with certainly, however,
the dark hair and eyes that Grace so much
admired.

The moment he now joined her, she
proceeded to inform him of the narrow
escape those tresses had had that had so
often been the subject of his muse.

His eyes flashed fire at the recital—
" What, think of such a spoliation!" he
exclaimed; " by Heavens 'tis well she did
not commit it! But," and he placed himself by her on the sod seat, and passed
his arm round her waist, " I am come
with heavy tidings, Grace," he said; " the
long-expected mandate is arrived from my

uncle, and to-morrow I leave this fe
England, to embark for India!"

"How vexatious," said Grace, "whe
we were to have such a pleasant dan
next month in the village!"

"It is," said William, with a de
sigh; "but then, the sooner I depart tl
sooner I shall return."

"Well, there is some consolation
that; but come, that I may have son
thing to keep for your sake——" a
whipping out her scissars, she cut off
look of his hair.

"And am I to have nothing in retu
to preserve for yours?" asked Willi
involuntarily, perhaps unconsciously, dra
ing her still closer to his heart as he spo

"Oh yes, you shall have one of th
happily-preserved tresses;" and with
little ceremony as she had used in cutt
off the lock from his head, she severe
ringlet from her own; then, having pl
ed and secured it at each end, she desi
him to hold out his wrist, that he mi
have it bound round it.

William dropped on one knee as he obeyed her.—" And with life," he exclaimed, " shall this precious token of regard be guarded! and by the radiant skies above—by the verdant earth below, I swear, that no other than the lovely bestower of it shall ever be the lady of my love!—But will you not promise to wait for me, Grace?" he demanded in a softened accent.

" How long do you think you will be away?" asked Grace.

" Seven years probably; in less time I think it hardly possible I can have realized any thing sufficient for an independence."

" That is a long time. But let me see, I am only fourteen and two months now, so I sha'n't, even at the end of that, be very old; so yes, I will promise to wait for you for that time, let what will betide."

When the ecstacy occasioned by this promise had a little subsided—" But will you not also promise to write to me?" said William.

" Yes; but I should not know how
send my letters."

William gave her the necessary instru
tions; and the plan of a corresponden
being thus settled between the youthf
lovers, Grace, after a little hesitation, sa
that when he did write, if he could co
trive to send her a bottle of the attar
roses, she should take it quite as an ob
gation; for she had heard that it was
guinea a drop, and was quite longing
it in consequence.

William, but not without a smile
the reason she assigned for wishing for
assured her, that as she would live in
thoughts, she might rely on his missi
no opportunity of sending her over wh
ever he thought might be agreeable
her; but as these might vary, he desi
her to mention what she was most an
ious for.

" Why I should be quite delighted
get one of the beautiful ivory fans,"
said; " and the shawls are so graceful,
—but I suppose you'll think it quite r

culous to mention such a thing—however, some time or other, I suppose, when I get a little older, I shall be allowed to go to an assize ball, and then a gold muslin would be so enchanting!"

" Then a gold muslin you shall have," said William.

" Shall I ?" cried Grace—" then you are a dear, darling creature!" throwing her arm round his neck; " and I don't care if I promise to wait for you a little, little longer than the seven years."

The lovers unconsciously wandered on to a darksome glen, where all was wild, romantic, and secluded—where the thick trees, and the shaggy banks, threw a deep shadow on the verdure, and the babbling of a brook was the only sound that met the ear. Here William internally exclaimed, as he held her to his throbbing heart—" Oh to find her when I return what she now is—all innocence, all loveliness, heightening, by her unconsciousness of it, the feelings she is so formed to inspire!—will it not be a compensation for

all of early suffering,—the grief of e
bereavement.—the pangs of dependenc

"How I shall miss you in winter!"
Grace.

"No, not near so much as in summ
returned William; "for this delicious
son was, you know, Grace, our seaso
highest enjoyment, when we could i
ble where we pleased, and loiter as
as we liked amidst this enchanting
nery, watching the last gleams of day
dually fading from the hill-tops, and
tening to the closing chant of the b
Oh! how fondly will my imaginatio
vert.—how will it delight to linger
the recollection of our twilight walks.—
delicious calm of the hour of sunset
—when heedlessly we have wandere
to some wild and heathy scene, or fo
some ruin amidst its dreary dells—

   ' Whose walls more awful nodded
   By the religious gleams'

of parting day—

'While all the air was hush'd, save where the weak-
    eyed bat,
With short shrill shriek flitted by on leathern wing;
    Or where the beetle wound
        His small, but sullen horn,
    As oft he rose 'midst our twilight path,
    Against us borne in heedless hum !"

Grace was in excessive sorrow for the
departure of William. The raillery of
Eugene, however, united to the consolation she derived from the presents he had
promised her, had soon a salutary effect
upon her; while her thoughts were still
further diverted from the circumstance
she regretted by the renewed attack of her
aunt. Determined on pursuing her plan,
she rested not till she had, by stratagem,
obtained an opportunity of examining, as
she called it, the *cranium* of Grace. Under the pretext of adjusting her hair for
her one day, which a walk had disordered,
she succeeded in procuring this; and
having committed to paper her remarks
on it, she proceeded, after a slight exor-
dium, explanatory of the deep regret and
remorse she felt for the sufferings she had

inflicted on Grace, by punishing her
faults which she *now* saw it was not
her power to have avoided committing
ask her so and so.—" Pray, my love,
you ever feel so attached to any one as
think you could break your heart
them?"

"Yes," was the reply, the thoughts
Grace at the moment reverting to p
William.

"Right!" in an ecstacy exclaimed
aunt; "I'd take their word for a thous:
pounds! Here stands *adhesiveness* la
indeed: and by the map of Gall a
Spurzheim, I see the functions of t
faculty is to give attachment.—And pi
my dear, when you set your childish v
to work to play me a prank, or dist:
the repose of the family by personatin
ghost, or something of the kind, did y
ever intrust any one with your scheme

"Very seldom indeed, except for
sake of getting assistance, to afford m
fun."

"Right again! *secretiveness* very sm

—And how do you feel towards yourself?"

"Feel towards myself! I don't comprehend you, ma'am."

"Why, do you think well—do you admire, or think highly of yourself?"

Grace laughed, and blushed, and cast a glance towards the glass, as much as to say it would be odd if she did not.

"So I see *self-esteem* very large indeed. —And when commended, do you feel much pleasure?"

"Yes, great—especially if I am praised by those I love or like myself."

"Right again! here it is—*love of approbation* very great.—And when opposed in any project, can you readily bring yourself to relinquish it?"

"No, not by any means; when once I have made up my mind to any thing, I cannot bear to be thwarted or disappointed."

"Second Daniels, upon my life! Yes, here it is—*firmness*, large indeed, and *sanguineness*.—That is, when you hope for a thing, what or how do you feel?"

" As if I had what I wish for already
possession."

" Right, right—still right, divine pl
losophers! what—what skill,—what kno
ledge—what science have ye not displa
ed in your chart, or map, of the hum
skull!"

So far all was well, with the excepti
of *firmness*, which, according to Gall a
Spurzheim, when too energetic, produ
obstinacy, stubbornness, and *infatuatio*
but, in opposition to the bumps indicati
of *candour, benevolence, warm-hearte*
ness, and *love of approbation,* there w
others, such as *amativeness,* and so for
from the propensities *they* betrayed, t]
Miss Agnes Flora Judith, determined,
in duty bounden, the application of t
metal cap, reminding her of the am
compensation she would have for the tr
sient loss of an ornament, that time wo
restore, by the lectures this would be t
means of saving her, and the further stru
gles it would put an end to between |

good and bad inclinations.——"Constructed
so as to press upon the bumps indicative of
the latter," she continued, "you will, with
out further struggling, or scolding, or stri-
ving on your part, by its mere application,
become all that is wished. How then, my
dear Grace, with the good sense you possess, can you hold out against what would
be the means of saving so much trouble
and anxiety to all parties? Gall and
Spurzheim have clearly proved that we
cannot help what we do, however contrary
it may be to our sense of right, no more
than a coach can help going down a precipice if dragged thither by horses; but
from the horror of the thought we are relieved, by the re-organization which the
discovery of sir Toby Tickletoby enables
us to obtain for ourselves."

But in vain she argued—Grace was as
inexorable to her coaxings and reasonings
at the winds to the supplication of the
alarmed mariner; and in a rage at her obstinacy, the consequence of the bump of
firmness not having been suppressed, Miss

Agnes Flora Judith proceeded to decla
that since she would not yield by f
means to what would be so much for l
advantage, she should by foul ones.

At this threat, Grace, in alarm, as
she already felt the despoiler's hands up
her hair, started up, and retreating a lit
way from her aunt—" What, conser
she exclaimed, " to have my hair i
merely cut off, but my head shaven, a
cased up in an iron cap! No!" she cri
while her very eyes flashed fire at the
deous idea: " you have told me I poss
firmness, and to prove you not incorr
in the statement, I now protest—may
swear, by the memory of my great anc
tor, that nothing but force, outrage
force, shall ever obtain the submission y
require!" and with these words she fl
• out of the room.

" So, so!" said Miss Agnes Flora
dith; " then since I cannot use force
must have recourse to stratagem;" and
she had previously determined in case
being reduced to such a dilemma, she i

mediately sent off a message to Mr. Barney O'Rooke, requiring to see him at a
certain hour that evening at the castle.

CHAPTER IV.

"Make the doors fast upon a woman's wit, and it will out
at the casement; shut that, and it will out at the key-
hole; stop that, it will fly with the smoke out of the
chimney."

BARNEY O'Rooke was the descendant of
one of the retainers of the great O'Neil,
and had been born and bred in the village,
where, according to his statement, upwards of a hundred generations belonging
to his house had flourished and faded,
though all living to a good old age.

" Why, Barney, my boy, how can you
make that out?" inquired the lieutenant
one day, on hearing him repeating this
assertion; " if so be as it is as you say,
why, by the head of Neptune, your fa-

mily must have come straight out of tl
ark to settle at St. Doulagh's!"

" Oh no, no, admiral, your honour
the title by which the lieutenant w
alone known in the village, from beir
one which it was there perhaps conceiv
he had a right to, " we don't count
high," said Barney; " our family histor
does not go higher than the Conquest."

" Family history!" repeated the lie
tenant, with a whistle; " why, what tl
devil, do you pretend to a history of yo
family?"

" Yes, that I do! and by St. Patri
I'd sooner lose my right hand than be d
prived of it, seeing the value that mu
have been set upon it by my ancestors,
have been preserved through all tl
changes and chances that took pla
amongst them, and the storms that pass
over this unhappy land! I don't go
deny, to be sure, that some people mig
only call it a journal, or memorandur
book, of all the chins that were shave
but I contend, and insist upon it, it a

swers all the *intints* and purposes of a history by the dates. Now, as I was stating to your honour, according to these, I know nothing certain of my family before the English invasion, at which time I find one of my great ancestors, A. D. 1172, had the honour of bleeding and blistering the great Strongbow."

"The devil he had! Well, I should like now to see that memorandum; for that is, I suppose, in what you call your black letter, that the learned make such a piece of work about it?"

"Ay, black enough once, I dare say; but this is not the only honour my family have had to boast of. Another progenitor, equally fortunate, was the person employed to adjust the glibbs of the four Irish kings that were called to a conference in Dublin with Richard the Second; and a third, I discover, was appointed shaver to the commissioner Mordaunt; on his coming over to value the church lands."

"He was! Then I hope the devil took

him, for not shaving his head off, wh
he had him in his power."

" The Lord save us !" cried Barn
crossing himself devoutly, for, like all
race, he was a *bon* Catholic; " how cou
you say such a thing, admiral? It's lo
ago, I trust, his precious sowl was d
vered out of Purgatory, and is now in 1
radise."

" What! is it for letting such a vill
escape ?" demanded the lieutenant, wl
in the simplicity of his heart, gave im]
cit credit to all the other told him, for 1
purpose of trying how far he might ex
cise his inventive powers upon him ; " :
would not the life of the great O'N
then have been spared ; and with him,
protect them, would not all his rich lar
and dependencies here, come down to .
descendants, instead of being parcelled c
among strangers, to their utter impoveri:
ment, not to say ruin ?"

O'Rooke could not deny this, and wi
the greatest dexterity endeavoured
change the subject, ready to bestow a 1

nediction on himself for having started one on which the lieutenant could never think or converse with patience.

Mr. Barney was now pretty well stricken in years, but still hale, strong, and hearty; having always made a point of taking good care of himself, and letting nothing trouble him, if possible. That he was not over scrupulous, may be inferred from what has been already said of him; he bore a fair reputation, however, in the village, where, from being the chief, if not only practitioner on the chin, as well as the only individual that knew any thing of the art of medicine, he was looked up to as a person of some importance; which the knowledge of his being able to argue with the priest, and having a well-stuffed purse lying by him, did not tend to lessen.

Miss Agnes Flora Judith's message threw him into something like a flutter. There was a mystery in the delivery of it that set him about conjecturing—" To slip in the back way, and see there was

no one minding me:' why then sure s
not being after taking a fancy to me;
what, in the name of St. Patrick, can
be wanting with me in private, if 'tis
to be telling me some secret? and if
did not ogle me the other day, whe
was after dressing the forehead of her l
ther, the devil's in it! Ah then, Barr
my boy, you are made at last, may
and sure wasn't there my ould aunt W
lan, that was a bit of a witch, tould
I'd make my fortune yet by marriag
and under the flattering idea of being
garded with a favourable eye by Miss .
nes Flora Judith, he set about adonia
for the approaching interview, though
trouble of dressing was one he by no me
liked. Armed at all points for conqu
or, as he conceived, for securing the q
quest he was induced to think he
made, his best suit on, his black ho
hair wig bushed out, and he little
that was perched on the top of it pine
into sharper cocks, he set off at the
pointed hour for the castle: but what

was the delusion under which he entered
it, it was soon dispelled by the manner
of Miss Agnes Flora Judith, who never
for a moment lost sight of the dignity of
the O'Neils, or forgot the homage due to
a woman of her superior endowments; not
but that she was, in some degree, condescending on this occasion to O'Rooke,
in consequence of the purpose for which
she had summoned him, motioning him
to take a seat in a distant window.

Having secured the door, to prevent
the danger of interruption, she then proceeded to business; and after a few intro-
ductory compliments, explanatory of the
opinion she entertained of his learning and
fidelity—" I presume, doctor," she said,
(a title by which she now chose to address
him, in order to deceive herself into a belief that she was not absolutely conversing with an inferior,) " that, as something
of a professional man, you have read, studied, and inwardly digested, that sublime
treatise, or system, of doctors Gall and
Spurzheim on phrenology ?"

After the high compliments she l
paid him on his learning, Barney wa
little confused at being obliged to ackno
ledge ignorance on any subject; aw
however, that to attempt to deceive l
would be unavailing, he forced himsel
confess he had never heard of these c
tors before; which, to be sure, seen
very strange to him, as he thought
ancestors had made it a point to m
mention in their history, or memorandi
book, of all the great doctors of their d:

" Their day !" repeated Miss Agnes l
ra Judith, with a smile of contemp
" ah, doctor, these are very different c
tors from those of their day. Little
the time you allude to, was it dreaml
that the period would arrive in which r
should discover, as they have clearly l
ved to be the case, that he was mol
creature of mechanism than of free w
but I will explain."

This she accordingly proceeded to
with all the delight and enthusiasm
spired by the subject. Having conclu

—" Well to be sure !" exclaimed the astonished O'Rooke, " it may well be said, wonders will never cease. Who would ever have thought' of such a thing !"

" Ay, who indeed !" said the lady ; " but how unhappy, doctor, should we have been rendered by this discovery of Gall and Spurzheim, but for that of sir Toby Tickletoby, well entitled to be styled the benefactor of mankind ! since by that, you perceive, it is in our own power to rectify whatever is amiss, or likely to lead us astray, in our construction. For instance, when we would have a girl truly virtuous, we must have the hollow in the metal cap intended for the bump of *amativeness* very small indeed ; and the reverse with regard to the organs of *benevolence* and *righteousness*, that they may be allowed to shoot up to the utmost luxuriance. By stratagem I have succeeded in obtaining a map of my niece's *cranium*, and find, that promising as she appears to be, she has still many dangerous *organs*, that if not timely suppressed, or corrected,

may eventually lead her to destruction:
but so great is the bump of obstinacy, that
she will not hearken to any thing I can
say about the metal cap, which I have already given private orders to the black-
smith to prepare, though with tears I
have implored her to allow the application
of it: now what I want of you, since I
find it hopeless to conquer her opposition,
is to mix up a sleeping potion for her a-
gainst the cap comes home, that, without
further trouble or delay, you may be enabled to shave her head for it."

O'Rooke wiped his face, and took a long
pinch of snuff—afraid to refuse the lady,
yet equally so to promise to oblige her.—
"There's nothing I am not bound, I'm
sure, to do for you and yours, my lady,"
he said; "but what would the admiral,
and master Eugene, and Miss Grace herself say, if I was to do what you require?
I'm sure my cheek tingles now at the
thought of the box she once gave me on
it, tiny as her hand is, for having cut her
hair too short; and didn't her brother and

William Delamere weary the life out of
me almost, for some time, for having
vexed her? Wasn't I near being blown
up, like the figure of Guy Vaux on a rejoicing night, by one pinning a cracker to
my wig? and didn't the other almost
frighten the *sowl* out of my body, by crying like a *banshee* one night at my window? Besides, in the whole course of
my life, never did I hear of an attempt to
mould the *osseous covering* of the *centre
of nervous energy;* all that is ever done,
is carefully to close the *cranium,* and to
attempt more, I humbly and respectfully
declare, would be a certain means of destroying the child. Sorry am I to be
obliged to differ from a lady so deeply
and profoundly read as your ladyship; but
I do aver and protest, that the safest and
most expeditious method of correcting any
thing wrong, in either master or miss, is
a good birch rod!"

"You think so!" said Miss Agnes Flora Judith, with a look of ineffable contempt; " but, Mr. Barney O'Rooke, I

did not send for you here to think, but to
act; or, in other words, receive my instructions, and promise attention to them; but
through my condescension, in explaining
what I have done, I suppose you have
been tempted to imagine the contrary.
Understand now, that it is a trouble I
would not have taken, had I thought you
the stupid old fool you have proved yourself! You are one of those ignorant, be-
sotted beings, I see, who are so wedded
to old notions, as to consider all improvements innovations not to be tolerated; but
does not the great suggester of metal caps
justly observe, that ' trees, left to their
own mode of growing, always delight to
luxuriate in the wild irregularity of un-
shapely and unpruned branches; though
it is well known to the skilful gardener,
that they can be made to assume the form
of a fan or a cone, on walls, or expand
horizontally on espaliers, at the pleasure
of their early instructors, and still, after
all, be trees, and bear fruit better than in
their wild, uneducated state?' Now I.

will not do my fellow-creatures the injustice to suppose that they are less susceptible of cultivation than plum or cherry trees, or that the bony covering of their thirty-two propensities is harder than holly or boxwood, or more untractable than the teak, or ' knotted oak.' But further illustration is unnecessary—the thing carries conviction with it to the mind, except where the bump of *stupidity* overwhelms the other thirty-one; so let me hear no more contradiction from you, but at once say you are ready to obey my commands."

" Certainly, my lady—surely, my lady; that is, in all reasonable matters; but to go for to commit such an act upon the head of Miss Grace!"

" You refuse then!" exclaimed Miss Agnes Flora Judith in a rage; " but I see how it is," and snatching up Gall and Spurzheim's map of the human cranium, now her constant study, with one hand, she, with the other, to his equal terror

and surprise, pulled off poor Barney's wig,
and rubbing her hand over his bare skull—
"ay, it is as I imagined," she said; " here
are the bumps of *stupidity* and *arrogance*
indeed of a size to account for all. But,
in spite of them, I will be obeyed, or Mr.
Barney O'Rooke must expect, for the future, to have his services dispensed with
here."

. Barney, through life, had made it a
point to make his own interest his first
consideration; this threat therefore was not
without its due effect; in short, upon Miss
Agnes Flora Judith's promising to reward
him most liberally, for doing what she required, and to take upon herself the re-
sponsibility of it, he consented to oblige
her, and the spoliation of poor Grace's
head was finally settled.

On the cap being brought home, the
potion prepared by Barney was adminis-
tered, and advantage taken of the deep
sleep into which she was thrown by it, to
divest her head of its beautiful tresses.
She did not, immediately on rising the

next morning, perceive what had happened, her head remaining confused by the
effects of the dose she had taken; but
when, on pulling off her nightcap before
the glass, she discovered it, who can describe her rage and horror! she shrieked
aloud, and, overcome with passion, fell
senseless on the floor.

The whole house was alarmed; all hastened to her chamber, where, at the sight
which was exhibited to her view, Miss
Agnes Flora Judith began to think she
had gone a little too far. She had meant
to have been by on Grace's awaking, to
prepare her, in some degree, for the shock
that awaited her; but being little accustomed to rise early, was not up time e-
nough for the purpose.

When tranquillity was a little restored,
and the young lady given up to the care
of Nell Tierney, her rage returning whenever her aunt approached her, the astonished lieutenant desired to know the
meaning of all that had happened—what
poor Grace had done, to be treated in the

barbarous manner as, it seemed to him, she had been.

"Ah! so you think," replied his sister, "judging, like other short-sighted mortals, from appearances; but when I explain, perhaps you'll be of a contrary opinion;" and she proceeded to gratify his curiosity, first reminding him, however, that though he had reserved to himself a right of control over Eugene, he had entirely resigned Grace to her management.

The lieutenant listened to her with unutterable amazement.—"Well," he cried, "of all the whims, or fancies, Agnes, that ever entered your noddle, this exceeds them all! Bumps! why didn't I see the poor girl's head as bare as Salisbury Plain? and if there was a bump or a lump on it, I'll consent to be shot for a coward! No wonder her poor little heart should be vexed, to be docked in such a manner. To be sure, if she was of an age, like yourself, to mount a false covering—but——"

"Brother, brother," exclaimed Miss Agnes Flora Judith, with a rising flush,

" I must say you speak in a most extraordinary manner! how often have I told you that personal allusions are extremely offensive!"

" Well, well," with a sly wink, "there's no harm done," cried the lieutenant; "for you know there's nobody by; so let it pass this time: but, by the Lord, Agnes, you put me in mind of the vane upon the mainmast top, that is sure of being twirled about by every blast! here, not long ago, you wanted to make me believe that nothing would save the girl from destruction but turning swaddler; and now you say that her salvation depends upon having a brass helmet clapped on her head!"

" Yes, and contend for it," replied his sister, " as you would yourself, could you be made to understand the system I have been endeavouring to explain to you; but in vain, I perceive, some minds being unfortunately so *opaque*, that nothing can enlighten them. Do not attempt, however, to abuse the system because you cannot comprehend it, as most ignorant people in general do what they cannot understand. You are yourself to blame for whatever is amiss in your children's *craniums*, and therefore it is an incumbent duty in you to support any thing that has a chance of rectifying what is wrong in their construction. Yes, you may stare! but had you, when you thought of marrying, given yourself time to discover what qualities you were deficient in, and whether the lady you were about to wed possessed those you lacked, by marrying accordingly there would have been an improvement, and what is obstinacy in you, would, in that case, have been but proper firmness in your children. Ay, you may give one of your polite whistles, but this is not, as I see you are on the point of exclaiming, one of my own ridiculous suggestions, but the suggestion of some of the first philosophers of the day. They argue naturally, if animals, for instance—if the breed of sheep, and horses, and dogs, is improved by cross breeds, why may not that of man? but in vain do they devote their time and abilities to researches beneficial to their species, while passion is allowed to predominate, and a man marries to please his eye, without any thought about those that are to descend from him."

" By the head of Neptune, Agnes, 'tis enough to make one mad to hear you talk so foolishly! why, what the devil can be more natural than for a man to marry to please his eye? and I'd be glad to know how any thing that's natural can be blamable?"

"Ah! fine doctrine! a fine way of teaching your son! Brother, I am astonished at you! I shouldn't wonder if, through your means, your son became one of the greatest profligates in the place."

" Oh, no danger of that! But, Agnes, ain't you afraid of Grace's being revenged for what you have done to her? By the Lord, I shouldn't be surprised if she served your head just as you served hers."

Miss Agnes Flora Judith turned pale at the thought, and involuntarily applying her hand to her head, as if to feel that all was secure there—" Dear, I should hope—I should trust," she said, " that she would never suffer herself to forget——" but her agitation was too great to permit her to finish the sentence, and in extreme confusion she left the room.

Grace certainly had, in the first transports of her rage, vowed vengeance against her aunt for the trick she had played her; but the violent agitation into which she was thrown by the circumstance brought on a fit of illness, that confined her for some days to her chamber; and the time that was thus allowed for the subsiding of her passion, was not without its effect in meliorating it. Her heart was too good, and she had profited too well by the religious principles that had early been implanted in her mind, to be capable of long harbouring revenge against any one. She determined, however, not to forgive, or in other words, be reconciled to her aunt, except she received a positive promise from her, never to serve her again in such a manner, or attempt

annoying her as she had latterly done:
This promise was readily given by Miss
Agnes Flora Judith, glad to get off so
cheaply, having been in no little dread of
what might ensue on the recovery of
Grace, from the spirit she knew she possessed.

A shyness however for some time after
existed between them, which rendered the
addition that was just about this time
made to the establishment at the castle a
very agreeable circumstance to both. Miss
Agnes Flora Judith, with all her attainments, aware that in those days of refinement there were many things she was not
capable of instructing her niece in, and
anxious to have her, not only learned, but
truly accomplished, engaged a young girl
who had been brought up for a governess
to assist in the completion of her education, and whose manners proved so very
amiable, as soon to render her a general
favourite in the house, and with none
more than her pupil, who, ardent and af-

fectionate in her nature, soon loved her as
if she were a sister, finding in her society
a substitute for the loss she had sustained
through the departure of her friend, or,
as he would have preferred being styled,
lover, William.

CHAPTER V.

" Oh, come not ye, near innocence and truth,
Ye worms, that eat into the bud of youth!
Infectious as impure, your blighting pow'r
Taints in its rudiments the promis'd flow'r."

BUT the system of Gall and Spurzheim
was not to be abandoned because of opposition, or disappointment, in the first
instance. Miss Agnes Flora Judith still
continued to make it her study and her
theme. She at length succeeded in awa-
kening the curiosity of her nephew, whose
mind was naturally inquisitive; and the
result of his investigation of it, was his

becoming a convert to it. He was just
of an age and temper to be caught by any
thing new; and in this there was something so ingenious and specious, as completely to captivate him.

How often was the world surprised by
sudden aberrations in those whom it believed almost incapable of error! and was
not this a convincing proof of the truth of
the system? for if we could help it, would
we, so often as we do, commit acts which
we know we must not only be condemned
by others, but ourselves for, and which at
times we could hardly account for?

The examination of his *cranium* was no
longer opposed; on the contrary, he had
an eager curiosity to know what he was
likely to be; and with what delight did
his aunt proceed to it, with the map of
Gall and Spurzheim before her—a delight
only allayed by the reflection, that if she
found any bumps requiring suppression,
it was now too late for the application of
the metal cap.

" That which I once took such pains to

impress upon your mind, my dear boy,"
she began, " namely, that man possessed
the power of controlling his passions,
through reason, religion, and education, I
find to be all nonsense; the new discovery
of Gall and Spurzheim clearly and satisfactorily proves the reverse to be the case;
exciting certainly some degree of terror,
by the consideration of what we may yet
be tempted to commit; but, on the other
hand, relieving us from a weight of re-
sponsibility—since if we cannot help, from
our construction, what we do, should we
be punished for our actions? No, assuredly—it stands to reason *that* would be both
cruel and unjust; but, notwithstanding
this, it is so natural for us to wish to be
amiable, that we cannot too soon enter
upon the study, not of our minds, but our
craniums, that, according to the bumps,
or, in other words, *organs* of *thought* and
volition, we find upon them, we may endeavour to regulate our conduct so as not
to arouse, but keep under those that have
a tendency to lead us into mischief. For

instance, the organ of *anger* is large; you must, therefore, as much as possible, avoid cause for irritation, since, when this opens, its effects are often productive of the most fatal consequences—a man, at such moments, not being able to distinguish right from wrong; but if such will occur, as indeed it is hardly probable to imagine they will not occasionally, you must then fly to the organ of *benevolence* for succour; and thus the mischief to be apprehended from the other will be prevented.

" *Combativeness* and *destructiveness* are also large, and I should rejoice at this, from the proof they afford of your possessing all that magnanimity that leads to glory, could I be assured they never would be allowed to flow but in the defence of your country, or some other equally just cause, when we call them courage, which is that magnanimity by which man is enabled to achieve such actions, as by reason of the obstacles to be surmounted are impracticable to the pusillanimous, and the performance of which obtain for a man the name of hero; but the great danger of these organs is, the strife, fierceness, and revenge, to which they may also lead.

" *Firmness* is of a good size; but except in battle, there are few other things to call it into action; as I conceive there are but two natural evils in life—the death of those we love, and our own; these are the only two that require any mental strength to sustain them—a very common share of fortitude, or perhaps that which does not deserve the name of fortitude, will suffice for the rest; but the loss of a dear friend, or relative, who was the object of our tenderest affection, is a stroke of adversity that will be sure to call forth the full contents of the organ of firmness.

" *Constructiveness* too is of a good size, as is also *the love of applause;* the *first* will be of service to you in the profession your father is desirous of placing you in, as enabling you to devise plans and stratagems, which the spirit flowing from the *second* will assist you to carry through.

" Here is an organ, *acquisitiveness*, also large; this, in business, would be of great service, but can never be of much in the army or navy, where, in general, a wreath of laurel is all that is to be reaped, and that too often at the expence of life and constitution. In other pursuits, where wealth is to be attained, this organ, as I have already observed, would be invaluable. Not, my dear boy, that I would wish you to have a regard for riches for themselves alone—far from it; because I consider such a failing base and ignoble; but gold and silver being, by general consent, the key of commerce, and the instruments by which all our wants are supplied, it would be folly to disregard any *fair* opportunity that may occur to enable us to become independent. Sorry am I to be compelled to say, it is the *mammon* that guides too much the actions and considerations of mankind in the present day; for I never knew a man or woman who were wealthy, who was old, or ugly, or wanted wisdom and virtue; such is the

effect it has in blinding the eyes, and deceiving, the judgment. I have remarked
a strange *trait*—so it appears to me—in
some characters I have met with in the
course of my journey through life—that
is, to magnify the fortunes of all they are
acquainted with, and look up to people
known to be wealthy, with all the obsequiousness of slaves, even though, from
their own knowledge, of a description that
would not give a doit to save the life of
a human being, and whose moral character should have made a good man fly from
their presence. It is therefore evident
riches possess the magic power of throwing a thick veil over their possessor, so as
to render all defects invisible.

" I have ever admired a bold, manly,
open disposition, considering candour one
of the finest *traits* in human nature; it
therefore follows, that I must be much
pleased by the small size of your organ of
secretiveness.

" Now, my dear lad, the metal cap, as
suggested and advised by sir Toby Tickle-

toby, that great benefactor to mankind,
being declined, and which would have
rectified your evil affections and expanded
your good, all that is left for you to do, is
earnestly and carefully to watch over
them, and by perseverance, endeavour to
correct them yourself, by opposing the
one to the other; so that you will be able
in time, as I fervently hope and trust
may be the case, to bring them to a tone
of union and harmony, that will enable
you to pass through the world free from
the perplexing, jarring conflicts, which
are the cause of all the unhappiness in
this life. I cannot conclude these remarks,
however, without adding, as it would be
unfair, when no fault of ours, that the
idea of self-accusation should torment us,
that if you find, on close examination,
your evil affections in some instances out-
weigh your good ones, you have no right
whatsoever to attach blame to yourself for
any actions you, from that cause, commit,
be those actions what they may; for it
would not be according to the rules of jus-

tice, if you were condemned for that o
which you had no control. For instan
suppose your organs of *combativeness* ι
destructiveness overpowered that of *be*
volence, and you killed, in a passion
man—what then? no possible blame ou
to attach to you! but if you had any ot
organ sufficiently strong to have calle
the aid of benevolence, that would h
checked the other two, and you did
take advantage thereof, then, and in s
case, and no other, you would be m
answerable both to God and man! Bι
look with a lively hope and confidence
the day, and anticipate its pleasure, tho
I should not live to see it with my own e
when, through the laws of propagation
laid down by Gall, or in other words, thro
the merits of cross-breeding, all human
facts will, by degrees, be avoided, and fut
generations produced perfect. Then s
commence the British millennium, and
revival of the golden age. It is impr
unions, indeed, that have caused so m
divorces. *Nature*, pointing out the

per objects, no matter whether married or single, for affection and love, they are insensibly attracted towards each other, as the needle to the magnet. To condemn such creatures for their actions, by attaching crime to their intercourse, would be to fly in the face of the Most High; since it was not any intention in them to commit an error, but their organs of *love* and *affection*, that propelled them into conduct they may afterwards deplore, but had no power to avoid at the moment."

Thus did this infatuated woman proceed in endeavouring to destroy, root and branch, those pure principles of religion and morality she had before taken the greatest pains to implant in the lad's mind, traversing her own work in a manner that was most extraordinary. Eugene became perplexed and disturbed by her arguments; as a mind of any reflection must ever do when an attempt is made, by a person on whose judgment they have a reliance, to make the worse appear the better reason. His own opposed her arguments. There

was something in this new doctrine altogether inconsistent with the ideas he had
formed of the goodness and justice of the
Almighty; but, as his aunt observed, this
was the age for discoveries, and what was
he, a raw and inexperienced youth, that
he should attempt to set himself up in opposition to men of deep research and profound knowledge? in a word, he became,
as already stated, a convert to the system.
There was something pleasing to a youthful mind in taking up a cause that would
require all its subtlety to support, and
equally so in thinking, that if we did err,
we should not have ourselves to blame
for it.

CHAPTER VI.

> " Plac'd for his trial on this bustling stage,
> From thoughtless youth to ruminating age,
> Free in his will to choose, or to refuse,
> Man may improve the crisis, or abuse :
> Else, on the fatalist's unrighteous plan,
> Say, to what bar amenable were man ?
> With nought in charge, he could betray no trust,
> And if he fell, would fall because he must ;
> If love reward him, or if vengeance strike,
> His recompence in both unjust alike."

THINGS were going on in this way at the castle of St. Doulagh's; the aunt and nephew were completely engrossed by the new system that had so captivated their imaginations; Grace, possessing a strong, comprehensive mind, and anxious for improvement, was steadily pursuing her education with her young friend; and the lieutenant, as usual, was seeking amusement for himself in rambling about the neighbourhood, and listening to the traditions connected with the memories of his great ancestors, when a letter arrived from an old friend, just appointed to a ship ordered on foreign service, with whom he had served many years, offering to take Eugene on board as a midshipman.

The joy this offer afforded the poor father was great indeed, his ambition not going beyond seeing his son a British officer. No time was lost in preparing matters, and in the course of a few days after the receipt of this welcome letter, Eugene was on his way to Portsmouth.

Ardent, enterprising, full of the most sanguine expectations of glory, longing to know something more of the world than as yet he knew from books—

" Or swains, whose feet came wand'ring o'er the nightly dew,"

and an enthusiast about the profession he was entering, from the glowing colours in which it had been depicted by his father, the delight of Eugene at his appointment was unutterable. The vessel sailed soon after his joining, and it was

not long ere an opportunity was afforded
him of witnessing a specimen of that valour on which his father had so often
dwelt with pride and rapture. The feats
he saw performed this day fully equalled
any he had heard of, and as he joined in
the shout of victory, he again exulted in
the thought of being the comrade of such
heroes.—" My aunt," he said to himself,
" laid great stress upon the size of the
bumps of *constructiveness* and *destructiveness* on my skull; but, hang it, from the
captain to the powder-monkey, which is
including several hundred men, every
man seems to possess organs of equal dimensions!" But when would the time
arrive in which he should be able to especially distinguish himself—to take the
lead—to set the example, instead of following it? It was yet distant, and all he
could do, in the interim, was to fit himself
for the occasion, by diligent attention to
the duties of his profession.

But these did not prevent his occasionally attending to others, and the system

of Gall and Spurzheim still continued to
be his favourite one, or rather every day
took deeper hold of his imagination. Infatuated by it, instead of using his reason
and discretion in regulating his conduct,
he was feeling the bumps on his skull to
account for it; and whenever reprimanded
for faults committed, conceived himself
most barbarously treated, from the cruel
injustice there was in censuring him for
-actions over which he had no possible control—" But such must continue to prevail in the world," he would exclaim, " till
all become equally enlightened; then, and
not till then, shall we relax in our severity
towards each other !"

At length, after serving about two
years, during which opportunities occurred
for his visiting many celebrated places, the
long wished-for one, as he conceived, arrived, for permitting him to signalize
himself. Observing a ship lying at anchor under the protection of a battery at
the mouth of a harbour, blockaded by his
own vessel, his active and enterprising

temper made him immediately call upon his organ of *constructiveness*, and having formed a plan for cutting the enemy's vessel out of the harbour, it was submitted to his commander, with an earnest entreaty that he might be allowed to achieve the exploit. The imminent hazard attending it rendered it difficult for him to obtain the requisite permission.

At length his supplications prevailed; the captain, unwilling to disappoint or check the ardour of so daring a spirit, gave the desired consent, provided he could get a sufficient number of men to volunteer in the business with him. This was not a hard matter; twelve gallant fellows instantly stepped forward; and at the destined hour, that is to say, as soon as the shades of darkness had overspread the hemisphere, the pinnace, was lowered, and the party, armed with pistols and cutlasses, descended into it, all determined to conquer or die.

Eugene, on their way, observed a sentinel beneath the fortress; could this man be put out of the way of giving an alarm, it would be doing wonders ; accordingly, ordering the boat to lay to under the rock on which the battery was erected, he landed by himself, and, after much difficulty and danger, succeeded in clambering up the sides.

On reaching the top, he stooped down, and creeping cautiously along, till he came to the box where the sentinel was stationed, obtained possession of his firelock, and had a pistol clapped to his breast ere he knew whom he was attacked by. The astonished wretch implored mercy. Eugene hesitated a moment; but the organ of *benevolence* prevailing, he satisfied himself with obliging the soldier to descend into the boat with him.

On reaching the object of attack, it was immediately boarded. A desperate conflict ensued, the numbers in the vessel more than doubling the assailers, but notwithstanding which Eugene finally succeeded in cutting it out. This desperate exploit was hardly achieved ere the fort, by this time alarmed, commenced a brisk cannonading.

Flushed with success, Eugene entirely lost sight of discretion, and would have the prize brought opposite the fort, for the purpose of silencing it. While the men were endeavouring to obey this rash order, the tide changed. Advantage was immediately taken of the circumstance by the enemy; they put off in boats, well armed, and after a sharp conflict, succeeded in retaking the vessel, and making prisoners of most of the party; Eugene, and the few that escaped with him, being indebted for the circumstance to their skill in swimming.

On regaining his own ship, he was summoned into the presence of the commander, where he met with a severe reprimand for the rashness he had been guilty of.—" I should be sorry," continued his gallant adviser, " to dishearten a youthful spirit, but I deem it an incumbent duty to endeavour to impress upon your mind,

that valour without discretion can never
be regarded in any other light than as a
species of madness.   Conduct, in every instance throughout life, is requisite, but
more especially when the safety of others
is committed to our care; but I can too
well understand the cause of your error,
however, not to be able to prevail on myself to forbear making any further animad-
versions on it, with this remark, that I
should conceive it utterly inconsistent
with my duty to pass over the repetition
of it in a similar manner."

After the expectations he had indulged, it would be ridiculous to say that Eugene was not stung to the very quick by
this rebuke; with the greatest difficulty,
notwithstanding what he knew of the
strict rules of subordination, he kept the
bump of *anger* from operating on him
whilst listening to it; nothing indeed perhaps enabled him but the consideration
that it was the friend of his father that
was addressing him.

Some time after this, a project, similar

to the one which had been attended with so mortifying a result to Eugene, was planned by the first lieutenant, and amongst those who volunteered on this occasion, our hero was the foremost; but on a nearer approach to the fort, which it had previously been deemed practicable to surprise, the utter impossibility of a thing of the kind, from the not-till-then discovered additional outworks that had been thrown up, was so evident, that the lieutenant very wisely relinquished his intention.

The reasons he assigned for giving it up were sufficiently conclusive to have satisfied any rational being; it must therefore be inferred, that Eugene did not merit the name of one exactly at the moment, as he was absolutely outrageous at the disappointment of his hope of renown; for he had hoped the present would have afforded him an opportunity for obtaining that distinction he had previously been disappointed of attaining, and to be deprived of it, therefore, was more than he could bear with patience.

Forgetting that his duty was passive submission, he proceeded, from remonstrances to angry expostulations on the subject with the lieutenant, opposing, with the utmost violence, the return of the boat to the ship.

The lieutenant, a cool collected Scotchman, of long standing and experience in the navy, after hearkening to him for some time, with a supercilious smile, observed he was a poor silly boy, who knew nothing of the subject on which he was speaking.

This was more than Eugene could bear; his organ of *combativeness* was full at the moment, acted upon by that of *self-esteem*, which we need not say can bear no slighting or lessening remark, and in the fury it excited he struck his superior officer.

His sword was of course directly taken from him; and on the affair being laid before the captain, on their return to the vessel, he confirmed his arrest, and took the necessary measures for having a court-martial held on him, on entering port;

but it was with the greatest regret he found himself compelled to the performance of this imperative duty, more especially as the offence committed was one that rendered the offender liable to the punishment of death; so great was the fancy he had taken to the lad, and such the friendship he felt for the father.

Being brought to a court-martial, on being called upon for his defence, Eugene arose, and, to the surprise of a crowded court, thus began—" I rise, gentlemen, filled with wonder, that a set of educated men, in this enlightened age, should act in such a manner, as to place me in the situation in which I now stand. I am accused of striking lieutenant Macintosh—'tis an accusation I do not deny—I could not if I would, my organ of *secretiveness* being too small to permit me. This act you are pleased to call an offence—I deny its being so, because it was merited; but supposing it were what it is designated, or even a crime of the greatest magnitude, why should I be punished for that which

I could not help? The legislature, you
will tell me, contemplates it in so heinous
a light, as to have apportioned the punishment of death to it; but, gentlemen, this
was at a period when, with all their wisdom, our legislators knew very little of the
real organization of man; it remained for
this, the age of deep discovery, research,
and science, to positively prove and ascertain this, and once proved and ascertained,
it must be self-evident, that all acts tending to severity should be abrogated, as
cruel and unjust in the extreme, or regarded as the dead-letter ones of barbarous periods.

"It is an admitted fact, beyond controversy, that all things human are in a progressive state, nothing under the sun being at a stand. We see by history this
remark verified. From the grossest ignorance and darkness, like the world itself,
that was produced out of chaos, the descendants of the original inhabitants of
this island gradually emerged, till, in the
course of time, they gave place to a set of

beings, learned, polished, and otherwise enlightened; until, at this day, we stand the first nation in the civilized world. But this state of perfection was not accomplished all at once—it took several years to be brought about, gradually proceeding, step by step, and as we advanced, we looked back with surprise, that those who had gone before us could have walked in such profound darkness, in respect to the sciences in particular, which at this day stand upon the highest grounds. Invention follows invention, discovery discovery, till we are almost led to believe a miracle wrought. How would queen Elizabeth, that enlightened princess in her day, have stared to have seen her fleets moving majestically along, in spite of wind or tide, to meet her enemies, merely through means of a boiling kettle of water; or Mr. Sadler mount up into the very heavens themselves, through those of an inflated bag of silk! Now, since what then would have been conceived im-

possible has since been accomplished, why
should we deride, or scoff at, or deny, our
belief to the discoveries that are daily taking place? Amongst these I hold that
of Gall and Spurzheim, to which, I make
no doubt, you are aware I previously
alluded, one of the most beneficial that
has yet taken place for mankind, tending
as it does to early enable man to obtain a
knowledge of his own propensities, a matter of all things the most important and
desirable to him. What time was heretofore wasted in endeavouring to learn the
natural bent, or bias, or, in other words,
disposition of a child! whereas, all that is
now necessary for a parent or a tutor, is to
examine his *cranium*, and act accordingly.
But this is not the only benefit likely to
result from this discovery. Noble as is our
constitution, fine as are our laws, yet has
our penal code long been stigmatized for
severity; revision after revision has been
attempted by some of our most enlightened legislators; but hitherto those efforts
of divine philanthropy have failed of suc-

cess; but can we suppose this will be much longer the case? No; as this sublime system gains ground, which, for the sake of humanity, I am happy to say it is gradually doing, depend upon it the desired amelioration will take place—for how could our legislators pretend to Christian principles, to feeling, to justice, if they continued to keep in force, or enact statutes for the punishment of crimes, which it is *now* proved we involuntarily avoid, or, commit, according to the construction of our *cranium*?

" That I am a disciple of Gall and Spurzheim, 'it must be superfluous to declare, after the arguments I have made use of; as such, I protest against the rules by which I have been tried, since, in common justice, I conceive, ere I was accused, or, in other words, brought to trial, it should first have been ascertained whether I could have avoided what I did. How would a member of the Phrenological Society have addressed you on the occasion? he would have said—

'Look at that bump, gentlemen, upon his head;
Pray feel its brother on the other side,
And say, if in the range of possibilities,
This man here could avoid the act,
Bearing such *striking marks* about him.
———————— feel your heads,
And if there is a knob upon your skulls
That militates to justice, you cannot
Give up this much-wrong'd man to punishment.'

"But, gentlemen, I have done, feeling that I have already trespassed too much on your time. For the patient attention with which I have been hearkened to, I beg to return my sincere thanks, and to assure you, that whatever may be your decision respecting me, I shall remain, to the last moment of existence, impressed with the deepest sense of gratitude for the indulgence shewn me.

"Should I be destined to become another victim to scepticism and ignorance (pardon the expressions, but I know of none others to make use of on the occasion), I trust in the organ of *firmness* I shall not be found wanting; though, like Douglas, I may perhaps feel a pang of regret, in closing my brief life, at the quick termination of that career of glory, which never mortal was more fond to run."

Here Eugene made a low bow, and sat down.

The court remained for some minutes, after he had ceased speaking, absolutely overwhelmed with astonishment; proceedings were then resumed, and, after a discussion of some length, it was agreed to find the prisoner guilty, on his own confession, but recommend him to mercy, as a person of incompetent judgment, or as the French would have it, *sans discernment.*

This was accordingly done; the recommendation was attended to, and at the same instant Eugene was restored to liberty, he received his dismission from the service.

Thus ended his short career in the navy, for which he had to thank his aunt, and her mad passion for the system of Gall and Spurzheim—a lesson to those intrusted with the care of youth, how they play

with their feelings, or attempt bewildering their judgment.

His captain, deeply feeling for the disappointment of the poor father, addressed
a letter to him on the occasion, in which
he said every thing that was possible to
soften this, as he feared to him, terrible
blow, assuring him, that though Eugene
was not fit for the navy, he knew of no
profession to which he would not do honour, from his bravery, his humanity, and
kindly affections.

This letter, which preceded by some
days, as the writer intended it should,
Eugene's arrival at the castle, was one of
the greatest puzzles that ever fell in the
way of the lieutenant. How Eugene
should possess all these qualities, that were
so absolutely essential for the profession
he had entered, and yet not be fit for it,
was more than he could comprehend; and
after perplexing his brains for some time
to no purpose, he at length applied to his
sister for a solution of the riddle. This
she was not long in giving him; in a mo-

ment she surmised the cause of what had
happened. She guessed it was owing
either to some hasty impulse on the part
of Eugene, or some firmly maintained
opinion, and she gloried to think of the
courage which, in either case, he had given
proof of.

The lieutenant however listened to her
with dismay.—"What! after all I told
him of the striet rules of the service? By
the head of Neptune, if he has mutinied
against his captain, he deserves——"

"Pooh, pooh! don't talk nonsense, brother; why should he not assert himself?
which is, as I surmise, the whole front of
his offending. Eugene has courage, integrity, spirit—all necessary for an officer;
yet is he not fit for the navy! The meaning of this is, that his organs of *thought*
and *volition* are not formed by nature for
the drudgery of a sea-faring life—some
other must consequently be struck out for
him; but for my own part, I had always
a presentiment, that such would be the end
of sending him into any profession in which

he could not be his own master; for who but the most stupidly ignorant could sup-- - pose a youth of his uncommon genius, his poetic imagination, his lofty and enthusiastic turn, could submit, all his life, to be bound to perform the duty of an old blind mill-horse, that is for ever going the same dull round? As some professions are regulated, I consider the men belonging to them as nothing better than machines; and with his high intellectual endowments, his powers of discrimination, what a sin—what a shame would it have been, had he quietly allowed himself to be converted into one! No—I rejoice as it is, that ere the vigour of his faculties was deadened, he has burst the chain that would have fettered him to ignorance and stupidity. Returning here, he will resume those studies, that only require to be a little longer pursued, to enable him to burst out upon the admiring world, as another luminary in the regions of literature. Let any one examine his *cranium*, and however fitted he may be to command, I'll defy them to prove he is fitted to obey; take my advice, therefore, brother, and endeavour to reconcile yourself to what has happened."

"Why, that I suppose I must," said the lieutenant, "whether I will or no," with a sigh from the very bottom of his heart. "Yet let me tell you, Agnes, after looking to see the boy, if not an admiral, at least a post captain, it is no trifling disappointment; but if so be it is, as you say, that he is so given to mutiny, why, it is as well as it is."

This argument, however, could not immediately reconcile him to the circumstance. He was restless and unhappy for some days after the discomfiture of his favourite project; but at length his happy temperament prevailed over disappointment, and though now and then a sigh of regret would heave his breast, at the thought of there being an end of all further prospect of being the father of an admiral, he forbore any further complaints.

CHAPTER VII.

> " Beside the dewy border let me sit,
>   All in the freshness of the humid air ;
>   There in that hollowed rock, grotesque and wild,
>   An ample chair, moss-lin'd, and overhead,
>   By flowering umbrage shaded ; where the bee
>   Strays diligent, and with th' extracted balm
>   Of fragrant woodbine loads her little thigh."

EUGENE was now upwards of three years
away. Short as is this period in review,
yet what a change is it calculated to produce in persons very young ! yet was it
only maturing and perfecting what Grace
early promised to be. The wild romping
girl was now changed into the animated, interesting young woman, full of animal spirits, but chastened and restrained by the natural sensibility and softness of her sex. No
pains had been spared in her education,
and the advantages bestowed on her were

not thrown away ; few of her age could boast of a mind more richly cultivated, and in all the ornamental accomplishments she excelled ; while a native ease and grace, in all she said or did, imparting a charm to the merest trifle, would have rendered her a creature of captivation, even though less alluring to the eye than she was ; but

" Her form was fresher than the morning rose,
When the dew wets its leaves ;"

while her eye's dark charm 'twere vain to tell, or the kind of dazzling radiance that high-toned feeling and intellect diffused over her enchanting countenance.

Her young friend, Rose Cormack, the young person who had been taken by Miss Agnes Flora Judith to assist in the ornamental parts of her education, had not profited less than she had in the course of these few years. She was the daughter of a miller, who had lately taken up his residence in the village of St. Doulagh's ; while yet a mere infant, a widow lady of some consequence took her under her protection, with an intention of educating her for a governess. Ere her education was completed, however, her benevolent benefactress died, without the power of doing any thing for her. One of the conditions of her accepting the situation at the castle was, her being allowed to take lessons with her pupil from the masters who attended there, to which Miss Agnes Flora Judith superadding her own, Rose grew up, in every sense of the word, a highly-accomplished young woman.

The deference which she paid to her abilities, and her facility in acquiring knowledge, soon made the old lady love her almost as well as her niece; the only quarrel they ever had being on the subject of phrenology, which Rose steadily set her face against; nor did the sweetness of her temper, and her obliging disposition, endear her less to the other inmates of the house, while by the warm-hearted

Grace she was absolutely regarded as a sister.

But it was not merely in mental attainments that Rose equalled her friend; nature had not rendered her less attractive to the eye. Like the Maria of Sterne, she was of the first order of fine forms, her air easy, graceful, and commanding; more that of a superior than a dependent. Her complexion was inclining to paleness, but the slightest emotion tinged it with a crimson glow, as fugitive as bright; her countenance was of the Grecian outline— her brows arched, her mouth small, her lips red and pouting, her teeth regularly set and beautifully white, her eyes of the darkest hue, and her hair, which in rich profusion was braided round her finely-formed head, of a corresponding colour.

Her temper and disposition, as already intimated, equalled her external appearance. She had a natural flow of spirits, though she was not without her anxieties, that kept the castle alive; but withal a simplicity and purity of heart that knew

no guile, nor entertained the most distant
notion, by such mirth, of levity; her sentiments were never twisted or turned to answer any particular purpose—she spoke as
she thought, and acted as she felt. Her
loveliness seemed to set at nought one
of Miss Agnes Flora Judith's systems,
her father, the miller, being a cross, black-
looking, little old man, and her mother,
she understood, for she had been dead
some years, was not more amiable in her
appearance; yet here, in their offspring,
was a paragon of beauty; but extraordinary cases will sometimes occur, she reflected.

But for the society of Rose, heavily, at
times, would the days have passed with
Grace; and even as it was, she could not
help, at times, from the little company
they saw, sighing at the absence of her
lover and her brother. The former kept
up a constant correspondence with her,
nor were the promised presents forgotten;
but his letters were often nearly as calculated to afford her pain as pleasure; for

though William would not have willingly
caused affliction to the heart of her he
loved, yet the gratification inseparably
connected with the idea of unbosoming
one's self to those of whose sympathy we
are sure, made him confide all his vexa-
tions and grievances to her; and these
were not a few, his uncle being a man of
an austere temper, little adapted to conci-
liate or soften the bitterness of dependence.

A severe shock was experienced by
Grace on hearing of Eugene's dismission
from the navy; but when she reflected on
his disposition, and that she might assure
herself from it he never would have turned
his face again towards home, had he done
any thing to discredit or dishonour his
name, she in a degree got the better of it.
The precise moment of his return was not
known; he therefore surprised his aunt
one day, when all the rest of the family
were out. Had she met him by chance,
she would hardly have recognised him, so
great was the alteration a few years had
wrought in his appearance; from a slight,

delicate-looking boy, he was now changed into a fine, tall, manly youth of nineteen, with a pleasant, ingenuous countenance, dark, sparkling eyes, and short, thick, curling hair, that set off his expressive features to the greatest advantage.—" Well, here I am, my dear aunt and kind instructress !" he cried, clasping the old lady in his manly arms, and giving her a hug of the most affectionate nature, " your poor sailor boy, turned adrift, to seek his fortune where he may, because, forsooth, he would not bow and cringe, and relinquish his own opinions ; but, by Jove, that is a meanness I would not have descended to, though the world had been all before me, where to choose my place of rest !"

" Then it is as I imagined," said Miss Agnes Flora Judith, as soon as she had recovered from the effects of surprise and the hug ; " but explain, my dear boy, explain, before we are likely to be interrupted."

This was succinctly done ; and Miss

Agnes Flora Judith was vehement in her exclamations on the injustice he had met with—" But console yourself for it, my love," she cried, " by the reflection of the glory that ever attaches to persecution in a just cause; and that, as nature did not form you to be a slave, these men, or petty tyrants, have only been instruments in the hands of fate, to turn you back into that path which will lead you onward to the accomplishment of your high destiny. Had your father taken my advice, instead of the few last years having been wasted, as they have been, amidst strife, and ignorance, and stupidity, you might even now, young as you are, have been a rising star in the horizon of literature, and successful competitor with ' the Great Unknown;' but n'importe, no great time has been lost, and ere long, I triumphantly anticipate seeing your brows bound with bays, instead," with a smile, " being shadowed with that odious hairy cap, like your late comrades, all tar and roughness."

"What, turn poet, my dear aunt!"
cried Eugene, as he doffed the offending
covering of his head; "ah, that might be
all very fine, if I had nothing to do but
to write sonnets ' upon a lady's eyebrow,'
as if this was the golden age of softness
and sentiment! but in these, our iron
times, something more forcible must be
had recourse to. I have been injured, and
I feel my injuries: they have wrested the
sword from my hand—but a pen shall supply its place; and if I do not ring a peal
about their ears, disclaim me for a descendant of the great O'Neil! We boast,
that the moment a slave sets foot on British
ground, his chains drop off—so they may;
but while ignorance is the order of the
day with those who govern us, they will
be used to fetter the enlightened amongst
us who dare leave the beaten track of science, as Galileo was imprisoned by the
pope for teaching that the earth turned
round on its axis! But what signifies the
freedom of the limbs, if the mind of man
be manacled? But perish the dastard,

with ignominy for ever attached to his name, who should submit to an attempt of the kind, though whips, and stings, and all the arrows of outrageous fortune, were levelled at him for his opposition to it! No, my dear aunt, I will not give up the system which, under you, I have embraced. Justly it has been observed—and thinking this, am I not bound to support them?—that Gall, and Spurzheim, and Combe, have done more, or, in other words, thrown greater light on the nature of man, than all the other philosophers put together since the world began, leaving now little or nothing to discover in the moral and intellectual geography of the head of man. Shame on those whose indolence, or whose bigotry, keeps them still in ignorance of their system! but while this ignorance prevails, we, my dear aunt, their disciples, must expect to meet with ridicule and opposition; but which, encountered in a cause so approved of by our reason, we shall laugh at, as the gods laugh at the petty follies of mankind."

Hardly had Eugene, concluded this *ti-rade*, which, delivered with full force and animation, raised him in the estimation of his aunt to the very heaven of heavens, ere Grace and Rose burst into the room, to welcome his return. While yet the former was clasped to his heart, his eye was turned on the latter, and with astonishment he beheld the improvement which a few short years had made in her appearance. But he was diverted from his eager contemplation of her by the entrance of his father. The lieutenant meant to have received him with reserve, but nature overpowered the resolve; and when Eugene thought, that to the new system he had adopted was owing the tear of mingled affection and disappointment that fell upon his cheek from his father, as he pressed him, with eager emotion, to his breast, in the pang of the moment, he, perhaps, notwithstanding all he had recently said on the subject to his aunt, bestowed a benediction upon it that might have astounded her.

Eugene had returned more wounded

by his dismission from the service than he would have chosen to acknowledge; but vexation, anger, disappointment, all were forgotten in the society of Rose; she had burst upon his enchanted vision as a being of a superior order: loveliness was around her as light—her every word was treasured, her every glance was dwelt on; while listening to, while looking at her, it was impossible to feel aught but pleasure; and, in short, ere he was aware of it, he became as very a lover as ever sighed " upon a midnight pillow."

To indulge in the meditations, and give utterance to the poetical effusions she inspired, the most lonely parts of the adjacent scenery became his favourite haunts; in particular, he fixed on a romantic cave at the opposite side of the mountain, leading to Nell Tierney's cottage, for his study. From this sequestered spot the scenery was wilder, and more romantic, than at the other side: at the foot of the hill, bordering on a high mountain, ran a narrow glen, chiefly occupied by a torrent, sur-

rounded by scenery indescribably wild, all
things being abrupt and rugged, as the
torrent foamed over its rocky channel in
this hollow abyss, half obscured by trees.

After crossing the torrent, over felled
trees cast across the glen, which passage
filled the mind with terror, from the depth
at either side, a narrow and rugged path
led to the ruins of an ancient monastery,
through hanging groves of oaks, ash, and
beech, spreading over the precipitous sides
of the ascent. These ruins derived a peculiar beauty from the height and boldness
of their situation, elevated upon the side
of a high mountain, and darkly shaded by
oaks and elders, well suited to religious
solitude; as behind the building rose in
succession mountain after mountain, as
if closing it in from the busy world on
that side; while the trees, that formed the
bridge across the darksome glen, only required to be withdrawn, to equally cut off
access to it in front.

From these ruins a bowered walk,
suited to the genius of the place, led to an

opening, called the Lover's Leap. The
screen the wood formed at times totally
precluded the slightest view of the country beneath, while at others, through a
chance break, the eye caught a view of a
deep, gloomy valley, the bed of a winding and foaming torrent, that, as it rushed
along, was now completely lost, now half
revealed to the sight, through obscuring
foliage. An angle in the wood suddenly
turned, an opening, awful in the extreme,
was presented to the view, from the tremendous depth down which an incau-
tious approach must have occasioned precipitation, from the sides of which pro-
jected pointed rocks, and tangled shrubs
and thickets growing out of their fissures.
This was denominated the Lover's Leap,
and numerous were the tales on record of
the catastrophes that had taken place here.

That such scenery was not calculated to
dissipate the feelings that had taken possession of the mind of Eugene may easily
be imagined; the romantic effect of the
deep gloom of the woods, the solitary

ruin, the voice of waterfalls, the roar of torrents, the murmurs of the mournful breeze, sighing through the streaming foliage of dilapidated ailes, served to render still more powerful the impression that had been made upon him. But in indulging his passion what was his aim? what did he hope for? to what look forward? In vain he tried to evade the question, and, with black despair, acknowledged to himself, that without fortune, without interest at either side, to form the union he sighed for would be downright madness. But then, to give up the object of his adoration—to see her perhaps in the arms of another—another, who might not estimate her virtues, her transcendant loveliness, as he did—No—there was distraction in the thought! Yet, to drag her into lingering wretchedness, through his ungoverned passion—the idea was still more insupportable; and sooner than do this, he would heroically resign her. But there was no occasion for such a sacrifice; they were both still young

enough to wait some years for the completion of their happiness, and with such
a stimulus as love for exertion, such a reward in view for them as Rose, what should
he not be able to make—what difficulties
to overcome—what wonders achieve?

But these ideas were only the feverish
dreams of a suddenly-inflated imagination, which a little reflection tended to
sober or dissipate. –Supposing he had abilities deserving of encouragement, yet,
without interest to procure patronage, of
what avail would they be to him? for
though he had not, as yet, seen much of
life, yet he had read sufficiently to know,
that unfriended genius has indeed but a
poor chance of making its way in the
world. After the fate of a Chatterton, a
White, a Burns—that fate over which his
youthful eye had so often melted in sympathy, at which his breast had so often
flamed with virtuous indignation—what
hope could he indulge to buoy his spirit
up to enterprise? No—it would be but

G 3

to deceive, to delude himself, to add another to the list of those heart-broken victims, whom cold neglect, and biting scorn, had crushed into untimely graves—and Rose must be relinquished.—" And this is existence," he would exclaim, seized at these moments with sudden misanthropy, " to see our budding hopes withered and destroyed, and a long, thorny path, desolate of all that can cheer and invigorate, stretched before us, our journey through life impeded by obstacles we do not deserve to meet with, till our temper becomes soured, our spirit broken, and after unsuccessful struggles with fate, we fall exhausted into the ocean of eternity!"

The loss of his profession stung him to the soul; but still he would not allow the justice of his sentence, conceiving, from the unhappy persuasion he had imbibed, that he had been most cruelly dealt with. At length, after many struggles with himself, the necessity of giving up Rose became too evident, not to induce him to determine on the conquest of his passion.

In consequence of this determination, he began to absent himself more than ever from the castle, convinced that it was only by abstaining from her society, that he could hope to succeed in his efforts for the purpose.

What credit did he not give himself for his resolution on this occasion, quite overlooking the anxious impatience with which he would listen for the first sound of the dinner-bell from the castle, from the pretext it afforded him of returning to her, and the thrill of delight he felt when Grace would insist on his being their companion in some evening ramble! How delicious were these rambles—after walking till perhaps fatigued, sitting down in some romantic spot, they would digest the studies of the day, or talk over such works of fancy as might have fallen in their way! Hence too they would compare the scenery of their favourite poets with nature, and so appreciate its truth and justice.

At the close of day, encircled by an

amphitheatre of black and lofty mountains, which seemed to exclude all intercourse with the rest of the habitable world,
would these youthful fancies picture and
describe to each other the fairy castles the
mists of the valley formed at times on
their sides, or the extraordinary chimeras
portrayed by the clouds, as they slowly
moved along the void, before the sun had
declined too low in the west to have its
beams obscured by these stupendous mo-
numents of nature: while it remained
above the horizon, it gave to the scene
the aspect of a pleasing retirement; but,
as this bright luminary of light and life
gradually withdrew its cheering rays, the
prospect began to assume a gloom that,
from the awe and terror it created, often
rendered it an exertion of courage on the
part of the females to remain where they
were. It was then Eugene exercised his
invention, or memory, in wild and horrific
tales.

Sometimes Nell Tierney, by chance,
would join the youthful trio, and her gob-

lin and fairy tales were, at such hours, a high treat to her auditors, enriched as they were by her own remarks, and enlarged by her imagination. The ghosts she spoke of she protested she had heard and seen herself, wailing, and gliding amidst the ruins of the monastery, and a thousand and a thousand times the good people, the tallest of them not higher than her little finger, dancing within their own rings in the meadows, attended by the glow-worm.

Eugene had made a mystery of his hermitage, but at length it was discovered to the girls by Nell Tierney; and, under the idea of teasing him, believing him to be engrossed in study there, not a few were the interruptions he began to receive from them. For the philosophy with which he bore these we shall give him no credit, believing, as we do, that they did not put his temper to any severe trial.

At first he became alarmed by these visits of Rose to this romantic retreat, as striking down the supposed barrier he had

raised to his growing passion; but in a
short time, he began to persuade himself,
nothing could be more calculated to cure
him of it. Before, on his return to the
castle, his soul was all fire and agitation
on beholding her; but now, almost con-
stantly in her company, this agitation had
begun to cease. Little, however, did he
imagine, because his fears of losing her
began every moment to lessen, that love
was fixing her image still more firmly in
his heart; and that, although he might
have been able to support a separation
from her, while his soul trembled with
apprehension, such could not be borne
when an imaginary security had made her
his alone. But either the subtle passion
that possessed him blinded his judgment,
or he chose to hoodwink it himself.
When we feel that we shall be compelled
to make a sacrifice by opening our eyes,
how studiously do we try to keep them
closed!

Grace was sometimes detained by her
aunt on private matters. Not having

her company, however, did not prevent
Rose from strolling to the hermitage; she
knew of no harm in doing so—was not
Eugene as a brother to her? and why
. should she deny herself the pleasure of his
converse when left to herself? These were
the moments that should have convinced
him of his danger—these the occasions on
which Eugene lost his balance: without
intending it, he would express his admiration of her beauty, her talents, rail at
fortune, and express terror at the idea of
a separation between them; to all which
Rose would reply, she supposed he was
rehearsing a scene with her he proposed
representing through his muse; would
even tell Grace of his fine compliments
to her, and affect to laugh him out of his
mad pranks, as she called them : but
a secret pleasure thrilled through her
veins while listening to him, that might
have assured her she would have felt
sorry had she really considered his compliments in the light she pretended to do.

CHAPTER VIII.

"Oppos'd to love, alas! how vain are vows!"

TIME rolled on unheeded; Eugene became every day more deeply sunk in the
passion that absorbed him; he no longer
struggled against it—he believed, or persuaded himself, it was useless, and eagerly
caught at the idea, as a pretext for indulging in the delicious pleasure it afforded
him.

When he could not engross Rose to
himself, he bent his steps to the ruined
monastery, or the Lover's Leap, that there
might be no interruption to his dwelling
on her idea. Rose herself still continued to
laugh at him whenever he seemed serious, and to try and deceive herself with
regard to the real nature of her sentiments.
for him, endeavouring to persuade herself

that it was owing to the gratification she derived from listening to his poetic effu- sions, which he was in the habit of read- ing to her there, on the spot where they were composed, that she took such plea- sure in going to the hermitage.

They were sitting here by themselves one evening (a thing now not very unusual with them, Grace, just at this juncture, being a good deal engaged in looking over some papers for her aunt), when suddenly throwing aside the poem he had been reading—" How cruel is your conduct, Rose!" said Eugene; " if I seem serious on any subject, or solicit your opinion, you laugh in my face, or——"

" Well, what is the subject on which you want my opinion?" interrupted Rose, but with a tremulous motion about her lip, that but too plainly indicated her not being unsuspicious of it.

" Why, you know, I was asking you, the other day, what you thought of early marriages?"

" Oh dear, yes—I recollect—and I told

you I had never yet bestowed a minute's
consideration on the subject."

" Well, but I ask you now to do so?"

" Well, if I must then—why, I think
them very foolish things—yes, positively
and decidedly, a very silly thing for a
boy and girl, ere they know their own
minds, to slip their necks into a noose
from which they cannot withdraw them."

" You are not in earnest?"

" I am indeed; I think a man should
never marry before he is——"

" Twenty," said Eugene, laughing in
her face, and seizing her hand.

" No, thirty-five or forty, and a woman
until she is thirty."

" What, wait till all the vividness of
the imagination—till all the fine sensibilities of the soul are deadened or destroyed,
by the flat realities, the harshnesses, the
anxieties of life? No, if we desire happiness in the marriage state, let the union
be formed while yet the dewy freshness
of youth is possessed by our hearts, our
minds, our faculties—for 'tis then only, free

from the sordid and debasing considerations that influence at other periods. We wed from the pure disinterested motives that can alone constitute felicity. It is then alone the enamoured pair can with truth exclaim—

' ———————What is the world to them,
Its pomp, its pleasure, and its nonsense all,
Who in each other clasp whatever fair
High fancy forms, and lavish hearts can wish?'

Besides, the chances are against a man or woman ever living to see their children brought up, who wait until a late period of life to marry. There is a proverb, my charming Rose—' Late children are early orphans—what an afflicting idea to their parents! By an early marriage, a man has not only the happy prospect of seeing his children, but his children's children, comfortably settled in life; and what——"

"What a patriarchal idea!" said Rose, trying, under a laugh, to conceal the emotion excited by the subject. "But supposing a fortune was wanting, as the early

season of life is the period for commencing
efforts to acquire one?"

" Well, and what would be so likely to
render those efforts successful, as a man's
having a lovely and adored being depend-
ing on him for comfort and happiness?
Do you think his own mere wants or necessities could ever prove such a stimulant to a generous and enthusiastic spirit,
as this consideration? no; to make a man
truly exert himself, let the happiness of a
beloved being be early confided to him—
let her, with all the lovely helplessness of
her sex, be cast upon his bosom for succour and support, and to what will he not
be roused—to what will he not be equal!
Oh, how cheerfully could I toil through
all the day, ' if, when I returned at eve,'
sure of the smiles of my sweet girl!" and
the arm which had involuntarily, perhaps
unconsciously, encircled her waist, gave all
proper emphasis to these words, by drawing her still closer to his throbbing heart,
as he was uttering them.

Rose began to feel the danger of her

situation—" I can see to work no more," she said, rolling up a bit of muslin, on which she had affected to be busy; " and as this is quite a poetical hour, I will leave you to your musings."

It was indeed a poetical one, and Eugene knew too well the effect of such an hour on the feelings, to let her escape in this manner —that it was at such moments as these love makes impressions never to be effaced. The day had been uncommonly warm, the sun sinking behind the distant mountains, rendered the shade delightful in the extreme; the air was all balm—the woods all melody; all, in short—the gorgeousness of sunset—the lengthening shadows of the mountains—the dying sounds of busy day, borne to the ear upon the fluttering breeze —the buzzing of insects in the parting ray—the vesper chant of the wild choristers of nature—tended to tranquillize the soul to peace and harmony.—" No," said Eugene, catching Rose by the arm, as she attempted to leave him, and drawing her back with gentle force to her seat beside him; "I cannot let you go; half the enjoyment of this delicious hour would be lost were you to do so—this hour of enchantment; when the deepening tenderness, when the awakened sensibilities of the heart, make it instinctively seek for the object of its adoration, to participate in its feelings: oh, Rose——"

But what he would, or might have added, was prevented by the sudden appearance of Grace at the moment.—"So, a pretty pair you are," she exclaimed, "to be sitting quietly here, instead of coming to meet me, as I fully expected you would do, that we might have taken a long walk together, after my being pent up with my aunt the whole day, as I have been! Upon my life, Eugene, I have a great mind to lay violent hands upon your sonnets, for detaining Rose in such a manner!"

"No, you would not be so ill-natured," said Eugene, fondly kissing her; "besides, I am not to blame—it was Rose kept me here."

"I kept you here!" exclaimed Rose.

" Yes, you know it was," replied Eugene, with an archness of look that recalled the fugitive blush that had just left her cheek.

" Ah, I believe you, to be sure," said Grace, as she skipped out before them, little aware of what was then passing in their hearts.

After this scene, Rose could no longer think of visiting the hermitage by herself; an innate sense of modesty, of propriety, forbade her; though still she tried to believe Eugene had no serious meaning in what he said; but no longer could she try to persuade herself she was uninterested or unconcerned on the subject,

" And all the tenour of her soul was lost."

The anguish occasioned by a passion that she was convinced must be hopeless, was aggravated by the impossibility of her bringing herself to repose confidence, in this instance, in her friend Grace. Agitated, distressed, unable to converse as usual, she now sought as much as possible to be alone. Like most girls of her age, she was romantic, and the passion that pervaded her soul did not render her less so. The ruined monastery now became her haunt, whenever unaccompanied by Grace. Here she could freely indulge her feelings; and here, when she thought it would not be likely to create alarm, she loved to linger, when the full-orbed moon shed its shadowy light upon the face of things. More than once she was surprised here by the impassioned lover; but it was each time with Grace so close on his steps, that all he had time to do or say, was to snatch a hasty kiss, press her gently to his breast, and whisper a remonstrance for her cruelty in thus absenting herself.

On finding she no more came to the hermitage by herself, and equally avoided all opportunities that tended to allow him to speak to her alone, he grew restless and unhappy, uncertain to what this conduct was owing, whether to indifference, or a persuasion of the necessity of repressing his passion : there was distraction in the former apprehension, and some way or other he must be put out of suspense.

He had always made it a point to place himself opposite to her at table, for this was the feast of his soul. The opportunity which this situation afforded him, of contemplating her countenance, of observing every look, was now more eagerly, more anxiously than ever profited by. The manner in which she now strove to avoid his looks—the blushes they called up when encountered—the confusion, the emotion occasioned by his suddenly addressing her—all tended to inspire him with hope; but this was not sufficient to satisfy a nature ardent, impassioned, as his was—nothing short of an absolute confession of her love would do this; but how was this to be obtained, eluding, avoiding him, as she did?

At length one evening, as she and Grace were rambling with him, in the romantic vicinity of the castle, the latter was sud-

denly sent for by her aunt. On her withdrawing her arm from her brother's to
obey this summons, Rose, alarmed and
agitated at the idea of being left alone
with him, prepared to attend her, but this
was opposed by Eugene's firmly keeping
hold of her arm, while Grace said, there
was not the slightest occasion for her returning with her, as she did not expect to
be detained long by her aunt, and if she
were, there was no reason why she should
also lose so lovely an evening.

Thus prevented doing what prudence
dictated, Rose endeavoured to assume an
air of carelessness, and the tumultuous
throbbing of her heart was in some degree
stilled by finding Eugene made no attempt to take advantage of the circumstance that had thrown her into his power.
But he only commanded himself till he
had got her more completely into it: step
by step he drew her on towards the Lover's Leap, diverting her attention from
the path they were pursuing, till, suddenly, the awful gap appeared before them.

Eugene stopped, and looking steadily in her face for a moment, relinquished her arm; but it was only to throw himself at her feet.—" Cruel Rose," he exclaimed, " to compel me to have recourse to stratagem, to obtain an opportunity for speaking to you !—nay, there is no use in struggling— I will be heard !"

" For Heaven's sake, what do you mean by this conduct? what will Grace think of seeing you in this attitude, should she surprise us? Rise, I implore—I beseech you! you know not how you agitate me by this behaviour !".

" Never, though the world were to collect around us, till you tell me what I have to hope—that you are not indifferent to the passion which, you must be sensible, you have kindled in my soul."

" How you distress me! but supposing I felt what you wish, for what purpose would you draw the confession of it from me, aware, as you must be, of the obstacles that are opposed to our thinking seriously of each other?"

" I know of none but what your indifference may create."

" What, not in the disparity of my
birth ?"

" Speak not of a mere chance circumstance proving one," exclaimed Eugene,
with vehemence.   " No, Rose, you should
be convinced, from the love, the reverence
borne you by my family, they never would
consider it as such."

" Ah, Eugene, you speak as you wish.
But do I not know your aunt's sentiments
respecting birth? do I not know what her
pride of ancestry is ?"

" Say but you regard me," cried Eugene, with pleading tenderness in his
looks and tone—" acknowledge a respon-
sive sentiment for me, and I swear there
can be no obstacles to our union that will
not, that shall not be overcome!   Did I
not think so, do you imagine I could urge
you in this manner ? · No, by Heavens I
would not have to accuse myself of trifling
with the feelings of a heart like yours, to
be lord of the universe!   Speak then, my

angel—I rest upon you for happiness; one word can elevate me to the summit of bliss—one word sink me into the very depth of despair!"

Poor Rose! her resolution faltered; she felt there was no safety for her but in flight, and flight was prevented; her frame trembled—her colour varied; and Eugene, believing she was on the point of fainting, hastily quitted his kneeling attitude, to support her in his arms. The scene that followed may be guessed: any further attempt at concealment was useless—the secret of her heart was betrayed; and the agitation and regret that followed the conscious discovery, were soothed, and gradually subdued, by Eugene's solemn assurances of truth and sincerity.

When composure was a little restored, Eugene ventured to acknowledge he did not desire their attachment to be yet known to his family, lest the knowledge of it should induce them to think he meant to abandon those exertions that were so essential for him.—" The moment I have struck out a feasible plan for myself, that moment," he added, " I shall demand the hand of my sweet Rose; but till then, we'll let the secret of our hearts be locked up within them."

Rose could make no objection to this suggestion ; on the contrary, she was rather pleased than otherwise at it, from the raillery and jesting she conceived it would be the means of saving her. Had she known a little more of the world, however, or the general deceitfulness imputed to man, it might have caused some uneasy feelings. But suspicion was certainly not merited by Eugene, his intentions being truly and strictly honourable, although he had not assuredly been quite ingenuous with her in this instance. The fact was, he was not quite so certain as he pretended of his family overlooking the disparity of Rose's birth; and from the fear he felt of the effect of their opposition to their union might have upon her, wished to keep them in ignorance of their attachment, till he had succeeded in binding Rose, in some way or other, irrevocably to him.

Solemnly engaged to each other, as she conceived, and reposing the greatest confidence in his honour and delicacy, Rose no longer sought to avoid giving Eugene opportunities of conversing with her in secret. Doubts and anxieties would recur; but the moment she found herself listening to his soft persuasive accents, her soul became restored to tranquillity; no wonder then that she was not able to resist his passionate entreaties for these stolen interviews. The old dilapidated chapel of the castle was in general the scene of these, as the place where there was least danger of surprise, the terror in which it was held by the domestics being such, that not for all the wealth which they asserted being buried beneath it, would any one of them have approached it at the hour when it was visited by the lovers; while the other inmates of the castle, from its long desertion, hardly ever thought of entering it.

At each succeeding interview Eugene
gained a still greater, a still more dangerous ascendency over his lovely Rose;
but with a heart as full of truth and purity as her own. But a curious circumstance took place at this time at St. Doulagh's, that a little diverts us from him.

CHAPTER IX.

" ———— Foul deeds will rise,
Though all the earth whelm'd them from men's eyes."

On giving up the castle, Mr. Mordaunt,
the recent proprietor, requested permission
to still retain two or three apartments,
in a remote part of it, it not being
convenient, just at that time, to remove
some articles he had deposited in them.
This was readily granted; these rooms
being amongst the number of those the

family did not mean to use, and entirely out of the line of those prepared for occupation.

Months, years, rolled on, and nothing further was heard on the subject, and the circumstance might almost have been forgotten, from these rooms being in a part of the castle that was utterly abandoned, but for the allusions of the people about St. Doulagh's from time to time to it, accompanied by dark and mysterious hints of there being something in these chambers that should be inquired into; and to which was owing, they asserted their confident belief, the strange noises that were heard in them.

At length so much injury was done to this part of the castle by a violent storm, that the lieutenant deemed it advisable to apprize Mr. Mordaunt of the circumstance, lest any thing should happen to his property from what had occurred. By return of post he received a polite answer from him, thanking him for his attention in acquainting him with what had happened, and mentioning his intention, in consequence, of immediately proceeding to Ireland, (for his chief residence was England,) to have the apartments cleared, and resign the keys of them, with many apologies for their long detention.

Just about the time this letter was received, Eugene was obliged to go to a distant town, to give orders about some matters required at the castle. His return that day was uncertain ; but in hopes of meeting him, when the evening was somewhat advanced, the girls walked out in the direction he must come : chatting of one thing or another, they proceeded much farther then they had at first intended, and might have gone on, but for a sudden shower that surprised them, obliging them to run down a little, narrow, straggling glade for shelter, in which stood the ruins of one of those innumerable old churches that are scattered over Ireland. They were in hopes that the present storm, like summer ones in general, might

soon blow over; but every moment it became more violent, the sky grew heavier
and heavier, till at last a pitchy darkness
overspread the hemisphere, while in awful
peals the thunder was heard rumbling
amidst the distant hills.

What to do they knew not; they were
now afraid to quit their shelter, owing to
the road they had to retrace being in many parts extremely dangerous; and yet to
remain much longer where they were,
would be to throw the family at home,
they feared, into the greatest consternation. While in this state of incertitude,
they heard the sound of an approaching
car; and the probability of its being one
sent from the castle for them instantly
occurred. In this agreeable persuasion
they were confirmed, on finding it had
turned down the glade, accompanied by a
lantern, the faint twinkle of which was,
every now and then, espied through the
bushes, with which the place was over-
grown.—" Thank God," cried Grace, in
the joy of her relieved heart, " that our

adventure is likely to end in this manner!" and was about raising her voice, to
call out to the supposed driver to hasten,
if possible, when Rose, laying her hand
upon her arm, bade her in a whisper be
silent, as the voices she heard were not
those of any one they knew.

Grace, trembling from head to foot, listened attentively, and soon distinguished
the voices of unknown men. The terror
of our poor damsels now became indescribable; no good purpose, they were convinced, could have brought any one, at
such an hour, to so solitary a place; and
crouching down together within the ruins,
they hardly allowed themselves to breathe.
In the mean time the car had stopped, and
some brands being lit, their red glare allowed the affrighted girls to see, through
the chinks of the wall behind which they
were concealed, three men, muffled up in
great-coats, with flapped hats, and something large, apparently a chest, upon the
car.

"Come, come, lads," cried one of them,

in a tone of impatience, on perceiving his companions employing themselves with the brands, as the wind threatened to extinguish them, " don't be delaying in this manner: consider what the consequence of being surprised here would be."

" Oh! as to that, master, you may make yourself pretty easy on that score; for who the plague, I'd be glad to know, would be likely to come here, at such a time as this? however, if we could once make out where the grave, or the pit is, we needn't mind keeping this blaze in.— I thought, Murdoch, you said you could point it out directly to us?"

" And so I could," said Murdoch, " only after digging it, I was obliged to cover it over with briers, to prevent its being seen; but—ay, here it is, right under the gable-end of the church; so bear a hand, my boy, and we'll soon finish the business."

The blazing sticks were immediately extinguished, and the two ruffians who had held them proceeded to lift the chest

from the car; as they put, or rather threw
it into the earth, a rattling sound was
heard within it, that made the girls shudder.

As they were loosely filling up the
chasm, and covering it over by the light
of the lantern—"Are you sure," demanded he whom they styled master, in a tone
of the most anxious alarm, " that there is
no danger of any discovery taking place
here?"

"Oh sorrow danger!" replied Murdoch;
" in the first place, myself will be here by
the first peep of day, to see that all is safe
and snug; and in the next, barring myself, I don't suppose there's a man in the
place would set spade in the spot, seeing
there's an ould story tould of a priest that
was buried in it, leaving a malediction to
any one who should disturb his bones."

" Well, I hope it may be as you say,"
was the reply; " but, should it prove
otherwise, remember, lads, what you've
sworn."

The girls did not permit themselves to

move till the rumbling sound of the car could no longer be distinguished.

As soon as she thought she might venture to speak—" Oh Heavens!" exclaimed Grace, " what have I not suffered! and you, Rose, I suppose are almost dead with fright too."

" I have been in a state of extreme horror indeed," replied Rose, " listening, as I am convinced I was, to ruffians concerned in some atrocious deed, of whose sacrificing us to their safety I had not the slightest doubt, if they discovered us."

" Good God! what a narrow escape we have had!" said Grace, shuddering. " Yes, there cannot be a doubt of what they buried being the body, or rather skeleton, of some murdered person, for the sound within the chest was evidently that of the rattling of bones: but what is to be done? I tremble to remain here another minute, and yet I am almost equally afraid to stir, lest of encountering those ruffians."

" I don't apprehend any great danger from the circumstance," replied Rose, " except in the immediate vicinity of this. At all events we must run the risk, lest their cowardly fears should make them return unexpectedly; and see, the moon is beginning to struggle through the watery clouds, so that we should hardly have any chance of remaining concealed from them if they came back."

"Let us fly then," said the terrified Grace; and seizing the arm of Rose, they hurried, with all the quickness of alarm, through the wet bushes.

On emerging from the glade, they looked cautiously about them, to see whether any one was lurking near it. They perceived no one, however, and hastening onward, hardly allowed themselves time to breathe, till they came within sight of the castle. Entering by the nearest gate to them, in order to avoid a round to the usual entrance, they had to cross the solitary grass-grown court, in which were the chambers still retained by Mr. Mordaunt, to the one in which the inhabited part of the castle stood.

" Stop," said Rose, suddenly laying hold of Grace as they were going on ; " don't I see the door leading to the rooms locked up by Mr. Mordaunt lying open ?"

" No, to be sure," replied Grace—" how could that be, when he is not yet come over, and has the key in his possession? and yet upon my word it is, and with a key in it! Some one has been here then—is it possible he could have arrived clandestinely? or, rather, have any motive for keeping his visit to these apartments a secret ?"

Rose staggered, and caught at Grace for support.—" A horrible suspicion crosses my mind," she said, " that what we witnessed this night is connected with them ; tales much to the disadvantage of Mr. Mordaunt have been in circulation, you know; and assuredly, now I am collected, the voice of one of the men we saw in the churchyard was that of a person of a superior description."

" You make me shudder !" cried Grace. " My very blood runs cold at the thought of any atrocious crime having been perpetrated beneath the roof under which we reside: but I'll tell you what we'll do—we'll secure this door, and without mentioning any thing of what occurred this evening, return, at an early hour in the morning, to examine the apartments by ourselves, when, if we find any further grounds for suspicion, we'll consider how we shall act."

Rose could make no objection to this plan, and the door being secured, they went on. Instead of finding all within in a state of alarm about them, as they fully expected, from the lateness of the hour, and the storm to which they had been exposed, they found them in a perfect state of composure. But the fact was, their absence was not known, Miss Agnes Flora Judith being engaged at study at the time of their going out, and the lieutenant having dined abroad that day, and the servant man, the only person who saw them leaving home, having taken himself off, the moment their backs were turned, to a dance in the village.

Their nerves were so agitated, that, instead of separating for the night, they continued together in Grace's chamber, talking, more than sleeping, of the extraordinary manner in which atrocious crimes were still brought to light, and the convincing proof this afforded of there being an omniscient eye, that never slumbereth or sleepeth, continually watching over us, so that he who says in his heart "there is no God," indeed completely deceiveth himself.

By the first dawn of day they were up, and stealing out, admitted themselves, with a feeling of mingled impatience and dread, to the chambers they were so anxious to inspect. They consisted of two large dreary rooms, forming part of a range that united two of the old mouldering towers that flanked the building, and were both lying open, containing, with a few articles of antique furniture (comprising a bed, a few chairs, and a table or two), several female

habiliments scattered about, of a description calculated to induce a belief of their
owner having been of superior rank. But
who was this owner, or who the last oc-
cupier of these desolate apartments, where
scarce the light of day could find admission, from the smallness of the high-raised
casements, and the gloomy curtain spread
over them by the dark tangled ivy?

But conjecture was vain on the subject.
The hints, however, they had heard, of an
unknown female having been confined in
the castle by Mr. Mordaunt, whom nobody ever saw, and who had been removed
from it with the same silence and mystery that she had been brought to it, did
not fail to recur to their recollection at
the moment, attended with a cold shudder,
from the idea of what they had seen the
preceding night.

"Could these silent chambers speak,"
cried Grace, "what a tale of suffering
might they not perhaps reveal! Yet is it
possible that Mr. Mordaunt could be guilty of what we are certainly now allowing

ourselves to suspect him? His character, even here, where he is neither liked nor loved, is not that of a dissipated man; on the contrary, he has always, I understand, been reckoned even a doting husband; and if the person supposed to have been confined here was not the victim of seduction, which, from what we have heard of him, seems improbable, what else could she have been? or whatever motive than her being one could he have had for spiriting her away? But, Rose, does not our stolen visit to these chambers remind you of some of the incidents in the Mysteries of Udolpho? in particular of Emily's midnight one with old Dorothee the housekeeper, to the apartments of her deceased aunt? Could we but find a lute, a picture, resembling one or other of us, and see a ghastly visage gradually rising, not above that pall, to be sure, but that counterpane, which, however, from the dust that has settled on it, does not certainly appear very unlike one, it would be quite similar."

" Hush !" cried Rose, in an under tone, " I think I hear some one on the stairs."

"Good God!" exclaimed Grace—and the temerity of which they had been guilty, in visiting these remote chambers, at such an 'hour, by themselves, all at once occurred to them.

They listened tremblingly. Rose's ear had not deceived. her; a heavy foot was plainly heard ascending; and Grace, in indescribable terror, involuntarily crouched down behind Rose, so as to be completely concealed by her.

Not less alarmed, Rose stood absolutely transfixed with fear to the floor, directly fronting the stairs upon which this chamber opened, her dark hair stiffened up above her brow, and the lifeblood forsaking her cheek, so that she might well, at the moment, from the imperfect light that still, from the earliness of the hour, prevailed within the chamber, have been mistaken by a superstitious mind or a guilty conscience for a tenant of the tomb.

Presently a man was seen ascending

the stairs; ere he had well gained the top, however, he suddenly paused, evidently owing to the figure that was facing him in the chamber.—" Merciful Heaven, do my eyes deceive me!" Rose heard him exclaim, betraying, by the voice in which the exclamation was uttered, his being the person who evidently was the director of what had taken place the preceding night at the ruins.

He appeared irresolute whether to advance or draw back; on a slight movement of Rose's, however, he precipitately retreated. A groan was instantly after heard, with a noise resembling that of a fall.

" Good Heavens! should he be killed!" exclaimed Rose, " for I am convinced he has fallen."

" Oh no, I hope not!" cried Grace.

They cautiously advanced to reconnoitre; he was gone, however, leaving the door open behind him, doubtless owing to the agitation he was in.

We need hardly say, that our damsels

did not lose any further time in speculating or surmising; they darted out, leaving the key as they had found it the preceding night.

Some time elapsed ere the flutter of their spirits at all subsided. At length, a little recovering herself—" Well," exclaimed Grace, " thus conscience doth make cowards of us all,' for to its influence I positively and decidedly believe was owing the precipitate retreat of this man, whoever he is."

" Why you don't suppose he took me for a ghost?" said Rose.

" I really am inclined to do so; the idea may appear ludicrous, but when we reflect on what we have heard of the effects of conscience on a guilty spirit—the deeds of horror it has been the means of bringing to light—the strong and powerful minds it has been the means of unnerving, making him who laughed at the battle's roar turn pale at a fleeting shadow, and shrink within himself at the whisper of a passing breeze—I do not think it de-

serves derision : it is, in short, the accusing spirit armed with ' whips and stings,'
the mysterious power of giving a threatening meaning to all we see or hear, that
is raised up against us the moment we wil-
fully violate the sacred commands of our
Creator. Like lady Macbeth, do you not
imagine that the shuddering murderer
must still fancy he sees his hand stained
with that fearful evidence of his guilt, that
must yet bear such terrible record against
him at the bar of the Almighty—or that
the cruel despoiler of the fatherless and
widow may not, in his most exulting moments, be often scared with the imaginary
groans of expiring misery ? Have we not
heard of nabobs, unable, from the way in
which the wealth was gained that acquired them that title, to pass a night in darkness or solitude ? and why, since all I have
stated is known to be a fact, why, I say,
should my suggestion about you this
morning be ridiculed ?—Oh my God !"
she suddenly added, dropping on her

knees, and raising her beaming eyes to
heaven, " since such are the horrors of
guilt, keep me ever from the knowledge
of it! strengthen me, that I be not led into temptation—for, let my destiny in life
be what it may, still, if the consolations of
an approving conscience are mine, it cannot be utterly a bitter one.   My path may
be lowly, but if, in the security of conscious innocence, I can inhale the sweets
of nature, and enjoy its beauties, will it
not still be one of bliss—for could all the
splendour of wealth make amends for such
fears, such horrors, as I have alluded to?"

The quivering lip and trickling tears of
Rose, proved her joining in this supplication.

> " So pray'd they innocent,
> And to their minds firm peace restor'd."

They had hardly done breakfast, when
a chaise and four drove up to the door,
and Mr. Mordaunt was announced.

The girls exchanged looks at the curious
confirmation which his arrival, just at this

juncture, was of the suspicions that had taken possession of their minds.

This gentleman had now attained the third season, or, in other words, the autumn of his days; but advancing age had only served to render his appearance more imposing: tall of stature, with a dignified, commanding air, he was what might be pronounced a magnificent-looking personage; but though his countenance was certainly handsome, there either really was a something sly, dark, dissimulative, in the expression of it, or else the girls fancied so, through the influence of the impression under which they laboured, that forbade those feelings of pleasure and confidence it might otherwise have inspired. The lieutenant and his sister had previously a personal knowledge of him; but Grace was quite too young at the time the negotiation for the castle was entered into, to have any recollection of him.

Compliments having passed between

him, her father, and aunt, she was introduced to him, and then Rose. It so happened, that until the moment of her being
presented to him, he had not observed
Rose, through her being obscured by
Grace, behind whom she had modestly
retired, to give her her due precedence.
The instant his eyes fell upon her he
started back, and—"Good God!" escaped
him; then recollecting himself—" I—I
beg pardon," he said; "but a sudden gid-
diness seized me: a—another niece, I
presume, ma'am?" with a kind of forced
smile, to Miss Agnes Flora Judith.

"No, sir, no kind of relation, though
quite as much loved as if she were; her
name is Cormack, as I have already told
you."

"Oh! ay—Cormack! Cormack!" and
he repeated the name several times, with
the air of a man perfectly unconscious of
what he was uttering at the moment;
then again recollecting himself in some
degree—"These sudden giddinesses are
terrible things," he said; "may I entreat,"

throwing himself into a chair, "for a glass of water?"

Rose was standing near a table, on which there was a glass jug of the pure lymph, clear and sparkling as brought from its native fountain; she directly poured out a glass, and presented it to him. He received it with a bend of acknowledgment; but at the very instant he was raising it to his lips, his eyes encountering hers, as she stood regarding him with a feeling of compassion—that compassion with which a virtuous mind cannot forbear viewing a fallen fellow-creature, such as she believed him to be, his voice, the instant it met their ear, having betrayed, both to her and Grace, his being the person who had caused them such alarm that morning—he suddenly rested it on his knee, and—"Gracious Heaven! what——". he stopped, gulped down the water, hastily rose, and walked to a window.

"You appear much indisposed, sir," said Miss Agnes Flora Judith, "and I advise you therefore to endeavour to obtain a little rest. When over-fatigued by study, I am sometimes subject to these kind of vertigoes myself; and on such occasions, always find a little repose efficacious. Since your intention of coming over was known, a chamber has been in readiness for you here, the accommodation at the village inn being but of a sorry description, and if you permit, my brother will now shew you to it."

" By no means, my dear madam," was the reply; " I feel myself quite recovered now, and have too much to do during the short time I can remain here, to permit me to lose a minute. Nor will it be in my power to avail myself of your kind hospitality to its full extent—I cannot sleep under this roof. But if I am permitted to pass the very few hours I shall have at my command here in the present society, I shall consider myself highly favoured."

A suitable reply was returned, both by Miss Agnes Flora Judith and her brother.

Neither liked Mr. Mordaunt; not absolutely from any personal enmity to him, but chiefly his being a descendant of him to whose treachery they imputed the loss of the rich possessions of their famed and royal ancestor; but notwithstanding which, the politeness of one, nor the natural kind-heartedness and hospitality of the other, would allow them to shew him any slight, upon an occasion that seemed to have thrown him upon their attention.

Mr. Mordaunt resumed his chair, and the party began chatting on the topics of the day, till his servant entered with the keys of the long locked-up chambers, which Mr. Mordaunt had previously mentioned his having given orders to have cleared, and a small package, which, on being opened, was found to contain some costly ornaments for the aunt and niece, and a musical snuff-box for the lieutenant. A glance at Rose, at the instant he was opening it, seemed to imply vexation that he had not known of her at the time of his making these purchases; and his se-lecting a beautiful brooch from Grace's ornaments, and forcing it on her acceptance, proved this glance was not misinterpreted. Miss Agnes Flora Judith did not by any means like to be indebted to him for gifts of such a description. However, as she thought their positive rejection would savour of ungraciousness, she condescended to accept them for herself and niece.

Having given up the keys to the lieutenant, Mr. Mordaunt prepared to depart, but with a promise of returning in the evening.

The moment he was gone the girls flew off, all impatience to be at liberty to converse about what had occurred.—" Well, what do you think now?" asked Rose, anxiously; " for that Mr. Mordaunt was not only the person that gave us such a fright this morning, but one of the men we saw last night at the ruins, his voice must, of course, have betrayed to you."

. " Yes, the moment he opened his lips I recognised him; and what I think is, that he certainly has been engaged in some transaction that shuns the light, but still which may not be exactly of the atrocious magnitude that we allowed ourselves first to imagine."

" He said he could not sleep under this roof; and, to my ear at least, he said so with emphasis: what a meaning may we not attach to these words!"

" We may indeed, a dreadful one; but still it seems so very improbable that a person in his rank of life, with his fair character, should have committed so terrible a deed as that you hint at——But this is going to confute all my own arguments this morning, in which I certainly did declare my belief of the emotion he betrayed at your sight being owing to his being under the influence of an accusing spirit."

" But as he could not, it is to be presumed, mistake me for a ghost when he saw me in the parlour, what do you infer from the emotion evinced by him on then seeing me ?"

"Why, either that you reminded him of some one whom he cannot think of without regret or remorse, or else that he was fearful you might have recognised him for the person whom you saw in your stolen visit."

"Yes, either one or other must be the case; but how have you decided—is it to keep silence on what we witnessed?"

"Yes, decidedly. I know the disposition and temper of Eugene too well not to be convinced, if acquainted with it, he would, regardless of all consequences, immediately set about an investigation of the affair; and in what trouble and difficulties might not such an investigation be the means of involving, not merely him, but all of us—causing our names in particular to be dragged forward in a way most unpleasant to the feelings, and all about a business which no way concerns us! We will therefore keep to ourselves the whole affair, with a firm belief, that if any action has been committed deserving of punishment, it will yet meet with it; Pro-

vidence, in its own good time, never failing to raise up efficient instruments to
bring to light the secrets of the guilty."

To the great disappointment of the
girls, who would have liked, but without
letting him know why, to hear what he
thought of Mr. Mordaunt's countenance,
Eugene, instead of returning this day,
sent word he should not be back till the
one after the next, that on which Mr.
Mordaunt had fixed for his departure,
owing to his not being able sooner to exe-
cute the business on which he went.

Mr. Mordaunt, as expected, came to
tea; there being no further surprise, for
he now knew who he was to see, there
was no further emotion. But nothing
could divert his attention from Rose; his
looks dwelt upon her, with an intenseness
that actually alarmed her, from the motive
to which she conceived it owing, namely,
his wishing to discover whether she had
any suspicion of him; since, if he did, she
had hardly a doubt, from what she had
been led to think of him, that the circum-

stance might be attended with danger to
her. In vain she sought to avoid his
eyes; move as she would about the room,
they still followed her; and that his
thoughts were wandering was evident
from the random answers he more than
once returned to Miss Agnes Flora Judith, who, with all her philosophical researches, had still a great curiosity to hear
about the world of fashion and bustle,
whenever she had an opportunity of asking questions about it.

Rose inquired of Grace, as soon as they
were again by themselves, whether she
had noticed the manner in which she had
been regarded by Mr. Mordaunt?

Grace acknowledged she had; and also,
that she attributed it to the same motive
that Rose herself did.

"How I should like to know," said
Rose, " what is passing in his mind, that
renders him so anxious to discover the
thoughts of mine! But that I fear it might
be a dangerous experiment, I should
like, by taking him to the old church-

yard, to put his conscience to the test, in something the same way that Hamlet did that of his uncle."

"It is better as it is," observed Grace; "since our attempting any thing of the kind would probably be productive only of something unpleasant to us."

Mr. Mordaunt could not say whether it would be in his power to dine at the castle the next day, but he promised to call in the course of the morning, to let it be known whether it would.

Rose happened to be alone in the parlour when he entered.—"How rejoiced I am at this!" he cried, the moment he perceived she was by herself, hastily closing the door, and approaching towards her; "I have been wishing for an opportunity of speaking to you without witnesses, and have now most happily obtained it.—Nay, don't be alarmed," he said, on seeing her turn pale, and recoil as he advanced, alarmed at what he intimated of his wish to speak to her by herself; "there is nothing in what I have to address to you to

alarm, or, I trust, offend. In short, not
to trespass unnecessarily upon your attention, I have, for this some time past, been
on the look out for an accomplished female, to whom I might, with confidence,
resign the care of a very young person,
about whom I am particularly interested.
Now, in you, it strikes me I have exactly
met with the object of my anxious search;
and as I presume, from the age of Miss
O'Neil, that your services here are no
longer required, if you will accept the situation I wish you to fill, you shall fix
your own terms, and may rely upon it,
that in every instance I shall endeavour
to evince the sense of obligation which
your acceptance of it will confer upon me."

"I thank you, sir," said Rose, coldly
withdrawing her hand, which, while speaking, he had taken, "for the favourable
opinion with which you honour me; but
I must beg leave to decline your offer. I
dwell here amongst mine own people, and
nothing could compensate for the pain of
quitting them."

" What, your friends here ?"

" Yes; the kindness with which they treated me has made me, long since, cease to regard them in any other light than that of dear connexions ; and so long as they wish to retain me with them, the world could offer me no bribe that could allure me from them."

" Happy beings," cried Mr. Mordaunt, " to have secured to themselves so charming a friend !"

" Rather say—happy she, who, wanting friends, obtained such ! A motherless girl——." The eyes of Rose filled with tears, and her voice faltered—" A motherless girl often needs protection !"

Mr. Mordaunt, without making any reply, turned abruptly away, and walked to a window.

Rose, wiping her eyes, was about leaving the room, to inform the family of his being there, which she concluded, from no one appearing, the servant had omitted to do, when, turning hastily round, he prevented her.—" Stop," he cried, interposing between her and the door. " Though no one can more admire the feelings that bind you here than I do, yet let me remind you, that a little abstracted consideration for yourself may not be amiss. The situation of a dependent—excuse the expression—however loved or respected, is still always a precarious one. There is no knowing the moment in which some change might take place in this family, to render your longer stay here unpleasant or impossible ; and, with such a possibility in view, would it not be as well for you to give my offer a little consideration, ere your mind was decidedly made up about it ?"

" It would be useless, sir ; my mind was instantly made up about it."

" To reject it ?—Well, I must say, I think this a little extraordinary. If you will not, however, be prevailed on to accept it now, promise, at least, that if any thing should occur to induce or oblige you to leave this, you will give it the preference to any other ?"

" No, sir ; I cannot promise what I would not do."

" Not do !" repeated Mr. Mordaunt, in an emphatic tone, and with a change of complexion ; " pray may I ask the reason? is it owing to any prejudice? to—to —any——"

Rose, alarmed at the idea of having betrayed too much, hastily interrupted him. —" I have already intimated, sir," she said, " that I should be most unwilling to leave the place to which I have been accustomed—to this you must attribute what I have said."

The searching look of Mr. Mordaunt, however, plainly intimated his not being satisfied with this excuse ; and something more he was on the point of saying, when, to the great relief of the agitated Rose, Miss Agnes Flora Judith, followed by Grace, entered the room, with a thousand apologies, for she piqued herself on her politeness and perfect knowledge of all the etiquettes of good breeding, for not having sooner waited on Mr. Mordaunt, but of

whose being there she had not heard till
the instant before.

Mr. Mordaunt, evidently without knowing one word she was saying, abruptly informed her it was not in his power to have
the pleasure of dining that day at the
castle, and then took a hasty leave, with a
promise of calling in the evening, previous
to his departure the ensuing morning.

The moment Rose found herself alone
with Grace, she informed her of the recent scene; anxiously asking her whether
she did not conceive the offer of Mr. Mordaunt meant for a lure, to get her into his
power, owing to some suspicion of her recognition of him?

Grace was very much inclined to think
so, but feared acknowledging this, lest of
alarming Rose; she therefore rather evasively answered—it might or might not be
so; that when people entertained a prejudice against any one, they were apt to put
the worst construction upon whatever
they said or did; but, at all events, it was
no matter, whether it was the dictate of

treachery or not, since she neither had or intended to accept it.

Rose protested she would not, if possible to avoid it, remain in the presence of Mr. Mordaunt again, so unpleasant to her was the scrutinizing earnestness with which he regarded her. Accordingly, on his being announced in the evening, to take leave, she made a hasty escape from the parlour by one door, as he entered by another; and with real joy, the next morning early, heard the distant rolling of his carriage wheels through the village.

The arrival of Eugene served to divert her thoughts still further from him. The short separation between the enamoured pair was, in love's calendar, an age; and, at the usual hour, a meeting was appointed that evening in the old chapel.

CHAPTER X.

" I scorn the chilling wind and beating rain,
      Nor heed cold watchings in the dewy ground,
If all the hardships I for love sustain,
      With love's victorious joys at last be crown'd."

IT was not without agitated nerves that
Rose kept these appointments; but not
even so much through the apprehension of
an unpleasant surprise, as the idea of acting with any thing like disingenuity towards friends who had such claims upon
her confidence; in particular, it was painful to a nature open and affectionate as
hers, to have any concealments from a
friend so dear as Grace.

As usual, Eugene received her trembling in his arms, and, as usual, was obliged to exert all his eloquence, to reassure
and compose her, ere her tremour at all subsided.

"Oh, what unhappiness have I not suffered during these few last days," cried Eugene, when he found she was again able to attend to him, "separating me as they did from you! If so miserable during an absence that I looked forward to have ended every minute, what will not my wretchedness be in a separation I cannot exactly fix the termination of! except, indeed, you consent to put an end to all further apprehension about our union, by binding yourself in such a manner to me as we shall both deem irrevocable."

"How do you mean?" asked Rose anxiously; "I thought you did not wish our union yet awhile to take place?"

"Nor do I publicly, till I have struck out some plan of independence for myself; but, in the interim, to put this blessed event beyond doubt, to set at rest all fears, all anxieties, on the subject, let us bind ourselves to one another here, by going through the marriage ceremony."

"Surely you are not serious?" said Rose, in a tone of unfeigned astonishment.

" By what right would you attempt to officiate on such an occasion?"

" By that of nature. What is the ceremony but a mere form, established by man. Think not I would be understood to speak with irreverence of the institutions of society—no, I consider them as the sacred safeguards of virtue, the checks of vice and immorality, and therefore to be upheld and supported, even at the risk of life. But I contend for it, the binding part of the ceremony, leaving worldly considerations out of sight, is the solemn appeal to Heaven, for the truth with which we intend to keep our plighted vows. I have a superstitious dread about me, that nothing can conquer but our pledging ours to each other, in its solemn and impressive language, plighted in this way; and I feel that you will indeed consider your engagement to me irrevocable. Come then, my love, approach with me the altar of our God; and kneeling before *Him* who sees into the inmost recesses of the heart, and consequently knows how to ap-

preciate virtue from vice, let us pledge ourselves to each other."

Rose trembled, but could not bring herself to oppose him, as he raised her from
the old tombstone on which they had been
sitting; how could she resist his pleadings
—how, indeed, resting as she did on him
for happiness, bring herself to refuse what
he led her to believe he should consider
binding them irrevocably to each other!

Amongst other vestiges of its original
destination that the chapel still contained,
was an antique altar. Before this the
youthful pair knelt, with the moon shining
in upon them in full lustre, through the
gorgeous window, beneath which the altar
was placed, and which, partly composed
of stained glass, still in perfect preserva-
tion, notwithstanding the hundreds of
years that had rolled by since the erection
of the building, threw a rich tinge of various hues upon the old banners, images,
and entablatures, that were scattered
throughout the place.

The purpose for which they knelt be-

fore the altar soon accomplished.—" Now,"
said the enraptured Eugene, as he raised
his trembling companion from the ground,
and with a bridegroom's ardour, indeed,
clasped her to his breast, " now do I consider, that in the sight of God, we are as
much man and wife, as if the ceremony
that should make us one, in the eyes of
the world, were performed by all the priests
in the universe!"

" Oh, Eugene!" cried Rose, dissolving
into tears, as she reclined upon his breast;
" I hope, I trust, we never shall have reason to regret our binding ourselves to one
another in this manner! but if your family
should yet prove adverse to our union——"

" I could chide you," said Eugene, interrupting her, " but that it would not be
consistent with my new character to do so,
for attempting to poison the bliss of this
minute, that tells me you feel that you
are mine, by giving way to tormenting
fears. I thought I had already said sufficient to render you easy on that head—
but supposing the reverse to prove the

case of what I have stated, sufficient unto the day is the evil thereof; and what shall we not have courage to contend with, or surmount, feeling, as we must, that in conscience we cannot permit ourselves to be separated?"

Scarcely had these words been uttered, ere a congregation of black clouds, that had for some time been gathering in the sky, the precursors of a thunder storm, completely hid the moon, leaving them in almost total darkness; whilst the wind rose to a hurricane, the thunder in successive peals rolled over the ancient pile, and the lightning ever and anon quivered through the gloom.

Rose, in a state of mind that rendered her easily agitated, instinctively clung to Eugene, and awful as he thought the storm, yet, as he clasped his fearful mistress to his bosom, he hardly knew how to avoid being pleased with what seemed to make her take shelter there.

As Rose, after a tremendous clap of thun-

der, raised her head from the shoulder of
Eugene, under the idea that the roof above
them was rent asunder, she saw, or fancied she saw, by the red glare of the lightning, that at that instant darted through
the aisle, a tall figure of a man, attentively watching her—" Good God !" she exclaimed.

" What's the matter — what affrights
you, my love ?" demanded Eugene, with
the quickness of alarm.

" Oh! did you not see it ?"

" No—what should I see ?"

" A tall apparition of a man—see there!
by that flash of lightning—how he frowns
upon me !"

" My love, this is silly—we'll leave this
place, since its effect is such upon your
imagination."

" Oh no, not till I have first tried to
ascertain what it is I have really seen——
But it is gone !" she said, in a relieved
tone, as a sudden drifting of the clouds
from off the face of the moon, allowed her
to see again distinctly within the place;

" and yet, I do believe it was nothing but the shadow of that old suit of armour I saw."

" Can you have a doubt on the subject —or, at least, can you imagine it was any thing supernatural you saw? Voluntarily do you suppose the released spirit would ever return to this world of care, of toil, and trouble, or that Heaven would permit our fears to be the sport of bugbears? but, at all events, since ' conscious,' as Theodore, in the Castle of Otranto, says, ' of having offended no good angel, we should fear no bad one."

" Ah, this is all fine arguing in a moment of calmness," said Rose, with a smile: " but I believe I have been silly; so let us say no more on the subject, but leave this dismal place, as you proposed, without further delay."

" But which will ever be dear to me, as the scene of our interchanged vows," said Eugene, as he proceeded to conduct her through the labyrinthian passages that connected it with the building.

K 2

There is a presumption in the season of youth, that gives a false confidence in its strength. The meetings of our lovers were continued, poor Rose forgetting the caution of the poet to her sex, not to trust their soft-believing moments to deceiving man: yet, of a premeditated idea of ever taking any unworthy advantage of the reliance she placed in his honour, Eugene was utterly guiltless; but, in short, both had soon reason to regret their confidence in themselves, and felt that nothing but the real performance of the ceremony that was to make them one, could restore them to tranquillity.

Eugene could no longer linger over the idea of quitting St. Doulagh's; all the energies of his nature were roused to exertion; and having by this time completed a treatise on the state of Ireland, with an address to his countrymen, some love sonnets, and two volumes of poems, on the plan of the ancients, he decided on regularly commencing author; the length

of time that would be required ere he
could be established in any other profession, now putting it out of his power to
think of any other. If there were dis-
couragements to his plan on one side, as
in moments of despondence he had suffered himself to think, what encourage-
ments were there not at another, in the
honours, the rewards, bestowed on some
of the existing geniuses of the day! and
having obtained from O'Rooke a letter of
introduction to a relation of his, in the
publishing line, as he said, in Dublin
(which, with no little ostentation, he promised to give him, should he ever make
up his mind to the disposal of his poems),
he forthwith announced his intention of
departing to his family, with a private assurance to his Rose, that the moment he
had secured to himself an engagement, or
settled a mode for the publication of his
works, he would return, to make known
their engagement, and claim her hand.

His aunt was the only person in the family who heard his intention without re-

gret; but in the results she anticipated
from it, it was utterly impossible for her
to think of it with any other feeling than
pleasure.—" Yes, my dear boy," she cried,
in the exultation of her heart, to which
the sanguineness of her imagination gave
rise, " in emerging from your native
shades, 'tis only, I feel convinced, to rise
another dazzling luminary in the hemisphere of genius. Should modesty, at
first, induce you to conceal your name, to
what speculations will not the circumstance give rise! how will ingenuity be
taxed to discover who the other *Great
Unknown* is, that has also started forward
to astound, transport, enrapture, an admiring world! As in former days the
name of O'Neil was immortalized by arms,
so will it now be by the pen. Hardly, I
feel persuaded, will your foot have touched upon the threshold of the temple of
fame, or rather, approached the base of
the mountain on which, according to
Pope, the glittering and alluring structure stands, ere you will find yourself

elevated to its very summit; for, without
flattery, I consider your productions deserving of unqualified approbation; and
this is not an age barren of rewards to genius—it is not now the fashion to wait till
the tomb has closed over the poet, to re-
compense him as he merits. What force
of language, what strength of argument,
what justness of reasoning, is there not in
your address to your degenerate countrymen, on the evils they have brought on
their native soil by their passion for expa-
triating themselves! while in your poems
I trace the wit of Horace, the elegiac softness of Tibullus, and the epigrammatic
points of Martial! Go then, my dear lad,
where, as some one, I don't know who,
says, where glory leads, and when you
have accomplished what you wish, that is,
opened for yourself a fair field of renown,
return hither, to intermingle the bays of
the scholar with the laurel of the soldier,
those green wreaths of victory, that, in
memory at least, must every flourish over
the tombs of your forefathers. Grieved I

am indeed—but what human joy is there without alloy?—that the descendant of the great O'Neil should be compelled to make an exertion for support; but since it is so, why, 'tis well as it is—that you have powers to make one in a line that will inflict no degradation. What remains of the patrimonial inheritance is not sufficient for two, and to let Grace be without a portion, would be out of the question. The twenty acres that remain to the family of their estates in Connaught, have always been intended for her."

" What, the twenty acres of bog on the top of one of the Cunnamara Mountains?"

" Well, bog or no bog, 'tis still twenty acres of land," cried Miss Agnes Flora Judith, a little flurried; " and that *sounds* well."

" Poor Grace!" with a bitter smile, said Eugene—" if that be all her portion, he who takes her must take her for herself alone; and if he have a heart capable of appreciating her real loveliness, and taste,

and genius, rich indeed will he consider
himself in her possession."

"Yes, she certainly is a fine creature!"
assented Miss Agnes Flora Judith; "she
has all that beauty," and she drew herself
up, and cast a pleased sidelong glance at
an opposite mirror as she spoke, "for
which the family were always remarked;
and though she would not permit the application of the metal cap for the suppression of her *bump* of *firmness*, yet, I must
confess, I never have had any great reason
to accuse her of obstinacy: but attractive
as she is, I trust *you* will yet give another
daughter as fair to the house of O'Neil—
that is, when you have the power of pro-
viding an establishment for a wife, suitable to the house to which you would ally her: sooner, would be cruelty both to
her and yourself; arguing selfish feelings,
or ungoverned passions, which sooner or
later meet their punishment; for how
could a man of any sensibility endure the
sight of the woman he loved struggling

with difficulties, and degraded from her natural station in society, through his means! I know, in the vernal season of youth, there is nothing that we think we cannot have strength to bear and courage to overcome; but, believe me, my dear lad, there are difficulties and privations that, even at this buoyant and elastic period, can crush the spirit, and harrow up the heart, rooting up the powers of enjoyment, till the feelings become numbed and callous, incapable of being revivified by a gleam of sunshine. Throw, therefore, the shield of prudence over your heart, I beseech you, for a time, and add what title you will to your name, do not add that of.' Benedict, the married man,' till a certain independence be yours."

Who that hearkened to this advice could have believed Miss Agnes Flora Judith capable of the wild ideas to which she, at times, gave utterance! but such are the inconsistencies in human nature—wise on some points, foolish on

others, according to our various caprices
and inclinations; even the decidedly insane at times astonish and deceive the
judgment by the sageness of their remarks.

Eugene, in this instance, did full justice
to the soundness of his aunt's arguments;
but he sighed from his uttermost heart,
that it was now beyond his power to attend to them.—" Can it be," thought he,
" that my aunt has renounced the system
she so warmly advocated? or has she only
lost sight of it for the time?" for they were
such sentiments as, in his cool, dispassionate
moments, his own reason had suggested to
him. The first idea struck him with actual
horror, recollecting the advantage he had
taken of unsuspecting innocence. After
a fearful pause, he falteringly asked if
phrenology stood as high in her estimation
as ever?

" Most assuredly !" with a stare of surprise.

Eugene was able to breathe again, for
on this stay alone now had he to depend

for consolation. The day, but not the exact hour, was fixed for his departure, in
order to avoid the pain of an absolute leave-
taking; he gave the family to understand
he would not set off till after breakfast,
but in his own mind decided on commencing his journey by early dawn.

CHAPTER XI.

" ————————From his tongue
Th' unfinish'd period falls: while, borne away
On swelling thought, his wafted spirit flies
To the vain bosom of his distant fair."

To avoid disturbance, Eugene had ordered his horse to a distance from the castle,
preferring this mode of travelling to the
restraint and confinement of a stage. As
he crossed the ancient portal, the crimson
glow of the eastern heavens, partially
screened by a long ridge of lofty mountains, announced the approach of the bright

god of day, rejoicing "like a giant to run his course."

Involuntarily Eugene lingered as he proceeded, and as his eye ran eagerly over the well-known objects, of hills separated by dingles, gloomy with shade, and watered by torrents, heightening the effect of this romantic scenery by their sound, in thundering amongst the stones that impeded their progress, the hours, the days of happiness he had passed within them, recurred to his recollection, and with a deep sigh he demanded, whether it was likely those hours, those days, would shortly be renewed?—" But yes, they will— they must," he exclaimed; " did I imagine the contrary, what would be the agony, the distraction of my soul at this moment! sorrowful enough, God knows, already, without wanting the aggravation of tormenting fears to render it still more so. Yes, confiding in the goodness of Heaven, I shall soon return, to press again my Rose to my longing heart, and restore to that angelic bosom the peace which I have injured. In the mean time, may she be the especial care of that Power, on whom I rely for my restoration to her!"

The voice of Martin suddenly roused him from his abstraction: he had followed with the horse, with which O'Rooke had undertaken to provide Eugene for the journey, and which Eugene had not before seen. On now casting his eyes upon it, his first idea was, that it was the ghost of doctor Syntax's, that of poor Rozinante being by this time, he supposed, completely laid.—" Why, in the name of all that's strange, where did you get that resurrection of a horse, Martin?" he demanded.

" Sure then, from Barney, your honour; didn't he promise to lend you his own hunter?"

" Hunter! what, a miserable animal, that does not appear to be able to move one leg before the other! I did not think O'Rooke would have played me such a trick; he assured me this was a most excellent horse."

" Ah then, sure it's natural enough to
speak well of an old friend; and it's many
a long day that he and poor Swiftsure
here have been acquainted."

" Yes, that is pretty evident, if both
have been acquainted since their birth;
however, this places me in a very awkward predicament, since, without a considerable delay, I cannot now procure
another horse."

" And if you could, the sorrow a need
would there be for you to do so; only
wait till the poor beast is put to his metal, to see how he'll get on !"

" His metal! if ever he had any, of
which I am very doubtful, it is long since
gone indeed. However, if I must, I
must; but it is with the greatest reluctance, and a firm conviction that I shall
be obliged to change him."

At length he mounted, and set off, but
not in the brisk gallop of impatience, but
in the slow pace of evident reluctance;
and on gaining the summit of a hill,
whence his eye ranged over scenes, every

one of which had, on some separate account, a peculiar charm or interest in
them, that he knew, on descending,
would exclude St. Doulagh's from his
view, he involuntarily checked the horse,
in order to take another farewell look at
that loved home, the delightful residence
of, to him, the dearest objects on earth.

Often as he had before contemplated,
with mingled awe and admiration, the
venerable structure, yet never, perhaps,
had its ancient grandeur, or picturésque
appearance, so forcibly struck him as at
this moment; but owing, perhaps, to the
influence of the feelings he was then under,
that heightened charm, that, in our fond
regret at parting from any object, animate
or inanimate, we are apt to see in them
at the instant. The rising sun was just
beginning to burnish its antique windows,
while the long streaming grass, that, in-
termixed with wild flowers and ivy, begirt its battlements, floated and fluttered
in the morning air, like the gay pennons

of a martial train, and all was indeed picturesque and beautiful.

Eugene, with a fervent, though silently-
uttered prayer for the peace of its beloved
inmates, at length forced himself to turn
away.—" Yet is it not hard," he cried, as
he slowly descended the other side of the
hill, that was to hide it from his view—
" yet is it not hard, that I should be compelled to tear myself away from all my
heart holds dear—the scenes of my youth,
my natural connexions, and her, without
whom life to me would be a desert? why,
since endued with these poignant sensibilities—why, since to separate from those
he loves is the pang of death to his heart
—why are the necessities of man so often
beyond his means? why, endued with
elegant desires, with noble aspirings, when
so often compelled to be the slave of sordid considerations—why, in short, are his
feelings and his hard destiny so often at
variance? But this is impious! are we
not assured, that all that now seems dark
and mysterious, harsh and unjust, to our

finite capacity, will yet be thoroughly accounted for, to the fully justifying the ways of God to man? that this is not our resting-place, but a scene of probation, to which, of course, therefore, trials are incidental? and even these trials, are they not often productive of felicity to us—such as, without them, we should not have tasted? If, for a season, we are torn from our friends, do not the delights of meeting compensate for the pangs of absence? do not the delicious tears of joy, that wet the glowing cheek of tenderness, as it reclines against the bosom from which it was separated, make rich amends for the bitter ones of agony that parting occasioned?—if, for a season, obliged to relinquish our domestic happiness, do we not, by its transient deprivation, better understand the value of that happiness? and could the mere possession of hereditary riches confer upon a man half the rapture that, when compelled to labour, he derives, from finding his efforts crowned with the success due to virtuous exertions? Yes, even by the light let in by my own reason upon my mind, I see, I feel, that all is for the best, ordained in infinite wisdom and benevolence. Never more, therefore, may I know what it is to cavil or complain; but firmly convinced of being under the care of a superintending Providence, cheerfully perform the part assigned me to the best of my ability. What reason indeed have I not for gratitude! and yet I have been murmuring—been complaining. My prospects are uncertain, and yet what multitudes would envy me the power I enjoy of gazing on the rising luminary of day, of inhaling the sweetness of the air that plays upon my cheek, of listening to the music of the bubbling brook, and feeling that I carry with me the prayers and wishes of devoted friends!"

Thus arguing, thus reasoning, or, as it might be said, silently conversing with himself, Eugene proceeded at a pace that certainly did not put his steed to any great trial; so that, whether he retained any of that metal of which Martin boasted, he yet remained ignorant, now too completely absorbed to attend to any thing, now insensibly drawn out of himself by the scenery. This chiefly consisted of a pleasing intermixture of wildness and cultivation, sequestered enclosures, skirted by hills, partly green with herbage, and partly darkened by overhanging woods.

Having purposely struck out of the public road, he crossed some romantic glens, gloomy from their awful depth, and the tangled shrubs and thickets that profusely covered their steep sides, while roaring at their bottoms, through all the impediments of broken rocks, and stumps of trees, was heard the mountain torrent, now playing in wild eddies amongst the branching roots of old trees—now foaming again over ledges of rock, as if impatient to gain the tranquil mazes of a smoother channel. — " Who can behold this scenery," thought Eugene, as he looked around him, " without being convinced it is the work of a divine hand? and if

Heaven takes such pains to clothe, to
beautify the earth, should not man be convinced of being under its especial protection? and should not this conviction banish all gloomy misgivings, and inspire
the mind with that strength and fortitude
that fits it to bear up with composure and
resignation against whatever may ensue?
How much more rational is this belief
than that latterly impressed upon me by
the system my aunt has adopted! by that
I am taught to believe myself a mere
machine, that, according to my construction, must act so and so, whether I will
or not, how contrary soever it may be to
my wishes, or ideas of virtue. The idea
is not reconcileable to reason, or what we
have been accustomed to conceive of the
goodness and justice of the Deity. If I
cannot help my actions, why should I be
accountable for them? and yet, that I
must be so, both to God and man, I am
well assured. Incongruous as this appears with divine justice, yet, if the truth
of the system was not satisfactorily proved,

can I imagine that a person so truly religious as my aunt, possessed of her clear,
comprehensive judgment, and enlightened
and superior understanding, would take it
up, and embrace it? No—the thing is
utterly improbable, not to say impossible;
she has had full leisure to give it a particular investigation—she has read, and most
attentively studied and compared the various opinions and discussions to which it
has given rise—and the result of all is, her
belief in the system being confirmed. The
great error of youth is to doubt the wisdom of age; instead of being guilty of
this error, let me endeavour really to understand my construction, so as to be able
to regulate my conduct accordingly; and
suppose, that what now appears unjust
and inconsistent, will, like other matters
that have at times appeared so, be equally
accounted for hereafter. Yet, I must confess, it is a melancholy reflection, that we
are no longer creatures of free will; and,
in this instance, it may indeed be fairly
said, that 'where ignorance is bliss, 'tis

folly to be wise;' for whatever benefit
may accrue to mankind from this recent
discovery, it certainly will not be productive to them of additional happiness. Yet,
if on one hand it impresses on them the
horrors of fatality, on the other, it relieves
them from those of remorse; for, to grieve
over what we could not help committing,
would indeed be weakness: as well might
a clock, if endued with sensibility, excuse
itself for a sudden stoppage, occasioned by
some error in its machinery, as a man, or-
ganized as it is now proved he is, for any
thing he did. For instance—how miserable should I now be, from self-accusation,
for my conduct respecting Rose, could I
blame myself for it! but I know, from
what my aunt told me, it was out of my
power to avoid it; and yet, knowing and
feeling this, it seems strange to me, that
if I discovered any man had taken a similar advantage of the confiding innocence
of Grace, I would pursue him to destruction. In short, I am not more comfortable for being enlightened, and must con-

fess, from the bewildering effect of this
new system upon my mind, I rather wish
I had been allowed to remain in ignorance
of it, and go on, as I had been brought
up to do, believing that if tempted, there
was still a way for me to escape if I
pleased, and a forgiving Creator, to whom
repentance was acceptable."

Day was drawing towards a close, when,
after having stopped several times in the
course of his journey, but more on account of the poor beast he rode than his
own, Eugene found himself approaching
a long, lonely hill, rising out of a dreary
and far-spread heath. Alighting, as
usual on such occasions, he left the horse
to follow as he pleased, while he slowly
walked on. In vain he longer struggled
to keep up his spirits; his thoughts, no
longer amused or occupied by varied objects, reverted to home, bringing back,
from the images they conjured up there,
to his imagination all that heaviness of
heart which had been experienced by him
at the instant of setting out. He was so

completely lost in his own reflections, that
he nearly reached the summit of the hill,
without noticing a traveller, who had for
some time been walking by his side, when
he was roused from his abstraction by the
fall of Barney's horse, with a hollow sound,
that made him believe the creature was at
the last gasp. He was hastily turning to
his assistance, when the sight of a person
so near him, rivetted him, through surprise, to the earth, not perhaps unaccompanied by a sensation of alarm; for the
stranger not only appeared to have stolen
upon him, but was certainly a suspicious-
looking personage, shrouded up in a large
flapped hat and loose great-coat, that prevented either his features or exact figure
from being clearly defined, with pistols in
the holsters that hung at the saddle-bow of
the horse, that he led by the bridle; and
Eugene was unarmed, with very little to
lose, to be sure, but his life; but still
what money he had could not be parted
with without very serious inconvenience
to him.

Both stood surveying each other for a minute in silence.—" An awkward accident this, sir," the stranger then said; " but I hope not a serious one?"

" I hope not, sir," was the reply of Eugene, as he proceeded to the assistance of his poor steed, which, to his great joy, he found, by this time, endeavouring to make an effort to aid himself. This being seconded both by Eugene and the stranger, he was soon upon his legs again.— " Poor fellow!" cried Eugene, patting his neck, and stroking him, " I would have saved your poor old limbs this day's fatigue if I could; but you shall be well fed and rubbed down for the night, and tomorrow sent back to your master, with an admonition against subjecting you to any thing of the like again."

" Why, it seems indeed full time," said the stranger in a satirical tone, " for him to be put upon the superannuated list. A bad horse, sir, where a fleet one would be required, as is sometimes the case in a journey, particularly in travelling over such lonely places as this, when one does not know the moment a dangerous rencounter may take place."

Eugene turned his eyes full upon him at this remark; not without an apprehension that it was but the prelude to something still more unpleasant.

"That we may get over this dreary hill without meeting with any thing of the kind, I believe I need not say I sincerely hope," added the stranger; "yet as this is considered a most dangerous spot, it is as well for us to be both prepared, in case of accidents. Accept this therefore, sir," he said, "as I perceive you have no arms;" taking, as he spoke, his pistols from the holsters, and presenting one to Eugene.

This act, restoring Eugene to confidence, as it was perhaps intended to do, he had no hesitation in informing him whither he was bound; nor, on his saying he was also going to Dublin, consenting that they should travel the rest of the way in company; finally it was agreed that they should put up for the night at a little public-house about two miles off, where the stranger assured Eugene he would be able to get a proper horse for the remainder of his journey.

Eugene soon conceived he had reason to congratulate himself on the adventure he had met with, his companion very shortly proving, by his style of conversation, that he was qualified to be at least a very pleasant travelling one; judicious, lively, and amusing in his remarks, with a perfect knowledge of every place that was mentioned to him. But notwithstanding this his knowledge of the country, there was something in his accent that persuaded Eugene he was not a native of the kingdom.

They had not advanced far, when the moon was seen rising above the distant chain of hills that skirted the heath. The air was still—the baying of the distant watch-dog was the only sound that met the ear, and all, in short, was calculated to heighten the placid effect generally pro-

duced upon the feelings by her mild shadowy light.—"What a melancholy reflection," said Eugene, after a silence of
some minutes, during which his eyes were
fixed upon this beautiful planet, "that a
man cannot, with that perfect tranquillity
it is so adapted to inspire, enjoy such a
scene as this, through fears of his fellow-
man breaking in upon his delicious enjoyment of it! but for these, or rather the
risk of being accused of romantic folly, for
wantonly exposing myself to danger, how
should I love to rove this heathy scene at
such an hour, watching the queen of night
in her progress through the heavens, a
thousand stars attendant in her train, and
listening to the night breeze sighing
through the chinks of the rock!"

"By which I am plainly to understand," said the stranger, evidently with
a smile, "that you are an enthusiast?"

"If to feel delight, amounting to rapture, in the contemplation of the works
of nature—if to hold in religious venera-
tion the memory of the mighty dead, and

kindle at the sight of the illustrious living
—if to derive pleasure from whatever
tends to lonely or abstracting musings, be
to deserve the name, I confess the justness of the imputation."

" With pride it should be confessed, for
it is inseparably connected with genius, or
rather genius is produced by it—for without a certain portion of it, nothing great
or glorious was ever achieved in life; it is
the true Promethean spark, that gives
life and warmth to the dull clod of clay.
Through its inspiring ardour, what cannot
man be able to accomplish? Animated
by this, no dangers can daunt, no difficulties oppose him. It is to it we are indebted for all that is matchless in song and
consummate in art; the heroism that has
awakened our astonishment, and the generosity that has thrilled through our
hearts; in short, you may esteem, you
may love the man who does not possess
it, but you cannot admire him."

" After this," said Eugene smiling, " I
shall ever consider the accusation of en-

thusiasm one of the highest compliments that can be paid me."

"Assuredly it must be considered so," rejoined the stranger; "for, as some writer observes, the mere man of business, by which is meant a person who abjures enthusiasm, and makes no claim to any thing beyond downright understanding, is no better than a farthing candle to the world, while enthusiasts are the Argand lamps that dazzle and enlighten.—But see, we have reached the Red Cow—our *auberge* for the night."

This was a long, straggling, thatched cabin, with a sod seat at the door; but not for the accommodation of the spinsters or the knitters in the sun, but the smokers; the Irish, like the Spaniards (from whom they so pertinaciously boast of being descended) delighting in basking in luxurious indolence in it, whenever they have an opportunity.

A barefooted boy and girl ran out to receive the travellers; the former took the horses, and the latter conducted them through a smoky clay passage, to what she called the parlour, a small room, with naked whitewashed walls, and a floor of yellow clay, like the passage, and containing four or five chairs, of different descriptions, with a table that seemed to have suffered in the wars, and a mouldering turf fire in the chimney, over which hung some prints of saints and martyrs, that, from their scarlet habiliments, led to the supposition of their having been coloured by the same pencil that drew the Red Cow.

Little Norah having deposited her bleared candle on the table, bobbed a courtesy, and desired to know what their honours would be pleased to have for supper?

" Now, my little lass, is not that an idle question?" cried the stranger, " when you know we can have no choice here? Come, tell me the truth now, though I am not your priest, and I'll give you a tenpenny; could we have any thing here but bacon and eggs, with a dish of *murphies*, which, by the bye, I smelt smoking hot as I was coming along the passage?"

Norah blushed and laughed, and bobbing another courtesy, said—"Yes, an' please their honours, they could have a fowl if they wished."

"What! steal upon the slumbers of unsuspecting innocence? Oh no; after going to roost, I bar all murders of this description. Not for the fattest fowl that ever fed at barn-door, would I have poor Chanticleer grieved, by missing one of his wives in the morning; so go, my little lassy, and let us have a supper of whatever you have in the house."

The order was soon obeyed, and mine hostess herself attended to lay the cloth, with an apology for her husband being out of the way, owing to his having gone to a fair that day, to make an addition to his domestic animals, or, in other words, to purchase a pig, to have fattened up, towards paying the rent.

The stranger's hat and great-coat were

now laid aside, and his figure and features
being, of course, fully revealed, Eugene
was quite struck by his appearance, conceiving he had never seen any one who
could boast of a more commanding air, or
greater intelligence of countenance; and
altogether, he could not avoid believing,
he certainly was a person accustomed to
move in the higher walks of society.
That he was a highly-talented being was
evident; but what were his propensities?
—"How I should like to know," thought
Eugene, "by the examination of his *cranium*, whether he has any against which
the keen satire that lurks underneath that
smile, the indignation which those dark
brows evince his being capable of expressing, might not be directed as well
against those of others!" The recurrence
of his thoughts to his favourite system,
imperceptibly led to the discussion of it.

The stranger listened with the greatest
attention to his arguments in support of
it, as he did indeed to his observations on
every subject. To a looker-on, indeed, of

keen remark like himself, it would have
been evident that he wished to thoroughly understand the character of Eugene—
what his real disposition and sentiments
were; but whether from the interest excited by his youth, or open and ingenuous
countenance and manner, was not now to
be determined.—" And you really believe
in this system?" he demanded of Eugene,
in a tone that seemed indicative of incredulity on the subject.

" I do," replied Eugene with serious-
ness, " truly and firmly. Weighing all
the consequences likely to result from it,
my doing so cannot make me discredit it.
There are few human discoveries that may
not lead to partial evil. I know you will
tell me that this has a tendency to make
us *fatalists*, and leads to the doctrine of
materialism, and that human nature was
quite sufficiently prone before to find excuses for its errors, without having the
additional one of believing them unavoidable; but still this cannot make me deny

my belief to the doctrine of Gall and
Spurzheim."

"Assuredly all this I should have told
you and more; I should have observed,
that discoveries that cannot benefit mankind, 'tis both the part of wisdom and philanthropy not to give promulgation to.
But to argue with enthusiasm," he added
with a smile, "on a favourite subject, I
know would be unavailing. Some few
years hence, however, when its fervour
perhaps has a little abated, should we
chance to meet, and the present one be
started, you may probably speak very differently of it to what you do at present.
You may, by that time perhaps, have had
some experience of the mischief the system is likely to do; and there is nothing
so apt to disgust a man with any particular opinion, as his suffering through the
adoption of it."

At length the travellers thought of retiring to rest, and were accordingly conducted, by their little barefooted attendant, to adjoining chambers, more comfort-

able than, from the sitting-room, they expected to have found them.

Transiently-banished reflections presently returned, and driving sleep from the pillow of Eugene, rendered him for some time restless. At length, through the profound stillness of the place, he was sinking into a doze, when he was roused by the voice of the stranger, speaking in his sleep. At first Eugene could only distinguish broken sentences, muttered in an under tone. At length, accompanied by deep groans, he heard more connected expressions, indicative of some deep internal trouble.

"Good God!" cried Eugene, after listening to exclamations that almost excited horror; "is it possible that goodly shrine can contain a guilty spirit? but no, it would be cruel to judge of the man by what has escaped him at such a moment as this, when we know the soul is often harassed by frightful imaginings. Besides, there are other causes for mental anguish than positive guilt. Imprudence

on our own part—deceit on that of others:
—loss of fortune—ingratitude of friends—
perfidy in a beloved object—all, or any one
of which, is quite sufficient to occasion
perturbation of mind.   There is something in this man that has so powerfully
interested me, that I should grieve if by
any chance I discovered he was the reverse of what I thought him."

He listened attentively, and finding
that all was again quiet in the next chamber, again composed himself to sleep, nor
woke till the swallow had at his window
bid good morrow.

He found the stranger in the sitting-
room before him.   It had been settled,
overnight, that they should recommence
their journey before breakfast; but this
intention was obliged to be relinquished,
in consequence of the horse which Eugene
had obtained, in place of Barney's, being
yet to be caught, and then wanting a shoe.

While breakfast was preparing, the gentlemen were invited into the garden, into
which the parlour opened, by the balmy

odours of the flowers, with which, to the astonishment of Eugene, he saw it abounded.—" How reviving is this fragrance," he said, " after a night of disturbed repose, such as mine was for some part of the night!—and I believe, sir, you fared no better."

The stranger started, and turned his quick searching eyes upon Eugene—" On —on what grounds do you imagine so, sir?" he asked, in agitated, confused accents.

" Merely from the restless state of your mind."

" My mind! my mind! and pray, sir, how do you infer my mind was restless?"

" By your groans and broken exclamations."

" Groans and broken exclamations! Good God! and could you understand? did you distinguish?"

" Yes; I heard you say——"

" Oh, I can well guess what—for now I recollect the frightful dream I had. I thought I was crossing the lonely hill,

where we met last night, by myself, and
that I shot a poor innocent man, who overtook me, under the belief of his being a
robber; and what you heard me uttering,
were my expressions of horror and remorse
at the supposed deed."

"Exactly so," said Eugene. "You
seemed, with the greatest compunction, to
be accusing yourself of some terrible act."

"Just so," said the stranger; "I assure
you I was so affected by the deed I fancied I had committed, that I was quite
glad when I woke to find it all a dream."

"No doubt," said Eugene; "and how
many, like you, would rejoice to find the
horrors that have haunted them by night
but unreal ones!"

The stranger turned of a deathlike paleness. Something he would have said, but
his quivering lip refused to give it utterance, and hastily turning away, he stooped down, as if to smell to a tuft of laven-
der. Presently raising his head, with
something of restored colour—" 'Tis rare,"
he said, applying as he spoke his hand to

his forehead, to brush away his hair, that at the instant appeared to lay damp upon it, " to see such a profusion of flowers in a garden belonging to such a place as this."

"It is," said Eugene; " I know not when I have seen a spot of the kind better laid out, or in finer culture; 'tis really a paradise of sweets—truly gratifying to the senses."

At this instant the landlord made his appearance from behind a little hedge, with a spade in his hand; and having expressed his hope that their honours rested well, proceeded to apologize for not being in the way when they arrived, to see that the good woman had every thing right for them.

" Oh, no occasion for regret on the subject," said Eugene, with one of his kind smiles—" there was nothing amiss. But, landlord, we have been admiring your garden—upon my word, it would do credit to the hand of an experienced gardener!"

The man gave a melancholy smile.—

" I had a pretty long experience in the business, sir," he said.

" You!" cried Eugene—" you surprise me! why, is it owing to *you* it is in the beautiful state it is?"

" It is, sir.   I was head gardener at lord G——'s."

" You surprise me still more," cried Eugene.   " Is it possible you could have relinquished the advantageous situation you must have held in his lordship's service, for such a one as your present?"

. " It might well astonish any one if I had done such a thing," replied the man— " given up such a situation as that, for the miserable one of an Irish innkeeper; but, about three years ago, my lord broke up housekeeping here, for the purpose of residing for the future in England, my lady saying, that there was no life to be enjoyed but there; and I, with all the other head servants on the Irish establishment, being discharged, I had no resource, to keep my family from starving, but taking this place, a poor one to be sure; but though I cannot boast of the Red Cow being a very good milch one, still she gives the children milk with their potatoes."

"Well, well, we must hope for better times," said Eugene, touched by the manner in which this simple little statement was given. " His lordship will yet see the folly of abandoning his natural home, and by returning, restore matters to their former condition."

"Ah, no, sir, I see but little chance of that—all is gone to wreck and ruin since his becoming an absentee; it being the plan now not to beautify, but to make the most of every thing; so that, of course, my lady would now dislike more than ever to live here. Ah, sir! if you knew the place well enough to be able to compare what it was formerly when it wasn't to careless underlings, or hard-hearted stewards, it was given up, with what it is now, it would wring your heart, as it has done mine."

Here a summons to breakfast interrupted the conversation, but without putting an end to the reflections to which it had given rise: the evils, the miseries, brought upon the country, by the desertion of so many of the landholders, became the subject of discourse.

Eugene expressed himself on it with all the warmth of a benevolent mind.— " I was in hopes," he cried, " that I should have found what I heard of these exaggerated ; but I am sorry to be compelled to confess the exact contrary is the case. I was in hopes my own observations would have enabled me to refute the statements; but, alas! they have only served to confirm them. I saw the rich shrubberies torn to pieces by the children for fuel, to dress their food—the sound of the axe proclaiming equal destruction to the ornamental timber of the demesne—the highways, nay, the very fields, desolate, for not a carriage or a passenger, save yourself (to his companion), did I meet in the whole of yesterday's journey—or scarcely a peasant did I see in the latter. I saw no hedger or ditcher—I saw no plough or harrow in

motion—not even a child, to frighten the
birds from the standing corn. I appeared,
at times, like my parent Adam, wandering alone in Paradise, on the first creation
of the world. There were flowery meads,
ripening fields of corn, and green pastures
well stocked. To what then, since it was
evident it was not to want of support for
man and beast, was this loneliness, this
appearance of all the busy flush of life being fled, owing? To the heartlessness occasioned by a want of interest in the country. Convinced that, if he did any thing
for the improvement of the little spot he
rents, it would be wrested from him by
the cruel middleman, at whose mercy the
expatriation of his landlord has left him,
the poor *Irish* peasant, having just secured the means of keeping life in his
wretched family, by sowing his potatoes,
ceases from any further exertion : wandering about in indolence, without any occupation for his thoughts, he has time to
brood over the misery of his condition ;
sullen indignation is the result—designing

benefited by them, may easily be calculated. With regard to agents—knowing
their tenure is always uncertain, they
make the most of every thing over which
they have any control, often realizing fortunes, to the utter destruction of those
who confided their affairs to them. In all
cases, however, there are exceptions; and
I have heard of middlemen and agents,
deserving both of esteem and admiration,
for their exertions to serve those de-
pending on them."

" As to Irish proprietors, natives of
England, who have large estates in both
countries, leaving the place of their birth,
to take up their abode in this country,"
said the stranger, " it is totally out of the
question; but it might be expected they
would from time to time pay it a visit.
Instead of continually travelling abroad,
let the noblemen and gentlemen who are
Irish reside for so many months on their
estates while parliament is up—let the
Catholics be emancipated—because being
satisfied, order must be restored—or, if not,

treat them with the severity hypocrites deserve, and I think there is a chance of tranquillity being restored, or rather permanently established, in this now-distracted country."

" As the poet says," cried Eugene, " that were a consummation devoutly to be wished ;' however, we must not despair ; good and generous spirits have taken up the cause of suffering humanity in this country, and from their exertions we may at last hope for the wished-for results."

Breakfast was by this time over, and the horses being brought to the door, the gentlemen took leave of the Red Cow.

They had not proceeded a great way, when Eugene's attention was attracted by a beautiful cottage, mantled over with honeysuckle and moss rose-trees, at the road-side. There was a small garden in front, with a prattling stream at the bottom of it, where shoals of minnows, or, as they are called in Ireland, pinkeens, were seen disporting

amidst the white pebbles, and over which
a fairy bridge was thrown; with a high
beetling hill, thickly planted with wood,
at the rear; the lawny spaces amongst the
trees covered with sheep; and at its very
summit, to which a stony path, enriched
with wild thyme and lichens, led in a zig-
zag direction, an old stone tower, nearly
overrun with ivy, looking down upon the
country.

Eugene involuntarily checked his horse,
to gaze upon this lovely spot, rendered
still more delightful to his imagination by
the air of profound tranquillity that prevailed about it.

" You seem pleased with that place?"
said his companion, at length breaking in
upon the reflections to which it gave rise.

" I am indeed charmed with it," replied
Eugene; " I was just thinking what a
delightful retreat it would be for an enamoured pair !"

" That thought savours a little of love,"
said the stranger, a little archly; " but

don't blush," he added, laughing; " 'tis a
passion natural to your time of life."

" If I do blush," cried Eugene, " 'tis
neither from shame, or anger at the suspicion—I do indeed confess myself as true
a lover as ever ' sighed upon a midnight
pillow."

" And, like all youthful lovers, conceive
that a cottage, with the object of your
adoration, would be all that could ever be
wanting for happiness. Alas! how short
would be the delusion! from the dream of
romance how soon do we awake, to be
astonished at ever indulging in such a
one !"

" I should pity the person," said Eugene,
a little warmly, " who was not capable of
indulging in such a one."

" Ah! this is the great error of youth,
to hug their errors. The greatest a young
man can commit, is to marry for love—
except indeed he has a fortune to sanction the folly."

" And because a man is not blessed with

riches, is he to remain a stranger to the delights of connubial tenderness?"

" By no means; but it is very possible for a man to enjoy these, without the complete sacrifice of his comfort, which must be the inevitable consequence of his marrying without a competence at one side or the other. It is natural enough for boys and girls to fall in love; but you know the old adage—' When poverty comes in at the door.'—If I was a young man, beginning life without a fortune, I should seek to turn whatever natural gifts I possessed to advantage, by looking out for a wealthy partner, instead of exposing myself, or dragging an innocent creature along with me into wretchedness; and what numbers of well-endowed dowagers and affluent maidens, who have suffered their youth to pass away in trifling with lovers, are to be found ready and willing to make the fortune of a handsome young man, by giving themselves to him.

" What, marry from interested motives —ally myself to a woman, the disparity of whose age to mine must convict me to the world of having done so?" cried Eugene.

" The most prudent thing a young man can possibly do," replied his companion coolly; " for, from what a variety of vexatious circumstances does he exempt himself by it, as a very judicious writer has observed—the caprices of youthful beauty—the distraction of children—the torturing fear of having the paragon he possesses so coveted by others, as eventually to be robbed of her—with many others, too numerous to mention; while, if he thinks the circumstance renders his taste liable to imputation, he has only to allow himself a little time for consideration, to be convinced of the contrary. For who has ever attempted to vilify the taste of Paris—of Henry the Second of France—or Louis the Fourteenth? and yet we all know the respective objects of their idolatry were all past the early period of life. If the classics are to be relied on, Helen was fourscore when Paris stole her away; while

Diana de Poitiers, many years after Henry's father had withdrawn his attentions from her, made a conquest of him, and to the last moment of his life had in him a faithful, jealous adorer; and Louis, after having rendered himself so remarkable by various means, by battles, by tournaments, and finally, by his triumphs over some of the finest women in Europe, at last became captivated by an old gouvernante, and sighed away whole years at the feet of his venerable mistress, as she worked in spectacles! The admiration which the renowned Ninon L'Enclos excited, is another proof of the truth, the writer I have just alluded to observes, of what he asserts—that we need not fear ridicule for paying homage at the shrine of matured beauty; as who does not know of the catastrophe occasioned by the passion which her son, ignorant of their connexion, conceived for her, when of course she must have been far past the bloom of youth— or her conquest, long after, of the polished abbé?

Eugene could not avoid believing his companion laughing all the time he was conversing in this manner; this, however, was not exactly the case.

About ten o'clock the next morning they arrived at the hotel in Sackville-street, to which Eugene's trunk had been directed. Here, of course, he expected his companion to alight, as he did, and in consequence was a good deal surprised at seeing him, instead of quitting his horse, preparing to go on.—" I thought you meant to stop here, sir?" said Eugene, anxiously, for he was unacquainted with any one in Dublin, and the intimacy he had formed with the stranger on the road, made him consider him something in the light of a friend.

" No, it is not in my power," was the reply; " we must part here."

" So soon—so abruptly?" cried Eugene; " but if we must, I hope not at least without a prospect of meeting shortly again?"

" Assuredly—of that there is not the slightest doubt—even sooner perhaps than

——but I see some one crossing the street
I want to speak to;" and ere Eugene
could give utterance to his intended request for his address, kissed his hand to
him, and touching his horse with his spur,
galloped off.

This seemed strange; but it might be
as he had said—he might have seen some
one he wished to speak with; and trying
to believe this, and that he would return
to apologize for his abrupt departure, Eugene entered the hotel, and lost no time,
after breakfasting, and changing his dress,
in procuring a boy to shew him the way
to the relation of O'Rooke, to whom he
had a letter of introduction.

CHAPTER XII.

" Such is the fate of simple bard,
On life's rough ocean luckless starr'd !
Unskilful he to note the card
         Of prudent lore,
Till billows rage, and gales blow hard,
         And whelm him o'er."

THIS bookseller, or rather bookbinder, Mr. Phineas Murphy, resided in a blind alley off Skinner-row, a short distance from the Castle. Eugene having introduced himself, and presented his letter, he forthwith proceeded to read it. This, however, was not as easy a matter as might have been supposed—Barney certainly not excelling in the art by which his sentiments were in this way explained.

Having puzzled himself for some time, in a vain attempt to decipher the pothooks

M 3

and hangers of his relation, he handed the letter to Eugene, for the purpose of making it out for him. The youth cast his eye over it; but finding himself in a similar predicament with the bookbinder, that is, unable to read it, he proceeded to explain what he supposed to be the contents, that is, its allusion to his works, and request to Mr. Murphy to point out the most eligible mode of disposing of them.

" Is it here?" exclaimed the bookbinder; " *och*, botheration, botheration, honey! Barney is thinking of *ould* times, totally forgetting that our parliament has been taken from us, and along with it nearly all that could read, or at least patronize literature; so that, *gra*, no bookseller in Dublin *now* will run the risk of publishing any thing on his own account. But let me have a side glance at your MS. because I have a notion, although I can't serve you in Dublin, I may be able to render you a kindness elsewhere, *jewel*— that is, in London, where I have a friend and relation living, one of the *biggest* publishers there, and that's saying a mighty great thing, where there are such thousands of other great ones: but, dear, you see Mr. C——— (the person I allude to), brings out works that the cowardly hearts of others would never dream of; he's the man who cares as little for law as gospel, and so has got on to be what I've tould you: but come, give me the papers; and while I am skimming over them, you can amuse yourself with the books there," pointing to some that were laying on the counter.

Eugene, with a little agitation, produced his M.S. from his pocket; but this was the first time it had ever been submitted to the inspection of an absolute stranger; and vulgar as Murphy appeared, yet still he did not doubt, from his long acquaintance with books, but that he might be shrewd enough to be a judge of the merits of one; and who can be waiting the review of a production, without some little flutter of spirits?

Murphy remained silent for some minutes; he then broke out into a violent exclamation—" *Hulla baloo!*" he cried, " what's all this about? ah! then, my *jewel*, as Barney might have *tould* you, it was useless for you to be after writing such an address as this to your countrymen, because as how, five-sixths of them never learned to read or write *at all at all*, and the other sixth, which are the Orange boys, seeing, by the titlepage, your object is to reconcile all matters, would never give a squint into it. So you see, *honey*, if a bookseller could be got to purchase it here, he'd have all the fun to himself— that is, no one coming to buy, which would never do: but it has pathos and force, ay, and a great deal of both, let me tell you; and if your poems, which I find you have not brought with you, possess equal spirit in their way, I don't despair of hearing your name shortly making a noise in the world: but, *jewel*, it's not by an *Irish press* you must hope to be introduced to the world—no, no, poor Ireland must now hide her diminished head: she may still give birth to genius, but it is not upon her solitary shores it can hope to raise itself to fame. But, to prove to you that it is not to be saving myself trouble I'd be telling you this—for there's nothing I wouldn't do to serve a friend of my cousin Barney's, and more particularly a young gentleman of such learning and parts—I'll go round with you to all the booksellers."

" By no means," said Eugene; " I have not the least doubt, I assure you, Mr. Murphy, of the correctness of your statement; and to confess the truth, I had some misgivings myself on this subject. I certainly feel more regret at the idea of a longer separation from my family than I at first contemplated by going to London; but as I see I must either acquiesce in the necessity of a journey there, or else abandon the object for which I have come so far, I shall gratefully avail myself of your proffered introduction to your friend there, and set off

without delay." Finally, he insisted on
Murphy's dining that day at the hotel
with him; and having, ere they parted,
received the promised letter from him to
his friend C———, penned in as strong
terms as the naturally-energetic mind of
Murphy could dictate, and addressed one
to St. Doulagh's, to apprize its beloved
inmates of the necessity there was for extending his excursion, he repaired, by
early dawn the next morning, to Howth,
and stepping on board the steam-packet,
in a few hours after found himself at the
Head.

On his arrival in London, he lost no
time in calling on C———, who, on pe-
rusing his letter of recommendation, addressed him most kindly, assuring him he
should have most particular pleasure in
attending to the purport of it; as a proof
of which, if he now left his poems with
him, he should have an answer respecting
them the ensuing day.

Not merely the youthful, but the human mind in general, has always a ten-

dency to hope; it is not till after a long reiterated series of disappointments, that this grand prop of suffering nature entirely gives way.

Naturally sanguine, a slight matter was sufficient to give elevation to the mind of Eugene, and in tiptop spirits he took his leave of C————. As he was walking on, in a state of mind that, humble pedestrian as he was, might have rendered him the envy, at the moment, of not a few, per- haps, of the occupiers of the brilliant equi- pages that passed him, he was suddenly accosted by a young naval officer, with whom he had served abroad. After chat- ting for some time, they separated, their routes lying in different directions, with a promise of dining together the next day.

The moment Eugene returned to the hotel, he sat down to acquaint his aunt with the brilliant prospects that were opening to his view, and the hope he con- sequently indulged of being soon again with the dear circle at St. Doulagh's; for a channel for the disposal of his works

once opened, he had nothing more to do,
he conceived, than prepare others for the
press.   But how did he regret, as he folded up the letter, that he could not accompany it with one for his Rose! but this
was out of the question; they had not
dared to make a confidant of any one, and
could not, therefore, hold any communication in this manner.

Never was morning more impatiently
longed for than the next one.   Eugene
was punctual to a minute: exactly as the
clock of St. Paul's was striking the hour
at which Mr. C———— had desired to see
him, he was entering his shop.—" Well,
sir," cried the man of business, after the
usual compliments of meeting were over,
" I have been looking over these papers
of yours, as I promised; but I am sorry
to tell you they won't do."

" Won't do!" faintly repeated Eugene,
changing colour.

" No, sir, they are not of a description
that would answer—they are, in short,"
and he laughed—oh, how the laugh seem-

ed to insult the agonized feelings of Eugene!—" too sententious, too—too moral for the taste of the present day ; but, certainly, they are still not destitute of merit. Yes, sir, it is evident you have abilities, which, if properly directed, might be turned to good account : for instance, if you were to write a treatise in favour of radicalism, or a ridicule on the Holy Scriptures, or a scandalous story of some man or woman of exalted rank, hitherto considered of immaculate reputation, or a libel on the reigning monarch, or a satire on the moral and religious character of a deceased one, and continue to supply me with *similar* productions, I should not merely willingly, but gladly, become a purchaser; and make no doubt, in a very short time, we should have reason to be pleased at our introduction to each other."

" No!" exclaimed Eugene, with a burst of indignation, " never—no, never will I prostitute my abilities to such vile purposes! never will I be guilty myself of what I have abhorred others for!—

> 'Curs'd be the verse, how well soe'er it flow,
> That tends to make one honest man my foe!'

But is it possible—can the age indeed be
so lost to purity and refinement, as to prefer what is gross and immoral to what is
chaste and refined?"

"Ah, sir, it is a sign you know very
little about it, or you would not ask the
question; but it is truth, upon my honour, sir, all that I have asserted, as a
very short residence in this great mart of
literature, and world in itself, London,
will prove to you."

"I am sorry for it," cried Eugene,
"from the very bottom of my heart," with
a sigh that proved him sincere in what he
said—"sorry for it, from the terrible de-
generacy it argues."

"And you persevere in your romantic
resolve? excuse the expression, sir; but
I really know no other to apply to yours,
so diametrically opposite is it to what self-
interest would prescribe."

"Perhaps so, sir; but," haughtily,
"that is my consideration."

"Assuredly, sir, assuredly, every one
to their taste and their principles; if they
pay for them, why, as you say, sir, that is
their affair. But we need not entirely part
in this way; here is a lighter volume of
poems, that I don't care if I take; so what
say you—will this," producing a few sovereigns, "answer for them? I am no hag-
gler, wanting to take advantage of any
one; so at a word, will this do?"

Eugene hesitated; he had built much
upon these poems; but his purse was very
low, and his spirits, in perfect sympathy
with it, equally so, and the glittering
gold, just fresh from the Mint, looked so
tempting, that, in short, the wish to grasp
it in his hand, as his own, was not to be
resisted; and accordingly, after very little
further difficulty, the bargain was closed.

"Well," cried C———, as he locked
the papers up in his desk, "before this
time to-morrow you will probably have
the pleasure of hearing your verses chant-
ed in a hundred different keys, in a hundred streets in Westminster."

" What, are you going to convert my
poems into common ballads ?" exclaimed
Eugene, the flush of indignant pride
crimsoning his cheek.

" Am I! to be sure I am. What else
could you think I meant to do with
such trifles? not bring them out on fools-
cap, hot-pressed! Well, d——me, that's
a good one, your being angry about them!
what signifies to you, or to me, my good
sir, how the *mocuses* be produced, so they
be produced? You recollect, no doubt
——but there is no occasion, I dare say,
to recall to mind your classical recollections; besides, was not the king of
poets of the same opinion? did he not
even sing his own verses through the
cities of Greece?—' Go to, go to,' as sir
Pertinax Macsycophant says, d——me if
ever you'll be a great man, if you don't
cast off at least a hundred weight of the
Irish pride you brought over with you!"

" Let me cast off what I will of it," said
Eugene, with a scornful look, " I shall
still always retain sufficient of it to make

me resent insolence and impertinence!"
and he was quitting the shop, when
C——, who was accustomed to those
hasty ebullitions of temper, from the intercourse he had with authors, and mind-
ed them no more than he did the effer-
vescence of soda-water, stopped him.——
"Come, come, we don't part in anger,"
he cried; "curse me if I meant to offend
you! so come, let me have your address,
and perhaps you may hear from me in a
few days."

Eugene hesitated; but an unwillingness
to do any thing that might raise up additional obstacles to his projects, at length
overpowered his reluctance to give it, and
he slowly drew forth his card.——"Yet what
can I hope from hearing from this fellow?"
he demanded of himself, as he began to
retrace his way in the lingering step of
disappointment; "nothing, but some new
mortification, or additional insult: and
thus end my shortlived expectations—
those expectations that were but yester-

day so vivid, so sanguine! but, as Wolsey says—

> 'This is the state of man; to-day he puts forth
> The tender leaves of hope, to-morrow blossoms,
> And bears his blushing honours thick upon him;
> The third day comes a frost—a killing frost,
> And when he thinks, good easy man, full surely
> His greatness is a ripening, nips his root,
> And then he falls, as I do.'

But what is to be done? had I not better make up my mind to return at once to St. Doulagh's while I have the means, and sink into the sordid obscurity to which I seem destined? But no, I will not so hastily abandon the oar, to suffer myself to be turned adrift: after the expectations my letter must have raised there, how could I bear to return without a further effort to do something? All the booksellers may not exactly coincide in opinion or sentiments with C——: I will try some more of them, nor relinquish my exertions till I see that longer perseverance in them would be folly."

But how cruel to his feelings the delay which this resolution must necessarily oc-

casion to his return to St. Doulagh's—
there, where love, honour, tenderness, all
united to recall him—how bitter—how almost desolating to his heart, the disappointment that rendered him unable to
attend immediately to this call!

He was ill at feigning what he did not
feel; accordingly, the dejected state of his
mind was soon betrayed to his companion
that day at dinner. The discovery led to
questions which shortly produced a disclosure of the cause of it. After a hearty
laugh.—" Well, I could never have
thought this," cried the other, " that a
young fellow like you, with such bumps
of *destructiveness, amativeness, constructiveness*, and in short, of all necessary to
make your fortune, should have given
way to despair in this manner! There is
an old saying—when one gate is shut up,
another is opened; so come, cheer up, my
hearty, as we say on board ship, since this
d——d dog of a bookseller won't employ
you, without your levelling your own
principles, we'll go to the play; after

which, I'll introduce you to a house in
Pall Mall, where you'll get as good drafts
on the Bank as any he could give you,
and in a much pleasanter and readier way."

They went to the play; but when, on
leaving it, Eugene understood that the
place to which it was intended he should
be introduced was one of those gambling-
houses not inaptly termed h-lls, declined
accompanying his friend thither; but not,
if the truth is to be confessed, without
doing some little violence to his inclination; but he had heard too much of the
mischiefs, the horrors, resulting from an
initiation into such scenes, not to see the
wisdom of avoiding them, and determined
to act accordingly.

His companion attempted, for some
time, to laugh him out of what he called
his quizzical notions; but finding the effort vain, he suddenly turned on his heel
with a contemptuous smile, and, without
the slightest intimation of a wish for another meeting, left him.

CHAPTER XIII.

" *Sir Tob.*—Come thy ways, signior Fabian."

" *Fab.*—Nay, I'll come; if I lose a scruple of this sport, let me be boil'd to death with melancholy."

SEVERAL successive days were entirely given up by Eugene to visiting the different booksellers; but without any introduction to them, an unfledged author literally, " to fortune and to fame unknown," the result was what might have been anticipated.

If there be any place that brings to mind the saying, that " gold maketh unto itself wings, and fleeth away," it certainly is London. When, at the expiration of this period, Eugene, in utter despair of succeeding in the object that had brought him over, came to examine his purse, with an intention of returning without delay to

St. Doulagh's, he found sufficient did not remain within it for the purpose. To describe his feelings at the moment would be impossible; he absolutely staggered under them. As he sat in the coffee-house, considering what was to be done, an isolated being, in the midst of busy thousands, away from friends, from kindred, from all who could feel for, or would sympathize in his forlorn situation, his eye was caught by an advertisement to the following effect, in a paper that lay before him; and which, the moment he had perused, decided him on calling again on C———, though with the greatest reluctance, not merely from his previous conduct, but having heard no further from him.—" Wanted, by a learned society, a secretary.—For particulars apply to Mr. C———," &c. &c.

On explaining to this gentleman the business on which he had now called on him.—" Bless your heart!" he exclaimed, " this is a thing that would not answer for you! I am sure I have had more than a hundred applications already for the situation, and probably may have a hundred more, ere a person be found qualified to fill it; so few thoroughly understand the science the society profess to study."

" Pray may I beg to know what that is?"

" Cranioscopy*, Craniology†, Phrenology‡!"

" Then, I flatter myself," said Eugene, " I am at home! each of these I have long made a particular study of, so that if I do not perfectly comprehend them, it must be through stupidity."

" Indeed!" but with rather a sneer— " oh! well, if that be the case, here's the president's address," taking a card out of his desk, and giving it to him; " but should you not succeed (though I see you expect it), let me know, as I was just on the point of writing a note to you as you came in."

Eugene, with new-flushed hopes, immediately set out according to the direction of the card. He found the president at

---

* Inspection of the cranium. † Discourse on the cranium.
‡ Frantickness.—Dr. Johnson.

home; and on announcing the business on which he had come, was instantly admitted to his presence. He was an old gentleman, full seventy at least, tall, and meagre in the extreme, and altogether such a personage as, in former times, if met at a suspicious hour, on a lonely heath in Scotland, might very well have been taken for a wizard. He received Eugene in his study, where, at the instant, he happened to be engaged in the examination of the *cranium* of an old lady, who was sitting with her head uncovered, on a stool by his side; her flaxen wig, one of the ornamental productions of Bishopsgate-street, laying on the table beside her.

Eugene, on discovering the extraordinary situation of the parties, conceiving the servant must have made a mistake, drew back, but was prevented finally retreating, by the old gentleman calling after him—" Come in, sir—come in," he cried; " you could not have arrived at a more fortunate moment, since I am now engaged on a subject that will give me an

opportunity of ascertaining whether you
are qualified, by knowledge, for the situation of secretary to our Phrenological Society. You must know, sir, there's a
cross organ here," laying his hand upon
the naked head of the old lady, "insomuch
that I know not how to decide on its de-
nomination. Now be so good as to consider it, and say whether you can illustrate
the matter ?".

"Sir," said Eugene, after due obedience
to this command, "I should pronounce
this the organ of *inhabitiveness;* but to
have doubts about it, need not be thought
to deteriorate from the judgment of any
one, since even the great Gall and Spurzheim themselves, if you recollect, sir, have
such on the subject, what they state respecting it being on *conjecture.* Now I
humbly suggest, in such cases as the present, the advisable mode would be to ascertain, from the subjects under consideration, how they felt, as to the nature of
the supposed faculty."

"As how, young gentleman ?"

" Why, sir, whether this lady has had
any passion for moving about—being careless of her place of abode, so it had novelty to recommend it—or contrary, so attached to one particular spot as not to be
able to leave it without pain."

" Give me your hand; a very Daniel
I pronounce you—just the enlightened
secretary the society want. Be here at
eight o'clock, and I'll invest you in an office, if not of great pecuniary emolument,
of vast importance to science, and, of
course, the world at large."

Eugene having promised to be punctual to the appointed time, was retiring,
when—" I beg your pardon, sir," said the
president, again stopping him, " but if
you'll seat yourself here, [the lady had, by
this time, risen, and was replacing her wig
on the block to which it had been transferred from Ross's,] I'll take a map of your
cranium, that it may be placed in the so-
ciety-room, for the study of the members."

Ere Eugene could take from his pock-
etbook one which Miss Agnes Flora Ju-

dith had made of it, as well as she could, without his having had his head shaved for the purpose—" I'll free you from this wig," cried the old gentleman, impatiently, and seizing Eugene by the hair as he spoke, with such violence as to cause an exclamation of pain from him. On discovering his mistake—" Bless my heart, young gentleman," he said, " this is a great omission! I should have thought, so great a phrenologist as you appear to be, would have had your *cranium* ready for inspection at a minute's notice! but this is a matter that can easily be remedied, so no more on the subject till we meet this evening."

But though Eugene did not view the recent scene in the light that others might, still adhering as he did to the system that had already led him into such errors, he did not feel, and he knew not how to account for the circumstance, any very exquisite delight at the idea of the appointment he now looked forward to. In a short time, however, he expected its emoluments would enable him to return home;

and longing, as he did, to find himself on his way there, he could not, accordingly, avoid hoping he might not be disappointed in his present expectations.

At the appointed hour, he repaired to the president's house, in which the society held their meetings.   The mansion, it seems, had formerly belonged to an eminent professional man, who had erected an extensive surgery at the rear, and it was in this the society assembled. A place better adapted for the purpose of examining the *craniums,* both of the quick and the dead, could not possibly have been found, being covered in with glass alone, so that a clear, bright, steady light, enabled the members, who met now by day —now by night, according to the whim of the moment, or the urgency of the occasion, to examine the most minute rises, bumps, or, as the great doctors term them, *organs* of *affection.*   The members consisted of each sex, and amounted to forty-two; if not of the first rank, at least, judging from manners and appearance, not

far removed therefrom; at all events the
street was filled with elegant equipages.
Round the room was ranged, in gilt
frames, maps of the *craniums* of the forty-
two members; with the name attached to
each of the party from whose head it had
been taken; and in the centre was a long
narrow table, strewn over with books, and
lighted by an immense chandelier of cut
glass, suspended from the ceiling; and at
each side of which the members were
seated—the ladies on one side, the gentlemen at the other, and the president, as
usual, at the head, in a chair somewhat
elevated.

Eugene being introduced into the apartment—" Ladies and gentlemen," said the
president, directing every eye to him,
" this is the young gentleman I have just
had the honour of mentioning to you, as
an applicant for the vacant situation of secretary to our society. From some observations which a particular circumstance
elicited from him, this morning, I am

inclined to imagine he is not without the requisite qualifications for what he aspires to; but as the examination that can alone establish this fact will take up some time, I move that we first proceed to the regular business of the meeting, and have the honour, therefore, ladies and gentlemen, to announce to you, that the house has resumed its sitting."

This was almost too much for the risible faculties of Eugene; but when, instantly after, he saw the whole *corps de phrenologists*, with as much alacrity and precision as a well-disciplined regiment would go through their *manœuvres* on parade, clap their right hand to their heads, and strip them of their artificial coverings, he must have electrified the whole assembly, by an absolute roar of laughter, but for the timely application of his handkerchief to his mouth.

" But how ridiculous is this," he said, with no slight indignation against himself, as soon as he had a little got the better of this convulsion—" I profess myself a disciple of this system, and yet I feel as if I were turning into ridicule those who are devoting themselves to the study of it! How much, how effectually may not their researches tend to remove whatever has hitherto had the effect of bewildering me on the subject! If I had any previous doubts of the correctness of the system, would they not vanish now before the high estimation in which I perceive it held—an estimation so great, as to induce even the softer sex to sacrifice their usual delicacy to it? Yes, that must be felt and considered right, for the investigation of which so much is done."

A gentleman now rose.—" On the last adjournment of the house," he said, " we left undecided the question, ' whether this recent discovery is not capable of being improved upon?' As every individual in this society is well versed in the rules by which we are guided, in discovering the different *organs* of *thought* and *volition*—so much so, that in the dark we can, by carefully passing our hands over the *cra-*

niums of our fellow-beings, decide infal-
libly the powers of their minds by the
bumps on their skulls—I respectfully suggest, that we should not stop in following
up this great system of Gall and Spurzheim, but, by a deeper search on the
skulls of each other, endeavour to make
some new discovery, as I can by no means
allow, that all the *organs* of *affection*
which humanity, no doubt, is in possession of, being set forth in the thirty-three
divisions which Gall and Spurzheim have
executed in the map of the *osseous* covering of the *centre* of *nervous energy*—I
say, it is my opinion that this map does
not go far enough, for I think room might
be found for thirty-three divisions more!
(Hear, hear, hear! from the opposite side
of the table.)   For instance, we know
that there are *dull*, and very *stupid*, and
even *insane* people in the world; yet there
is no *organ* of *stupidity* or *bump* of *dulness* (great murmuring), no *rise* or *de-
pression* to designate the *sane* from the
insane !" Here the noise became very

great, insomuch that the speaker was obliged to call the unruly members to order.

On the gentleman attempting to resume the argument which had been thus interrupted, several female members rose in a rage, to deliver their sentiments. Another tumult now took place, as to who had the first right to be heard. An appeal, as usual on such occasions, was made to the chair.—" Mrs. Déliré first caught my eye," said the president.

This restored order; the other ladies courtesied, and sat down, and Mrs. Déliré, with a triumphant smile, advancing a little forward, thus began :—" Mr. Speaker, I am sorry the honourable gentleman who spoke last forces me to enter on a subject that may tend to cause any misunderstanding, in a society that has hitherto proceeded in its affairs with such feelings of unanimity; but his attack is so clearly meant to my honourable friends who occupy this side of the table, that to vindicate them, as well as myself, from

'such insinuations, I feel to be a bounden
duty. It is represented, that the great Gall
and Co. have not entered deep enough into
the study of their theory, having left out
the bumps of *insanity* and *folly* in their
cranial maps. The honourable member
who has thought proper to advance this
new doctrine, did not, I am sorry I am
compelled to say so, do so merely out of
a pure wish to suggest inquiry, but to insult his sister members at this side; for
what can be clearer, in proof of this intention, than his adding—' *We know* there
are *dull*, and very *stupid*, and even *insane* people?' Who knows? Why, the
member and his friends at the opposite
side know that we are *dull, stupid*—nay
many of us *insane!* These expressions
were too forcibly emphatized by the
speaker's eyes and gestures, during their
delivery, to allow me to entertain a doubt
of their real meaning; and I do contend
for it, Mr. Speaker, and I am ready to
take the voice of the house on the occasion, that if personal allusions be allowed,

particularly of this injurious nature, there will be an end of all freedom of debate and concord."

The gentleman thus accused, or attacked, now rose to explain. In the most solemn manner he assured the honourable members at the other side of the table, that he had not the most remote idea of giving any one of them offence; his only object in what he had said being to start inquiry.

This a little appeased the offended part of the assembly; still, however, there were murmurs of dissatisfaction, and private discussions, which leaving the president's attention unoccupied for a moment, Eugene took advantage of the circumstance, to ask whether they had discovered any method of turning to practical use this theory of Gall and Spurzheim? and being answered in the negative, availing himself of the suggestion of sir Toby Tickletoby, received permission to address the society on the subject. Having stationed himself at the further end of the table, he thus began.

CHAPTER XIV.

" ——————————But tell me true, are you not mad indeed, or do you but counterfeit ?"

" Believe me, I am not; I tell thee true."

" Nay, I'll ne'er believe a madman till I see his brains."

" MR. President, and ladies and gentlemen, receive my acknowledgments for
the high honour conferred on me, by the
permission I have obtained to deliver my
sentiments before you; In entreating you
to accept them, permit me also to solicit
your adding to the kindness already
shewn, your bearing in mind, as an excuse for any thing in which I may be
found deficient, that I am but a young
and an inexperienced speaker, insomuch
that it is not without extreme diffidence I
think of addressing so erudite a body.
But not to trespass unnecessarily upon
time so precious, from the purposes to

which it is here devoted—ladies and gentlemen, I presume it must strike every one, that the theory of Gall and Spurzheim, like all other theories in general, could only be considered valuable to a certain extent, except the means of turning it to practicable account were discovered—that is, of being enabled by it to do more than ascertain on each other's skulls the indications of genius, or the want of it. Thinking so, and feeling assured that there must be a coincidence of opinion with me on the subject, it is with pleasure that I announce to this learned assembly, that a discovery of this nature has been made, and of which being duly appreciated, I cannot entertain a doubt; the production of genius being a much more philosophical subject of inquiry than the indications of it. (Hear, hear, hear!) It is a well-known fact, that the human *cranium*, in early infancy, may be moulded into any conceivable shape, from the elastic nature of the bones of which it is formed. As all the organs of *thought* and *volition* are as distinctly laid down in the cranial map of Gall and Spurzheim as we could desire, and as I have already expressed the practicability of compressing the *cranial bones,* at an early age, into any conceivable form, nothing more is requisite to give a new and definite direction to the *thoughts* and *feelings* of the next generation, than to mould the infant's head to a given form, by the simple application of an unyielding metal headdress, formed so as only to permit the developement of the required *organs.* If the elevation of the skull, at a certain point, be accompanied by the developement of a particular *organ* seated under it (and this is clearly demonstrated by the great doctors), there can be nothing more easy in nature, or in the brass or iron manufacturers, than to furnish metal caps, which, by repressing the growth of the injurious, and encouraging the expansion of the good *affections,* will invariably make all the future generations of Britons to think and act alike for the common.

welfare. In short, the thirty-three divisions into which the skull is arranged, and the thirty-three *propensities*, corresponding to these divisions, may be so modified, by adopting metal cases for the covering of the heads of the young, as to produce any quantity of talent required."

On Eugene signifying he had concluded, by drawing back, with a bow, from the table, the members, as if one and all were electrified, sprung from their seats, and gave three cheers, waving their wigs. On resuming their seats, after giving this mark of their approbation, one of them proposed that the thanks of the assembly should be voted to their learned secretary, as from that moment he was henceforth to be considered, for the perspicuous manner in which he had explained the means by which the system of the great Gall and Spurzheim might be turned to account, and the same entered on the journals of the house, as too much gratitude could not be evinced to the person, who, by his suggestion, or discovery, had probably

hurried on the British millennium some
hundreds of years.

Nothing was heard but the praises of
the young secretary, and congratulations
amongst the society, for having met with
so brilliant a genius to fill the situation.
In taking these plaudits to himself, as a
just tribute for the merit of a discovery
due solely to another, we must acknowledge Eugene was not correct; he certainly did not exactly assert a falsehood; but
then his not disclaiming what was attributed to him, was nearly as bad; but he
was young and unthinking, to be sure,
when the *organ* of *vanity* flows at a rapid
rate—perhaps also knowing his unfortunate country was considered only capable
of producing thick-headed blunderers, he
wished to prove, in that respect, as in
others, there was no general rule without
an exception. The question being put
from the chair—" Whether the thanks of
this honourable house be bestowed upon
Eugene O'Toole O'Shaughnessy O'Neil,
their secretary, for the suggestion of so

beneficial a discovery, as that of turning
the theory of doctors Gall and Spurzheim
to practical account, by the use of metal
headdresses, during the infancy of children, for the suppression of bad *affections*,
and encouragement of the good?" a member rose, and expressed himself concerned,
that, in justice, he could not give his as-
sent to so great an honour being conferred
upon any man, as that proposed to be
conferred upon their secretary, unless his
services were incontrovertibly proved to
be of importance to the community at
large, or who had, in some particular,
rendered their society some essential benefit; and therefore as this, in neither instance, was the case, he could not, although he felt for their worthy secretary
a respect for the genius and depth of reading evinced by so young a man, concur
in the vote he had been called upon for.—
" If," continued he, " the soul is independent of the body, as we are led to believe,
and which indeed we cannot doubt being
actually the case—if, I say, the soul is in-

dependent of the body, and if the *bumps* and *depressions* of the human *cranium* be the work of this invisible agent, it should be full proof that it can make room for the display of its peculiar faculties, without consulting the mass of matter, or the bones where it has its temporary residence. What possible benefit could mankind derive, in such cases, from metal headdresses? I am firmly of opinion, none. More, that the soul would most likely not choose to occupy a habitation moulded by these brass or iron caps to a certain shape; and further, that if forced to reside in a house she did not like, she might sit sullenly in her cell, and disappoint the expectations of those interested in her future display."

Several ladies here rose in an evident rage with the last speaker; but whether through being prepossessed in favour of their youthful secretary, on account of his manly beauty, or to vindicate the discovery they supposed he had made, we cannot venture to decide. As before, the

president was obliged to decide which had
the first claim to attention; and his voice
being in favour of Mrs. *Folle*, she stepped forward, and thus began :—

" The doctrine broached by the honourable member last on his legs, has filled
me with astonishment! He asserts, the
soul is independent of the body; but do
we not all know, that when the body is
worn out by sickness, or years, and ceases
longer to act, our natural life is at an end?
Do we not commit the body to the earth,
from whence it sprung? We know, for
a certainty, therefore, what is become of
the body ; but where is this separated being, the soul, to be found? Do we know
any demonstration of the soul, save through
the body ?. Is it not absurd, therefore, to
assert, that the soul is independent, when
it is nowhere to be found, save in com-
munion with its corporal body? Wine is
wine, whether in a cask or a bottle, and
soul can only be soul while it animates the
body. If however the honourable member can produce me any soul—nay, even

satisfy me, from unquestionable proof, that
he has ever conversed with one, *independent of a body*, then, but not until then,
can he persuade me that soul and body
are two distinct beings.   The soul comes
into the world as belonging to a particular body, and takes its departure with the
same; *ergo*, a body could not exist without a soul, nor a soul without a body!
What can be a stronger proof of this than
the old adage, when speaking of a person
whose fortune is small—' He has scarcely
sufficient to keep soul and body together?'
How then can any one pretend that one
can be independent of the other, when, to
make a whole, both must be united?   As
we are assured, by our great masters, that
the seat of the soul is in the *cranium*, I
must heartily concur in voting that the
thanks of this honourable house be bestowed upon our learned and ingenious
secretary, for so valuable and important
a discovery as that of a metal headdress."

" After the very brilliant, clear, and comprehensive speech of my honourable sister," cried another lady, hastily rising, "it is hardly necessary for me to intrude upon the attention of the house; nor should I, but for the impossibility I feel of avoiding following up her observations on the strange assertions of the honourable member who has opposed the tribute we conceive due to our secretary, for his most ingenious and valuable discovery.   To shew that the soul is not independent of the body, as has been attempted to be proved, I would ask if ever philosopher was heard of, who could invent theories, or illustrate facts, without the assistance of his stomach, and the apparatus contained in its thoracic cavity? (Hear, hear, hear! and great applause.)   And does not a cannon-shot through the breast put a stop as effectually to the operations of the soul, as if it had been directed to the head? (great and reiterated applause,) which proves, beyond a doubt, that in place of the soul being independent of the body, she occupies not only the head, but every individual part of the body, though her means of *thought* and *volition* are fixed in the *cranium*. What do we phrenologists contend for? Why, merely that particular powers of the mind, or soul, have been proved to manifest themselves in particular developements of the bones of the head; and all that our secretary's glorious invention (as I have no doubt, if not in the present, it will at least in after ages be termed) contends for is, that the growth and developement of these bones may in early life, from their yielding quality, be made to accommodate themselves to the display of any required faculty of mind. In expressing the pleasure I feel in giving my hearty concurrence to the vote of thanks, I cannot help taking this opportunity of noticing what lasting and great obligations this nation is under to many of his countrymen, for services that have immortalized their names.

> ' I saw Othello's visage in his mind,
> And to his honours and his valiant parts
> Did I my soul and fortunes consecrate!'

exclaims the beautiful Desdemona, violently enamoured of a gallant soldier: can we allow genius to affect our hearts less warmly than courage?" casting a fascinating glance.

> " ——— ———Oh, wise young secretary,
> How much more elder art thou than thy looks !"

This member sat down, amidst tumults of applause. The standing order being then read, that the whole house go into a committee on the study of skulls, the twenty-one ladies turned round on their stools as regularly as a regiment could to the right or left, and presented their *craniums* for inspection to the gentlemen at the other side of the table, who, having finished the investigation, and taken notes made of whatever alterations appeared in them since the last examination, in their turn underwent the same from the ladies.

" Prior to adjourning the house, I deem it expedient," said the president, " to take its sense, whether it is absolutely necessary for our secretary to conform to the general rules of this honourable society, by having his head shaved, and made ready against the next inspection, by mounting a scratch?"

This was carried *nem. com.* The house then adjourned to that day week, then to meet for the dispatch of business; but their resolution about his head had settled the business with Eugene. To return to his Rose in a wig! No—the thing was impossible; and, in consequence, lingering behind, he informed the president, that since the honourable society could not be satisfied with the map he had already taken of his *cranium*, he must beg leave to decline affording them an opportunity for making any other; he made him a parting bow, and retired.

With a heavy heart would he have done so, after the expectations he had been indulging, but for the hope held out by what C—— had said of his being about informing him when he called, of his having something advantageous to propose to him.

END OF VOL. I.

Printed by J. Darling, Leadenhall-street, London.

NEW PUBLICATIONS

PRINTED FOR

A. K. NEWMAN & CO.

LEADENHALL-STREET, LONDON.

[2 c

NEW PUBLICATIONS.

[7c

THE CASTLE CHAPEL.

A ROMANTIC TALE.

Printed by J. Darling, Leadenhall-Street, London.

THE

CASTLE CHAPEL.

A Romantic Tale.

IN THREE VOLUMES.

BY

REGINA MARIA ROCHE,

AUTHOR OF THE

CHILDREN OF THE ABBEY; BRIDAL OF DUNAMORE; CLERMONT; DISCARDED
SON; HOUSES OF OSMA AND ALMERIA; MUNSTER COTTAGE BOY;
TRADITION OF THE CASTLE; TRECOTHICK BOWER; MAID
OF THE HAMLET; VICAR OF LANSDOWNE, &c.

VOL. II.

LONDON:

PRINTED FOR
A. K. NEWMAN AND CO. LEADENHALL-STREET.

1825.

THE

CASTLE CHAPEL.

CHAPTER I.

"Stung with the thoughts of home—the thoughts of
    home
Rush on his nerves, and call their vigour forth
In many a vain attempt. How sinks his soul!
What black despair, what horror fills his heart!

Thinking o'er all the bitterness of death,
Mix'd with the tender anguish nature shoots
Thro' the wrung bosom of the dying man."

IN placing himself at the mercy of chance
fortune, by declining the situation that
was offered to his acceptance, Eugene
may be accused of folly, by the prudent

part of the world, to a certainty; but in extenuation of this folly, it should be taken into consideration, that Eugene was a very young man, just at that period of life, indeed, when trifling matters have an importance, which, at a more advanced stage, we are astonished we could ever allow them. The very few acquaintances he had in London were all young men, like himself, who considered the cut of the coat, shape of the hat, and polish of the boots, as matters of the most essential consequence. To expose himself to the ridicule of such, by consenting to have his head shaved for his support, was more, he felt, than he had philosophy to endure; but, above all, he was a lover, full of romance, and wishing to appear as ever in the eyes of his lovely mistress.

At an early hour anxiety led him to C———.—" Well," exclaimed the man of business, with an ironical laugh, as he saw him entering, " am I to congratulate you on your being appointed secretary to the *craniums ?"*

Eugene pretending to be looking over some books, replied, with affected carelessness, in the negative, though his blood glowed at the manner in which the question was asked.—" Then, perhaps," resumed C———, " since you can turn the outside of theirs to no advantage, you will have no objection to try what the inside of your own will enable you to do for yourself;" and he proceeded to inform him, that he had the unpublished manuscript of a deceased author lying by him, which, wanting revision, he would pay him handsomely for editing.

Eugene inquired the subject ; and finding there was nothing offensive, either to religion or morality, in the work, he readily closed with the offer ; and, with the first part of it in his pocket, returned with something of a lightened heart to his lodgings, impatient to enter upon a task, the execution of which would enable him to return to St. Doulagh's.

The wretchedness his Rose must suffer

till she saw him again, was too terrible to
his imagination, not to render him indefatigable in his exertions to restore her to
tranquillity ; he hardly allowed himself a
moment's respite, and scarcely ever went
out, except it was to C———'s, to whom,
according to his desire, he returned the
work in detached parts, now and then accompanied by trifles, such as essays, and
ballads, that, by way of relaxation, he
sometimes permitted himself to compose ;
and for which, instead of only receiving
two or three pounds, all he conceived himself entitled to for them, he was often very
agreeably surprised by getting a check for
ten or fifteen pounds.

He had gone on in this manner for two
or three weeks, when, late one evening, a
billet, to the following effect, was brought
him, by an unknown messenger, who vanished the moment he had put it into his
hand :—

" *To Eugene O'Neil, Esq.*

" If Mr. O'Neil will call this
night, at No. —, Pall Mall, between the
hours of ten and eleven, he will see a person who has a communication of very great
importance to make to him."

———

We may readily believe Eugene could
not peruse such a note without emotion—
who it came from, or what was the nature
of the communication it alluded to, he
could not form the most distant idea. For
an instant his thoughts glanced at Rose;
could she, fearful of his truth and constancy, have confided their story to some one,
for the purpose of having the cruelty he
was committing, in trifling with her feelings, by longer delaying his return to St.
Doulagh's, represented to him? but no,
this was too improbable, from what he
knew of her delicacy, her timidity, to be
imagined; he had a thousand reasons for
believing this could not be the case; and
at length, finding conjecture on the sub-

ject only distracted him, he determined on endeavouring to wait patiently for the elucidation of what was at present so perplexing.

He would, however, have gone out, for the purpose of inquiring who lived at —, in Pall Mall ; but just as he took up his hat, with this intention, a young friend, not knowing what to do with himself, came in, for the good-natured purpose of bestowing his tediousness upon him, and detained him till within a minute or two of the time for keeping the appointment.

On knocking, Eugene was admitted in the dark, but by whom, the manner in which the door was opened, and the hasty way in which it was closed, prevented his discerning ; but hardly had he heard it fastened behind him, ere he received a tremendous blow on the head, that felled him to the ground.

On regaining his senses, he found himself extended in a large parlour, through which the glare of a lamp, immediately fronting the windows, one of which was

lying open, diffused a sufficient light to
let him see about him; and, to his unspeakable horror, he beheld, at a little distance from him, a man stretched upon the
floor, weltering in his gore. He started
up, and flew to the door, but it was fastened; shouting aloud, he caught at the
bell-ropes, but, through the violence with
which he pulled them, they each gave way
in his hand. He then hastened to the
open window, and forgetful, through the
state of mind he was in, and his anxiety
to discover whether it was too late for any
assistance to be rendered to the ghastly
object within the apartment, or of the
depth of the area below, was stepping out,
when he was violently pushed back by the
pole of a watchman, who was passing at
the instant, and who naturally concluded
he could not be a good man or true, who
was making his exist from a house in such
a manner. An alarm was given, the
street-door was forced, and ere Eugene,
from the bewildered state of his senses,
well knew what they were about, he

found himself taken up on suspicion of murder..

· He passed the night in a solitary cell of the watchhouse, to which he was conveyed, and the next morning was brought before a magistrate, who, after a long and patient investigation of the affair, conceived himself fully justified, from the circumstantial evidence against him, in committing him to prison, to take his trial for the alleged offence. Nothing indeed could be stronger than this; steeped in blood, he was detected, apparently attempting to effect his escape from the house where the atrocious deed was committed; in vain he told his story, he protested his innocence—man can but judge from appearances, and these were all against him; even if the note, that had been the treacherous means of drawing him into this dreadful predicament, could have been of any service, he had it not to produce, having been taken from his pocket after his being knocked down. Who could be the contriver of this diabolical plot? or what the instigation to it? In vain he tried to conjecture, unconscious as he was of ever having done any thing to provoke enmity; but that he had, enmity of the rancorous, the most deadly nature, was but too evident from what had happened, and that he should assuredly fall a victim to it was equally so, for every circumstance, he clearly saw, must make against him.

Who can paint his feelings when the gloomy walls of Newgate came in sight— that dismal place, that even, when only contemplated as the prison of another, he never could pass without a kind of shudder! His despair at first rendered him frantic—repeatedly he dashed himself against the stone floor of the cell in which he was locked up. It was not enough that he was to be cut off in the very springtide of his youth, but an ignominious death was to be his.—" Why," he raved, " when tossed upon the foaming ocean, with but a frail plank between me and eternity, why was I not plunged be-

neath the whelming waves? Why, when
the balls of the enemy whizzed round my
unscreened head, was I not struck down?
was I only saved—was I only shielded—
was I only reserved for this?" reproachfully raising his manacled hands to heaven, " to meet a felon's fate! to die under
the agonizing idea of leaving an execrated
name behind me! Those I love will believe in the protestations of my innocence
—but that will not be sufficient to rescue
my memory from detestation! their belief
in them will be imputed to the fond credulity of affection—and their efforts of
course to induce others to join in it unsuccessful!"

But calmer thoughts succeeded; and
the visits of the chaplain, who was unremitting in his attentions to him, tended
not a little to the continuance of these, or,
in short, to gradually bring about a better way of thinking; either he really gave
credit to Eugene's solemn asseverations of
his innocence, or else, compassionating his
youth, he evinced a degree of sympathy

for him, that had no slight effect in softening the feelings of the unfortunate youth.

The first agony of distraction over, Eugene reflected he was not the first who
had innocently suffered, and that he had
no more right to fly in the face of Heaven, therefore, for permitting a thing of
the kind, than others who had gone before him. Even *He*, that divine being,
on whom *all* rely for intercession, with
every other virtue, what an example of
patient resignation under unmerited sufferings has he set his followers! with what
uncomplaining meekness did he take up
his cross, and submit to the most cruel
and ignominious death that could be inflicted! and should he then, a worm, a rep-
tile, in comparison, dare to outrage the
majesty of Heaven by murmurs and complaints! No, following the example of
his Blessed Saviour, he would humble
himself before it, and in his words say—
" Oh my Father, if it be possible, let this
cup pass from me! nevertheless, not as I
will, but as thou wilt!" Justly has it been

said, that religion is the anchor of the soul
—the moment we turn to it, in truth and
in spirit, for consolation, we receive it.—
" A broken and a contrite spirit I will not
despise," saith God ; and we feel the assurance confirmed in the innermost recesses of that spirit, the moment we lay it
prostrate before his throne.

As soon as ever Eugene was brought to
a frame of religious resignation, he became
comparatively composed, and sufficiently
collected to be enabled to do whatever was
requisite for himself. But his cares, or
thoughts, were not confined entirely to
himself; contemplating his death as certain, he prepared two letters, to be forwarded to St Doulagh's, by the chaplain,
after his execution. One was addressed
to his aunt, assuring her of his innocence
of the crime for which he suffered, and
making known the attachment between
him and Rose, whom he represented as
his wife by a private marriage, and for
whom he implored, in the most earnest
and pathetic terms, the continued protec-

tion and kindness of his family. The
other was to poor Rose herself, beseeching
her to support herself under the disastrous
stroke that separated them, and evince
her love to his memory, by exerting herself to supply his place to his afflicted relatives, and in particular to poor Grace, to
whom he addressed a few lines, recommending them, in the most forcible manner, to the love and care of each other.
But innocence is Heaven's peculiar care —
we may doubt and despair of its goodness, but let us patiently wait, and we
shall see the " ways of Providence justified to man."

Eugene's trial was almost on the very
eve of taking place, when three men were
taken up for a robbery, and committed to
Newgate. One of them, almost immediately after his committal, offered to turn
king's evidence : and being permitted, not
only confessed the commission of the crime
for which he and his companions were apprehended, but that they, that is, the other
two, had perpetrated the murder for which

Eugene was about being tried. It seems the house in Pall Mall, to which Eugene had been so insidiously decoyed, belonged to a gentleman of fortune, then abroad, and had been in the sole care of a confidential servant, of which circumstance the villains getting apprized, a plan for murdering him, and robbing the house, was concerted: with their hands reeking in his blood, they repaired, with as much of the property as they could carry off, to his, the informant's, lodgings, where, he averred, some part of it was still concealed. This being ascertained to be the case, very little more was requisite to fully establish the innocence of Eugene; and, in short, on the very morning that the forms of law obliged him to be brought up for trial, he was liberated.

What the overflowings of his heart were on this occasion, we presume may easily be imagined; but in the midst of his gratitude and joy, his heart was seized with sudden terror, at the idea of the awful predicament he had been in being by, this time perhaps known at St. Doulagh's, and the apprehension of the effect it might have produced there, although his letters were not forwarded. While considering how, under this apprehension, he should act, being most unwilling, if not already known to them, to let them ever learn the terrible situation in which he had been placed, he received a letter from Grace, of recent date, written with even more than her usual liveliness, and containing the gratifying assurance of all being well at home. He, of course, lost not a minute in answering it, that in case any unpleasant rumour should yet reach them, they might have this letter to turn to immediately, for the removal of any alarm that might be created.

Relieved from anxiety about those at home, he delayed not waiting on C———, the expenditure of all the little hoard he had lying by him rendering it impossible for him to quit London, as, after what had occurred, he would immediately, if in his power, without a reimbursement, which could only be obtained by finishing the task he had undertaken for C———.

This gentleman, who, though prevented from seeing him while in prison, by a severe fit of illness, had still been extremely attentive, in sending from time to time, to inquire whether there was any service he could render him, received him most kindly. After congratulations and acknowledgments had been exchanged, Eugene expressed his readiness to complete what he had begun; and accordingly the remainder of the work was handed over to him, with a few pounds.

If indefatigable before, Eugene was now, if possible, ten times more so, heightened as was his anxiety to quit London, by the apprehension of having a secret enemy there, who might again bring his life into jeopardy. But who was this enemy, to whose machinations he had so nearly fallen a victim? His conscience could not reproach him with injury to any one, except one, too good, too innocent, too tenderly attached, to harbour revenge or malice.

So much did his brain run upon the subject—so greatly did it perplex him, that he found it at times difficult to collect his thoughts sufficiently to go on with his task; but at length it was completed, and with a joyful heart he took it to C———.

"Well," exclaimed C———, on paying him the remainder of the stipulated sum, "what next shall we set about?"

"Nothing at present," replied Eugene, proceeding to inform him of his intention of immediately departing for Ireland.

"Are you serious?" demanded C———.

"Perfectly so."

"Well, this is wrong—very wrong," cried C———, "just at the moment when we were beginning to understand one another, and matters might have gone on so well."

"Well, perhaps our acquaintance may not end here," said Eugene, who encouraged a vague idea of returning again to London after his marriage; " but whether it does or not, be assured I shall not forget your kindness in many instances."

" Oh, I know to what you allude! but if you have positively determined on leaving this, I have a secret to disclose."

" I am then, positively."

" Well, then, not to take to myself what I do not deserve, though I will not do myself the injustice to say I am not capable of a liberal act, the remuneration you received for the little matters you from time to time brought to me for publication was not entirely out of my pocket."

" I don't comprehend you," said Eugene.

" Why, the fact is, you have a secret friend here."

" Indeed! well that is a very agreeable counterpoise, or counterbalance, to a secret enemy; but pray explain—who is he?"

" Why, really, I know very little more of him than his name. The circumstance altogether is a very romantic one, inso-

much that I think some day or other I
shall mention it to some one of my pet
authoresses, to see whether they cannot
work it into something of an incident for
one of their novels. Immediately after
your first visit to me, a gentleman of most
prepossessing appearance entered the shop,
and having inquired whether the young
gentleman he had seen quitting it was
not so and so (meaning you), proceeded to
introduce himself to me, as a person most
particularly interested about you; but
which interest, very peculiar circumstances
then preventing his making known to you
himself, he wished to make me the instrument of proving it, by lodging in my
hands a certain sum of money, to be given
in addition to whatever I might, from time
to time, myself give for any of your productions; of course I would not do you the
injury of not being his agent on the occasion, and the matter was soon settled between us, with an understanding that you
were to be kept in ignorance of it, except
any thing occurred to induce you to leave

this, in which case I had his permission
to acquaint you with it, and give you his
address, it being his wish to have a conversation with you ere your departure."

" This is a most extraordinary affair !"
said Eugene, impatiently holding out his
hand for the card of his unknown friend.
" Wilkinson! Wilkinson!" he repeated,
as he cast his eye over it—" No. —, Charlotte-street, Bedford-square ?'—I don't recollect ever being acquainted with one of
that name. However, I shall soon know
who he is;" and with a hasty nod to
C——, he darted off.

We need hardly say his steps were directed to Charlotte-street. He knocked
at the door of a handsome house, and had
the unspeakable satisfaction of finding Mr.
Wilkinson was at home. A servant in a
handsome livery threw open the door of
a back parlour, fitted up as a library, and
in the gentleman who rose to receive him,
Eugene instantly recognised the stranger
who had journeyed with him from St.
Doulagh's to Dublin.

CHAPTER II.

"——————————How many shake
With all the fierce tortures of the mind,
Unbounded passion, guilt, remorse!

Wrench from their hands oppression's iron rod,
And bid the cruel feel the pains they give."

"This is an agreeable surprise indeed!"
said Eugene, as he advanced to meet the
extended hand of Mr. Wilkinson.

"I am gratified by your allowing me
to imagine you feel it so," was the reply;
"for, I assure you, you have lived in my
remembrance since our meeting."

"You have given proofs of that, sir,"
said Eugene, "that I know not how to
express my gratitude for: but, pardon
me," a flush of pride mantling over his
cheek, "if I say I cannot remain perfect-

ly easy under a weight of pecuniary obligations."

"I know what you allude to; but if
you really wish me to believe you consider me as your friend, you will not touch
upon that subject again; it is the duty of
the old to aid the young, if they have the
power, more particularly the young and
enterprising; and all I regret is my being
so peculiarly circumstanced at the time of
your arrival in London, as to be compelled to make another the medium of my
goodwill to you: but come, be seated, and
let me account to you for what must have
surprised you so much, as my not returning to take a more particular leave of you
than I did at the moment of our parting
at the hotel in Sackville-street. You must
know then, that the person whom you
may remember I said I wished to speak
to, on catching my eye, fled. I pursued
him, nor gave up the pursuit till I found
he had baffled me for the present, by stepping on board a steam-packet, just then
on the point of sailing for Liverpool. The

fatigue I had gone through made me stop
at the place to which I had traced him,
and when I returned the next morning to
Sackville-street, to take a more formal
leave of you than I had previously done,
and express my hopes of a further renewal
of our acquaintance, previous to my departure from the kingdom, I found you
had embarked for England, but for what
port I could not discover, though I rather
conjectured, from some hints you had
given me of your plans; till by chance I
espied you coming out of Mr. C———'s.
Without flattery, I assure you, I never
met with a person who, upon so slight an
acquaintance, interested me more strongly; insomuch, that I should have felt a
lasting regret, if an opportunity for re-
newing, or rather becoming more intimately acquainted, had not occurred:
with difficulty I have so long curbed my
impatience, to avail myself of it; but for
this some time past I have not exactly
been my own master, the concerns of an
afflicted and very dear friend having al-

most totally engrossed me; but the restraint imposed upon me by his affairs being now at an end, Mr. C———, ·in the information he gave you this day, only anticipated what I meant myself to-morrow to have given you."

" Again, sir," cried Eugene, " I must say that I know not how to express what I feel for the kind interest you have evinced about me. I did not think I should have felt such a pang at leaving London; but I must be cold and insensible to kindness indeed, if I could depart from a place, containing a person I have such reason to esteem and regard, without a feeling of deep regret."

" Professions are fine things," said Mr. Wilkinson, with a good-natured smile; " but actions are the tests of sincerity I rely on. I shall see whether you indeed feel what you intimate, by your appearing to forget, from this moment, that we have not been longer acquainted; and making my house your home, should you return to London."

" I have now an inducement to do so, which will make me feel a sensation of disappointment, should I be compelled to abandon the intention," said Eugene.

" I am happy to hear you entertain such a one," replied Mr. Wilkinson ; " London is indeed the place for a person who has to make their way in the world. With talents, with genius, what a terrible thing for a young man to suffer himself to sink into obscurity, without a struggle for independence—that, without which there can be no real enjoyment! He that possesses it, has reached indeed the point of happiness, for independence is at once a shield and helmet; then does the soul walk uprightly, and proudly guard the dignity of its nature, because exempt from the cruel necessity that, under other circumstances, might compel it to bow to titled villany, and overlook an insult offered by a hand that was decorated with a sparkling ring."

" Be assured, sir, none can more highly

estimate it than I do," said Eugene—
" none be readier to undergo any possible
privation for its attainment; since without, I conceive it utterly impossible but
that a spirit endued with any thing of
lofty feeling, must speedily be crushed.
Good Heavens! as you say, to be compelled to stoop to those we despise—
oh, death—death to me would be infinitely preferable!"

" Perseverance is almost always, as indeed it deserves to be, crowned with success," resumed Mr. Wilkinson; " those
who are determined on reaching a certain
goal are seldom disappointed. But you
see how I practise what I preach—by
speaking to you as if indeed we had been
acquaintance of long standing."

" I consider your doing so as a kindness
and an honour, sir," said Eugene. " In
what estimation must a young, inexperienced man, like me, hold the advice and
suggestions of a person of your experience
and judgment!"

" Well, without perhaps allowing that

I entirely merit your compliment, I may, perhaps, from what I have seen of the world, be able to suggest hints that may be of service to a young person just entering it. But do you know, I am not clear that we shall part quite so soon as you now imagine—as I just mentioned to you, I am again my own master, and the tour which I proposed making through your Emerald Isle not being completed, I really think, if you can put off your departure for a fortnight, I shall accompany you."

Eugene hesitated, but it was only for an instant. His very soul was on the wing to his Rose; but after the kindness he had received, how could he refuse compliance with this intimated wish? no, the thing was impossible; and finally it was settled, they should set out together at the expiration of this period.

He was not suffered to take his leave until he had promised to return to dinner. As he slowly retraced his way home, how agreeable were the meditations in which

he indulged! every thing about Mr. Wilkinson argued his being a man of wealth;
and from the warm, the really extraordinary interest he evinced about him, who
knew but that there might be a speedy
end to all further occasion for intense anxiety about the future?—" And yet I
murmured so, and desponded!" cried Eugene; " really, after so often giving way
to repinings, I scarcely merit the good
fortune that appears opening to my view;
but I trust, in consideration of our natural infirmities, these will be forgiven;"
and with the usual proneness of all warm
temperaments, or romantic imaginations,
he set about castle-building, or, in other
words, erecting castles in the air; but as
the streets of London are not exactly the
places for buildings of this description, not
a few were the thumps and angry shoves
he met with in consequence, till at last he
was fairly compelled to rouse himself from
his waking dream.

He and his new friend dined *tête-à-tête*,
nor was there any addition to the party in

the evening, nor any indeed wanted, so
well qualified were both gentlemen for
supporting an unaided conversation.

From this day almost the principal part
of each was passed by Eugene at Mr.
Wilkinson's, no matter at home or abroad,
that gentleman having informed him that
he would always find his library open for
him. But though he went, it might be
said, at all hours to the house, he never,
by any chance, met any one there but
Mr. Wilkinson himself; nor did any thing
ever transpire from him to render him in
any degree acquainted with his connexions. These were circumstances that Eugene but slightly commented on, if at all;
there were many people, he knew, who
had a dislike to mixed society, and perhaps he had no connexions, or at least,
none sufficiently interesting to speak of.

A week had passed in this way, when,
one morning that Eugene called as usual,
Mr. Wilkinson informed him he had just
received a letter from the friend he had
before alluded to, entreating him to pass

a day or two with him at his cottage in Hertfordshire—" I am therefore just setting off," he said, " but in positive expectation of being followed by you—my friend's invitation extending to you, I assure you. You may feel surprised at saying follow; but the fact is, I am prevented asking you to accompany me, by having to call in my way at a house, where a recent calamity prevents my attempting to introduce a stranger. I know you have no horses of your own; and as I do not think those got at livery stables always safe, I shall send one for you early in the afternoon."

• Eugene thanked him for his consideration about him, and all matters being arranged, Mr. Wilkinson departed.

At his express desire, Eugene took an early dinner in Charlotte-street. He soon found, however, this need not have been hurried, as minute after minute passed away, and still no horse arrived. He was at length beginning to think something had happened to Mr. Wilkinson, and to get very uneasy in consequence, when he was informed the horse was come. The servant who brought it accounted for the delay, by saying a shoe had fallen off his own, which obliged him to stop by the way.

"That was rather an unfortunate circumstance, my lad," said Eugene, as he prepared to mount, "for I understand the road we have to go is a very lonely one, and there is no moon now."

"'Tis a safe road, for all that, sir," was the answer, and they set off.

They were within three miles of what Eugene understood was their destination, and a little way advanced in a dark, narrow glen-like lane, into which they had struck off of the high road, when the servant riding up to Eugene, informed him he was under a necessity of turning back for a parcel which he had forgot to call for at a house which they passed—"But I shall make great haste, sir," he said; "and at all events, you can't miss your way here, as there is but one turn in the lane that leads direct to the cottage."

" Of course not," was the reply, and the man rode off.

Eugene every moment expected to see the turn that had been mentioned to him; but he rode on, and on, till at last he began to think that this lane would prove a contradiction to the old saying, that " the longest has an end;" every moment it assumed a more fearful and savage aspect, both from the fast diminution of the light that still lingered in the sky, and the height of the beetling banks, completely overrun with thickets and trees, that in many places stretched from their summits across it.

Eugene had proceeded a distance that, from what he had heard, should, he conceived, have brought him to the end of his journey, when a pistol was fired across the path, and so immediately close to him, that he felt the ball graze his hat. The horse started, reared, and threw him, and for a moment he was so stunned by the

circumstance, as to be unable to rise. He
then quickly succeeded in regaining the
horse, and clapping spurs to it, galloped
back in the direction he had come, convinced that he had heard the person who
fired the pistol running up the lane, and
that therefore it would be the height of
imprudence for him to go forward. He
looked every moment to meeting the
groom; but he neither met him nor any
other person; and having regained the
high road, conceived, under all the circumstances, his best plan would be to return to town; a strange idea having taken
possession of his mind, that whoever was
the person that had fired the pistol, it was
the person whose enmity he had so unconsciously provoked. In vain he tried
to argue himself out of it, by reflecting
that he had latterly no kind of intercourse
whatsoever but with Mr. Wilkinson; and
the utter improbability therefore of this
secret enemy, if indeed still aiming at his
life, being able to know any thing of his

c 3

movements, so as to be enabled to contrive this scheme for his destruction; he could not divest himself of it, and, in consequence, resolved on having an immediate communication with C—— on the subject, and advising with him what steps to take, in pursuance of the suspicion under which he laboured.

It was about ten when he reached town, and on suddenly finding himself in the vicinity of Charlotte-street, he thought he had better at once leave the horse there than take any further charge of it. As the servant who answered his knock took the animal from him, he asked him whether he would not walk in? Eugene hesitated for an instant, and then thought he would just step in, to examine whether the ball had done him any other injury than that of merely grazing his hat. He accordingly proceeded to the parlour; but what language can do justice to his astonishment, when, as he threw open the door, the first object that met his eyes was Mr. Wilkinson, whom he at the instant imagined so many miles distant from town, seated in deep thought at a table!

Greatly as he was surprised, however, Mr. Wilkinson appeared equally so—perhaps from a similar cause; he started up with an air of the wildest perturbation, and—" Good God!" escaped him—" you here *again!*"

" I have surprised you, sir," said Eugene—" alarmed you" he was involuntarily on the point of adding; but was prevented by seeing Mr. Wilkinson, with an ashy paleness, staggering back against the wainscot.—" You are ill, sir!" cried Eugene hastily.

" Ill!—oh God!" and he dropped into a chair.

" What can I do for you, sir?" asked Eugene, making a movement as if to pull the bell.

" Stop—nothing—that is, a glass of water is all I require; there is some on the sideboard;" and having swallowed some—" I feel better now," he said— " pretty well recovered indeed, considering the shock I received. Yes, I fancied, on seeing you so unexpectedly, that—that—in short, I was but half-way to my friend's, when I was overtaken by a messenger, requiring me to return to town on business that could not be put off; but having sent on a servant to apprize my friend of the circumstance, and desire him to detain you, as I expected to be down with him the latter end of the next day at least, I could not help imagining, on seeing you coming in so unexpectedly, that something terrible had happened to him, as I know he is subject to fits, to prevent your stopping."

"Through my sudden return you need be under no apprehensions about your friend, sir," said Eugene; "the circumstance being owing to one by no means connected with him;" and he proceeded to explain the cause of it.

"Graze your hat! so near taking, and yet fail——" exclaimed Mr. Wilkinson.

"Of taking my life," cried Eugene, finishing the sentence for him: "I have had, indeed, a narrow escape, but which, with every other I have experienced, I must attribute to the watchful care of a superintending Providence."

"And what do you think? do—do you suspect? but, of course, you knew it to have been a robber."

" It is a natural supposition certainly," said Eugene; " but then, when, by my fall from my horse, he might have supposed he had killed me, why not come to rifle me?"

"Per—haps—when you fell—he—he— might have been so panic-struck by the deed he thought he had committed!"

" Oh no, my dear sir," cried Eugene, smiling incredulously, " that is not by any means an admissible idea! it is only when we commit a terrible deed, or occasion a dreadful catastrophe, through accident, not design, that we are apt to be panic- struck. The fact is, a strange persuasion has taken possession of my mind: I have reason to believe that I have some secret, deadly foe here, that lies in ambush for

my life; and I cannot divest myself of
the idea, however improbable it seems,
from my not recollecting lately my having mentioned any of my intended movements to any one but yourself, that it was
through him, not a stranger, this attempt
was made to destroy me."

" A deadly foe! You surprise me!
What reason have you for such a conclusion?"

" Are you then ignorant, sir," asked
Eugene, " of what recently occurred?
through the publicity it obtained through
the newspapers, I thought the reverse
must be the case, but that delicacy to my
feelings prevented your touching on it."

" No, really I don't know what you
allude to. I was so entirely engrossed, for
some time, by my poor friend, that I had
not even time for the perusal of a paper—
but I should be glad you would explain
yourself."

Eugene proceeded to oblige him. He
was hearkened to with the most profound
attention; and when he had concluded—

" 'Tis a strange affair indeed! a most extraordinary one!" said Mr. Wilkinson. " Have you any idea, any suspicion of who this secret enemy can be?"

" Not the slightest—I am happy, I am grateful to Heaven for being enabled to say—I am not conscious of having done any one an injury, to make such an enemy."

" Well, be that as it may, it seems you have one; I must, however, entirely dissent from you, in thinking the recent attempt on your life by him; for, except an invisible being, how, in the name of all that's wonderful, could he obtain a knowledge of intentions that were hardly known to yourself? for instance, this visit to my friend—it was quite a sudden thing, you know, and I believe not mentioned to any one?"

" Not to any one."

" Then I say," resumed Mr. Wilkinson, in an animated tone, " imputing this recent attempt on your life to any one but a common ruffian, is quite absurd, and I

therefore advise your not mentioning your
first idea to any one ; it would only be the
occasion of having late occurrences revived
in the public mind—which, between ourselves, are quite as well forgotten—and
having yourself beset and besieged by all
the police-men in town, under the pretext
of having taken up mysterious personages."

· " Well, sir, I believe you are right,"
said Eugene ; " and I shall relinquish
what assuredly was my intention in the
first instance."

Things reverted to their former channel, and every thing went on quietly for a
few succeeding days, when one morning
(within a very few days, as Eugene hoped,
of commencing preparations for their departure for Ireland) Mr. Wilkinson told
him he had just received a packet of papers from a friend in the country, requiring him to look over them, for the purpose of giving his opinion on the subject of
which they treated.—" I really would
wish to oblige him," he said, " but the
writing is of such a description, that I

might just as well hope to make out one
of the manuscripts of Herculaneum, as decipher it; but some people have a knack
of making out bad writing, and if you
are one of these, and have any time to
spare, you would greatly oblige me by
transcribing those papers for me, so that
I may be enabled to read them."

" With pleasure, sir," replied Eugene;
" and really," glancing his eye over them,
" I don't think the task will be so difficult
as you led me to imagine."

" *Tant mieux*," said Mr. Wilkinson;
" and that I should be no interruption, or
hindrance, to you in it, I shall take myself
off till you have finished it."

As Eugene proceeded in his task, he
felt happy it had not devolved to any
other person—of so seditious and inflam-
matory a nature were the papers he was
copying; so violent a *tirade* he had never
read against government—king, ministers,
and laws, were all libelled, and open re-
volt and rebellion preached up to the
people. Of course he communicated what

he thought to Mr. Wilkinson on his return.

" Well," replied that gentleman, " I am not surprised by what you tell me ; for, between ourselves, I have long ago suspected my friend of being inclined to radicalism. However, if I can help it, he sha'n't get his neck into a noose. I shall, as indeed desired, give my opinion of his papers, and endeavour to obtain his permission to destroy them."

When Eugene was about taking his leave in the evening, Mr. Wilkinson said, as it would not be much out of his way, he should be obliged by his taking the trouble of dropping a parcel for him, at such a bookseller's, in such a street—" It contains papers of consequence," he said, " for which he must therefore let you have a receipt ; and in return, beg of him to lose no time in their publication, and to cover the expences of which, give him also this," presenting as he spoke a bank-note of some amount to Eugene.

Eugene faithfully fulfilled the instructions given. He heard no more of the business for some days, nor expected indeed to hear more about it, when, to his utter astonishment, he received notice of information being filed against him, by the attorney-general, for a libel against the king and government. But if he was bewildered by this notice, how infinitely more so was he, when, upon inquiring into the business, he found that the papers which he had copied for Mr. Wilkinson were the identical ones which he had taken, by his directions, to a bookseller, with a positive order for their immediate publication! and which being supposed to be his, from the circumstance of his obtaining a receipt for them in his own name, occasioned what followed.

Hardly indeed had they made their appearance, than their seditious tendency, as might have been anticipated, caused their publisher to be taken up. He did all he could to avoid betraying the supposed author; but finding there was no alternative but his doing so, or submitting

himself to all the pains and penalties of
imprisonment, he at length gave him up.
In vain Eugene pleaded his innocence—
proofs, as in a former instance, were again
too strong against him, to permit his assertions of it to have any weight. He stated
the facts simply as they were; but they
were only considered aggravations of his
offence, from the tissue of falsehoods they
appeared to be, there being no Mr. Wilkinson to be found, or even heard of, to
corroborate his statements; the people of
the house where he alleged having met
him, declaring that they had never given
up the occupation of their residence to any
one, as could be proved by their neighbours; and that, neither directly nor indirectly, did they know any thing of a
person of the name he said he had met
there.

In short, Eugene being unable to deny
his handwriting, or invalidate, in any the
slightest degree, the testimonies against
him, was tried, found guilty (with a full
conviction on his mind of Wilkinson be-

ing the villain who had brought all this mischief upon him), sentenced to one year's imprisonment, and to pay a fine of one thousand pounds; and further, as usual, to be imprisoned till said fine was paid.

The instant he found Wilkinson was neither to be seen or heard of, that instant the conviction flashed upon his mind, of his being the secret enemy, who had, for some time, been labouring for his destruction. But how, in what way was it, he had provoked such deep and deadly malignity? had he unadvisedly said or done any thing that could have offended him in their journey from St. Doulagh's to Dublin? for whatever was the cause of his enmity towards him, it was certainly in Ireland it had been conceived.

His blood curdled when he thought of having sat so quietly with the fiend, who had so narrowly betrayed him to an ignominious death, and then attempted to take him off by assassination. His agitation on so unexpectedly seeing him, on the night he returned from Hertfordshire, was now accounted for; for no doubt, whoever was the person that had been employed to take him off, had been led to believe him killed, from hearing him fall from his horse. Twice had he been foiled in his machinations, but the third time had proved but too successful. A year's imprisonment was no great matter, but a fine of one thousand pounds was incarceration for life, Eugene knowing he might just as well hope to raise a million as raise that sum.

CHAPTER III.

> " Ah ! never again, in the green shady bowers,
>   Where my forefathers liv'd, shall I spend the sweet
>   hours,
> Or cover my harp with the wild woven flowers,
>   And strike the sweet numbers of Erin go Bragh."

COMMITTED to the King's Bench prison, a world within itself, Eugene was accommodated with an apartment at the top of the prison, whence his prospect consisted of the iron spikes surrounding the wall, the dome of St. Paul's, the top of the Monument, and the spires of innumerable churches. What a prospect for him, who so delighted in the wild beauties, the romantic solitudes of Nature, to

> " ——————wander o'er the dewy fields,
> Where freshness breathes, and dash the trembling drops
> From the bent bush, as thro' the verdant maze
> Of sweetbriar hedges he pursu'd his walk."

To him who loved the

> "———————valley sunk and unfrequented, where
> At fall of eve the fairy people throng,
> In various game and revelry, to pass
> The summer night, as village stories tell."

For him who loved to see

> " Among the crooked lanes, on every hedge,
> The glow-worm light his gem; and thro' the dark
> A moving radiance twinkle, while
> ———————a faint erroneous ray,
> Glanc'd from the imperfect surfaces of things,
> Flings half an image on the straining eye;
> And wavering woods, and villages, and streams,
> And rocks, and mountain tops, that long retain'd
> Th' ascending gleam, are all one swimming scene,
> Uncertain if beheld !"

As his wearied eye rested on the objects that now alone met them—" Is it not cruel," he involuntarily cried, " that man will not keep pace with the improvements of the day, and not, by remaining stationary, pursue systems that ought to be exploded ? Here, for instance, am I confined in a prison, though an innocent man, because, forsooth, ignorant people choose to adhere to the practice of ancient times—

that of placing the innocence or guilt of a man at the mercy of twelve men as ignorant as themselves; who hear evidence, and on that, whether a man is innocent or guilty, decide his fate. Now had they proceeded on the system of Gall and Spurzheim, by examining the cranium, how differently would they have acted with regard to me! As my aunt has stated, my organs of destructiveness and inventiveness being so full, I never could, *in that case,* have had a chance of being sent to pay this visit to prison, because I could have no control over my actions. Gracious Powers! amongst the hundreds of unfortunate beings I passed through in the yard, how many are probably as innocent in fact as I am! debt is the crime the major part are accused of; but has it ever been ascertained by the new system whether they could have avoided incurring this? I'll answer for it, not; so that, by thus confining them, they actually are men ' more sinned against than sinning.'

For instance: suppose a man had a very large organ of *profusivedness*, which made him spend, in a very short time, all he had in the world—what then? is that any premeditated fault of his? certainly not, because he had no control over it. In the next place, that his organ of *acquisitivedness* was proportionably extended, which made him go instantly to work, to gather where he could provision for his organ of *profusivedness*—was this not proceeding according to nature? are we not told, necessity is the mother of invention? why not *profusivedness* the mother, or father, of *acquisitivedness*? And do we live in this enlightened age, to see our fellow-beings cast into prisons because they follow the dictates of nature—more especially when it is really impossible they could avoid it? We are told, the fear of imprisonment prevents many men from obtaining money when they well know they can never repay it; but how is that proved? does not every day testify the contrary—establishing still more fully the

correctness of the system of Gall and
Spurzheim, that though prisons are staring men in the face, with wide-extended
jaws ready to swallow them up, yet, however desirous they may be to avoid such
unpleasant places (and that every man
must be anxious to do this is is but natural to imagine), yet it is totally out of
their power, in consequence of certain organs, that propel them to lay their hands
upon cash wherever they can find it?
Nay, does not the organ of *inventiveness*
drive one on, at times, into scenes the
most extraordinary, for the sole purpose
of supplying the never-to-be-satisfied organ of *profusivedness* with what it requires from time to time? And all these
matters are visited as crimes upon the
heads of men, who, if they had no such
organs, would have walked quietly through
life, without ever dreaming of touching
their neighbours' goods.

"And what benefit does this severity
do society? I'll venture to tell what in-

jury it will, to a certainty, be the consequence of to the morals of the people; a
man of the best principles, well educated,
who mixes in the first society, and who
would sooner run the risk of losing his
life—that is, being shot through the head
—rather than allow any man to call his
word or honour in question; this man,
unfortunately for him, has a large organ
of *profusivedness*, which, in spite of all
his care, runs him in debt to a large
amount; he is suddenly called on for pay-
ments which he cannot make, and, without ever ascertaining whether these engagements were contracted in a fair or
foul manner, by the examination of his
cranium, they cast him forthwith into
durance vile. Very well—now let us
see the result: in this sink of iniquity, a
prison, he remains for some length of
time, agreeable to the terms of the insolvent act (it is wonderful the legislature
have been sufficiently modernized to establish even this little benefit); during this
period, this *Corinthian* pillar of society

loses much of its polish; and when he enters the world again, proves, by the tameness with which he bears the sneers and scoffs he may encounter, that much of the *exquisite sensitiveness* of his feelings is lost, the first and most certain indication that can be given of relaxation of principle; efforts are no longer made to curb the organ of *profusivedness*, but rather the contrary, while care is taken that *inventiveness* shall keep *acquisitivedness* close up to it, so that it should not languish for want of succour; and this is the benefit having a new exerciser of his wits cast upon the public, that the community derive from clapping people in prison!

"He gets out, however; but, for me, there is no insolvent act. Here I am lodged for life—here shall I see seasons return, but not for me, with their varied sweets or sources of enjoyment—for me no more the cheerful hearth of home—fireside enjoyments—the incense-breathing morn—the wildly devious walk with her I love—for me no more

' Domestic happiness, that only bliss
Of Paradise that has surviv'd the fall!
The nurse of virtue, in whose arms
She smiles, appearing, as in truth she is,
Heaven-born, and destin'd to the skies again!'

no; to satisfy my royal creditor, there is
no other mode save through purse or
prison—were the twenty acres of bog on
the Cunnamara Mountains mine, all would
not produce sufficient for my ransom. We
talk of the laws of our country, that guard
us from tyranny; but can it be denied,
that a fine imposed upon the subject beyond his means of ever paying, knocks
down, at one blow, whole barriers that
secure us from being swept away by
the overwhelming torrent of despotism?
When I have so warmly advocated the
constitution of England, I was not aware
of this dangerous power in the hands of
our rulers.—Oh, my beloved! and is it
come to this? must I be content to resign
thee, or see thy beauty and thy fragrance
wasting away within the confines of a prison? But, no, it cannot be; with thee,
in a thatched hovel, even on the bleak

side of the Connaught Mountains, I could be happy; but here, to behold thee amidst vice, misery, depravity of every kind— amidst the horrors of the gloomy gaol—

———————————Where misery moans—
Where sickness pines—where thirst and hunger burn,
And poor misfortune feels the lash of vice'—

no—no; and you are lost to me for ever!"

The die was cast—it was useless to repine; but as there was no hope, no prospect of liberation, he deemed it expedient to acquaint his friends at St. Doulagh's with the fatal end of his career. He had hitherto kept them in expectation that his journey to London would be crowned with advantageous results; but now, that it would be both cruel and deceptive to insinuate any longer this belief, he decided on coming to an explanation with them.

This truly painful task over, he tried, as much as possible, to fly from thought; and in his efforts for the purpose, he was aided by the variety of characters he met with. He had not long been confined

before his abilities were spread through
the prison; in consequence of which he
was beset with a host of followers, each
asking some favour at his hands. The
first that approached him for this purpose
were a set of young men who professed
themselves Radicals, without well knowing what it meant; but considered, as he
was confined on the score of having written in their favour, their society must be
acceptable to him, and a pleasure felt in
obliging them. Memorials, petitions, re-
presentations of all kinds, to people in
office and out of office, were what they
required the exercise of his abilities in;
and, but that he had an exhaustless fund
of good-nature, they certainly would have
deprived him of all patience, so heavily
and incessantly did they tax it.

But these were not the only suitors who
bowed at his levee; he was also annoyed
by a set of young half-pay officers, complaining of cruel creditors, and overlooked
services. One morning, a dashing Bond-
street lounger, but whose perambulations

were now confined to the rules of the
King's Bench, through the unreasonable
conduct of a Jew tailor, entreated an au-
dience; and on being admitted, presented
himself, accompanied by this Philistine of
the shears.

- It seems captain B———, having got a
remittance from an uncle, had prevailed
on all his creditors, save the one who now
accompanied him, to compromise their
debts for five shillings in the pound; and
having heard much of the cleverness and
eloquence of Eugene, conceived, if he
could but obtain his interference with
him, he might be brought into terms like
the others.

Eugene could not decline what was requested. After some arguments on pressing the composition on the Jew—" Blessh
my heart!" he cried, assuming a countenance of astonishment, " but it'sh wonderful how preposterish the affairs of thish
vorld are managed! naturally von vould
imagine, de interesht of a few should give

place to the interests of the many; but no such a thing——"

"Why, how do you mean, Mordecai?" demanded captain B——.

"Vy, vat I mean ish, if there were more examples made of young shentlemen for running in debt, above their means to pay, they vould not be so apt to do so."

"And what the devil then, do you think, if they didn't, you'd have got on as you have done? do you think, if the lads came down at once with the ready shino to you, they'd let you make up the bills you do against them? No, no, my buck! so don't abuse what's the making of your fortune, as well as that of all the other knights of the goose."

"Blessh my heart, to hear how you runs on! Make our fortunes!—Here comes a young shentleman, and he orders so and so; and when, like de honeslit man, I begin to tell him vat the cost of such and such articles will be, he saysh—'Oh, d——n the expensh!' and to be sure he may vell care little about it, vhen I finds he never pays: and then comes another——."

"Oh, d——n it, Mordecai, no prosing! long bills are the devil; but long speeches are worse, if there be any thing worse."

"Ay, all ish bad, vhen ve come to speak about our monies; but vhen one young shentleman meets anoder, with a fine, stylish new coat on, does he not lay his hand upon his shoulder, and cry, 'Who shuffers?' and does not the oder say, 'Oh, cursh it! the rascally tailor, to be sure?"

"My good friend, supposing this to be the case," cried Eugene, "that there be a want of principle in some instances, are the innocent to be punished for the guilty? Both by captain B——'s shewing, and your own allowing, you have got a good deal of his cash; it is therefore evident, that he never meant you should suffer through his means; that is, when he contracted a debt with you, it was not without an intention of discharging it."

"Yesh, I don't dishpute I have got some of his monies; vhen firsht he came

to me he had de long pursh; but, blessh
my heart, no pursh could have stood his
calls upon it! Firsht he get de cottage
ornee near town, den he get the housh in
town itself, den de carriage, den de shoot-
ing-lodge in Norfolk, den de marine villa
at Brighton, den de fine——"

"Come, no more of your dens, if you
please, sir!" said captain B——.

"No, no more dwelling on such matters," resumed Eugene; "but supposing
captain B—— can really be accused of
extravagance, are you certain (without
being which you should not condemn
him) that he could help it? in short, did
you ever examine his cranium, to ascertain how his organs of *thought* and *volition* stood?"

"Hish vhat?" cried the Jew, staring.

"His *cranium*—before you arrested
him, did you examine his head, to see
what his *organs* were?"

"My goot sir, my businessh ish vid
de body, not vid de head; that belongs

to the hatter, as the veet and legs do to
the shoe and bootmaker."

" Ay, poor devils, we are all cut up
amongst you," said captain B———; " one
seizes this part, and another that part; and
by the time you are all done with us, we
are dressed with a witness."

" Am I to understand," again resumed
Eugene, " that you know nothing about
the system of Gall and Spurzheim, that
has made so much noise in the world—
that is, that you know nothing of phrenology ?"

" No, nothing—nothing at all at all,"
replied the Jew, shaking his head.

" I am sorry for it, from the liberality
it inculcates; not that I can permit myself to doubt, finding you possessed of all
we can expect or desire. You must know,
my friend, from this, that the old mode of
proceeding against our fellow-creatures,
when they happen not to perform their
engagements, agreeable to their promises,
should now be laid aside, it being clearly
proved by it, that they could not help the

conduct or actions that occasioned their incurring such engagements. *Formerly* it was understood we were reflecting beings, each in possession of a certain proportion of reason, to guide us through life, and thereby rendered accountable, both to God and man, for our actions. But this is *not* all proved to have been an error; by the discovery of those enlightened philosophers, it is now ascertained that we are more mechanical than rational creatures. Hence the cruelty, to say nothing of the injustice of coercion, or incarceration of any kind. Had you therefore, my friend, been acquainted with *this system*, and in consequence studied the cranial map of captain B——'s head, I make no doubt you would either not have permitted his name to blot your ledger, or else, having done so, would have patiently borne whatever might have been the consequence, for I do rather conceive, that you would have found his organ of *profusivedness* so large, that *in terror* you would have refused opening your book for his orders. As the business is, however, now done, and cannot be recalled, I will hope, that after this explanation, you will not refuse acting as we wish, more especially when I render you happy by shewing—for I perceive, by your own statement, you are a man of great organs of *philanthropiness* —that captain B——'s having squandered, as you call it, large sums in building, and so on, may rather have done benefit than mischief to society. May not a shilling spent by such a man, in what the world denominates folly, be picked up by a man whose organs, fortunately for him, are under better control? It is therefore not lost. You say my friend here has built fine houses, and furnished them richly, has lived in them expensively, and in a few years has ruined himself; but the masons, carpenters, smiths, and other honest tradespeople, have they not by him been assisted in maintaining their families? so who is it actually he has injured by this conduct but himself? Under all these considera-

tions, therefore, I am persuaded you cannot any longer hesitate about coming into the proposed terms."

" Vell, I do believe your advish is for
the besht," said the Jew, " and so I will
not refush to acquiesce in it. As vell as
I understhands vat you have been speaking
about, tish that the vise vay ish to look
to the outside of man, to shee vat they
are, and tish ish vat I've always done,
and never yet found myshelf mishtaken."
With a profound bow, he then said he was
ready to attend captain B——, and retired
with him.

If " hope deferred maketh the heart
sick," what must the extinction of hope
do? When Eugene reflected on his last
days of happiness—when he compared the
cheerful past with the miserable present,
and the dreary future, his soul shuddered
within him, and loathing life, he wished
to have resigned it. It was not enough
that he was separated from her he adored,
the reflection was aggravated by the consciousness of having brought ruin upon

her—ruin for which he could make her no reparation.

In vain, arguing from the notions he had imbibed, he tried to persuade himself he was not to blame for this—it is not, in the moments of bitter sorrow and repentance, fallacious reasoning will prove efficacious; the tortured heart requires some other unction than can be derived from it, to allay its agony. Gradually he began to doubt and to deride what he had before so obstinately adhered to: Conscience awakened restored him to his reason; and to his aunt's sudden refutation of all she had early and previously taught him, he now clearly saw all the inextricable misery in which he was involved was owing; but for the doctrine to which she had made him a convert, he never would have been capable of the rashness and presumption that deprived him of his profession, and turning him adrift upon the world, exposed him to all those temptations and snares that eventually proved his ruin.

But retrospect was useless—oh, could time past be recalled, where is the mortal that could say there was not some portion of his he could wish to live over again! As the poet says—

> " How readily we wish time spent recall'd,
> That we might try the ground again, where once
> (Through inexperience as we now perceive)
> We miss'd that happiness we might have found!
> Some friend is gone, perhaps his son's best friend,
> A father, whose authority, in shew
> When most severe, and must'ring all its force,
> Was but the graver countenance of love;
> Whose favour, like the clouds of spring, might low'r,
> And utter now and then an awful voice,
> But had a blessing in its darkest frown,
> Threat'ning at once, and nourishing the plant.
> We lov'd, but not enough, the gentle hand
> That rear'd us. At a thoughtless age, allur'd
> By ev'ry gilded folly, we renounc'd
> His shelt'ring side, and wilfully forewent
> That converse which we now in vain regret.
> How gladly would the man recall to life
> The boy's neglected sire ! a mother too,
> That softer friend, perhaps more gladly still,
> Might he demand them at the gates of death."

But the tide may roll back, to throw into our arms that which we have lamented; but there is no ebb or flow of time, to restore to us that which we have lost in its silent progress. Eugene believed his fate inevitably fixed. Oh, the sinking of his heart, as his eye, wandering round the high walls of his prison, contemplated them as the enclosure of a living tomb, that interposed between him and all he loved on earth! oh that he was but one of the sparrows that sat upon their top, that he might fly away to the bosom of his Rose! oh that but for one hour he could be indulged with seeing her, to kiss away her tears, study her wishes, and learn whether she could be content to share his wretched destiny! But, no, no, no, this was a felicity he never more expected to enjoy; and the distraction which, in these moments of despair, he gave way to, led to an idea that his intellects were at times disordered: but we must now leave him to his sorrowful reflections, to look in upon our friends at St. Doulagh's.

CHAPTER IV.

"I have a silent sorrow here, a grief I'll ne'er impart—
It breathes no sigh, it sheds no tear, but it consumes my
　　heart;
This cherish'd wo, this lov'd despair, my lot for ever be,
So, my soul's lord, the pangs I feel be never known by
　　thee."

ON deciding to acquaint his friends with his unfortunate situation, Eugene conceived it would be difficult to make them clearly comprehend how he should be cast into prison, although perfectly innocent of the crime for which he was tried, without entering into a detail of his supposed enemy, which, wishing to avoid, lest of adding to their unhappiness about him by the excitement of vague fears, he made up his mind, after some further little consideration, to merely inform them that he was to be imprisoned a year, and fined a thou-

sand pounds, in consequence of its having
been proved against him that he had libelled the British government. Gladly would
he have concealed the disastrous circumstance, and would have made every effort
for the purpose, had his sentence been for
any specific period; but as he considered
it in the light of one for life, he deemed it
absolutely necessary to prepare them in
time for his returning no more to his native home.

On the news arriving of the fate of this
beloved relative, to describe the scene that
took place at the castle of St. Doulagh's
would be impossible. The lieutenant,
when he could comprehend that his son
was imprisoned by order of the king, for
high treason, as he called it, raved about
like a frantic bedlamite; while Grace and
Rose dropped lifeless from their chairs;
Miss Agnes Flora Judith, to whom, as
already stated, Eugene's letter was addressed, having, in the indignation it excited, communicated the distressing information it contained without the slightest

preparation. The servants, frightened at all they saw, at all they heard, ran about, without well knowing whom first to call in to assist.

At length the young ladies being recovered—" Well," said Miss Agnes Flora Judith, wiping away the tears from her eyes, with as much carelessness as the really-agitated state of her mind would permit her to assume the air of—" well," she said, " our immolated dear one is not the first of his family who has suffered in the cause of freedom, and for the good of his country. The great O'Neils often struggled to free their native land from the authority of the English throne altogether, and many of their royal race have fallen in the glorious effort. Why should we take to heart, therefore, his having met with a similar fate? I make no doubt his name revived old animosities. As for one year's imprisonment, that would be nothing; but the fine keeps him in confinement for life; but this, their laying such a one upon him, only proves more strongly than ever the cold blood of these Sassanachs. There was a time when the Irish kings would not have allowed such a set of upstarts to sit at table with them! What a state of darkness was England in between the first and second century, when this " lovely green isle of the ocean" flourished in religion, learning, and arts! As to St. Patrick being the founder of Christianity in this land, it is false; while our opposite neighbours, therefore, were involved in the most profound darkness, going through the horrid rites of Druidism in their woods and groves, we were an enlightened people, and should, accordingly, ever have been the most respected ; for it is proved, beyond controversy, that when he visited Ireland in the fifth century, it was merely (as was customary in those days, according to St. Paul's recommendation) to review the churches, and report accordingly ; and in so pure a state did he find them, treading so immediately on the footsteps of the apostles, that it is a well-ascertained fact, he took bishops from hence to Scotland, to preach the word of salvation there. Nay, they have it recorded, so high was the estimation in which Ireland then stood in foreign countries, that their youth of quality were sent over here for education, to what they termed the Island of Saints, being chiefly for instruction in religious knowledge. In those days each province was governed by different monarchs, whose courts (where the greatest luxury, refinement, and beauty, were to be found), were visited by the most enlightened nations. They possessed both gold and silver, as their coins, extant to this day, can verify. The prerogatives of royalty were exercised by O'Neil, in spite of all the attempts of England to subjugate that great prince, down to the latter end of the fifteenth century. Here," continued Miss Agnes Flora Judith, opening a small casket, " here is a gold coin of that reign, on which may be perceived an impression of that king's head, and on the reverse the cross, with the inscription declaratory, in the charac-

ter called *Ogham Croabb;* and as I never
met with any of a later, or so late a date,
belonging to any other of our Irish kings,
this is a proof to me, that our royal house
was the last that became completely sub-
jected to the yoke of England. But for
its long resistance, what a revenge is now
taken! for to the recollection of this, I am
persuaded, is owing all that has now happened."

"Stuff, stuff!" exclaimed her brother
impatiently, who had been pacing the
room all this time, attending to her as
little as he would to the whistling of the
wind. "By the Lord, Agnes, you are
enough to drive one mad, with your old
coins, and I don't know what: by what
right, I say, did this young rascal attempt to find fault with a government
looked up to by the whole world as a model for imitation?"

"By the right which Heaven gave him,
in enduing him with reason! and let me
tell you, that if you find fault with him,

for what is natural to man, political jealousy, or an aptitude or propensity to suspect and inquire into the conduct of those
who rule us, being inherent in our nature,
you oppose nature herself. How ably is
this proved by doctor Benjamin Franklin,
from the most faithful of all histories, the
Holy Bible! Hear what he says in illustration or support of the argument.—' The
Supreme Being had been pleased to nou-
rish up a single family, by continued acts
of his attentive providence, till it became
a great people; and having rescued them
from bondage, by many miracles performed by his servant Moses, be personal-
ly delivered to that chosen servant, in presence of the whole nation, a constitution
and code of laws for their observance, accompanied and sanctioned with promises
of great rewards, and threats of severe pu-
nishments, as the consequence of their
obedience or disobedience.'

  " This constitution, though the *Deity
himself* was to be at the head (and it is
therefore called, by political writers, a theo-

cracy), could not be carried into execution but by means of his ministers. Aaron and his sons were therefore commissioned to be, with Moses, the first established ministry of the new government.

" One would have thought that the appointment of men who had distinguished themselves in procuring the liberty of their nation, and had hazarded their lives in openly opposing a powerful monarch,.who would have retained that nation in slavery, might have been an appointment acceptable to a grateful people; and that a constitution, framed for them by the Deity himself, might, on that account, have been secure of an universal welcome reception. Yet there were, in every one of the thirteen tribes, some discontented, restless spirits, who were continually exciting them to reject the proposed new government, and this from various motives.

" Many still retained an affection for Egypt, the land of their nativity; and these, whenever they felt any inconve-

nience or hardship, though the natural
and unavoidable effect of their change of
situation, exclaimed against their leaders,
as the authors of their trouble; and were
not only for returning into Egypt, but for
stoning their deliverers.   Those inclined
to idolatry were displeased that their golden' calf was destroyed.   Many of the
chiefs thought the new constitution might
be injurious to their particular interests—
that the profitable places would be *engrossed by the families and friends of
Moses and Aaron;* and others, equally
well born, excluded.   In Josephus and
the Talmud we learn some particulars not
so fully narrated in the Scripture.   We
are there told, that Corah was ambitious
of the priesthood, and offended that it
was conferred on Aaron, and this, as he
said, by the authority of Moses only,
without the consent of the people.   He accused Moses of having, by various artifices, fraudulently obtained the government, and deprived the people of their li-
berties, and of conspiring, with Aaron, to

perpetuate the tyranny in their family. Thus, though Corah's real motive was the supplanting of Aaron, he persuaded the people that he meant only the public good; and they, moved by his insinuations, began to cry out—' Let us maintain the common liberty of our *respective tribes*; we have freed ourselves from the slavery imposed upon us by the Egyptians, and shall we suffer ourselves to be made slaves by Moses? If we must have a master, it were better to return to Pharaoh, who at least fed us with bread and onions, than to serve this new tyrant, who, by his operations, has brought us into danger of famine.' Then they called into question *the reality of his conference* with God, and objected to the privacy of the meetings, and the preventing any of the people from being present at the colloquies, or even approaching the place, as grounds of great suspicion. They accused Moses also of *peculation*, as embezzling part of the golden spoons and chargers that the princes had offered at the dedication of the altar,

and the offerings of gold by the common
people, as well as most of the poll-tax;
and Aaron they accused of pocketing
much of the gold of which he pretended
to have made a molten calf. Besides peculation, they accused Moses of *ambition*;
to gratify which passion, he had, they
said, deceived the people, by promising to
bring them to a land flowing with milk
and honey—instead of doing which, he
had brought them *from* such a land; and
that he thought light of all this mischief,
provided he could make himself an *absolute prince*. That, to support the new
dignity with splendour in his family, the
partial poll-tax, already levied and given
to Aaron, was to be followed by a general
one, which would probably be augmented
from time to time, if he were suffered to
go on promulgating new laws, on pre-
tence of new occasional revelations of the
Divine will, till their whole fortunes were
devoured by that aristocracy.

" Moses denied the charge of peculation, and his accusers were destitute of

proof to support it; though facts, if real, are in their nature capable of proof.—' I have not,' said he (with holy confidence in the presence of God)—' I have not taken from this people the value of an ass, nor done them any other injury.' But his enemies had made the charge, and with some success among the populace; for no kind of accusation is so readily made, or easily believed by knaves, as the accusation of knavery. From all which we may gather, as the doctor observes," continued Miss Agnes Flora Judith, " that popular opposition to a public measure is by no means uncommon; or, in short," concluding the remark in the way that was most agreeable to herself, " that the ruled have always a right to inquire into the conduct of the rulers."

We are told that " the grief that cannot speak, whispers the o'erfraught heart, and bids it break." We may therefore be led to imagine, from this long tirade of Miss Agnes Flora Judith, that hers was not exactly of this description; but there

is no rule without an exception; she was
indeed absolutely overwhelmed with affliction, by the terrible situation of Eugene, whom she loved with even maternal tenderness, and had long looked up
to as the pride and ornament of her
house; and whatever aggravation her distress was capable of receiving, it met with,
in a dawning idea of being, in some way
or other, the cause of his misfortunes.
But acute as were her sufferings on his
account—acute as were those of his sister,
who could not even have heard of a stranger being doomed to so rigorous a fate
without pain and commiseration—what
were they, when compared, in bitterness,
with those of the distracted Rose—she
who had such reasons, such manifold reasons, for anxiety for the return of Eugene!

As already hinted, the nocturnal meetings in the chapel—the unbounded love
experienced for Eugene—the unlimited
confidence reposed in his honour—had
proved fatal to her repose; disgrace, from
which nothing but her marriage with him

could save her, was staring her in the face; and all hope of this being now at an end, she resigned herself to despair. She had no one to consult with in this dreadful emergency—no one to whom she could venture to intrust the secret of her indiscretion. Having previously withdrawn her confidence from Grace, she had no right now to torture her with the knowledge of her situation, more especially knowing, as she did, that Grace possessed not the power of affording her the assistance it required; but had the reverse been the case, how could she bring herself to impart such a secret to her?—how endure to meet her eye, after seeing her cheek kindle with the blush of shame for her disgrace? No—the thought was not endurable; and happen what would, she resolved that Grace should not be the repository of her wretchedness. She had a father certainly at hand; but to think of crossing the threshold of his cabin, either for consolation or protection under her present circumstances, was out of the question, he never having evinced any thing like the tenderness or interest of a parent for her, owing, she conceived, to her having been brought up in tenets different from his by her early protectress and benefactress; besides which, knowing as she did, the even romantic notions which the *Milesians* entertain of the sacredness of female chastity, she was convinced, that to reveal her misery to him would be to have herself spurned with maledictions from his door. How, in this agonizing moment of utter desolation, did she deplore the absence of the affectionate creature, to whose maternal care she had been consigned almost immediately after her birth, through the inability of her mother, who died while she was yet but an infant, to perform the part of one to her! Had Margaret Brady been near, she would not have wanted a friend in the sad hour of necessity; but, alas! her fond nurse was far distant from the Emerald Isle, having gone over to the West Indies, to reside

with a brother there, shortly after Rose's
adoption by her late benefactress; not
willingly, certainly, but from necessity;
as she would infinitely have preferred, for
the sake of being near her darling, to have
remained the manager of Cormack's cabin;
but unfortunately, as it so happened for
poor Rose, some missionaries travelling
through Ireland had so completely satisfied Mrs. Brady of the errors of the Popish
persuasion, that her absolute recantation
of it was the result. There being nothing,
perhaps, however of the martyr in her
composition, this was a step she rather
felt solicitous to keep from the knowledge
of Cormack, from the consequences she
apprehended from its disclosure; but all
her precautions for the purpose were unavailing; partly through the hints of some,
the positive assertions of others, and his
own observations, Cormack came to a
knowledge of the truth, and finding that
neither he, nor, what was more, father
O'Dogherty, could succeed in bringing
her back to the path from which she had,

strayed, made up his mind to expelling her from beneath his roof; which resolution he carried into effect, with all the zeal and alacrity of a true defender, as he conceived, of the faith, by turning her into the road one night, just on the eve of Christmas, and in the midst of sleet, snow, and darkness, when even an enemy's dog might have moved one sufficiently to compassion not to drive him from the door; taking care, previous to her expulsion, to secure two bottles of holy water from father O'Dogherty, that the house might undergo a purification immediately after it had taken place, lest otherwise it might become the abode of those that shall be nameless.

Young as Rose was at the period of her nurse's departure, she had never ceased to recollect her, omitting no opportunity of writing to her, and sending her little remembrances of her regard; among these was her picture, at the particular desire of the affectionate being, shortly after her taking up her residence at St. Doulagh's.

What would she not have given that she
was now within her reach—now, when she
so much wanted a confidential friend, a
maternal bosom, to receive and shelter her!
But she was far, far away, little recking
the fate of her she loved as her own.
In the first moments of her distraction,
a thousand wild plans suggested themselves to her; one instant she thought of
writing to Eugene—the next of flying to
him; but the design was hardly formed,
ere it was abandoned, with the same precipitation it had been conceived. No,
since she had not previously acquainted
Eugene with her unhappy situation, as
the daily, almost hourly expectation she
had latterly been in of his return, had prevented her, she would not now, when no
aggravation of misery was wanting to crush
him to the earth. She knew him too well
not to know what the result of the torturing communication would be; but
how, at the very moment when, stopped
in his career of fame and fortune, he must
be indebted to the kindness of his family

for what he could no longer supply to
himself by his own exertions, how could
she bear to throw herself, with her help-
less burthen, upon him? No, death was
preferable to the thought, and to death
she now looked for relief from her woes.
But she did not only weep her fatal imprudence—with equal agony she wept
over the idea of no more beholding him,
for whom, if possible, the tenderness of
her heart was redoubled, through his misfortunes—her affianced husband in the
sight of Heaven, with equal the idea of
what she was well aware he was suffering
on her account, though unacquainted with
the full extent of her misery. Oh that
he could burst his way through his prison, and flee with her to some wild solitude, though the bare earth were all their
resting-place, its roots their food, some
cleft their habitation; or, oh that, unknown, she could be near him, to creep to
his bosom, pour the balm of love into his
distracted soul, and kiss him to his rest!
But these were but the delirious wishes of

despair; she should never more behold him: if he returned, he would seek her, but he should not find her. But he never would return—never would his adventurous foot scale his native hills again—never would he again stray through those green shady bowers, where they had passed so many delicious hours together; his youth, his beauty, his talents, would waste and wither away within the gloomy limits of a prison—and when he died, English dust would cover him, and a nameless grave receive him, once so loved, so valued!

Her deep dejection was, at first, rather imputed by Grace to her sympathy in the sorrows of her friends, but observation shortly tended to convince her, that there was yet a more powerful cause for it; thus confirming a suspicion, previously excited, of a partiality in her bosom for Eugene, through the flutter, or variation of colour, which, from the moment of his departure, any allusion to him occasioned; but if she had forborne before touching on the subject, from a fear of the opposition an at-

tachment between them—and of Eugene's
she had all along been aware, if not from
her father, at least from her aunt, whose
prejudices in favour of birth she knew to
be unconquerable—she would not now attempt doing so, when, from the predicament in which Eugene was placed, a union between them must be downright madness; but dearer than ever did she feel
Rose to her heart, from the idea she had
conceived of her affection for Eugene, and
with feelings, in consequence, easier to be
imagined than described, soon perceived
her health declining, the rose grow pale
and leave her cheek, and all her natural, her
wonted spirits utterly forsake her. Oh
how was the affectionate heart of Grace
torn at this juncture! by what conflicting
feelings, by what clashing interests, was it
occupied and rent! Sisterly affection
would have urged her to fly to the poor
prisoner—to try if, by her attentions, she
could do any thing towards alleviating the
bitterness of his fate; but at the very moment she had almost made up her mind

on the point, she was drawn back by the state to which she saw her father and aunt reduced through their affliction for him; while again she was called away from them, by seeing her, her sweet companion, her adopted sister, the friend of her heart, to whom she had looked for support and consolation, in some degree, under this heavy calamity, fading away before her eyes, like a blighted flower. Oh, it required more almost than human fortitude to enable her to bear up under such sorrows! but she had recourse to that which is never disregarded, prayers to Heaven, for strength to be enabled to perform the sad duties which had devolved upon her.

CHAPTER V.

"No more she cherishes sleep's balmy hour,
　No more she feels the joy of soft repose;
She breathes her anguish in the roseate bower,
　And to the murmuring stream reveals her woes.

"Oft by the moon's pale lustre was she seen,
　In pensive mood, upon the dewy lawn,
Or wand'ring lonely in the midnight scene,
　Or prostrate low beneath the silver thorn."

In the first transports of his indignation
against his son, for having committed
(what was in his mind, though not construed so by laws too merciful) high treason, the lieutenant vowed he would neither see, nor have any intercourse with
him, till, by two or three years confinement, he had in some measure paid the
penalty of his guilt; and, in consequence
of this quickly-repented vow, remained
stationary at St. Doulagh's, as would not

otherwise have been the case; but all the
gay hilarity of his spirit, the happy con-
tentedness of his mind, was gone, and instead of any longer appearing to take interest in any thing about him, he passed
his hours in gloomy wanderings, repent-
ing and reproaching himself for having
denied himself the melancholy consolation
of sympathizing with his poor boy, by the
vow he had taken.

The unhappy family consulted together,
to see if there was any way by which the
sum required for his liberation could be
obtained; but, upon the most minute survey, saw that, without exposing themselves to the horrors of absolute want, all
they possessed in the world would not be
sufficient for that purpose, and as it was,
with shuddering sensations, feared their
means would be found inadequate to the
supply of his necessities.

Every thing of value in the house, it
was determined, should be disposed of, to
obtain a fund for this. The first sacrifice
made for the purpose was by Grace col-

lecting all the little ornaments she possessed, though many of them were most
precious in her estimation, as memorials
of the affection of William Delamere,
whom, if she did not regard as a lover, she
yet loved with the truest fervour as a
friend, and dispatched with secrecy to a
town at some distance, to be disposed of.
But this was not all—she began to turn
in her mind how, unknown, she could exercise her abilities for him; for she could
not divest herself of the pride appertaining to her station—the pride of a delicate
and sensitive mind, that would shun

> "————————the cruel scorn
> Which virtue, sunk to poverty, would meet
> From giddy passion and low-minded pride."

But wretched as she and her father were
about poor Eugene, still the unhappiness
of Miss Agnes Flora Judith, on his account, exceeded theirs, heightened as it
was by self-reproach; for in vain she tried
to fly from the idea, she could not evade
it, that she had been the cause of his ruin,

by the notions to which she had made him a convert. To rashness and presumption were to be attributed the loss of his profession ; and of these, with feelings of the deepest self-remorse for the change she had wrought in his disposition, she reflected he had never given any indications till she had taken him in hand ; and surely, in a system productive of such consequences, there must be something wrong. In this persuasion she began to be still further confirmed by a simple circumstance that took place about this time, but which, simple as it was, had still perhaps a greater effect upon her than the eloquence of a Cicero would have produced.

It appears, after Eugene's departure, Miss Agnes Flora Judith feeling a great vacuum in the want of a person to instruct in the new system, cast her eyes upon Martin, the son of one of the cottiers of St. Doulagh's, a deep shrewd young rogue, who served in the castle in capacity of footman. He had dived into the character of the old lady, and conceiving her mad, decided within himself on humouring all her whims and fancies, under the persuasion, that he should thereby reap unto himself no small advantage.

In this conclusion he was soon justified, by seeing himself gradually becoming a favourite with her. At length, one day, she promised to buy him a silver watch, provided he consented to have his head shaved by Barney, in order that she might be enabled to take a map of his cranium. The bribe she offered for his compliance was so great, that any thing, short of having the head itself shaved off, the delighted Martin would have consented to oblige her in.

Accordingly, his skull being prepared for her inspection, by being rendered as bald as the Scalp in the county Wicklow, she proceeded, in all due form, to its examination. In a little time—" I feel, Martin, that you have got here a bump of *philo-progenitiveness* large; this is an exceeding amiable trait in your character, Martin, indicating that you will be an affec-

tionate father : but here is one of rather
an opposite description, *combativeness*, also;
are you fond of fighting?"

" There isn't a lad in the parish, man or
boy, but I'd give a black eye to if he vexed me."

" Correct—*constructiveness* large again;
how do you feel on that head?"

" Ah then, mistress *jewel*, what may
that be?"

" Why the organ of contrivance; when
at a loss for any thing, you are ready at
invention."

" Faith and troth, mistress, if this is the
way you are going on, you'll be getting
more out of me than ever father O'Dogherty did, with all his cuteness; but let
me alone for helping myself—'tis I that
was never at a loss at a pinch! the *ould
one* himself would hardly be up to me,
when I set my wits to work!"

" Good again!—*acquisitiveness* ; ah,
this is of a size indeed, exceeding all the
others!"

Martin put the usual question to her.

"Why the intention of nature, Martin," was the reply, "in bestowing this organ upon you, was to inspire you with the desire of acquiring, so that, in consequence of its activity, you might have what you required, and not be left to the uncertain provision that could be made from the mere dictates of reason, after tracing a long chain of consequences. How stand your feelings as to this organ?"

Martin was silent; which Miss Agnes Flora Judith imputing to his not perfectly comprehending her, as was really the case, proceeded to render herself more intelligible, by stating, that this faculty, if not controlled by superior powers, produced theft.

"Oh now, any how, mistress, but you are going the lengths with me! Maybe it's after telling the master you'd be, and getting me to be sent to prison if I answered?"

"To prison, you foolish boy! for what? for yielding to the influence of a propensity which you could not help? No, that

would be treating you barbarously indeed:
and so you acknowledge——"

"Oh no, mistress, no!" said Martin,
alarmed; "don't be after going to say as
how I ever confessed stealing any thing,
and so get me clapped up into prison!"

"Haven't I already told you, if you
had been convicted of any thing of the
kind, you shouldn't be blamed for it, from
the size of your bump of *acquisitiveness*?"

"Well then, *troth* and *faith*, and upon
my *conscience*, and that's as good as if I
bibled it, myself never stole any thing;
because father O'Dogherty *tould* me I'd
go to hell, after being hanged for it, if
ever I meddled or made with my neighbour's goods; though I won't go for to
say, that my fingers haven't often and
often itched to touch what didn't belong
to me."

"Father O'Dogherty is a stupid old
fool," cried Miss Agnes Flora Judith,
"ignorant of all he should know; but
send him to me, and I'll soon shew him,

that if you committed any act he thought wrong, you should not be blamed for it, because, from your organization, you could not help it."

This was most agreeable information to Martin, who had long cast a longing eye upon some valuables of Miss Agnes Flora Judith's, contained in a casket that stood upon her dressing-table, and which the bump of *curiosity* had more than once made him examine, while that of *acquisitiveness*, dazzled by the splendour of the contents, consisting of brilliant earrings, necklace, and several diamond rings, strongly tempted him to appropriate them to his own use. The dread of the gallows, however, as well as of future punishment, as held up *in terrorem* to him by the priest, to deter him from the commission of such a crime, still prevented him from giving way to this evil inclination, and with a sigh of regret, he would close the box.

The case was now altered. Relieved from all further apprehension of punishment, by what Miss Agnes Flora Judith

told him—assured by her that he might
laugh at the threats of father O'Dogherty,
and set a gaol at defiance, he determined,
with a heart beating with delight, on no
longer delaying to secure to himself what
would be the making of his fortune for life,
without the necessity for any further exertion; and accordingly possessing himself
of the long-coveted casket, decamped with
it early the next morning. There was
but one jeweller's shop in the town, to
which he repaired from the castle, where
producing his prize, the master of it very
naturally concluded he could not have
come by such articles honestly, and took
him before the mayor, who discovering, on
examination, how they were obtained
(not a very difficult matter, partly through
the fright Martin was thrown into, partly
through his confidence in what Miss Agnes Flora Judith told him), he committed
him to prison, and sent off an express to
St. Doulagh's, to acquaint the family
there with what had occurred.

Miss Agnes Flora Judith was absolutely overwhelmed with shame and confusion by the intelligence; she rested not till she had obtained the liberation of the poor ignorant being she had so helped to delude, by pretending that what had happened was all through a mistake; and having seen him, for the purpose of endeavouring to undo the mischief she had done, gave him a sum of money, to enable him to seek his fortune elsewhere, as, after what had taken place, he could no more be admitted to the castle.

This simple fact worked wonders in the mind of Miss Agnes Flora Judith against the system she had adopted; she confined herself almost entirely, for some days after, to her closet, for the purpose of giving it a full and patient investigation; when, being fully satisfied and convinced that this hypothesis of human actions is indeed ill calculated for the subsequent improvement of our species, but, on the contrary, has a direct tendency to lead to the doctrine of materialism, she abandoned it altogether; but with what bitter regrets for ever having adopted it, from the ruin and misery in which the circumstance had been the means of involving those who were so dear to her!— "Oh that on me, on me the punishment due to error had alone lighted!" she cried; "and yet, could any personal infliction equal the agony of thinking I have been the cause of suffering to others?"

The intensity of her feelings brought on a severe fit of illness, and nothing could in any degree sooth or compose her, but consulting with Grace on the means of obtaining the power of administering to the comforts of Eugene. But, notwithstanding the way that Rose lived in the castle—notwithstanding her being considered as almost a second Grace, the pride of Miss Agnes Flora Judith not brooking that she should know the absolute necessity there was for these distressing consultations, she was often, in consequence, left for the greater part of a day to herself, through her exclusion from her apartment.

These welcome hours of freedom were passed by Rose in the indulging absorption of her deep despair, fast approaching to insanity; the wildest, the gloomiest, the most savage haunts about the castle, were the spots she sought, the moment she found herself at liberty to stray where she pleased. Here, unmindful of all that, in other days, was wont to delight her innocent mind, occupied by one fearful, one terrible idea, she would remain, forgetful of the lapse of time, heedless of the lengthening shadows of evening, the gathering cloud, the pelting shower, till sought and found out by the alarmed Grace.

With the most appalling intention, the unhappy girl often struck into the walk leading to the Lover's Leap, that spot where first the light of love had broke upon her soul. As long as sufficient reason remained, enabling her to govern her actions, her deep sense of religion, on consideration, proving if she was not warranted in self-destruction, she surely could not be so in taking the life of another, had hitherto operated in preventing the execution of her rash design, such reflections ever rushing on her mind as she came in sight of the awful gulf, down which she proposed precipitating herself—a cold shuddering would come over her—she would draw back with dismay and horror, and precipitately hurry into the embowering walk leading from it.

At length, the consciousness of the enormity of the act she had committed wrought with such intensity on her feelings, that they, at times, would overthrow the noble faculties of the mind; yet, during these paroxysms, there was a method in her actions not a little surprising. One evening she stole forth, determined on destruction—never had it appeared so inevitable as at this moment. After a course of the most distressing reflections, she proceeded towards the fatal spot: with a degree of calm composure, that she had long been a stranger to, her step was

firm; all proclaimed a state of mind fit for
the dreadful purpose. She suddenly turned the angle—the opening stood before
her; she no longer shuddered, or suffered
herself to draw back; but for one moment
she paused, and that was but to raise her
hands to heaven. Advancing, she stepped
upon the projecting rock—that fatal point,
which once to have touched would have
made her senses reel with terror, and her
blood freeze within her—

> " All pensive on the margin as she stood,
>   Contending passions tore her wo-fraught breast;
> With tearful eye she gazes on the flood,
>   With longing eagerness she pants for rest."

Her arms were extended, when, as she
tottered on the extreme brink of destruction, she was forcibly dragged back. The
suddenness and violence of this shock recalled her scattered senses; but rendered
desperate by her situation, she struggled,
but to no purpose, to free herself; and
after a few more unsuccessful efforts, with
a sudden conviction that it could not be
Grace that held her in so firm a grip, she

turned to see who it was, and beheld the tear-bedewed countenance of an elderly woman. Who was she? was not a necessary question, the stranger, by, suddenly clasping her to her heart, with a burst of rapturous tenderness, proclaiming herself; and Rose, overpowered by the sudden revulsion of her feelings, the undeserved kindness of Heaven, in sending such a friend to her aid as her beloved nurse, at the very moment she was so impiously doubting its goodness, sank, to all appearance, lifeless, on the bosom that throbbed with such maternal solicitude for her.

The return of Mrs. Brady indeed was not more providential than sudden and unexpected; her brother dying, left her at liberty to do again as she pleased, and accordingly she made the best of her way back to Ireland, where, the moment she landed, she set off for St. Doulagh's, and, without announcing herself at the castle, inquiring for Rose, was directed where to find her by a servant, who had chanced to meet her in her way to the Lover's Leap.

Fortunately for Rose, this faithful friend was a woman of firm nerves, else she must have stiffened into stone with horror, at the sight that presented itself to her view on gaining this spot—horror not merely at the sight of a human creature tottering on the brink of destruction, but of that creature being the one on whom she alone depended for all she hoped to taste of happiness in this life, death having swept away all her own natural connexions.

The observations which she had an opportunity of making, while endeavouring to recover Rose, gave her a suspicion of the cause of the rash act she had meditated; yet perhaps it might not be so bad as she apprehended. She had stopped at different cabins in her way to St. Doulagh's, to make inquiries at them concerning the family there; and from what she had heard amongst them, had been led to conceive that an attachment subsisted between Eugene and her darling—"And who knows," thought she, "but a private marriage may have taken place between them, and that fear of its being discovered, from the situation he is now in, may have driven her to the despair she must be in, to think of what I saved her from?" Anxious to be out of suspense, on a subject so interesting to her feelings—" Then, perhaps, after all, my darling," she cried, on Rose's reviving, "it is not for Rose Cormack, but Rose something else, I should have inquired at the castle?"

The blood which had forsaken the cheek of Rose now rushed to it, her very forehead was crimsoned, at the idea of the secret she had to disclose, as, burying her face in the bosom of the good woman, she faintly murmured—" No—no."

" Well, well, all in good time, my darling," said Mrs. Brady, affecting more cheerfulness than she really felt at the moment, the discovery she had made being a terrible shock to her feelings, having looked forward to a very great match for Rose, from her beauty and accomplishments. She made up her mind that Eugene was a complete young reprobate, persuaded nothing but the most insidious arts could have effected the destruction of her child. But this was no time to ask questions; she was convinced, from all that had occurred, that Rose's unhappy situation was as yet undivulged to any one, and she immediately determined on taking her away, where there would be no chance of its being discovered, her honour being even more precious to her than her life. Some little indignation was certainly mingled at the moment with her feelings—" But to comfort, not upbraid, is the duty of a Christian," she reflected: "independent of the blindness of love, forgiveness is the more readily claimed, when we behold such strong symptoms of contrition as this poor darling has manifested." But then all her prospects were closed for life, and tears of disappointed pride and affection, spite of all her efforts to suppress them, gushed from the eyes of poor Mrs. Brady. She was a woman of a strong mind, however, and good natural understanding; and aware therefore, that it is not by mere lamentations we can remedy what is wrong, she speedily exerted herself to explain to Rose, that she was come to take her away for some time from St. Doulagh's.—"After our long separation, they can't grudge, I am sure," she said, "letting you pass some time with your poor old nurse. I shall only stop there this night; to-morrow I shall be off, to get every thing ready for you, in a place I have in view; and as soon as I have done so, which will be, I am certain, in the course of a few days at farthest, will be back again for you with a mountain car."

She should have the shelter then, the concealment she required, to recompose her distracted mind, enable her to make her peace with offended Heaven, and prepare herself for whatever might ensue; and bursting into tears of grateful joy, the afflicted Rose again threw herself upon the bosom of her maternal friend.

Mrs. Brady exerted all her eloquence to sooth her, anxious to leave a spot where she could not look around her without shuddering. At length they repaired to the castle, where Mrs. Brady received the kindest welcome from Grace, the only one of the family who appeared. Far from starting any objection to her proposal respecting Rose, she expressed herself delighted at it, from the benefit that she conceived it likely she might derive from change of scene, and the soothing attentions of a person who had the power of devoting herself entirely to her.

Every thing was done as settled by Mrs. Brady; she went away the next morning, and at the expiration of a week, passed by Rose in a state of comparative, though melancholy, tranquillity, from the relief her mind experienced, freed, as it now was, from those torturing apprehensions that had so long agonized it, returned with a mountain ear for her.

Rose took leave of all but Grace over-night; but when in the morning she was bidding her farewell, then indeed was the renewal of sorrow. An ill-divining spirit whispered to her that she should see St. Doulagh's no more, or, of course, her friend. Under the terrible thought, she returned again and again to press her in her arms, to weep over her, to kiss her hands in agony. At length, dropping on her knees, with her own trembling hands uplifted to heaven—"Oh God!" she inwardly prayed, "let peace and happiness be restored to this house, though I shall not live to witness it! restore to it him, without whom neither can be more enjoyed within it, though on my cold bosom the sods of the valley will soon be pressed!"

At last Mrs. Brady, alarmed by the prolongation of such a scene, interfered to terminate it, and more dead than alive, Rose was placed upon the car. They had proceeded some way ere she was able to rouse herself from the state of affliction in which she had left the castle. At length the consideration of what was due to the kind friend who was making such exertions for her, and the reason she had for thankfulness, operated to induce her to make an effort for the purpose, and, by degrees, she began to enter into conversation, to the no small delight of her companion.

It has been remarked, that when the mind is at ease, the body is delicate, or, in other words, that when we have no cares to perplex us, trifling matters will be deemed of consequence, illustrating the story of the luxurious Sibyrite, who could not rest because a rose-leaf was crumpled under him.

The mind of Rose was too much occupied, or rather entirely engrossed, by its sorrows, to allow her to think of personal inconvenience, or else perhaps she might have complained a little of the fatigue of the present journey.

She soon found, from the track they were pursuing, that Mrs. Brady had completely deceived them at St. Doulagh's, with regard to their destination—a cir-

cumstance that tended to confirm the suspicions previously entertained of her already guessing all she had to communicate.

Their course lay, for some length of
way, through roads made alone by the
torrents that in winter came rushing from
the mountains; it may therefore be easily
imagined how they must have been shaken and jolted on such a vehicle as an
Irish car, without springs, in proceeding
through those deep gullies, rendered rough
and dangerous by the stones brought down
by the violence of the floods from the
mountains. Such were the sudden shocks
they received, that nothing but having
firm hold of the bars of the car prevented their being flung off amidst the briers
and nettles that fringed the way.

At length, after crossing several hills,
that elsewhere might have passed for to-
lerable mountains, they found themselves
without any other direction to proceed,
than was afforded by the tracks of cars a-
long the sides of the mountains, employed
some months before in drawing turf from

their summits; and in many places rendered hardly perceptible through the fern and moss that had grown above them. Here and there this road, if it could be called one, sloped down into deep glens, at the dark bottoms of which foamed noisy torrents, creating a degree of awe and terror in the mind, from the idea of danger they awakened; in some places, it being impossible to ford them, the trunk of an old tree, or its intertwisted branches, were thrown across them, which the boy who drove the car, by way of dissipating any fears of the females, generally expressed his hope they would not find rotten, as many a one to be sure had done before them, to the loss of many a poor man's horse. On these occasions, with admirable dexterity, he took the wheels from the car, thus reducing it to a sledge, the only mode in which it could be got over.

The travellers, however, got on without meeting with any accident; and but for their apprehension of something of the kind, would have found this part of the

journey agreeable enough, the road being
over a soft moss, or heath, the latter per-
fuming the air around, while the views,
though wild in the extreme, were still
highly romantic and interesting; but
when all became lost in confusion, or rather, was only sufficiently seen to let
them perceive the risks they ran in their
advance, when, in short, night overtook
the travellers, amidst rocks, and gullies,
and roaring torrents, the case became very
much reversed.

In the silence imposed by terror, they
proceeded for about a mile, when Mrs.
Brady, with a sudden exclamation of
thankfulness to Heaven for their escape
from all the perils of the way, threw her
arm round the neck of her companion,
and fondly kissing her cheek, told her
they had got to the end of their journey,
pointing out to her, as she spoke, a long
thatched cabin, or cottage, at a little distance.

Rose, however, was by this time so
completely overcome by the fatigue she

had undergone, and the restraint she had imposed upon her feelings throughout the day, on account of her kind friend, that she was unable to join in the gratulations occasioned by the circumstance. She was lifted from the car in a state of exhaustion, that made Mrs. Brady conceive it would be advisable for her immediately to retire to bed, to the great disappointment of Judy, the girl hired by way of attendant, having anticipated no small degree of *plause* from the nice manner in which she had cooked the supper. Instead of partaking of this, however, Rose swallowed a basin of white wine whey, which operating as an opiate on her, soon threw her into the sleep she so much required.

She woke from this much refreshed in the morning; but still, with something of the restless impatience of sorrow, hastily rose. As she cast her eyes about her chamber, she was rather surprised by its neatness; and still more agreeably when, on drawing back the white dimity window-curtain, she found the cottage was

situated at the entrance of a beautiful valley, instead of being seated at the side of a
bleak mountain, as she had rather conceived, from the imperfect view she had alone
been able to obtain of objects the preceding
night, was the case. There were no other
habitations immediately in sight, but in the
centre of the vale were the extensive ruins
of a very ancient monastery, rendered picturesque in the extreme by a high tower,
completely mantled over with ivy, rising
from the centre of the building, the roof of
which having given way to the destroying
hand of time, and thus permitting the
light to traverse the interior, its numerous
pillars, arches, and receding aisles, begirt
with long streaming grass, wild flowers,
and ivy, were displayed to the greatest
advantage, impressing upon the mind peculiar interest and grandeur.

The valley was enclosed by stupendous
mountains, many of them clothed to the
very summits with wood, others skirted
with hanging groves of oak, ash, and
beech, while tufts of elder trees clustered

about the ruins; and innumerable streams, gushing from the sides of the steeps, meandered in wild mazes across the paths, or collecting in natural reservoirs, formed limpid wells under the shadow of the rocks.

The cottage of Mrs. Brady was not unworthy of its situation; it was a commodious building, for one of that description, though somewhat ancient, as the houseleek and moss upon its thatch denoted, but still in good repair, and consisted of a neat parlour, kitchen, and three bed-chambers, honeysuckles and rose-trees covering part of the front, and behind it a delicious garden, that is, from its situation, stretching up a sunny hill, in every nook of which was a profusion of wild flowers or aromatic herbs. Nothing that could conduce to the comfort of Rose was omitted, and could she have steeped her senses in forgetfulness, she might, she would have been happy! but

" Remembrance wak'd, with all its busy train,
Swell'd at her heart, and turn'd the past to pain."

The requisite confidence was soon reposed in her friend, and the weight on her heart seemed in some degree lightened by the circumstance.

Aware of what she would suffer if she conceived herself under any restraint, Mrs. Brady always affected to be busy, that she might feel herself at liberty to do as she pleased, except when she actually saw that she had an inclination to converse with her.

The ruined monastery soon became the favourite haunt of Rose. Here, where the want of animate objects, the dead silence that reigned around, the solemnity of the venerable pile itself, formed a combination well calculated to give rise to pensive reflections, all was in union with her present feelings. Yet, absorbed as she was in these, there were moments when she was almost stolen out of herself by the admiration and curiosity excited by this romantic ruin, and the pleasure she took in involuntarily examining every part of it—its pillars, its arches, the cu-

rious and elaborate tracery of its windows,
and exploring the very minutest of its recesses, for

> " Each proper ornament was there,
>   That should a chapel grace;
> The lattice for confession fram'd,
>   And holy-water vase."

But as the excitement of novelty ceased
as all became familiar to her eye, this effect ceased to be produced, and the increase of her melancholy, the air, the look
of utter despondence with which she returned to the cottage, after passing hours
amidst all the silence, the dreariness, of
long-drawn ailes and fretted vaults, so
alarmed Mrs. Brady, that at length she
interfered, by endeavouring to prevail on
her to bend her steps in a different direction when she went out.

But the scene congenial with its feelings is the one the mind will cling to.
Rose could not be induced to forego her
visits to this lonely pile, so adapted for
sorrow, that sorrow seemed soothed by
being indulged within it; and where, if

any thing could steal her for a moment from the contemplation of her woes, it was the objects of interest by which she was here surrounded.

CHAPTER VI.

"No wounds like those a wounded spirit feels,
No cure for such, till God, who makes them, heals.
And thou, sad sufferer, under nameless ill,
That yields not to the touch of human skill,
Improve the kind occasion, understand
A father's frown, and kiss his chast'ning hand:
To thee the day-spring, and the blaze of noon,
The purple ev'ning, and resplendent moon,
The stars, that, sprinkled o'er the vault of night,
Seem drops, descending in a shower of light,
Shine not, or undesir'd and hated, shine,
Seen through the medium of a cloud like thine:
Yet seek Him—in his favour life is found—
All bliss beside a shadow, or a sound.
Then heaven, eclips'd so long, and this dull earth,
Shall seem to start into a second birth;
Nature, assuming a more lovely face,
Borrowing a beauty from the works of grace,
Shall be despis'd and overlook'd no more."

"BUT was he ever—was her Eugene for ever to remain in confinement?" the anguished Rose at length began to demand of herself; "was there no way to be thought of—no plan to be suggested, for freeing him from it? She had conceived the most exalted opinion of the nobleness, the generosity, of the British character, and could not therefore believe, that if his story were made known, some exertion would not be made to effect his liberation. No; she could not bring herself to imagine, that those who had torn the fetters from the oppressed African, who had come forward with such enthusiasm to aid the glorious patriots of Spain and Greece, would permit a fellow-subject to languish away his life in a prison, for what was excusable on the score of youth and inexperience, exclusive of any consideration of the fallibility of human judgment! No—the thing was impossible: but who was the person—where was the friend, that was to take up the pen in his cause? In vain she bethought her, till she at length came to the resolution of becoming his advocate herself. She was aware her address would contain no subtlety of argu-

ment; but then she believed that a simple
statement of facts would be a resistless appeal, and accordingly sat down forthwith,
with all the eagerness of newly-excited
hope, to compose a pamphlet, which,
when finished, she immediately dispatched
to one of the most eminent booksellers in
London, with an accompanying letter,
entreating he would print and publish it
without delay, and add to the obligation,
by letting her have a line of acknowledgment on its receipt.

Full of the most delightful anticipations—for of the result being all she wished she would not permit herself to entertain the shadow of a doubt—she suddenly
evinced a degree of cheerfulness that absolutely astonished Mrs. Brady, ignorant as
she was of the cause; Rose, in order, if
possible, to add to the joy of Eugene's
unexpected liberation, having decided on
imparting to no one what she had done,
till the purpose for which she had exerted
herself was effected. She no longer objected to varying her walks a little, as her

kind friend had before proposed in vain,
nor sought to decline having her company
in them.

Restored to comparative tranquillity,
she was now able to do full justice to the
beauties of her present abode. In this
wild, but, to her, enchanting spot, in
what happiness, what bliss, she thought,
could she pass her days, were her Eugene
restored to her! and might he, would he
not, after all that he had suffered, be easily induced to settle with her in retirement, far from the " meddling crowd's
ignoble strife?" and if he were, where
could a more delightful one be found than
this? Mrs. Brady's cottage was large
enough for the accommodation of all, and
with her to be a mother to them, what
felicity might they not enjoy! true—

> " No powder'd pert, proficient in the art
> Of sounding an alarm, would assault their doors;
> ————————no stationary steeds
> Cough their own knell, while, heedless of the sound,
> The silent circle fan themselves, and quake;"

but here the needle " would ply its busy

task," the poet's, or historian's page, by
one be made vocal for the amusement or
instruction of the rest, while

> " The sprightly lyre, whose treasure of sweet sounds
> The touch from many a trembling chord shakes out;
> And the clear voice symphonious, yet distinct,
> And in the charming strife triumphant still,"

would beguile the night; and, in short,
she gave herself up to the most enchanting day-dreams, the most soothing reveries.

Her eyes no longer wandered mechanically over the grandeur of the dilapidated
monastery; with all the rapture of gratified taste, they ran along the lines of Gothic pillars, sweeping beneath sublime
arches, to take in the splendid relics of
the eastern window, the grand termination of the choir, the length of the nave,
the height of the walls, the aspiring form
of the pointed arches, the exquisite delicacy of the tracery of the windows, clothed
or ornamented by the hand of time, with
gay shrubs, flowers, and ivy, which, closing the perspective, gave something of
the appearance of a twilight grove to the

'further end. But as the time approached
for bringing the expected letter from
England, she again became restless; and
when day after day passing away without
any thing but disappointment to her, led
her to believe she had completely deceived
herself by the hope she had yielded to,
again sunk back into despair—a despair of
a still deeper, gloomier nature, if possible,
than that she had previously indulged,
the anguish of her feelings now being in-
creased by the bitterness of disappointment, as darkness seems more profound
after a transient flash of light.

In vain her maternal friend argued with
her on the impropriety of the feelings she
was now giving way to—in vain represented to her that it was the duty of a
Christian, one of the strongest proofs they
could indeed afford of being what they
professed themselves, to suffer with patience; there were moments when, in the
black despair of her soul, Rose almost regretted what she had before considered

the providential interposition of her friend
at the Lover's Leap.

But the time was now fast approaching
that was to give her a name that, under
other circumstances, she would have rejoiced at. As it drew near, Mrs. Brady
became extremely perplexed how to procure her the requisite assistance without
exposure. Barney O'Rooke was the person whom she would have called upon on
the occasion, but this would be attended
with utter ruin to her darling; and at
last, after lying awake night after night,
revolving what she should do in this puz-
zling dilemma, she finally made up her
mind to sending for a gentleman in his
line but a few miles further off.

On the arrival of the hour that rendered
it expedient her doing so, she dispatched
two lads, whom she had in her pay, with
the necessary instructions for him. But
poor Mrs. Brady, in her calculations, had
quite forgot to take into consideration the
possibility of his being out of the way.
This, however, actually proved to be the

case, and her messengers, in consequence, were quite at a loss what to do, till they suddenly recollected O'Rooke, which having done, they forthwith proceeded to his habitation, with a determination of treating him exactly as they had been instructed to treat the other.

The night was a cold, damp one, and after solacing himself with his pipe and glass of whiskey-punch, over a large turf fire, Barney had betaken himself to bed, where he was comfortably snoring at the moment he was aroused by a violent knocking at the door.

Hastily rising, as soon as he was convinced, by a repetition of the knocks, that he had not been dreaming, he opened his window, and popping his well-defended head out of it, demanded who the devil was there? In reply he was informed, that a gentleman's carriage had been overturned just at the entrance of the village, and his services immediately required, in consequence of some very severe contusions the gentleman had received.

Barney hesitated; he was very unwilling to go out at such an hour, but still more so to lose the handsome reward which he made no doubt he should receive from a gentleman for his rest being disturbed; and accordingly, hastily doffing his nightcap, and slipping on his greatcoat and *brogues*, he unbolted the door, and sallied out.

The lads, lest of his suspecting a trick, had bribed a person with whom he was acquainted to call him, and with him Barney was trotting on at a brisk pace, from his impatience to grasp the sovereign, or sovereigns, that, like the ideal dagger of Macbeth, were glittering before him, the expected remuneration for his trouble, when, just as he reached the head of a solitary green lane, two men bolted out upon him, and having gagged him, and put a bandage over his eyes, forced him upon a car, and placing themselves one on either side of him, drove off with all speed.

Not a few, nor slight, were the struggles of Barney to extricate himself—but all were useless; and at last he was told by one of his companions, he had better take his advice, and be asy—" For, to tell you a secret, my lad," he cried, " I am lieutenant Moonlight, and my friend at your tother side is ensign Starlight, and we are the boys, you may know from our names, that are not to be daunted or disappointed in any thing we take in hand, and we have been ordered to bring you to the assistance of captain Rock's lady, who is about producing an heir to that renowned commander, righter of wrongs, and redresser of grievances; and who knows but, if he takes a fancy to you, he may keep you by way of family surgeon ?"

Poor Barney trembled, both in flesh and spirit, on hearing this intimation, captain Rock being the complete Bluebeard, or Raw-head and Bloody-bones of the neighbourhood, and quite overawed by it, ceased all further efforts to liberate himself.

The journey was pursued in silence; and from the roughness of the roads, or rather, the up-and-down-hill work, Barney was convinced, to a certainty, that they were taking him to some one of the numerous mountain-fastnesses of captain Rock. He was endeavouring to think how the adventure might end, when, pretty near the end of the journey, the car coming in sudden contact with a huge stone, was upset, and Barney, with his companions, flung to a distance from it. The latter soon regained their legs; but Barney, being fat and unwieldy, lay sprawling amidst the nettles amongst which he was thrown, till he suddenly heard the lads in pursuit of the horse, who, frightened by the accident, had made off as fast as he could, with all that remained of the car. Barney no sooner became sensible of this, than he thought it would be a good thing for him also to make off too, and accordingly rising, with greater alacrity than he had conceived himself capable of, he quickly succeeded in ungagging his mouth, and unbandaging his eyes.

Day was now just beginning to break, and by its faint light, on looking about him, he saw a neat cottage, at a little distance; and after a little consideration, thither he thought he would bend his steps, to entreat shelter, till he could obtain some safe conveyance back to his own village. Hardly had he come to this resolve, when an old crone, the wretched inmate of a miserable hovel he had not before noticed, so completely, through time and neglect, was it incorporated with the mud bank in which it was inserted, came out with a pitcher for water; and of her Barney, on seeing her, conceived, as appearances were sometimes deceitful, he might just as well, ere he proceeded to it, inquire who the owners of this cottage were.

Her answer filled him with astonishment, being led to imagine, from what he had heard at the castle, that Mrs. Brady was gone in a very different direction. Something was wrong, it instantly struck him, and having the most important reasons for ascertaining, he repaired, with the old woman, to her cabin, where promising her a liberal recompence for concealing him for a few hours, he succeeded in obtaining from her all the information he wished (unfortunately for the inmates of the cottage, or at least for poor Rose, she and the girl engaged by Mrs. Brady for an attendant being quite intimate)—information of such consequence, from the reward he was aware he should receive for it, as would have made him willingly undergo infinitely more than he had already to obtain it.

The old woman declaring her readiness to take her book oath that she had neither seen nor heard him, on the lads coming back to seek him, they made up their minds that he was fairly off, and after a little consultation, agreed, since matters had turned out so, to say nothing about him at the cottage, their minds, prior to the accident, beginning to misgive them, that after all Mrs. Brady had said to them

about secrecy, she would not be pleased by
what they had done in bringing him.

How Mrs. Brady, after this disappointment, managed, it matters not to say;
suffice it, Rose gave birth to a lovely infant, but which hardly opened its innocent eyes to the light, ere it closed them
for ever—a circumstance that, though considered fortunate by the hapless mother,
yet excited such feelings in her breast, as
considerably retarded her recovery. But
at length she was again able to leave her
chamber; but so pale, so attenuated, from
illness and affliction, as to have more the
appearance of a shadowy than a corporeal
body. She now never stirred out, except
to visit the ruins, and there it was she
now passed almost the whole of her time:
it was there she often first beheld the kindling light of day—there she sheltered
herself from the sultry heat of noon—
there she often saw the evening yielding
the world to night. It was at twilight,
indeed, she particularly loved to be there,
but more especially when there was a

moon, to shed her pale lustre over the surrounding scenery ; it was then she liked
to find herself within the dreary pile, from
the recollections at such an hour it recalled—recollections which deluged her in
tears, as she indulged them, seated on a
fragment of the building, or some marble
covering of the dead—perhaps the grave-
stone of some holy father; now sainted in
the calendar; or some fair sister, born " to
waste her sweetness in the cloistered cell,"
but who, spotless of crime, wedded to her
God, had passed away in the blessed hope
of everlasting happiness.

The evening sun was on the fields, the
newly tedded hay scented the air, and all
was delicious sweetness and serene beauty,
when Mrs. Brady joined Rose one evening in the ruins. She found her, as usual,
absorbed in sorrow ; but without appearing to notice this, she seated herself by
her, and entering into conversation about
the stories and traditions connected with
the building, gradually succeeded in engaging her attention, Rose being just in

that state of mind when the excitement occasioned by the marvellous is particularly agreeable to the disturbed imagination.

" If a body was to believe all they hear," said Mrs. Brady, " many a screech and a sigh was heard here that no one could account for; and indeed I myself know people that have seen sights here, that they could never think of after without shaking in their skins; but of all the curious stories of the place, that is the most curious of a young woman that was buried here—did I never tell it you?"

" No," replied Rose; " I don't recollect any thing of the kind."

" Well, first I'll shew you her grave," resumed Mrs. Brady. " It was the fashion, many a long day ago, to come to visit it; but, *och hone!* I don't know how it is, this place, like all about it, may be well said to be gone to decay;" and as she spoke, she drew her companion out from amidst the ruins into the open space about them, marked by many a grass-grown grave and mouldering tombstone. Wading through a complete bed of nettles, they came to a grave, in a remote corner, almost lost amidst the weeds that overrun it, and contiguous to a fragment of the wall that had once enclosed the place, and in which were still to be discerned the piers of a gate that had opened to a a small village now lying in ruins. The rebellion of 1798 had brought destruction to the place, the insurgents having intrenched themselves here for some time, so that all that now remained of a once neat village,

" Where health and plenty cheer'd the lab'ring swain,"

were the gable ends of a few houses, some roofless cabins, and shattered barns, but amidst which some wretched beings still found shelter, betrayed to the astonished stranger by filthy dunghills, stagnant pools of water, a sudden burst of smoke, the grunting of a pig, or cries of squalid children.

" In this grave," said Mrs. Brady, " lies

Kate Roonan, reckoned in her day one of
the prettiest girls in this village. Her father was a comfortable farmer, with but
her and a son to provide for. Kate was
always a good child, dutiful and affectionate; but the son was always a trouble to his
father, idle and headstrong; and finding he
could make nothing of him, he at last sent
him to sea; and when he died, two or
three years after, took care to shew what
he thought of the difference of his daughter's behaviour, by leaving her more than
the half of what he had, together with the
house they lived in, in the village, that
old shattered one just opposite to us, in
the gable end of which you may still see
a window remaining. Well, all this added to her beauty, brought Kate not a few
admirers. Out of so many, it would have
been strange if she hadn't found one to
please her; and, about a few months after
her father's death, every thing was settled
for her marriage with a young man belonging to the place. Just about this
time her brother returned from sea, and

though he had never been a very kind one
to Kate, yet she was quite delighted to see
him, thought she could never make too
much of him, and added many things to
what he was entitled to by his father's will.

" Well, the day for her wedding was
fixed, and it was expected there would be
quite a gathering at it, when, lo and behold, within a morning or two of it, Kate
was found lying dead in her bed ! You
may well suppose the consternation this
occasioned, and the strange talk it at first
gave rise to ; but, after a close examination of the body, no marks of violence
could be discovered on it, and it was at
length supposed she had died by the visitation of God ; and, after being waked the
usual time, she was buried here without
more ado. Her brother, of course, came in
for all she had been left ; but after living a
few months here, after her death, he suddenly took it in his head to set his place,
and go and settle in another part of the
country. The house was accordingly shut
up, and the key given to a neighbour, to

shew it to any one that might like to take
it.

"Just about this time there was a mill
built here—you may see the remains of it
on the hill yonder. The chief person employed about it was a stranger in these
parts, a man by the name of Dickson; he
took a cabin at the further end of the village, and was thus obliged, in his way back-
wards and forwards from it and the mill,
to pass the gate that was then standing
here, and indeed, till the year 1798, when
it was destroyed, together with all that remained of the old ivyed wall, by the army
in their attack on the rebels, who had taken possession of this, as well as every
other place in the neighbourhood. His
hours were very irregular through his
business; sometimes it was dark night before he returned home; and at last he began to be surprised by seeing a woman,
regularly as he passed this at night, come
out at the gate, and keeping at the other side
of the way, walk on with him to his cabin,

where she always disappeared, he didn't
know how.

" Once or twice he thought of mentioning the odd circumstance to his neighbours,
but then if it was any trick they were
playing him, on account of his being a
stranger, why what good would this do
him? and so he made up his mind to trying to satisfy himself about it, entirely
through his own means; and accordingly,
one night that, as usual, he saw the woman coming out at the gate, as he was
passing, instead of walking on straight, as
he was used to do before, he crossed over
to her, with the intention of speaking to
her; but without allowing this, she directly turned back to the gate. He followed,
nor lost sight of her till they reached this
identical spot, when, suddenly turning
round upon him, she gave him a sorrowful look, and then seemed to sink into the
earth before him. Well, after this, to be
sure, he could no more doubt what he had
seen; and it was natural enough he should
tremble a little; but he had a stout heart

and a good conscience, and so presently
getting the better of his fright, he stuck a
bit of a stick he had in his hand in the
grave, convinced that something wrong
had happened, which, some way or other,
he was chosen by Providence to bring to
light.

"The next morning, at cock crow, as
he was going to the mill, he espied an old
man digging a grave here, just close to
the one he wanted to know about; so he
stepped in, and after a little chat, he asked
whose grave that was, meaning poor
Kate's, making the fine garlands of cut
paper, with which it was hung, the excuse for asking.

"The old man suspending his work, re-
counted to him her sad story. Dickson
was all attention, and when the story was
finished—' So,' said he, ' the house in which
she died is to be let—well, I should like to
look at that house, for I'm thinking I sha'n't
be long without taking a wife, and then,
you know, one would be wanting a larger
place than the one I have now.'—' Very

well, neighbour,' said the old man; ' whenever you like it, you can see it, for I have
the key;' and so it was settled, that by the
first opportunity Dickson should view it.

" Well, this wasn't long wanting, for
he was all curiosity, as you may well conceive, in consequence of what had happened. He got the key, and went to
look at it by himself, the old man being
busy when he called. The house was
part of an old-fashioned one, that had
belonged to a great family in the place,
and was a queer straggling kind of building, built all in ins and outs—nothing of
which was lost upon Dickson, who was a
shrewd fellow, and from being a good
scholar, knew a good deal about the nature of these kind of buildings. He had
had her chamber particularly pointed out
to him, and there he went searching about,
to try if he couldn't discover some secret
means of gaining entrance to it—but no
such thing; and he was just on the point
of leaving it, when a hook in the wall
caught his coat, and in the jerk he gave.

to pull it away, he dragged down a panel,
and what should he behold behind it,
but a narrow stair within the walls, leading down to an old building filled up with
rubbish. Well, upon this discovery, he
was convinced there had been foul play
here; so, deciding how he would act, he
returned the key, and told the old man
he thought he would go off to Roonan,
and try if he could not get a better bargain of the place than he had the power
of giving him; so off he was, as good as
his word; and when Roonan heard his errand, he made him kindly welcome, and
asked him to stop the night with him;
and in compliment to the stranger, two
or three neighbours were invited.

"In the midst of their chat, after
supper, said Dickson, addressing himself to Roonan—' Every man, to be
sure, is the best judge of his own affairs,
but I can't help wondering that you should
prefer the place you are now living in to
the one you are about letting, since, to my

mind, one is not to be compared with the
other;' and that was very true indeed, the
house Roonan then resided in being a very
poor one, on the edge of a dreary bog.—
'That's no lie,' replied Roonan; 'but as
you've said, neighbour, every one has their
own reasons for what they do.'—'To be sure
they have,' said Dickson; 'and, between
ourselves, I am in two minds about taking
this place of yours, for I have met with
something that troubles me in the village.'
—'Have you?' cried the other; 'why
then, if it wouldn't be making too free,
may I be after asking what that is?'—
'And welcome,' was the reply; 'indeed
it will be an ease to my mind unburthen-
ing it;' and so he told him all about the
figure he had seen coming out of the
churchyard, and vanishing in it, keeping
his eye upon him all the time he was
speaking; and sure enough, he saw
him turn all manner of colours as he
went on, and his hair, at last, as it were,
bristled up, and the perspiration trickled
down his face in large drops—'And more

than this,' continued he—but this was all
an invention of his own—' the same woman, that vanished from me in the churchyard, appeared to me in a dream, and told
me, that, as she was lying asleep in her
chamber, dreaming of no harm, either to
herself or any one else, a person got into
it by a secret door!'—But here the fall of
Roonan, with a deep groan, from his
chair, put a stop to any thing further; and
when he was brought to himself, which
was not without great difficulty, he desired every one to leave him but the stranger; and as soon as they were alone, he
fell on his knees before him, and told him
he saw what he was really come about—
not to bargain about the house, as he had
pretended, but to prove to him that the
watchful eye of God is over all; and, without further delay, confessed the murder
of his sister, partly through avarice, partly
revenge, at her being left more than he
was by their father. Administering an
opiate to her, on the night he had deter-

mined on the perpetration of the atrocious
deed, he availed himself of the secret entrance to her chamber, unknown to all
but himself in the place, and by means
of melted lead, poured in at her ear, destroyed her; trusting, by the method he
had had recourse to for her destruction,
and the precautions he had taken in exe-
cuting the foul deed, no suspicion would
be entertained of the truth. 'But see,'
he added, 'how vain is the hope of the
sinner! the guilt which he flatters himself hid for ever, God will himself, if man
does not of his own accord discover it, contrive means to bring to light.   But what
punishment can I meet with from man,
for my crime, equal to that which my
own secret consciousness of it has inflicted
on me?   From the moment I murdered
my sister, peace has been a stranger to
my heart; and had I had seas of molten
gold, and mines of diamonds, I would
have given them all up to have recalled
her to life.   From that moment she has
never ceased to haunt me—go where I

would, do what I might, there she was still regarding me; but not with a sweet, kind smile, as in her days of life, but with a threatening aspect. It was on this account I left the village; but I could not leave my guilty conscience behind me. The first thing that met my eyes here was the spirit of my sister — here, on the dreary bog, has she glided before me in her windingsheet—here, at the cheerful hearth, has she stood frowning on me— here she woke me at the dead hour of midnight, to make me feel that there is no rest for the murderer!'

" In short," continued Mrs. Brady, "not to make a long story of a short one, he was committed, on his own confession, to prison, tried, found guilty, and sentenced to meet with the punishment due to his crime; and noise enough, as you may believe, the affair, attended with so many extraordinary circumstances, made in the country. Often and often have I heard all the particulars of it from old Dickson himself, for he was old at the time that I

was quite a child, and heard them from
him, like all children, I believe, being
fond of the marvellous, and therefore never
tired of questioning him on the subject,
though I never listened to the story that
my teeth did not chatter and my nails
turn blue, and that I did not lie all the
night smothering up in the bed-clothes,
longing for the first glimpse of day, lest poor
Kate's grimly ghost should meet my eyes,
frowning on me as she had done on her
guilty brother.—But this is not all I could
tell you," said Mrs. Brady, either in a particularly gossiping humour, or else induced to go on, by conceiving she was amusing her companion, " of this place. It
is said that immense riches were hid here
in the troubles, but more especially in
those of Cromwell's time, and some have
from time to time been discovered here,
by means of dreams and apparitions. I
myself knew a man, who, from being so
poor that he was obliged to sleep under
hedges and ditches, get all of a sudden so
rich—no one could tell how, except by get-

ting a pot of money here, as every body believed to be the case—as to be able to take one of the best farms in the neighbourhood; and two lads who, in consequence, came to dig here, but who were so frightened by a violent hurricane that came on just as they came in sight, as they said, or a trap-door, that they ran off; and since that, I believe, no one has ever searched here for money."

" I am not by any means one of those," said Rose, " who deride every thing that is marvellous; on the contrary, from the extraordinary discoveries we have heard of, brought about through the agency, as we have had reason to believe, of supernatural means, I conceive it would be stupidity to do so. What we are speaking of, reminds me of a curious article I met with in an old magazine; it is an account written by the dean of Christ Church, in England, in the year 1726, of a gentleman of the name of Reynolds, when he was at school at Eton, who dreamed that his father was deceased, and

that he was walking in the meadows very
melancholy, when a strange woman came
up to him, who told him she was his mother, who, it seems, had died soon after
he was born; she said to him—'Yes, your
father is dead, and your mother-in-law has
had too much influence over him; he has
left all the property to the younger sons;
but there is an estate he had no right to
leave away from you, the writings are in
(mentioning some acquaintance of the family's) hands, and you may recover it.'
Reynolds, hearing no news from home of
this description, soon forgot his dream.
About a year after he went down to his
friends, and found his father very well;
but, at the time of Reynolds's dream, he
had been extremely ill, and recovered beyond expectation. The first to whom he
related his dream, when he described to
him the person of the woman who appeared to him, said, they who had been well
acquainted with his mother's person could
not have described her more correctly.
About a year after his father fell ill again,

died, and left all to his younger children. Upon this Reynolds's dream came into his mind; he went to the gentleman named to him by his mother in his dream, and found that it was exactly as he had been told; namely, that this gentleman had the papers of the estate which had been unjustly left from him, and by which he was enabled to recover it."

"Wonderful, to be sure!" said Mrs. Brady; and as one story of the kind generally brings on another, they continued conversing in this manner till the increasing darkness warned them to return to the cottage.

CHAPTER VII.

"Farewell awhile, I will not leave you long,
For in your shades I deem some spirit dwells,
That from the chiding stream, or groaning oak,
Still hears and answers to Matilda's moan."

Mrs. Brady finding that she could not detach Rose from her lonely haunt, endeavoured to let her be there as little as possible by herself; but in spite of all her anxiety to this effect, she was sometimes prevented following, or at least joining her there, as quickly as she could have wished, having many matters to attend to at home, and being frequently called away to a distance from it, by the claims of the miserable cottiers in the neighbourhood on her charity. It was upon one of these latter occasions, that, detained out till a late hour, by the dying infant of a poor woman who had besought her to

come to her, that Rose, uninterrupted in
her melancholy ruminations, quite forgot
herself in the ruin.   There was a time,
that to have even thought of remaining
till such an hour in such a place, by herself, would have scared her imagination;
but what would then have been repelling,
was now inviting or unheeded—grief, carried to an excess, rendering us incapable
of those sensations natural to us at other
times: thus she who would once have
shrunk from darkness and solitude united,
no longer had a fear of visiting the habitation of the dead at unseasonable hours.

  Having roved about the dreary aisles till
she was weary, she had seated herself on
an old tomb, and with her eyes steadfastly
fastened on the recumbent effigy on it,
though without being conscious of what
they were rivetted on, was giving way to
the most sorrowful reflections, when she was
roused from her reverie by a deep-drawn
sigh; she instinctively looked up—but
what words can paint her feelings, when,
by the moonlight gleam, she beheld, al-

most close to her, the selfsame figure that
had appeared to her in the chapel of St.
Doulagh's, on the night—the fatal night,
at least to her, that Eugene had prevailed
on her to exchange vows with him! The
apathy in which, but the minute before,
she had been wrapt, as to external objects,
instantly vanished; she started up, and
with a faint scream, receded: the spectre,
for such it had every semblance of being,
advanced. Rose, at this, uttered a still
shriller cry, and dropped lifeless on the
pavement.

On recovering, she found herself supported in the arms of Mrs. Brady.—" So,
I suppose," said her alarmed friend, as
soon as she saw she was in a condition to
attend to her, " you have seen something
at last in this dismal old place to frighten
you ?"

" Seen !" repeated Rose somewhat wildly, and casting her eyes shudderingly
around her; " and did you yourself see
nothing to frighten you when you entered ?"

"Yes, enough, I am sure; for I saw you stretched on the ground, to all appearance a corpse."

"It had vanished then!" resumed Rose; "or else to me alone are its visitations."

"What vanished? What do you mean, my dear child?" exclaimed Mrs. Brady, in absolute agony, conceiving Rose was becoming delirious.

"Nothing," replied Rose, trying to check herself, but unable—"nothing, but that, as I am a living being, I saw an apparition here to-night!"

"Pooh, pooh! this is nonsense—folly!" cried Mrs. Brady—"entirely the effect of the fancies you have been giving way to for some time past. I thought, by humouring you a little in them, I might be doing you a service; but I now find I was mistaken, and I must positively therefore prevent your coming here as usual."

"If you hear all I have to tell you, you won't deride what I have now mentioned to you. Amongst the circumstances I had to disclose to you, there was one I concealed, lest you should think I was raving. On the night that Eugene prevailed on me to kneel before the altar in the chapel of St. Doulagh's, I saw an apparition, and the very same I have seen this evening here."

"No, no; don't suppose I will be induced to believe any such thing," said Mrs. Brady; "don't I know what the effects of people going about pining and moping by themselves are?"

"Yes; but I was neither pining nor moping at the time I saw this figure at St. Doulagh's."

"No; but then you had done what was very wrong; or, at least," said Mrs. Brady, recollecting herself, "what, by your own account, you thought so; and when that is the case, the imagination is easily disturbed."

"But don't you yourself believe in supernatural appearances at times?"

"I won't answer another question," said Mrs. Brady, "till we leave this. Here you are trembling like an aspen leaf, and as cold as death. These goings on will never do; I blame myself very much for having allowed them so long; but the case must now be altered."

She did indeed believe, that, owing to the melancholy to which she had given herself up, the imagination of Rose was beginning to be affected; and from the turn she seemed inclined to take, she grieved that she had told her the stories she had done; but it was through a good motive—partly through a hope that she might by them render her perhaps loth to be as much as usual at the abbey, and partly a wish to divert her thoughts. She did all she could to argue her out of the belief she saw with such alarm she had conceived; and Rose, at length, weary of contesting the point with her, seemed to give it up; but notwithstanding this, Mrs. Brady would have been happy for a time to have sent her from so lonely a spot as the cottage, and would accordingly have proposed to return to St. Doulagh's, but that she knew poor Grace was still too much engrossed there by her afflicted aunt and parents, to be able to watch over her

in the manner she still thought requisite;
and all she could accordingly decide on
was, to attend to her more closely than
ever herself, and try to find amusement
for her.

When Rose came to reflect on what
had occurred, how did she lament her
want of nerve on the recent occasion!
Her judgment was certainly in a degree
unsettled, by the mental struggles she had
been long enduring; and firmly persuaded, by what she had seen at the ruins, of
the reality of what she fancied she had
seen at St. Doulagh's, how did she regret
that she had not had strength of mind
sufficient to enable her to bear the awful
sight without shrinking! It had then
evidently come on a warning errand, and
had probably appeared again for a similar
purpose—to caution her of some new danger; or perhaps point out to her some
long-buried treasure, that, brought to light,
would effect the liberation of her Eugene,
and restore both to happiness. Cold incredulity, or hard-hearted scepticism, might

laugh at the idea; but what extraordinary things had we heard, had we read of, discovered by Providence through the medium of dreams, or agency of spirits? have not, in both instances, crimes of the greatest magnitude been detected, and their perpetrators brought to punishment? have not treasures been pointed out through the means of the one and the other?—" Does not what I have lately been listening to from Mrs. Brady," she continued, arguing the point with herself, " go to prove the faith that should be placed in such things? was not this very place the scene of a supernatural visitation? did she not hear, and see, and speak, with the person who, by means of the kind, was made the especial instrument of Providence for, bringing guilt to light? and have not riches been discovered here in a similar way? why then should I strive to discredit the evidence of my senses? or in allowing their testimony to be correct, permit myself to suppose that this apparition that has twice appeared to me has done so, or rather been allowed to do so, from any other than a benevolent purpose? I am miserable, afflicted, beyond measure; I see the man I consider as my husband imprisoned, without a hope of obtaining his liberation—I behold the friends who have supplied to me the place of every natural connexion involved in wretchedness I cannot remedy, and my heart is consequently abandoned to despair. God is never so near us as when we conceive ourselves utterly forsaken by man. He that regardeth the prayer of the poor destitute, may he not, in his infinite mercy, at length have taken compassion on my sorrows, and permitted a visitation that may be the means of ending them? yes, I do—I will believe so; and under this persuasion, will find courage to visit the ruin again."

But her resolve to do this she was not able to carry into effect so soon as she wished, so closely was she now watched by Mrs. Brady. Whenever she saw her preparing to go out, she was sure to be at her elbow, and instead of allowing her to bend her steps towards the abbey, always turned them in a different direction. But at length a message was received by Mrs. Brady one evening, requiring her presence in the cabin of a poor woman, at some distance from the Vale, one of whose children had suddenly been taken ill.

Mrs. Brady could not avoid attending to the urgent request she had received, and accordingly the car was ordered. Before setting out, however, she took Judy aside, to lay an injunction upon her not to stir out during her absence, except Rose went from home, when she was to follow, and keep close to her, let her say what she would to the contrary.

Judy promised, nay swore upon her conscience, that she might depend on her; but no sooner had she seen her mistress fairly out of sight, than whipping up to Rose's chamber, she abruptly asked her—
" Was she going out ?"

" Why do you ask ?" demanded Rose,

raising her head from a book on which she had been trying to fix her attention.

" Why, Miss, I'll tell you — because the mistress has charged me not to put a foot outside the door, if you went out; but if you were going to stay at home, I'd just be after running over to ould Nell Flannagan's wake, because I know I'd be back again before her; and sorrow such a wake, they say, there has not been hereabouts these twenty years! for Nell had the *stocking*, and her ould man says that's himself will do the *ginteel* thing by her, seeing she'll never want any thing more from him."

" Well, you may go," said Rose.

" Yes, Miss; but it's yourself that won't be after telling on me to the mistress? for I gave her as good as my *affydavy* that I wouldn't put hand or foot out of doors till she came back; so it's *kilt* myself would be by her, if she found I broke my word wid her."

Rose nodded, and away scampered Judy, only stopping till she put on her best cap, to be off to the wake.

As she had watched her mistress out of sight, so Rose watched her, and then very deliberately walked out herself. It would be superfluous to say her steps were directed to the ruin; yet with all her impatience to find herself again within it, her steps began to falter as she drew near it, and a cold dew to gather on her brow.— "But this is no positive failure of courage," she said; " nothing but the common infirmity of human nature: and, after all, what is this (as an able writer has demanded) that so alarms and terrifies the human mind, at a visit from those who are merely gone a journey before us, which sooner or later we are all destined by nature to take? Is it not the will of God that our mortal bodies be laid aside, when the soul is to enter into real life? we may fairly consider ourselves but preparing, in this state, for living for ever; we are not completely born until we are dead; why then should we fear a visit from a mem-

ber of that happy society, which it is our
earnest wish, and ought to be the whole exertion of our mortal lives to endeavour to
merit a place amongst ? Are we not spirits?
Bodies are lent us, while they can afford us
pleasure—while they can assist us in acquiring knowledge, or doing good to our
fellow-creatures; when they become unfit
for those purposes, we get rid of them
through death. Why then apprehend
such terror, when visited by a former
friend and companion ? We may rest assured, if Providence permits our return
here, it is not to injure the living, or for
any idle purpose, but for some wise, some
good end;" and reassured by this argument, she advanced within the building :
but all was dread silence here, and undisturbed, " nor eye, nor listening ear," an
object found, but what was familiar to
them.

She went on towards the innermost recesses of the place, but still pausing almost at every step, to look around her, or
listen, but without seeing any thing but

the shadows of the pillars, or hearing any sound, save that of the rustling of the long streaming grass that begirt the walls, in the night breeze, as it swayed it to and fro.

At length, just as she was beginning to give up the expectation that had again allured her to the spot, she suddenly saw the spectral figure before her, as if risen from one of the tombs. For an instant she drew back; then seeing the figure receding, but with a gesture to follow, she rushed forward—" It invites me to follow—to speak to it!" she cried; but the excitement of her feelings was too much for her—her head grew giddy, and with a faint exclamation, she fainted away.

Mrs. Brady tarried not a minute longer than she was absolutely obliged—she felt a restlessness, an inquietude of spirit, that made her think she should never get back again. The instant she entered the house, her first inquiry was after Rose.

" Oh, she's up in her room, snug

enough!" replied Judy, making herself
sure of this being the case, for she had
not had time to ascertain, having only got
in a minute before her mistress; "sorrow
foot either of us stirred out since you went
away!"

"Well, you sha'n't be the worse for keeping your word with me," said Mrs. Brady,
taking the candle from her to go to Rose's
room—but the bird was flown; she searched all the other chambers without finding
her, and in utter consternation returned to
the kitchen.—"Why what's this you have
been telling me," she said, "of no one
having gone out while I was away? I
can't find Rose high or low."

"Ah then, mistress honey, how can
that be," cried Judy, with a well-counterfeited look of surprise, "when myself, as I sat spinning here in the kitchen,
must have seen her, if she went out?"

"You young jade!" exclaimed Mrs.
Brady, now noticing her cap, which in
her flusteration, as she called it, at finding her so close on her heels, Judy had

forgot to take off, " I see how it is—you have been to the wake ; and while you were away, my child took the opportunity of going by herself to the abbey! Go call me Pat directly!" the boy who drove the car, and was now putting it up.

A lantern was lit, for it was now quite dark, and giving it to Pat, the greatly-alarmed Mrs. Brady set off with him for the ruin. But no sooner did Pat understand whither they were going, than he would have given all he expected to earn for years to come, to have been fairly off, in such terror at this hour did he hold that dreary place—in so much, indeed, that with all his dread of captain Rock, he would infinitely have preferred encountering, at any time, this self-appointed ranger of the Irish hills and mountains, with even all his merry men at his back to boot, than have been obliged to visit the abbey in the dark. However, knowing he could not avoid obedience to his mistress, he tried to summon all his courage to his aid; but in spite of his efforts, he trembled at every blast of wind that shook the bushes surrounding the place, expecting the next instant to see the ghost stalking forward that had occasioned the noise; and when, holding up the lantern, at the west entrance, he cast his eyes fearfully forward, and saw the long double row of receding pillars, appearing like so many sheeted spectres to him, with their flowing drapery, or loose tresses, if it might be so styled, of ivy, wafted about by the night breeze, he stopped in an agony of fear.

"Why don't you come on?" demanded his mistress impatiently.

"By my blessed namesake, St. Patrick, mistress, but I can't!" was the reply; "but the Holy Mother have mercy on my sinful soul! if there was but one ghost, or two, but if I don't think all the ghosts that the churchyard contains are now before us!"

"Ghosts, you silly fellow! where?"

"Oh, mistress *jewel!* there, just right *far'nent* you! just—the Lord save us, and defend us!—like a parcel of White Boys coming down the hills!"

"Come, come, this is no time for playing tricks, Pat!" cried his agitated mistress, seizing him by the arm, and dragging him forward. "I wish," laying her hand upon one of the pillars, "we may meet with nothing else here to frighten us than these." She then called aloud upon the name of Rose; but no Rose replied to the call: "My child! my darling!" echoed through the building, but to no effect.

At length, having traversed every part of it, examined into every nook and corner, and through all the gloomy cloisters, Mrs. Brady began to tremble with apprehension of her having turned her steps in a still more dangerous direction that evening. In their recent walks, she recollected her having, more than once, stopped to gaze upon some dangerous spots among the mountains; and in particular, her making an observation on one of a particularly appalling nature, that occasioned her to hurry her away from it, with a determination never to let her approach it again, if possible.

As this alarming circumstance recurred to her recollection, so at the same moment did the terrific scene at the Lover's Leap at St. Doulagh's; and rushing from the ruin, in absolute distraction, she called to Pat to follow with all quickness to the *Rent*, a frightful fissure in one of the adjacent cliffs, reported to have been caused by an earthquake, and at the bottom of which was a deep abyss of water, apparently of the colour of ink, from the almost immeasurable height from which it was viewed, and the ivy and fern that crept about the bleak rocks that formed the reservoir.

She was within a few yards of the horrid spot, when Pat, who was unassailed by her sickening apprehensions, and whose courage had gradually revived as he receded from the abbey, suddenly springing before her, exclaimed, with a shout—" I have her, mistress! here she is !" stooping

as he spoke; but, to his utter disappointment, instead of a human form, merely
grasping a long cloak, that lay stretched
upon the cliff.

Mrs. Brady instantly knew the cloak to
be Rose's.—" She has been here then !"
with a shriek, she exclaimed; and in the
height of her distraction was about making
an attempt to scale the precipice, for the
purpose of looking down the chasm, forgetting, from the state of mind she was in,
both the danger and uselessness of such
an attempt, at such an hour, when she was
prevented by Pat.—" For the Lord's
sake, have mercy upon yourself, mistress !" he cried, holding her firmly by the
arm. " What good would it do Miss
Rose for you to be getting yourself dashed to pieces, as to be sure you must, if
you attempted scrambling up the cliff at
such a time as this ?".

His remonstrances, however, were lost
upon her, and desperation lending her
strength, he would not much longer probably have been able to prevent her rash

design, had not a neighbour, passing that
way, come to his assistance, and enabled
him to convey her home, where she was
kept by force till morning; when, at its first
glimpse, they all hasted away to the Rent.

Midway the cliff the bonnet of poor
Rose was found, and immediately within
the fissure a fragment of her gown, as if
caught and torn away by the sharp pointed rocks, at the moment of her throwing
herself down.

Of the horrible catastrophe that had
evidently taken place, no doubt, after
this, could be entertained. Mrs. Brady
was conveyed back to the cottage, in
strong convulsions, and for a fortnight
after, her life was despaired of: she then
slowly recovered, if recovered it could be
called, to feel that she must ever after bear
a wounded spirit about her.—" Oh, how I
grieved," she cried, from time to time,
wringing her hands, " when I thought my
child was dying here! how I prayed to
Heaven to spare her! but had it been the
divine will then to take her, amidst all my

grief, I should have had the comfort of seeing her laid quietly in holy earth! not as now, as I do continually before me, wounded, bleeding, dashed to atoms, through her own means!"

The cottage had now become hateful to her, and accordingly, the moment she was able to travel, she shut it up, and set off for St. Doulagh's, convinced, if capable of any consolation, it would be in the sympathy she would there meet in her affliction.

CHAPTER VIII.

" Society, friendship, and love,
   Divinely bestow'd upon man,
Oh, had I the wings of a dove,
   How soon would I taste you again !

" My sorrows I then might assuage,
   In the ways of religion and truth,
Might learn from the wisdom of age,
   And be cheer'd by the sallies of youth."

AN ancient author compares life to a voyage, in the progress of which we are continually changing our scenes; we first leave childhood behind us—then youth— then the years of ripened manhood—then the better or more pleasing part of old age. The passage recurred to the recollection of Eugene one day, and led to a train of the most melancholy reflections—what change, what fluctuation should he experience ! youth, manhood, age—each would be

equally unenjoyed by him! equally un-
marked by opportunities of evincing that
change of feeling, that alteration of sentiment, which their advance upon one another naturally produces. The energies of
youth as yet unimpaired, a life of even
stormy indifference would have been preferable to the idea of the dull, the cheerless, the monotonous one to which he
seemed doomed; his spirits, sinking before, now began utterly to fail him; and a
long interval of silence from St. Doulagh's,
by alarming him about its beloved inmates, did not tend to raise them.

In vain he tried to shake off the melancholy that oppressed him; never had he
felt so sick, so sad at heart, as on the
evening of this day; and it seemed a curious thing, that this was the very evening, as he afterwards ascertained, on which
the fatal catastrophe of poor Rose took
place. In vain he tried to divert his
thoughts by reading; books, for the first
time, were but formal dulness to him. At

length, the following exquisitely beautiful and sublime lines fixed his attention, but only to excite a still intenser feeling of melancholy in his soul :—

THE TREASURES OF THE DEEP.

What hid'st thou in thy treasure, waves and cells ?
Thou hollow-sounding and mysterious main !
Pale glistening pearls, and rainbow-colour'd shells,
    Bright things which gleam unreck'd of and in vain.
        Keep, keep thy riches, melancholy sea !
            We ask not such from thee.

Yet more—the depths have more ! What wealth untold,
    Far down, and shining, through their stillness lies !
Thou hast the starry gems, the burning gold,
    Won from ten thousand royal argosies.
        Sweep o'er thy spoils, thou wild and wrathful main!
            Earth claims not these again.

Yet more—the depths have more ! Thy waves have roll'd
    Above the cities of a world gone by !
Sand hath fill'd up the palaces of old,
    Sea-weed the halls of revelry !
        Dash o'er them, ocean, in thy scornful play !
            Man yields them to decay.

Yet, more!—the billows and the depths have more!
　High hearts and brave are gather'd to thy breast!
They hear not now the booming waters roar,
　The battle-thunders will not break their rest.
　　Keep thy red gold and gems, thou stormy grave—
　　　Give back the true and brave!

Give back the lost and lovely! those for whom
　The place was kept at board and hearth so long;
The prayer went up through midnight's breathless gloom,
　And the vain yearning woke midst festal song!
　　Hold fast thy buried isles, thy towers o'erthrown—
　　　But all is not thy own!

To thee the love of woman hath gone down,
　Dark flow thy tides o'er manhood's noble head,
O'er youth's bright locks, and beauty's flowery crown;
　Yet must thou hear a voice—" Restore the dead !"
　　Earth shall reclaim her precious things from thee—
　　　" Restore the dead, thou sea !"

A kind of holy horror thrilled through
his frame, if the expression may be allowed, at the conclusion of the last line, and
closing the volume that contained the
poem, he retired to bed. Here he had not
been long, when he fancied he heard the
chamber door open, and saw a woman enter; she walked round the bed, and com-

ing to the opposite side, drew back the curtains, and looked in at him; and at that instant he discovered that it was Rose he beheld; but a different Rose indeed from her he had left behind him—pale, sorrowful, and ghastly. He started up in his bed, with a sensation of mingled surprise and joy, to enfold her to his breast—but she eluded his grasp; and on his repeating the attempt, retreated in seeming displeasure. He followed her from the room, out of which she hastily passed, through intricacies of the building he had not before any knowledge of, till he suddenly found himself beyond it, in a wild and dreary scene of rocks and mountains, over which he continued to pursue her, with astonishment at the fearless celerity with which she passed them, till they came to the edge of a horrible chasm, where she vanished, he knew not how, from his view, and stooping down, he found, on the spot where she had disappeared, a pair of funeral gloves.

The impression made upon his mind by

this dream was so great, that not even the
return of daylight could dissipate it, and
in agony at the idea of something afflicting having happened at St. Doulagh's, he
addressed a letter to Grace, entreating to
hear from her without delay, as he had
been tormented the whole of the preceding night by dreams about them at the
castle.

By return of post he received an answer
from Grace, in which, in a general way,
she said they were all well at St: Doulagh's, and intimated a hope of some one
of his family seeing him ere long.

The period to which he had been nomi-
nally sentenced to confinement was now
drawing to a close, but the exact day on
which it would expire was forgot by him,
through the agitated state of mind he was
now in, as a matter indeed of no consequence to him to remember; so that it
might, on its arrival, have passed by entirely unheeded by him, but for his being
reminded of it by some of his fellow-pri-
soners. He smiled, in bitterness of spirit,

at its announcement, and almost instantly after retreated to his room, to conceal the feelings occasioned by the circumstance.— "It is come then!" he cried, gnashing his teeth, and pacing the room with impatient steps. "but only to mock me—the day which, under other circumstances, I should to have longed for, so have hailed with rapture; but which has now only arrived to add additional bitterness to my feelings, by the exposure it occasions of my being a poor, miserable wretch, destitute of the means of relieving myself from a cruel and unmerited imprisonment!"

Hardly had these words been uttered, when a person belonging to the place entered, to inform him, in due form, that his fine was paid, and every thing arranged for his immediate discharge.

Eugene stared wildly, incredulous of the truth of what he heard.—" Are you serious?" he demanded of the man; " but yet, no one would—could have the barbarity to trifle with the feelings of a person situated as I am!"—But who was the

kind friend who had so unexpectedly opened the prison-gates for him—to whose generosity he was indebted for his despaired-of
liberation? This, however, was information no one could give him; the affair
had been conducted in a way that completely set all inquiries on the subject he
was anxious about at nought. He could
not, however, rest, without endeavouring
to surmise, and at length, after long puzz-
ling himself in vain, it suddenly struck
him that C———, who had continued to
keep up a friendly communication with
him, frequently visiting him in prison,
and from time to time affording him the
means of replenishing his purse, by doing
little matters for him, was the man.
Under this impression, he proceeded
straight from St. George's Fields to his
house; but, to his extreme disappointment, he was out of town, gone on a kind
of desultory tour, so that a letter might
not possibly reach him, nor expected back
for a fortnight.

In consequence of this information, Eu-

gene, notwithstanding his impatience to
find himself again at St. Doulagh's, decided on putting off his immediate departure for Ireland, conceiving himself bound,
both in gratitude and honour, to see his
kind friend ere he left England, that some
arrangement might be made for the at
least gradual discharge of his pecuniary
obligation to him. Having made up his
mind on this, he lost not another moment
in acquainting them at St. Doulagh's with
what had occurred, desiring them, at the
conclusion of his letter, not to be uneasy
if they did not see him exactly at the time
specified, as ·C——— might not perhaps
be punctual to a day in returning.

The next morning, as he was saunter-
ing about St. James's Park, enjoying the
delicious privilege of loitering where he
pleased, he was suddenly accosted by one
of those gay young men with whom he had
occasionally, previously to his committal,
been how and then in the habit of associating with in the coffee-houses about
town. Having warmly congratulated Eu-

gene on his liberation—" You are the very man," he added, " I wanted to see; I was at the King's Bench last evening to look for you, but the bird was flown; and as I know your friend C——— was out of town, curse me if I could tell where to find you!"

" And pray," asked Eugene, with some little degree of surprise, " is there any particular cause for the anxiety you expressed to see me?"

" Yes, faith, a wish to serve you."

" As how, pray?"

" Why, I know you sometimes amuse yourself with your pen, and so, on a very particular friend of mine asking me if I could recommend any one to him qualified to look over and prepare some poems of his for the press, I thought I would speak to you on the subject."

" I am much obliged by your thinking of me," said Eugene; " but my departure from London is now so very near, that if they would take up much time——"

" I am certain they wouldn't take up

more than a week, or ten days at the
farthest; and a hundred pounds will be
your remuneration for your trouble."

"London is a terrible place," cried Eugene, with a smile, "for making one
selfish. Since you say they will not take
up more time, I readily undertake the
task," he added, not a little pleased at the
idea of obtaining a sum that would enable
him to take over some little presents to
St. Doulagh's; "so let me have them immediately."

"Fair and softly, my good sir; you
little know the person to whom they belong, or you would not conceive it possible he would intrust them to such a hairbrain as he considers me; but call on me
in the course of an hour, and you shall
have a letter of introduction to him,
which, as you are so limited for time, I
advise your delivering without delay."

Eugene gave the requisite assurance,
and they parted.

On calling, he found the promised letter ready for him, directed to a gentleman at Hoxton. For this Eugene immediately set off in one of the stages, and was set down at a very large, handsome mansion, enclosed within iron gates. A well-dressed footman answered his knock, and to his demand of his master being at home, answering in the affirmative, ushered him into an elegantly-furnished parlour. Here he had not been many minutes, when an elderly, grave-looking gentleman, with any thing but an air that Eugene would have taken for one of genius about him, made his appearance. Bows being exchanged, he begged to know to what he was indebted for the honour of the present visit.

Eugene replied to this interrogation by respectfully presenting his letter.

The stranger, casting his eye over it—"Oh, ay," he exclaimed, "I see how it is.—Well, sir, and you know the purport of this letter?"

Eugene bowed.

"Right, quite right—I am satisfied."

"I hope, sir," said Eugene, "you will

have reason to consider yourself so. I am aware, of course, that my friend has spoken favourably of me; all I am afraid of is, his having mentioned me in higher terms than I merit. If I fail, however, in answering the expectations he may have raised, it will not, I assure you, be for want of due exertions."

"Oh, I make no doubt. But come, suppose you take a walk in the garden and grounds before dinner; it will cool and refresh you, after your ride in a hot stage-coach."

"Excuse me, sir," said Eugene; "but my time is so limited, as I observed to my friend, that if you could conveniently let me have the papers now, with your instructions——"

"Oh, I see—but it will be time enough after dinner to speak about business; and, in fact, I am particularly engaged just now. In the interim, I advise you again to breathe the fresh air of the garden; it will be cooling, and of course salutary for you;" and without further ceremony he

rung the bell, and ordered the servant to
conduct the gentleman to it.

Eugene, though extremely vexed, every
moment being so precious to him, yet
knew not how to resist what might be
owing to good-nature, and accordingly
suffered himself to be shewn to the
grounds as directed. He found them extensive, and well laid out, and could not
avoid thinking all he saw a great encouragement to genius, if indeed owing to
its exertions; but of this he had very
great doubts, from the appearance and
manner of the stranger, and began, in
consequence, to fear that he had undertaken a task that would prove more disagreeable than he had previously anticipated.

He had not strayed about long, when
he met several ladies and gentlemen, most
of them walking by themselves; and as
he could not imagine they were all one
family, he concluded they were guests invited to dinner, and felt still more disconcerted by the supposition, owing to the
still greater delay he conceived the cir-

cumstance would be occasion to his returning to town.

For some time he appeared to be unnoticed; but at length, a gentleman coming up to him, begged to know, with a profound bow, whether he could favour him with any account of the ascent of a balloon that had very recently taken place—"Of course I knew," he said; "I should see nothing of the process of inflating; but I did flatter myself I should have seen it majestically sailing over our heads here. However, the wind suddenly shifted—nothing so fickle, you know, sir," with a laugh; "as the wind, except a lady's smiles—and bore it, to my extreme disappointment, quite in a contrary direction."

" No, indeed, sir, I cannot," replied Eugene; " I was not so fortunate as to witness the ascent."

" Then, sir, we may condole with each other on the circumstance."

" As to that, sir," said Eugene, laughing; " very little condolence is requisite about a matter that one does not regret; having seen one or two ascents, my curiosity is perfectly satisfied, there being nothing of interest to keep it alive in them."

"Nothing of interest! you astonish me, sir! What, no interest excited by seeing your fellow-beings soaring and penetrating into the regions of boundless space,—those regions to which our longing eyes were once raised, hopeless of ever ascending to them?"

"No, sir; because I conceive no benefit can result to mankind from their possessing the power of doing so; could balloons, indeed, be rendered stationary, or——"

"Sir—sir, this is a conclusion that a scientific mind would never be capable of!" cried the other hastily interrupting him; "should not—must not time be allowed for improvements in every discovery? It is not the moment one is made that we can take in or comprehend all the results that may be the consequence of it, —it is progressively all sciences advance to

perfection :: astronomy was not at once
what it now is; how long were we mistaken with regard to the form of the
globe, and the nature of the planetary
system! and arguing by this, is it not fair
and natural to imagine, that the fourth
element may yet be rendered as subservient, and as much under the control of
man, as the other three have been, by his
attaining the means of steering and navi-
gating a balloon through it? You may
smile, sir; but be pleased only to recollect
how many things have been scoffed at in
one age, that the next have proved possible beyond controversy, by accomplishing
them—be pleased, I say, only to cast
your eyes a hundred years back, and think
how they would have sneered at and de-
rided the idea of our being enabled, in the
ensuing century, to traverse seas of cold
water, merely by means of a little hot,
light our streets with smoke, and travel at the rate of a hundred miles an hour
through the air, seated snugly beneath a
puffed-out bag of silk, filled with the same

light vapour! I say, sir, do this, and you will perhaps not deem what I have now said so ridiculous as you seem to intimate your thinking it."

Eugene could not immediately reply. Had the stranger been a person at all acquainted with him, he would have conceived he was indulging a laugh at his expence, so exactly similar were the arguments he made use of to those he had himself advanced, on an occasion that he could never think of but with shame and confusion.

"Yes, sir, I say," continued the stranger in a triumphant accent, misconstruing the silence of Eugene into something of conviction, "that balloons may not only yet, but immediately, be rendered subservient to the control of man, I myself having devised a project for the purpose: it is nothing more than having so many fathom of line attached to them, which retained below, to draw them gently back on a given signal, will allow of their tra-verging the heavens to an almost immeasurable distance!"

"That is to say, sir," said Eugene, again laughing, "you will allow them to travel the length of their tether?"

The stranger frowned.—"It is as much as to say, sir," he cried, "that I can at once render them serviceable; and once rendered so, what glorious discoveries may not be anticipated from the circumstance! We are told, there is no part of space unoccupied: and if this be the fact, may not the adventurous *æronaut*, in his almost celestial voyage I may call it, possibly discover some glorious creatures, forming the link between us and those more spiritual ones, that walk, as we are assured, the earth unseen?"

"Why, certainly, sir," said Eugene, again giving way to his risibility, "as we know there are such a number of castles elevated in the air, it would not be very unnatural to suppose they had inhabitants."

"Oh, you are pleased to be facetious sir! but a sneer won't deter me from say-

ing what I think; so, not to dwell upon
what to me is, I assure you, of no weight
—as discoveries, we must suppose, are the
suggestions of the Deity, how do we
know but that this of balloons may be for
the benevolent purpose of opening an intercourse between us and the inhabitants
of the other planets, and thus finally
amalgamating us all into one happy har-
monized family of love and concord? I
know, in refutation to this idea, you will
begin to argue philosophically of the attraction of the earth, and of the millions
of years which it is computed a cannon-
ball would take in flying from one star or
planet to another; but, sir, in reply, I
say, with regard to the first observation,
there is nothing too difficult for science to
surmount; and with respect to the latter;
that when the computation was made, it
was at a period when the facility with
which we can now bolt into the air was
unknown. Conceive, sir, if it be possible
for you to do so, what, should such eventually prove to be the case, must be the

transport of the traveller, at finding himself going with as much ease from one
planet to another as ever he did from one
place to another here—what his sensations
must be when, for the first time, he finds
himself within the ring of Saturn, and pe-
netrates the belts of Jupiter! what will
the interest created by the discoveries of
captain Parry, or captain this, or captain
that, be, compared with what his will excite, after his visiting the elegant inhabitants of the moon—the more beauteous,
but perhaps not more interesting ones, of
Venus—the fiery and animated ones of
the more torrid planet Mercury, and so
on! Oh, sir, I could envy the antedilu-
vians their prolongation of existence, from
what I anticipate being yet discovered to
man!"

Eugene knew not what to say or think;
but from his perplexity about this he was
speedily relieved by the sound of the dinner-bell—a sound that was no sooner heard
than every one hasted from the garden,
leaving him to follow or stop as he pleased.
He was slowly doing the former, when a

servant came out to meet him, and by
him he was conducted to the dining-room,
where he found the master of the house
already seated at the head of the table,
with his guests ranged at either side of
him. He merely noticed Eugene by a
nod, and motion to sake a seat.

But if Eugene was surprised by what
passed in the garden, how much more
was he by the conduct observed at dinner! no one speaking, not a mouth being
opened, except for the positive purpose of
receiving food. But this was not all;
some of the guests distinguished themselves in a way that was equally curious:
one lady made a sudden grasp at a pud-
ding, but which she dropped the instant
she caught the eye of her entertainer; and
as another was raising her fork, with a bit
of chicken, to her mouth, a gentleman
dexterously turned it aside, and put it in
his own; and altogether Eugene began to
form strange surmises as to where he was.
They were, however, perhaps, wide of the
mark; but when, by a short conversation

after dinner with the supposed poet, he actually ascertained he was in a private mad-house, as we make no doubt the reader has by this time conjectured, what his feelings were at the circumstance we leave to be imagined—his feelings, at the almost appalling idea of the inveterate enemy, that had previously aimed at his life and character, not being yet satisfied with what he had made him suffer; since to his contrivance he of course at once attributed what had now happened; and working, as he did, in the dark, like an invisible agent of mischief, knew not how he should be able in any way to cope with him.

The enemy we know where to face we in some degree lose our fear of, but something like a freezing sensation of terror accompanies the idea of one whom we in vain endeavour to detect, while still convinced they are hovering about us. But leaving him in this deplorable place, to chew the bitter cud of reflection on the errors, or misconduct, that had either been

the means of raising him up this enemy,
or, at least, of enabling him to plan suc-
cessfully against him, we shall, for the
present, bid him adieu, and pass over,
though without either the aid of a steam-
boat or a balloon, to St. Doulagh's, having
always thought the time for visiting our
friends was indeed when they were in sorrow, as was now the case with the family
at the castle.

CHAPTER IX.

"Do you love me?"
"Troth, no—no more than reason."

ERE Mrs. Brady's arrival at St. Doulagh's, she had fully decided on concealing from all, save Eugene himself, the fatal catastrophe of poor Rose, lest otherwise a suspicion of the circumstance to which she entirely imputed it should be excited, and thus a stain cast upon the memory of her lost darling. To Eugene she considered its disclosure but a merited punishment for his conduct, and accordingly determined, should they ever chance to meet, on pouring into his bosom all the bitterness of her own lacerated one; for though Rose had done all in her power to exculpate him in her eyes, still she would not, could not be induced to believe but that he had been terribly to blame.

From the effect of her melancholy tidings upon the family of St. Doulagh's, in particular upon Grace, she rejoiced in not having heightened the shock these imparted, by a full confession of the truth. Against such a one Grace would hardly indeed have been able to bear up; as it was, she was, for a few days, completely overpowered by the loss of her adopted sister, the sweet friend of her heart, and confidant of every thought; nor even then perhaps would have had power to make a struggle against her absorbing grief—a grief aggravated by her belief of the early death of Rose being imputable, in a great degree, to the undermining effect her hopeless attachment for Eugene had upon her health, but for the consideration she knew due to the feelings of others, and the kind attentions of some friends in the neighbourhood; but while life remained, she felt Rose must be regretted, and that no succeeding friend could ever fill up the void she had left in her heart.

Persuaded of this unfortunate attachment being returned by Eugene, she dreaded, with his ardent feelings, and situated as he then was, without any friend at hand to reason with or console him on the subject, imparting to him what had happened, and hence her evasive reply to the letter occasioned by the agitating dream he had had in prison. She simply stated to him that all were then well at St. Doulagh's, aware that, as he knew not of Rose's departure from it, he would by this statement be quieted about her; for whatever was the alarm he was under, the manner in which he inadvertently expressed himself in one or two parts of his letter, had betrayed its being about her, a circumstance that occasioned a kind of strange inquietude in the mind of Grace, arguing, as it seemed to do, our receiving some secret intimation of the sorrow that is approaching; for, from the date of Eugene's letter, she saw that it was on the very night of poor Rose's death that he had been thus disturbed about her. But

there were some matters that Grace deemed too curious to enter upon; and, as
much as possible, she tried to divert her
thoughts from dwelling on this.

Hardly had she come to the resolve of
not making known, for the present, the
death of poor Rose to Eugene, when the
letter, announcing his liberation, through
the kindness of an unknown friend, arrived. A few weeks before, and what
transport would this announcement have
communicated to her feelings! but now,
how was the joy it imparted alloyed and
imbittered by the conviction of the sorrow
that awaited his return home—a sorrow
of which she had such apprehensions, that
she almost felt it as a kind of respite his
departure from England being a little
longer delayed. But still, notwithstanding her dread of what he had to endure
on his return, there was real, substantial
comfort in the thought of his restoration
to his family, such as had, by degrees, its
effect upon her feelings, lightening and
relieving her heart of the intolerable load

of anguish that had for some time previously oppressed it.

Hardly had the agitation occasioned by Eugene's most unexpected liberation been recovered from, when Grace was given to understand that William Delamere might now be daily expected at St. Doulagh's. More than seven years had now elapsed since his departure from it—seven years! what a period to look forward to, and yet how quickly is it passed! Long before its expiration, Grace would probably have ceased to think about the foolish promise that had passed between them, but for the continuance of their correspondence, and the manner in which he, from time to time, alluded to this. Led, from the way in which he reverted to it, to at length believe he viewed it in a serious light, she at last began to feel as if engaged to him, and make up her mind to their being yet united. The idea excited no kind of emotion, one way or other: she still loved William quite as well as she had ever done, but still it was with that kind of

affection that, while it prevented any repugnance to the thought of being his,
would equally have prevented any unhappiness at the thought of his being married
to another, provided she was certain that
other had as sincere a regard for him as
she herself had.

Thus thinking and feeling, she received
the following letter from him, about a
year previous to the period of which we
are now speaking; the result of which
was, the immediate termination of the
affair between them.

" To Miss O'Neil.

" Geneva, 18—.

" MY DEAR GRACE,

" Should this letter prove neither
a very connected, nor a very long one,
impute the circumstance to the agitation
of spirits under which I write. I have at
length, in the course of successive conver-
sations with my uncle, discovered that he
has all along had a particular alliance in

view for me, on my acceding to which depends the realization of those flattering expectations I was so long permitted to encourage. Of course I could not learn this without some little discomposure; but do not be alarmed—destitution will not be the consequence of refusal; the small patrimony of my father, redeemed on his decease, from the creditors that had seized it, by my uncle, and already restored to me, still affording a competence. And now, my dear girl, as a competence with you is preferable to affluence with any other woman, do not let me hear you say you regret the promise plighted to me; or, in other words, that you have ever considered the affair between us in any other than a serious light: neither permit yourself to think, that any thing I relinquish for your sake can be regarded by me as a sacrifice, since, if I understand the meaning of the term, nothing can be denominated a sacrifice that is not attended with pain to our feelings. Let me hear from you without delay; but when

did I write to you without requiring
this? I am now, however, more anxious,
if possible, than usual, for your attending
to this request, our stay here being quite
uncertain; so that, if you delayed writing
immediately, I am fearful a tedious time
might elapse ere I received your letter.
Remember me, as usual, to all kind friends
at St. Doulagh's, but in particular to those
of the castle; and believe me, your more
warmly than ever devoted

" WILLIAM DELAMERE."

———

Grace had hardly come to the conclusion of this letter, ere her determination
was taken as to the purport of it: the little hesitation she had on the subject was a
convincing proof to her of her attachment
to Delamere not being of a nature to entitle her to the sacrifice he meditated for
her sake, and perhaps she was not altogether sorry to have a fair pretext for extri-
cating herself from an engagement she had
somehow got herself entangled in, with-

out exactly liking the idea of it, there
being minutes in which she could not
help thinking something more than esteem was requisite for the person to
whom one thought of allying themselves
for life.

Had she been inclined to waver in her
decision, the unqualified approbation it
met with from her aunt, to whom, through
the force of habit, she was still accustomed
to look up, would have prevented her.
In his kind tokens of regard for Grace,
William did not forget Miss Agnes Flora
Judith, and who accordingly, from very
much liking his remembrances, always
felt a fidgety kind of impatience for the
perusal of his letters, to see whether any
thing new might shortly be expected.
Impelled by this, she hardly permitted
Grace to finish this letter, ere she demanded it from her.

Grace handed it to her without any
comment; but not without comment did
Miss Agnes Flora Judith peruse it.—
" Good Heavens !" she exclaimed, " I am

really quite agitated! and so, after his
being allowed to draw you into an engagement to him, here's an end to all his
expectations! well, really I never knew
any thing so——"

"No, my dear aunt," cried Grace, hastily interrupting her, "there is not an end
to his expectations, at least as far as I am
concerned in preventing their termination,
as on my account I certainly shall not permit of any relinquishment."

Her aunt asked her to explain herself.
Grace obeyed her; and the mind of Miss
Agnes Flora Judith became immediately
relieved from extreme alarm, being sadly
afraid that, with the romance usual to girls
of her age, Grace would have persisted in
her engagement, now that she saw it was
likely to meet with opposition, to the utter discomfiture of the only hope she (Miss
Agnes) now had of the retrieval of the family consequence, through means of her
beauty and accomplishments, believing she
only required to be seen to be admired, and

an introduction into life, to make a conquest of some man of illustrious birth and fortune. —" Well, really I am rejoiced," she cried, " to find you determined on acting so rationally, determined on not throwing yourself away."

" No woman," said Grace, with warmth, " could be accused of throwing herself away, by allying herself to such a man as William Delamere, even though he did not possess a shilling! but though such is my opinion, I should still, from a variety of reasons, think myself highly culpable if I could now consent to marry him!"

But again becoming a little alarmed— " Thinking so highly of him as you do," cried her aunt, " may you not be persuaded, in spite of all your objections—in short, am I to believe you serious?"

" My letter shall convince you," replied Grace, unlocking her desk, and sitting down to it as she spoke, to address herself as follows to William :—

" To William Delamere, Esq.

" St. Doulagh's, 18—.

" MY DEAR WILLIAM,

" It was not indeed necessary to request an immediate answer to your last, as my anxiety to prevent any act of imprudence that might be laid to my account, would have been sufficient to prevent any delay in replying to it, even though unsolicited on the subject. That I feel as I ought the sacrifice you would make for my sake, I hope I need not say ; but I should hold myself unworthy indeed of the sentiments that prompt it, could I permit any thing of the kind. No, my dear William, I cannot, I will not! on this point my mind is unalterably made up! Nothing, I protest, I declare most solemnly, most sacredly to you, shall induce me to recede from the resolution I unhesitatingly came to on the subject. To be plain with you, I feel that I have no claim upon you to make such a sacrifice—a sacrifice that would occasion you to be stigmatized at least, to say nothing on the score of ingratitude to your uncle, with the imputation of folly—for what could your attachment to me be denominated, but a mere boyish impression, unsanctioned by any subsequent knowledge of me? in short, my regard for you is of this description, that I could willingly see you become the husband of another this instant, were I only assured that other was truly worthy of you.

" This declaration may perhaps wound your feelings for a moment, and occasion you to demand—why then, this being the case, did I allow myself to hearken to your wish for our union? In answer I shall reply—because, having seen no one who had inspired me with a warmer feeling, I entertained no repugnance to the thought, or rather, perhaps, because the very affection that would make me rejoice to see you happy with another, made me feel pleased at the idea of rendering you so myself. But I shall attempt no further vindication on the subject, feeling, that to do so, would probably be only to confuse you and myself. This only I will further add, that if my fate to have become yours, I hope and trust you would have found in me all the faithfulness and affection you would have had a right to expect in a wife. But, as might naturally have been expected, had we suffered ourselves to reflect on what was likely and probable, your uncle has formed very different views for you, from those you formed for yourself. That you will evince your good sense, by your acquiescence in them, I sincerely hope, and equally so ensure your felicity; but of this I have very little doubt, since I cannot for a moment imagine, that your uncle would have fixed upon any one for you, not sufficiently amiable to deserve your regard and admiration.

" Your next letter will, I trust, be to claim my congratulations on your happiness; none other, at least none attempting a now forbidden topic, will I notice; merely as a friend, it will always afford me the highest pleasure to hear from you —but only as a friend can I henceforth be induced to hold any correspondence with

you, or allow you to consider your affectionate

"GRACE."

———

This letter was perhaps one of the cru-
ellest shocks the susceptible feelings of
William ever received.   That Grace was
altogether as much in love with him as he
could have wished, he did not perhaps always allow himself to imagine, but that
her regard for him was sufficiently strong
to have prevented her losing him without
regret, much less giving him up without
hesitation, he certainly did flatter himself.
Some little demur, from her natural delicacy and generosity of feeling, about permitting the sacrifice he meditated for her
sake, he perhaps anticipated, but certainly nothing like the letter he received—a
letter so plain and positive in all its assertions, as entirely to preclude his throwing
himself upon the kindness of his uncle, for
indulgence to his passion.   No, he could
not ask to be indulged in withstanding his

wishes, for the sake of a woman who had
plainly told him she would as soon see
him the husband of another as herself.
No, after this galling, this almost insulting avowal, he would not, even though
commanded, renew his suit to her; but it
was not without a bitter pang-he thought
of relinquishing the hopes in which he had
been so long indulging.

The hold which Grace had taken of his
imagination was not easily to be shaken
off, strengthened and confirmed as was
the impression she had made upon his boyish fancy, by all he had subsequently heard
and understood of her, from the accounts
of others, and her correspondence with
him. If, as an " unlesson'd girl, unschool'd,
unpractis'd," she had been so captivating,
what must she be, he conceived, as she
grew up—finished in all those graces and
accomplishments that at once affect the
heart and inspire love ! in short, wherever
he went, whatever he did, her idea was
still present to him, occupying his imagination, and delighting his fancy ; but

there was now an end of any further
thought about her—she had thrown him
back the heart that had been so long devoted to her as a valueless deposit, and
pride and reason now alike instigated him
to forget her. But why did he write to
her on the subject of his uncle's intentions?
because he had flattered himself her letter
would have furnished him with a pretext
for appealing to his generosity ; if he had
not done so, they might still have continued mutually deceived—he with regard to her real sentiments for him, and
she as to their positive nature ; and could
he—he who felt that

> " ————————nought but love
> Can answer love, and render bliss secure,"

could he really have wished to remain undeceived on this subject ? No ; and with
all the pain inflicted by the acknowledgment of her indifference, he still rejoiced
at the timely discovery of it.

Her letter of course sealed his lips with
regard to her to his uncle ; and soon after
its receipt they left Geneva for Lausanne :

and here it becomes necessary to mention that his uncle, who for a series of years had held a highly-lucrative situation in India, was hardly joined by him there ere he made up his mind to quitting the country altogether, and passing some years in travel in Europe, for the retrieval of his health, injured by his long residence in India. To the inquisitive mind, and ardent imagination of William, no plan could possibly have been more agreeable, and several years of real enjoyment were, in consequence of it, passed by him.

In the course of their short journey from Geneva to Lausanne, his uncle became more communicative, and at length acknowledged that the person he had selected for him was no other than his own daughter, the offspring of a connexion which, from being infinitely beneath him, pride had hitherto induced him to conceal from his family. He represented the young lady as having received every advantage education could bestow. On the death of

her mother, a Swiss governess, she had
been sent over, then quite an infant, to
her deceased parent's family at Lausanne,
with whom she had been brought up, with
no pains or expence spared on her education; and altogether, he spoke of her in
terms of the highest delight and affection

The expectations which he raised concerning her were not disappointed: Del-
mere found her amiable, elegant, interesting—in short, well calculated to efface
the idea of the unkind Grace, and accordingly soon found no difficulty in paying
her those attentions that were so agreeable
to his uncle. The young lady received
them with complacency, and in becoming
his guide about the romantic and enchanting environs of Lausanne, afforded him
all those opportunities that could be wished for, for paying them. With her he
visited the adjacent lake, wandered about
the rugged coast of Chablais, and viewed
the principal beauties of the Pays de
Vaud, deriving additional pleasure from

those delightful excursions from the companion he had.

The manner in which she often fixed her large black eyes upon him, led him to believe she was trying thoroughly to understand his character; nor was he mistaken in the surmise, though from a very different motive to what he ascribed the circumstance. But she was soon explicit with him—she only delayed being so till assured of his being capable of being the generous friend she required. Once convinced of this, she had no further reserve from him; and with some slight emotion of pain he learned, that she had neither heart nor hand to bestow, both being already given to a young Englishman of the name of Langrish, who had for some time taken up his residence at Lausanne, and who, fearful her father would never sanction his addresses to her, from the inferiority of his fortune to that she expected, had at length prevailed on her to become his in private.

Delamere did not disappoint the confidence she had in his kindness and generosity; he at once undertook to break what she had disclosed to him to her father, and intercede for her. But, for a length of time, his zeal in her cause was unavailing. Mr. Delamere was one of those characters that could never patiently bear disappointment, and he had long set his heart upon seeing the whole of his immense fortune centred in his two nearest and dearest relatives, his daughter and nephew. In the first paroxysm of his fury, on hearing what she had done, he vowed a shilling of that fortune, from the certainty of which he concluded she had acted as she had done, should never be her's; but at length, the serious reflections brought on by a dangerous fit of illness, seconded as they were by the renewed importunities of William, and the certainty that, neither with regard to family or character, Mr. Langrish was unworthy of her, effected what William had been so long previously labouring to bring about in vain. But the reconciliation did not take place without his daughter being informed, that, from this period, she must make up her mind to but half of his property being hers, it being his determination that her cousin should not suffer through her conduct.

He kept his word—William finding, on his decease, which took place some months after, his fortune equally divided between them. The Langrishes were quite as little displeased as surprised by this division of it: they knew their obligations to William—were perfectly aware that, but for his zeal in their cause, they would, in all probability, have been entirely cut off from any part of it, and accordingly felt neither envy nor displeasure at his being an equal sharer with them in the wealth of the deceased. They by this time quite regarded him in the light of a brother; so much so, that Mr. Langrish, who happened to be an isolated being, expressed a wish to settle wherever he did; and accordingly, it being William's determination to have what he should consider his permanent home in

Ireland; they all set out for that kingdom, shortly after the decease of Mr. Delamere.

Either from early prejudice, or, in reality, knowing of no place that surpassed it in romantic beauties, William felt that St. Doulagh's was, of all places, the one he should like to settle in, and thither accordingly it was decided the party should repair, after a short stay in Dublin, for the purpose of ascertaining whether their wish for taking up their abode there could be gratified.

All that is already known to the reader was already known at St. Doulagh's, and in consequence, not a little was the bustle which the announcement of William's visit to it occasioned. This announcement took place through the medium of the dissenting minister and his wife, Mr. and Mrs. Hamilton, by whom he had been brought up, and with whom he had kept up a constant correspondence from the period of his departure, feeling for them something of the kindly feelings of a son, as they did for him those of parents.

Mr. Hamilton was a quiet, unobtrusive, excellent-hearted man, of good sound, sense, and well educated; but though well calculated, by learning, for conversation, infinitely more inclined to commune with himself than the world. Not so Mrs. Hamilton—that is, she had no objection to commune with her own heart; nor why should she, for it was a happy, contented heart, at peace with itself and all the world?—but to be still was another thing; in short, she was all bustle and activity, fond of knowing all that was going on in the world, and equally so of partaking, as far as she could, of its pleasures. A game of cards was her delight, and a social gossip with a neighbour one of her greatest recreations; but neither her love of cards, or gossiping, occasioned the slightest neglect in any of her duties; and when this is the case, a little love of pleasure is excusable. It was impossible to find a thriftier housewife, a better wife, or a kinder neighbour; and if she did like to know the affairs of others, it certainly was not out of any invidious motive.

But, with all her excellences, she did not meet with that general attention at St. Doulagh's she was so deserving of. The fact was, most of the frequenters of the meeting-house belonged to what was there considered the second class, and as she could not but be intimate with them, from motives of policy, to say nothing of any others, she was, in consequence, rather looked down upon by those who regarded themselves as the first. Amongst these was Mrs. Mayfield, the rector's wife; though no one more aimed at being thought amiably condescending than she did. A kind of intimacy was indeed, by the desire of her husband, who had a high respect for the minister, kept up between her and Mrs. Hamilton; that is, she now and then invited her to tea, when there was no one with her she cared about; and in return, once in the course of the winter, accepted an invitation from her; but when she had what she called her select party, poor Mrs. Hamilton might just as

well have hoped for an express invitation
to St. James's, as to obtain admission to
the rectory. Still no offence was taken,
Mrs. Mayfield so contriving it as to prevent her omissions on these occasions from
appearing any way pointed; so that,
though poor Mrs. Hamilton could not but
regret her not being of parties where she
knew she should have been certain of
meeting with such excellent whist-players,
she never once thought of taking offence
at the circumstance.

But at length a change took place:
Mrs. Mayfield, either beginning to estimate Mrs. Hamilton as she ought, or else
through some other cause, suddenly began to pay her the greatest attention, and
not only to invite her to the parties from
which she had heretofore been excluded,
but absolutely to make such on purpose
for her. This agreeable change took place
very shortly after the welcome tidings of
William's succeeding to the half of his
uncle's fortune, and his intention of short-

ly paying her a visit, had reached her;
so that Mrs. Hamilton hardly required
it to render her happier than she was.
But this was not all: not satisfied with
having her when invited, Mrs. Mayfield
began to call her unkind if she did not see
her of her own accord. If a day now
passed without bringing her to the rectory, one or two of the young ladies, with
their coaxing ways, were sure of being
with her, to see what had become of her;
and then, such caps, and frills, and bas-
kets, and pin-cushions, and reticules, as
they commenced working and making
her, that, in short, she might have set up
a repository if she pleased.

All was received as proofs of regard;
but there were some in the village who
slily laughed, and affected to think, that
but for William, she would not have had
to return thanks for such. But where is
the place in which people are to be found
who will not now and then be sarcastic,
and inclined to impute the actions of
others to other motives than they choose

to avow? Poor Mrs. Mayfield having five unmarried daughters, all ready for preferment, as Mrs. Hamilton said, was the cause of this innuendo, or insinuation; besides which, she had two married ones, and two sons, the eldest his father's curate, and the youngest studying physic at Edinburgh; so that, altogether, her family was certainly large enough to occasion some little maternal anxiety. But then, two of the girls were already well married; and amiable and accomplished as the others were, and so well taught and disciplined, as to be ready to take the first good offer that was made them, there was no occasion to fear their not being yet well established in life.

To aid any natural advantages they might possess, she had omitted no pains; they played on the harp and piano, warbled, if not very sweetly, at least very scientifically, and, in short, it was quite the fashion to admire, and hold them up to imitation, according to their mamma's assertion, being not less amiable than ac-

complished. But while, in some way or
other, she was always contriving to bring
them forward, it was remarked by some,
that she did not do equal justice to the
merits of others. This was a remark,
however, ascribed by her friends to envy,
that is still excited by superior merit.

But though Mrs. Hamilton could not
fail of being flattered by the attentions of
a family so universally looked up to, and
considered the very first in St. Doulagh's,
her self-elation had not the effect, as is
but too often the case, of rendering her
neglectful or inattentive to those to whom
attention was still due, and accordingly,
the family at the castle still, as usual,
never found a day pass without seeing
her. Her attachment to them indeed was
of a description not easily to be shaken—
a variety of circumstances had contributed
to confirm it. In the first place, she had
always received the kindest and most unremitting attentions from them; in the
next, she had long contemplated a union
between Grace and William, whom she

loved as a son, as a certain thing; and in
the third, Mr. Hamilton, to whose judgment she paid the highest deference, had
repeatedly declared he knew not a family
any where more deserving of estimation.
Through his means it was that they were
kept in ignorance of all that befell Eugene
in London; he was the first that heard of
the terrible predicament in which he was
placed there, and immediately set about
exerting himself to have it kept from their
knowledge. But this was not the only
obligation which they were, unconsciously,
under to him and his wife; the discovery
of this, however, was not requisite to add
to their regard for them, having long considered them in the light of their first
friends.

At length came the long wished-for letter from William, announcing his arrival
from Switzerland, and intention of being
soon down at St. Doulagh's, accompanied
by his cousin and her husband. Hardly,
however, had the flutter of joy into which
it threw her a little subsided, ere Mrs.

Hamilton began to feel herself in a state
of terrible perplexity, from not having
the power of immediately accommodating
the party under her own roof, owing to
the house being then undergoing some
repairs.—" Was ever any thing so unfortunate," she thought, " just at this time
to have the place in such a state!"   But
there was no use in fretting about the
matter; the bricklayers, and plasterers,
and carpenters, had got in, and to get
them out time enough to have every thing
ready for the reception of the travellers
was out of the question; so all that could
be done was, to consider where she could
bestow them for a time.   This, however,
required more consideration than she was
at first aware of, there being very few
lodgings at St. Doulagh's, and those of a
very sorry description, and no inn of any
consequence, the village not being a tho-
roughfare.   She would have had no hesitation in asking accommodation for them
in that barrack of a place, as she called the
castle, with its numerous suits of cham-

bers, but after what had occurred between Grace and William, this could not be done with any propriety.

In the midst of her dilemma on the subject, in walked Mrs. Mayfield, with the young ladies—a real compliment, if she knew but all, as they had just been on the point of turning their steps in a different direction, to pay a visit at a house of some consequence, when a whisper of a letter having been received from William reached them, and occasioned them immediately to change their intention.

Mrs. Mayfield entered with her usual honied smile, but which vanished the instant she beheld the thoughtful looks of Mrs. Hamilton, and with an eagerness not usual to her, her feelings and passions being generally in a state of excellent subjection, so much so as to permit it seldom to be known what was passing in her mind, she demanded what had happened—whether there was any ill news—whether, in short, William had entirely put off his long-expected visit, or——

"No, no," replied Mrs. Hamilton, "no such thing—it was not because he put off his visit, but because he's about paying it, that you found me cogitating in this manner;" and she proceeded to explain the dilemma she was in.

"And is this all!" said Mrs. Mayfield, her countenance immediately brightening up, like the sky after the passing away of a thunder-storm; "you really are a sad woman to cause one such a fright; for really, from your looks, I was quite afraid Mr. Delamere had abandoned his intention of coming here, and that would have been such a cruel disappointment to—to you, I know, that really I was quite pained at the thought; but really I don't know how I shall forgive your allowing yourself to be teased and perplexed in this manner, when you must know you had friends here, who would feel it quite a happiness to accommodate any friends of yours."

" Yes, that I knew right well," replied Mrs. Hamilton; " and I certainly should have gone up to the castle, to have asked a few nights' lodging for my visitors, but for this coolness between William and Grace."

" Tut, tut !" cried Mrs. Mayfield, a little impatiently, and with a slight contraction of her brow; " when I spoke of your friends here, it was not the family at the castle I alluded to, but the family at the rectory. After the ill usage William received from Miss O'Neil—her breaking with him in the abrupt manner she did, without rhyme or reason, it certainly would be insulting to him to attempt bringing about any renewal of his former intimacy at the castle."

" Well, I don't know that he would think that, or rather that he really considers there's an end of his intimacy there. Grace's not choosing to marry him is no reason why he should quarrel with her family—a family who were always so fond of him; but, however, that's not the question at present."

"No, certainly not," said Mrs. Mayfield, again a little impatiently; "if Mr. Delamere chooses to put up with what is generally considered most unworthy conduct to him—conduct I should blush to think any of my girls were capable of—that's his affair, not ours."

"Certainly; but indeed, my dear friend, when you come to hear and understand every thing, you'll find my sweet Grace has not been so much to blame, if at all, as you now seem to imagine."

"Well, perhaps so," a little peevishly; "but to return to what I was saying—how could you think of perplexing yourself in such a manner, about accommodation for your friends, when you must know you had only to acquaint me with your distress, to be relieved from it?"

"Yes, I know that; but then such a thronged family as you are in yourselves: besides, didn't I hear you dictating a letter to Miss Harriet the other day, in re-

ply to one from your old uncle, saying he
wished to come with his daughters to pay
you a visit, to excuse yourself, on the score
of room, from receiving him?".

"Why, yes, undoubtedly you did,"
replied Mrs. Mayfield, with a slight blush,
and after a momentary hesitation; "but
the fact is, I actually had no room to
spare just then, owing to a—a—an apprehension of one of the girls being taken ill, or
indeed the whole set of them, for I thought
the complaint Anne was getting was the
measles; But that alarm is now over, and
so I shall have the greatest pleasure in the
world in having your friends with me."

"Well, since not inconvenient, I shall
be obliged by your letting Mr. and Mrs.
Langrish have a chamber for a night or
two; but as for William, I don't think I
need trespass upon you for him, for in
some nook or corner I think I shall be
able to make up a bed for him myself
here."

"No, no, I positively insist against any
thing of the kind; there are two unoccu-

pied chambers now at the rectory, and so leave this I will not, till you write to him, to let him know what arrangement you have made for him and his cousins."

Thus urged, Mrs. Hamilton sat down to write the required letter, which having perused, Mrs. Mayfield undertook putting in the post-office herself, lest of any disappointment to her plan.

"Well, I think we have him secure," said Mrs. Mayfield, talking over the matter with her eldest married daughter; "his taking up his abode here will afford a pretext for monopolizing him, in a way that can scarcely fail, I think, of leading to an agreeable result. I wonder which of the girls he will most like! if very intellectual, I think Charlotte will be the one; but if apt to be struck by beauty, our darling Myra will have the best chance."

"That would be unfortunate," returned Mrs. Neville, "after the lengths she has gone with Falkiner; why, she confessed to me having absolutely engaged herself to him."

"Pooh, pooh! what signifies? do you think she would be fool enough, or that, if so inclined, I would permit her, as to reject such a match as Delamere for the sake of a person so inferior in fortune as Falkiner? Should the former take a fancy to her, and the latter not be inclined to give up his pretensions, why your father and I, who have hitherto pretended to be ignorant of the affair, in order that we might not be accused of encouraging a son in disobedience to his parents, must then come forward, to extricate her from him, under the pretext of disapproving of what is clandestine. However, as in him she certainly would have a very good match, I should much rather Delamere took a fancy to any other of the girls than to her. Should she, however, be his choice, I hope we shall be able to manage matters so as to keep Falkiner among us. I know very well, that neither Bell nor Bab would object to him, and am positive, that had not Myra come in his way, he would have become particular to the

latter. I now see the bad policy of bringing out more than two or three girls at a
time."

By return of post a letter arrived from
William, stating the precise day on which
he might be expected; but that, owing
to a slight indisposition of Mrs. Langrish's,
his cousins would not accompany him,
though it was their intention soon to follow; and with his acceptance of her kind
offer of a bed for a few nights, requesting
Mrs. Mayfield to be assured of his gratitude for her kindness in offering it.

Grace could not help smiling, a little
sarcastically, when she heard of this offer,
from pretty well knowing the motive to
which it was owing. What she thought,
however, she kept to herself. The keenness of her observation would not permit
her to join in the warm encomiums it was
the fashion to bestow on the family at the
rectory; but no one ever heard an ill-natured insinuation against them from her;
she was indeed particularly guarded in
what she said about them, lest of being

accused of pique or resentment, so little
was the attention she received from them,
or rather so slighting, in general, was their
conduct; but she was too much calculated
to excite admiration not to occasion envy,
while her want of fortune prevented her
being of any consequence in their eyes.

That William was seriously offended
she could not doubt, from the total cessation of this correspondence with her, and
grieved at the idea, from her sincere regard for him, she had long looked forward with impatience to his present visit
to St. Doulagh's, from the opportunity
she conceived it likely to afford her of endeavouring to bring about a reconciliation
between them; but in her hope of this
she began very much to fear she should
be disappointed, on learning the arrangement that was made for him—a fear that,
of course, made her regret the circumstance; for, from the object she was aware
the family at the rectory had in view in
inviting him to their house, she was convinced they would do all in their power

to prevent the renewal of any intimacies
that might be likely to detach him from
them.

At length the subject of all this specu-
lation and anxiety arrived, and as he dashed through the village in his handsome cur-
ricle, with the usual accompaniment of
attendants, the whole place seemed to be
thrown into commotion by the impatience
there was to behold him. He stopped at
Mr. Hamilton's; but hardly had the first
affectionate greetings been over between
him and his much-valued friends there,
ere Mr. and Mrs. Mayfield made their appearance to claim him as their guest, and
without more ado, bore him off in triumph to the rectory, with Mr. and Mrs.
Hamilton.

Grace could not help being thrown into
a little flutter on hearing of his arrival;
she knew not how the welcome she was
so longing to give him might be received,
and felt that she could not quite compose
herself till she had ascertained whether, in
addition to the resentment she had occa-

sioned him, change of circumstances had effected any change of manner. She was not immediately, however, to be put out of suspense on this point; nor indeed did she altogether, from her knowledge of the Mayfields, imagine she should.

He arrived early in the morning, and the day advanced without hearing any thing more of him than that he was come, except it was the work that was making about him at the rectory. Miss Agnes Flora Judith had again got into the clouds, so she made no comment on the circumstance. Not so, however, her brother; he had always dearly loved William, and could not help therefore feeling sensibly the indifference, which his being so many hours in the village without looking in on his old friends at the castle, manifested about them. A fit of the gout, from which he was just recovering at the period, did not tend to render him more patient under any little vexation, and with downright indignant bitterness he

spoke of William's seeming unkindness.
—" Well, well, times are altered !" he
said; " there was a time when Mr. William wouldn't have passed these gates
without stopping, if he could have helped
it; but he wants no further attention from
us: he knows how matters have gone on
here, and so, like the world in general,
' no longer pipe no longer dance;' he has
given us up for those who can better entertain, and afford him more amusement !"

" Let us not judge him prematurely,
my dear father," said Grace; " I can hardly think we shall find him so much
changed as you seem to imagine."

" Tut, tut! that is a sign you know
nothing of the world, child, or you
wouldn't say so: as the barometer rises
and falls according to the changes of the
weather, so your friends' regard is very
apt to increase or decline according to the
increase or decline of your fortune. But
there is one thing I am determined on,
and that is, to let him know my mind.
Yes, I'll take care, as soon as I get on

my legs again, to brush up the memory
of my gentleman, in such a way for him
as shall make him blush, if capable of
blushing. But if we had any doubt of his
being altered, wouldn't his having given
up entirely writing to you be a proof that
he is?"

Grace was on the point of saying no,
but checked herself, from the reflection of
the explanation that must have followed
the assertion, deeming it as well, since
there was an end of the affair between her
and William, that her father should know
nothing more of the matter than he already
did, and that was only that if she had
liked to give him encouragement, she
might perhaps have had William for a serious admirer.

"One wouldn't like to be thought impatient, Grace," resumed the lieutenant,
"by complaining; but somehow one can't
help feeling a little sore at seeing every
one getting on, as it were, in life but one's
self! Here's this jackanapes, for what I

know to the contrary, Delamere, come flourishing down amongst us, who went away a dependent on the kindness of a capricious uncle! and here's the rector getting his daughters married, and his sons established in life! while here we are just as we were seven long years ago, or rather much worse, for my expectations about Eugene were not then disappointed? but don't cry, Grace—don't cry; it will fret me if I think I have said any thing to vex you. God knows you have had but too many tears lately, my poor girl; your trials indeed commenced early. In your spring-tide, a nipping frost has fallen upon your young hopes! Yet—no, I will not think so; I will trust that they will yet bud and bloom out as freshly as ever. Now, don't shake your head in that manner, Grace; I cannot bear—I mean, I don't like it, it puts me so much in mind of poor Rose!" and the lieutenant drew forth his handkerchief from beneath the bolster of the sofa, on which he was reclining; " that's the way she used to shake her head latterly, whenever I tried to cheer her, by saying she would yet be as blooming and merry as ever. I always liked that poor child; but," and there was a slight break in his voice, "I never thought, or rather knew, I loved her so well, Grace, till we lost her."

Grace was applying her handkerchief to her fast-falling tears, when she was startled by a sudden bustle in the hall, and the sound of a strange voice; she listened attentively—could it be? Yes, she was sure it was the accent of William; and under the idea of its being him she heard, she was darting to the door, when, happening to brush against her father's elbow, the part in which the gout had just then lodged itself, he seized her by the gown, to demand what she was about, declaring that she had nearly killed him by what she had done.

"I beg your pardon, my dear sir," cried Grace, gently struggling, as she spoke, to disengage herself—" but I really think——"

" If you wish to save me from dying,
rub my elbow!" cried her father, interrupting her, " for I am in agony."

Grace, without a further effort to release herself, knelt down beside him. In
a minute after the door behind her opened;
she tried to glance round, but her father's
hand was resting on her head, and that
prevented her. Presently the lieutenant's
eyes were raised from following the motion of her hand as she rubbed his elbow,
and—" Bless my heart!" he exclaimed,
" who have we got here?"

Grace now instinctively turned round
—" And who have we got here indeed!"
she was on the point of repeating; for in
the tall, finely-grown, elegant-looking
young man that stood before her, she
could hardly bring herself to believe she
beheld the identical William that seven
years ago had left St. Doulagh's. But,
yes, it was him; his smile—the lurking
smile at the surprise he excited, betrayed
him. And—" Really you are so im——
so altered," said Grace, correcting herself,

as, after standing a minute to enjoy the stare he occasioned, or else through some other cause, he stepped forward to receive her extended hand, and raise her from her kneeling attitude, "that I should hardly have recollected you elsewhere."

"Altered!" exclaimed the lieutenant; "yes, that you may well say, indeed; by the head of Neptune, but he has grown a proper fellow! but this comes of the books being thrown aside. Poor Hamilton, however, is not to be blamed for having kept you so close to the oar as he did; it was all along, I know, by the order of your uncle, who, if not obeyed, would have removed you to where you would not have received such kindness." But suddenly changing his tone, and drawing back on the sofa—"So at last, sir, you have found your way here, I perceive," he said.

"And that I did not sooner do so, I am not to blame," cried Delamere, dropping the hand of Grace to take the lieutenant's; "but really there was so much to

talk over with my friends, the Hamiltons,
and then——"

"So much at the rectory to render you
forgetful of every thing else, that——
Well, well, that's all natural; when a
young fellow gets amongst a set of pretty
girls, one can't wonder at his being unwilling to break away from them; and so
here's my hand, of my own accord, and
with it a hearty welcome back again to
St. Doulagh's; but come, Grace has told
you that you are altered—do you think
her so?"

"No; I perceive no other alteration in
her," Delamere calmly replied, "than
what might naturally be expected."

"That is, you left her little more than
a child, and you have found her a young
woman: and how many in the village
would be glad you found them the same!"
added the lieutenant with a laugh, for his
spirits had received quite a fillip from this
visit; "eh! what do you think, my lad?"

"Perhaps so, sir; but——"

"You were going to inquire about the

rest of us! Well; my sister is just the old thing still—a Socrates, or Plato, or any other philosopher you choose to name, in petticoats; and Eugene, he'll soon be here again, I suppose; but, God knows! I don't know how, but that it would be quite as well he staid away; for I am much afraid he is coming here only to afflict himself and us all. Ah, Bill," suddenly reverting to old times, "I little thought, when, perhaps as great a boy as you both, I shared or promoted your sports here, that that boy, then so promising, and every thing a father could wish, would ever have caused me the sorrow he has done!"

"Come, come, my dear sir, I must not hear any thing said against my friend Eugene."

"Well, well, I sha'n't say a word more against him; nor should I now, only to a friend like you. Indeed, you have reason to regard the poor fellow, for, next to his own family, I don't suppose there

M 3

is a person in the world he loves more
than you."

"I never doubted his regard, sir. No,
I never doubted Eugene's possessing a
warm heart—such a one as would render
him incapable of meeting the affection of
a friend with indifference."

His colour rose as he spoke, and Grace
caught what she thought a reproachful
glance from him. Well, it was only what
she had previously made herself certain of
being the case; she had offended him;
but being so long convinced of this, why
now feel herself so uncomfortable at the
thought? But William had always had
such a way of shewing resentment by his
eyes, and she found he had not lost the
trick. She began to feel awkward; William, after the first shake by the hand,
made no attempt to unbend towards her;
and uncertain whether, after all, the reserve of his manner was altogether owing
to resentment, or the absolute conversion
of his former sentiments into indifference,
she knew not how to make an effort to

enter into conversation with him. To relieve herself from the unpleasant restraint this imposed upon her, she suddenly rose, and said she would go seek her aunt. Ere she reached the door, however, it was opened by Miss Agnes Flora Judith herself, apprized of the visit of Delamere, and as impatient to see him as a person of her dignified habits would allow themselves to appear.

CHAPTER X.

"Silent and chaste she steals along,
Far from the world's gay busy throng;
With gentle, yet prevailing force,
Intent upon her destin'd course;
Graceful and useful all she does."

MISS AGNES was quite as little prepared for the alteration that had taken place in the appearance of William as were the others, and her looks, like theirs, testified the surprise it occasioned. Mutual greetings over, and a little incidental conversation ensuing, William at length rose to depart.—" What! leaving us so soon?" demanded the lieutenant. " Nay, this is unkind, after so long an absence; tea is just coming in, and you know you used to say there was no one in the world made it so well as Grace. Come, stay a little

longer, if it be only to see whether she
has lost the art."

William looked at Grace and smiled.

"As much as to intimate," thought
Grace, "that when he made that assertion,
it was at a time when he was weak enough
to think very differently of her from what
he now did." But let him have meant what
he would by the smile, his hat was thrown
aside, and down he sat again.

The lieutenant knew he had travelled
a great deal, and he now began to question him as to the places he had seen. In
the course of conversation, wanting some
observations illustrated, he called to Grace
to hand him down a bundle of maps, that,
enveloped in dust and cobwebs, lay upon
the top of a bookcase. Now the bookcase
was so high, that to attempt to get them,
without either running the risk of pulling
it down on her head, by her efforts to
reach them, or else mounting on a chair,
was out of the question; and as she liked
neither one or the other, she stood irresolute.—"Why, what's the matter with you,

Grace?" said her father a little petulantly:
" didn't you hear me?"

" Yes, sir; but——"

" Then why don't you do what I desire,
pray?"

Grace coloured, and so did Delamere,
either from being unaccustomed lately to
hear females treated or addressed in this
authoritative manner, or some other cause.
—" No, no!" he exclaimed, interposing
between Grace and the bookcase, as she
turned to it, and taking down the maps,
and at the same time drawing down a
whole shower of dust upon himself, he
presented them to her father.

The lieutenant laughed heartily at the
figure which he had made of himself by
what he had done.—" Well, you may
thank Miss Grace for this," he said; " and
the least she could do in return, I think,
for the figure you have made yourself for
her, would be to give your jacket a good
dusting for you."

" I am sure I am very sorry," said
Grace; " but——" Her hand was some-

how in the way of William at the moment, and there was a pressure of it at the instant, that either through surprise, or the indication this seemed to be of some little relenting towards her, caused an emotion that prevented her finishing what she was about saying, and made her resume her seat in silence.

Tea over, William again took up his hat to be off.—" So you are in a hurry to leave us?" said the lieutenant again, a little reproachfully.

" My dear sir, I really stole away."

" Well, what then? Perhaps you are not missed yet; and if you are, a few minutes longer delay can make no difference. I wanted to see whether you remembered any thing of the lessons I gave you at chess."

" Another time, my dear sir; but now really——"

" Oh, very well! I see poor Grace is to have no respite; for except some charitable person drops in to relieve her, which is very seldom the case, down she

is obliged to sit every evening to chess
with me."

Again the hat of William was thrown
aside, and—" Where is the chess-board?"
he demanded.—" And all these summer
evenings," he asked, as they were arran-
ging the men, " do you keep her pent up,
playing chess?"

" Why, what can I do?" replied the
lieutenant. " But my poor girl, I know
—I know she is lost amongst us."

From this moment the lips of Delamere became sealed, and he became so
evidently abstracted, that the lieutenant
at last thought it would be a charity to
release him; and accordingly pretending
a sudden twinge, that rendered playing
any longer unpleasant to him, he said
that he would no longer detain him.

For the third time then the hat was
taken up, but not for the third time to be
resigned.

" Well," said Miss Agnes, " who ever
would have thought that William would

have grown up so fine a young man! Not
I, I am sure."

" Nor I, I am sure," said Grace, with a
sigh.

" And then I think him pretty much
what he was with regard to good-nature.
If there was any little stiffness or shyness
in his manner, I certainly think it imputable to your breaking with him—to the
way in which his pride was piqued by that
circumstance."

Grace looked at her father; but he was
too much occupied at the moment, in
looking over a map, for some of the places
mentioned to him by Delamere, to be
paying any attention to them.—" Well,
perhaps so," she said; " but if so, pride is,
I believe, by this time, the only feeling
that remains at all hurt by it."

" It is not, however, altogether impossible for former sentiments to be revived,"
observed Miss Agnes a little thought-
fully; " and an alliance with William
would not be an undesirable thing now."

" Of that there is very little chance now,

I believe," said Grace, rising, and moving
to a window; " therefore, my dear aunt, I
beg you may speak no more of such a matter."

Delamere was not yet completely out
of sight. Grace involuntarily glanced
round the room; and what a contrast in
her imagination did the great old-fashioned, dusky apartment—did the stillness, the
solitude of the castle, whence mirth and
cheerfulness had long departed, form to
the pleasant abode, the gay domestic circle, to which he was hastening! No wonder he should be in such a hurry to depart
from a place where it was hardly possible
for the spirits not to be affected—and she
sighed heavily. Yet there was a time
when William would not have thought it
a punishment to remain with his friends
at the castle; but that time was passed—
their circumstances were altered, and so
were his; yet do not let her do him injustice—if his feelings for them were changed,
had she not to thank herself for it? Not
content with merely breaking with him,

had she not said every thing she could on the occasion to affront and offend him? Why not be satisfied with simply stating, that, after his uncle's explanation, she could not possibly think of any further encouragement to his addresses; without telling him she did not care one pin about him, which her declaration, that she would as soon see him the husband of another as herself, was certainly tantamount to; when, after all, she was actually any thing but decidedly indifferent about him? But if his attachment was of the deep-rooted nature he would once have led her to imagine——but man was proverbially an inconstant creature—always prone to change, and then so proud as not to be offended with impunity; and so, all things considered, the manner in which she had piqued him, and where he then was, surrounded by those whose object it would be to keep them asunder, she could not avoid thinking there was indeed very little chance or hope of the renewal of his addresses. But was there no indication

whatever of former feelings during his recent visit? and she began to run over
every look, and word, and glance, that
had escaped him. The motionless manner
in which he stood contemplating her on
his entrance—the sudden pressure of her
hand—the flushed cheek at her father appearing angry with her—his anxious interposition to prevent her running any
risk of harm; did not these circumstances
indicate something flattering—some little
struggle in his mind about her? but then,
opposed to this, was there not his anxiety
to depart? and his sudden abstraction, as
if his thoughts were any where but where
he then was? Ah, it was idle, ridiculous
to imagine he entertained a further idea
about her! Well, let things turn out as
they would, it was fortunate perhaps for
him, that she had not sooner understood
what her real sentiments for him were,
since, if she had, she rather doubted whether she could have absolutely relinquished him in the decided terms she had done;
and without her having done which, per-

haps he would have done something to provoke his uncle's displeasure on her account, and so probably have prevented the settlement ultimately made in his favour; and then where would be all the attention he now received, the ringing of bells, the blazing of bonfires, at his arrival at St. Doulagh's? how quietly, with all his worth, his captivating graces and accomplishments, might he then have stole in and stole out of the place!

The moment he was missed at the rectory, it was guessed where he was gone; to be out of doubt on the matter, however, Mrs. Hamilton was referred to.

Not a little was the perturbation of Mrs. Mayfield, at finding he was actually, as she had surmised, gone to the castle. In vain she tried to retain her usual placid brow and tranquil manner—she continued in a downright fever, till a significant look from one of the young ladies, who were all stationed at the respective windows of the drawing-room, commanding a full view of the road, dissipated the alarm she was in, of his having deserted for the evening, by announcing his return.

" Well, after all, his visit was not so very long a one; and perhaps, from the consideration of former intimacy, he thought an immediate one could not well be avoided;" and she forthwith proceeded to ring for the tea-urn, which she had not power before to do, notwithstanding the yawnings of poor Mrs. Hamilton, who always liked what she called an early cup of tea; and—" Been to see some of your old friends?" she said, with one of her sweetest smiles, and in her most dulcet tone, as he entered.

" Yes, I rank my friends at the castle amongst my very oldest."

" Well, and——" she hesitated, with all her anxiety to proceed, fearful of betraying that anxiety, " well, and——" after a slight pause, " you found wonderful alterations there I suppose?"

" No, by no means; so little alteration there indeed, that I could almost have fancied it was but the day before I had been there."

"Oh, that is with regard to the place itself, you mean; but with regard to the inmates—now Miss Grace, for instance?"

"Certainly no wonderful alteration with respect to her, for it couldn't be very wonderful to find a person you left a child, seven years ago, now a young woman."

"Assuredly—undoubtedly not!" assented Mrs. Mayfield, taking a sip of tea between each word, to conceal a something very like a feeling of discomposure at the coolness of this observation, or rather, perhaps, with which it was uttered. "Well, and young woman as you now find her, what is your opinion of her?—she certainly was a pretty child—but I don't know how it is, yet there are people who still think her rather prettyish."

"Indeed! well I could never agree with them in thinking so!"

"No!" exclaimed Mrs. Mayfield, with all the vivacity of surprise, and a wide

distension of eyes, sparkling with delight
—" no!"

" No."

Mrs. Hamilton laughed.—" You may
well look surprised," she said, addressing
herself to Mrs. Mayfield; " but when you
know this gentleman as well as I do, you
won't be taken in by him, as you have
now been.   I'll tell you the reason why
he couldn't join in opinion with those who
only think our Grace prettyish—because
he himself thinks her beautiful."

" Indeed!" said Mrs. Mayfield, affecting
a laugh, but with a slight variation of colour; " very well explained indeed!—And
is it so? (to Delamere) is it really as your
friend has intimated?"

" I wouldn't on any account be the
means of having Mrs. Hamilton's judgment or penetration called in question!"
replied Delamere evasively.

Mrs. Mayfield did not like this answer;
yet, after the manner in which he had
been treated by Grace, as she had contrived to learn from Mrs. Hamilton, who,

though fully her equal in plain good sense, was certainly not her match in subtlety, could he really retain any further prepossession for her? how she should have liked to be out of suspense on the subject! But supposing he did, was it likely he would continue much longer to indulge it, assailed, as he would now be, by all kinds of charms and allurements? no, she could not imagine such a thing; and her spirits reviving at the thought, she became quite as agreeable as ever.

By this time the pretty fair-haired Myra had taken her cue, or, to be more explicit, perceiving that depreciating Grace was not the way for any one to recommend themselves to the good graces of Delamere, had decided on acting quite a contrary part, allured to do so by the belief that he seemed more inclined to admire her than her sisters; but of what consequence could his admiration be to her, it might be remarked, having engaged herself, as she had done, to another? 'tis true she had

done so, but then it was when she had no
chance of making such a conquest as the
present, and to try and secure which she
determined to let nothing prevent her, certain of both the sanction and concurrence
of her mother and sisters in her efforts for
the purpose.—" La, my dear mamma,"
she exclaimed, " how any one could say
Grace O'Neil was only prettyish, when to
be sure, in my opinion, she is one of the
sweetest-looking girls!"

" Yes, and in mine too, my love," said her
mother, quite forgetting her insinuation
to the contrary but a few minutes before;
" but I never knew any one, indeed, to
whose pretensions you did not do justice.—
How amiable," she added, in a pretended
whisper to Mrs. Hamilton, but which, like
a playhouse whisper, was quite distinct
enough, and intended to be so, for every
one to hear, " for one pretty girl to praise
another! 'tis so seldom the case—but indeed, both by precept and example, I have
always tried to guard my daughters against
envy."

" Yes, that I am sure of," said Mrs. Hamilton; " but whatever cause you may have given for envy, I am sure you have had no cause to feel it, with your excellent husband, and your fine family, and every thing so happy, and comfortable, and thriving about you."

" Certainly, my dear friend, certainly I acknowledge myself a most fortunate woman—superlatively so with regard to my family; since, in point of disposition and abilities, and all indeed that can flatter the pride, and delight the heart of a mother," and she put her handkerchief for a moment to her eyes, " I believe I may say none can surpass them."

The contemplation of domestic happiness was always delightful to Delamere, and the felicity a man must enjoy with a partner selected from such a family of love as the present, appeared to have suddenly struck him. As the thought occurred, his eyes were involuntarily bent upon the fair sisters, and without being well con-

scious of it, he was minutely scanning the
countenance of each, when a sudden smile
from Myra drew him to her side, and a
playful flirtation immediately commenced
between them.   But though he certainly
was struck with her, and thought indeed
that any of the daughters of such a woman as Mrs. Mayfield must be considered as a prize, still his ideas wandered; and
at length returning to Mrs. Hamilton, he
seemed to forget there was any one else in
the room but her.

What would not the party have given
to have known what they were conversing about with such earnestness, and the
meaning of her evidently assenting nods
from time to time!—almost as much as to
have known his real opinion of Grace:
but at length patience becoming exhausted; Myra undertook breaking up the *tête-à-tête*, by asking him, in a rallying tone,
how he liked the song she had just sung?

"The song!" repeated Delamere, staring—"did you really sing?"

"Oh! a pretty gallant gentleman you

are, to ask me this, when here I have been doing my best to charm you this half-hour !".

" Perhaps I shall yet be able to prove to you not in vain," said William, rising, and drawing her harp to her, near which she had purposely seated herself as he spoke.

The moment he vacated his chair by Mrs. Hamilton, it was taken by Mrs. Mayfield; and who, in a very few minutes, succeeded in learning what he and his old friend had been conversing about; but no address was requisite for the purpose, as it was intended she should be made acquainted with it, without making any inquiry on the subject.

The fact was, all his former anxiety about her revived by seeing her, to say nothing of any other feeling. Delamere had proposed to Mrs. Hamilton making a pleasant party, for a week or a fortnight, on account of Grace, to a little bathing-place on the coast, about eight or nine miles from St. Doulagh's, though osten-

sibly for the purpose of seeking lodgings
there for Mrs. Langrish, under the pretext of there being none at St. Doulagh's
that would suit her. Mrs. Mayfield readily acceded to the plan, and the young
ladies were highly pleased with it, from
the amusement they anticipated from it;
and would have been still more so, but
for the explanation of Mrs. Hamilton.
However, it might be only out of mere
good-nature that he had thought of such
a thing for Grace.

Had he been questioned on the subject,
he certainly would have denied its being
through any other motive, wounded as
his pride and sensibility had been by her,
and determined as he was never again to
consider her in any other light than that
of a mere common acquaintance or friend.
Yet how inconsistent with this determination was the manner in which he suffered himself to dwell on her idea, and
the feelings he pictured to himself would
have been his, had he returned to St.
Doulagh's undeceived about hers! She

was so lovely, so interestingly lovely, even
beyond what he had conceived he should
find her, that he could not help dwelling
on the thought; and yet perhaps it was
the manner in which he found her engaged—her kneeling attitude, the mingled
expression of astonishment and pleasure
that pervaded her countenance, as her
head was thrown back to gaze at him,
that alone gave to her appearance that
kind of interest or character that fixed
him for a moment in an absolute trance
of admiration.

Made up as his mind was about her, it
was of no great consequence certainly for
him to ascertain, and yet he felt he should
greatly like to know what she thought of
him. Of the improvement in his appearance, the personal advantages he, in short,
now possessed, he was not unconscious—
had they produced any effect upon her?
did her looks betray any other kind of
emotion than that of mere surprise? He
thought he had observed a slight variation
of colour once or twice, a something indi-

cative of a little flutter, a resting for a minute or two of the long, dark eyelashes
upon the beautiful cheek, as if there had
been something beneath them to conceal.
But how ridiculous these fancies, or rather, what weakness, to permit himself
to draw any flattering conclusions from
them! was it to give her an opportunity
of again telling him she cared nothing
about him? no—he would not expose
himself to any thing so mortifying again.
Yet if there was a chance of subduing this
indifference——but, no, no; this was the
way, by yielding to delusive hopes, that
mankind lost the means of securing happiness; he really thought, and believed,
he had seen, in the pretty and elegant
Myra, a person perfectly adapted to compensate him for his first disappointment;
and how much wiser then to try and turn
his thoughts upon her, than suffer them
to wander or dwell where no return was
to be expected.—" Yet, cruel, cruel Grace,
to compel me to such a struggle with my
feelings!" he called her, as he paced to

and fro his chamber, utterly regardless,
contrary to the expectations of Mrs. Mayfield, of the many tasteful specimens it
contained of the young ladies' skill in
drawing and needlework, purposely collected and hung up there for the occasion.
If for a moment he paused, it was only
to station himself at the window, commanding a full view of the then-slumber-
ing village, gradually leading up to the
castle, on which so often he had stood
gazing at the same hour, or rather, sighing his soul toward it, like the lovesick
Troilus, " toward the Grecian camp,
where Cressid lay."

· The first thing that Grace heard the
next morning was, of his having gone,
accompanied by the family at the rectory,
to view a seat called Rockland, some
miles off, the proprietor of which, an absentee, it was understood had some idea
of disposing of it. Well, there was an
end of any hope of seeing him that day—
on her own account she did not much
mind that; but her father, so sincere and

affectionate himself—she knew he would
be vexed at this apparent indifference;
and she thought—yes, certainly she
thought that he might have spared a minute or two, if it was only to ask him
how he was, knowing he would be pleased
by the attention. But he was too much
engaged with, too much engrossed by his
new friends—for, long as he had known
the Mayfields, still they could only be
considered as such; for well she remembered the time when he might have wandered about the rectory for hours without
ever being invited into it—to think of his
old friends, now no longer able to contri-
bute to his amusement. She had taken,
the preceding night, she did not know
how, unconsciously she believed, the locket containing the raven lock of hair she
had despoiled his head of seven years ago,
in the moment of parting; it was now in
her bosom, and drawing it out, she was
almost tempted to throw it aside again.
But no, she would not give way to such
petulance, such irritation; and according-

ly returning it to its hiding-place, she tried to resume her work; but there was a something that dimmed her sight for a few minutes, that rendered the immediate attempt ineffectual.

The morning was not quite over when in came Mrs. Hamilton. Grace looked the surprise she felt.—" What, not of the party to Rockland!" she said; " how comes this about?"

" Na, na," cried Mrs. Hamilton, speaking in the broad Northern accent she sometimes chose to express herself in, " gadding about every day won't do; 'tis an old saying, and a true one—' If we wish to keep a house, we mustn't leave the house to keep itself!' I had something to do at home this morning; but the business being finished, and my good man being gone to dine with his friend Fowler, I shall take my chance here to-day, if you, Grace, promise to come up with me in the evening to the rectory."

Grace coloured violently.—" No, you'll excuse me," she said.

"And why so? why should I excuse
you?"

"Oh, it's no matter—I'd rather you
wouldn't ask."

"Yes, but I must ask."

"Why then, the fact is, I can't think
of going to a place where I have reason to
imagine my company not desired. I
should be sorry, extremely sorry, to be of
a captious temper, apt to misconstrue or
take offence—but where is the attention I
have ever received from Mrs. Mayfield?
what young parties is she not continually
making, and to what one of them has she
ever had the politeness, or good-nature,
or whatever you please to term it, to invite me? No, no, my dear ma'am, you
must excuse me indeed."

"But indeed I won't!" was the reply.
"This is not like my own Grace, to speak
in this manner—I am sure there must be
some mistake in this matter: perhaps before I knew Mrs. Mayfield as intimately
as I now do, I might not have thought so;
but now that I really know her, I give

it as my opinion that she is incapable of
any slight, or intentional neglect, to any
one, particularly to a person she esteems
and admires as she does you. She is a
charming woman indeed, and they are altogether a charming family; and William
thinks so as well as I."

The colour, which had begun to fade
from the cheek of Grace, again revived—
" Oh, he would be singular if he didn't !"
she said.

" Yes, he admires them all greatly,
but Myra especially."

" Really ! well, I—I——". and taking
up her scissors, Grace began to snip away
most unmercifully at the frill she was
working—" I don't wonder at that, for
she—she certainly is pretty."

" Yes, with her sweet flaxen hair, and
laughing blue eyes !—But, child, what
are you about ? you are cutting your frill
to pieces !"

" Oh, no matter," said Grace; but
blushing more deeply than ever—" it was
spoiled before;" and hastily crushing it in

her hand, she thrust it into her work-basket.

"But what do you think of our William himself?"

"Our William!" repeated Grace, with a supercilious smile.

"Well, my William—is he not grown up a bonny chiel?"

"Yes, he's grown up very well," replied Grace coolly.

"See how he has remembered me!" said Mrs. Hamilton, producing a very handsome watch as she spoke.

"He would have been ungrateful, could he have forgot you."

"Well, perhaps so; but I am not the only person who occupied his thoughts while absent: he has deputed me to present these tokens of regard to his friends here;" and as she spoke, she took out a box, containing a variety of beautiful trinkets for Miss Agnes Flora Judith and Grace, and a superb snuff-box for the lieutenant.

Miss Agnes Flora Judith had a feminine passion for trinkets, which she could not resist; William's presents were therefore not refused, though, as much as possible, she tried to give her accepting them the appearance of condescension; but Grace, after running her eye over those intended for her, positively refused taking them.

"Not take them!" exclaimed Mrs. Hamilton, much surprised; "why, William will take your refusal of them very unkind!"

"I don't care; he has other friends, to whom such things would be more desirable than they are to me. The pearls would be very becoming to Miss Myra; and, in short," suddenly drawing back entirely from the table, "upon my honour I will not accept them!"

"Very well—I shall of course then return them to him; but I hope I sha'n't find you in a disobliging humour about every thing this morning;" and Mrs. Hamilton proceeded to mention the party that was made for Strandmore, and Grace's

being included in it. William had positively charged her not to let Grace know
that it was on her account it was made;
but somehow Mrs. Hamilton was not always on her guard in her communications,
and though she did not directly disobey
him, she spoke in such a manner, that
Grace, ere long, began to surmise the
truth.

To find we have unjustly accused, or
suspected any one, never fails of making
us feel angry with ourselves, if we possess
any feeling. Grace could almost have
cried when she thought of the manner in
which she had inveighed against William,
in, her own mind—the anger, the resentment she had given way to, against him,
at the very moment that he was contriving
a plan for her health and amusement; and
how much did she now wish she had not
been so positive in her rejection of his
presents, undeserving, as he had now
proved himself, of any ungraciousness from
her! and almost she had a mind to ask for
them. But, after all, could she profit by

his present kindness? could her father
spare her? or daily expecting Eugene as
she was, and wishing to be on the spot on
his arrival, to try what she could do towards mitigating or consoling him under
the sorrow that awaited him, how could
she think of leaving home? But Mrs.
Hamilton obviated all her objections:
Mrs. Brady would supply her place: as
nurse and attendant to her father, and her
good man had given her a promise to drop
in every evening for an hour or two to
play chess with him; and it was rather to
be supposed they would hear again from
Eugene before they saw him; but if not
—if he should arrive unexpectedly, the
melancholy disclosure that awaited him
could very well be kept back, the distance
was so short to Strandmore, until she was
sent for; and finally it was settled that
she should leave St. Doulagh's on the
morrow, with the rest of the party.
She no longer refused accompanying
Mrs. Hamilton in the evening to the rectory, anxious to have an early opportunity

of trying to atone, by her manner to William, for the ungraciousness she feared he would accuse her of in refusing his presents

They arrived just as the party had returned from their excursion, having dined on a cold collation they took with them in the beautiful woods of Rockland. Mrs. Hamilton was rather expected, as they knew she would be impatient to learn whether there was any chance of William's getting Rockland—but not Grace, and seeing her was certainly not an agreeable surprise, a dance being settled for the evening, and arrangements altogether made, or at least expectations entertained, with which they much feared she would interfere; well knowing that wherever she appeared, she was still the magnet of attraction; but it could not be helped—this odious Mrs. Hamilton was always a busy over-officious person; and so veiling their real feelings with smiling countenances, all was kind greeting to Grace.—" An additional obligation to dear Mrs. Hamil-

too, our seeing you here, I dare say," said Mrs. Mayfield, with one of her sweetest smiles; "for I don't know how it is, but you are a terrible stranger here, Miss O'Neil."

"But she won't continue to be so, I know she won't," said Myra, skipping up to her at the moment, and laying her hand on her shoulder—"I know she won't, when she knows how we all love her so. Yes, indeed," she cried, passing her arm under hers, and walking her away to a window, "and we are all so delighted to think we shall have you for a fortnight at least amongst us. But what a good-natured creature this William Delamere is!" she said. "Do you know, that the moment I told him last night that we had been at mamma almost this whole summer in vain, to take us to Strandmore for a few days, he immediately decided on making a party to it. The girls are quite beginning to tease me about him; but, la! 'tis quite ridiculous to suppose that, knowing so little of me as he does."

". She might have saved herself the trouble of arguing the point, for Grace knew not another word of what she was saying; her feelings had undergone a revulsion. It was then for Myra, not Grace, that the party was made, and Mrs. Hamilton had quite deceived her by what she had insinuated; and she felt inclined to be very angry with her, but checked herself, for what motive could she have for deceiving her but good-nature? she thought a little change of scene would be of service to her, and so had recourse to a little artifice, to induce her to consent to it. Well, she would not disappoint her—she would not give way to this kind of captiousness she was beginning to experience. And what on earth was it she expected from Delamere? she had refused him decidedly as a lover, and yet it seemed to her as if she was angry because he was not still dangling after her! really it was quite ridiculous this feeling—quite preposterous to feel displeased at seeing the attentions she had declined transferred to another! Yet

notwithstanding this arguing with herself,
she rather allowed him to take her hand
than gave it to him, on his coming from
an inner apartment, where he had been on
her arrival, with a countenance all radiant
with delight, on learning from Mrs. Hamilton that she had consented to be of
the party he had made for her, and answered his inquiries after her father in a
manner that made him stare at her—for
what had he done to offend her?

His look made her recollect herself; and
blushing deeply, she was about asking
some question about the place he had been
looking at, calculated to lead to a recon-
ciling conversation between them, when
ere she could give utterance to it, Myra
gave him a whispered message to one of
her sisters, and under the pretext of being fearful he would not deliver it correctly, almost instantly followed him.

He was almost immediately surrounded
by the whole set, and from the gay badi-
nage that ensued, found it next to impossible to break away. And for what

should he? why should he leave those
who seemed to take pleasure in conversing
with him, to join a person who looked so
cold upon him as Grace? no, he felt offended, and would leave her to herself.
Yet, when dancing was about commencing, he could not help anxiously watching her, but she had no idea of dancing;
in vain she was asked and solicited—with
the sister of her heart, her beloved Rose,
so recently lost to her, she could not think
of joining in such an amusement.

Delamere seemed to enjoy every thing
—it was the least return he could make
for the kind hospitality he experienced;
but his thoughts, his looks, wandered—
he wanted to catch the accents of Grace,
to hear those remarks that seemed to give
such pleasure to those who, from time to
time, took a seat beside her.

If he watched her, Mrs. Mayfield watched him, and at length becoming absolutely provoked by the involuntary inattention which she was the cause of to his
pretty partner Myra, suddenly joined her,

and telling her, in an under tone, she was
sure merely looking on must be a stupid
affair for her, said, she would not press
her longer stay, in consequence of thinking so, if she had a mind to avail herself
of some the servant-men being about going
to the village.

Grace took the hint, and immediately
rose to depart: she did so with a heavy
heart, for she saw a very great likelihood of Delamere being entangled in
the net she was aware would be spread
for him, and there was hardly a connexion he could form she could more have
disliked the idea of, than one with the
Mayfields, since there was hardly one, she
was certain, that would be more likely to
detach or estrange him from all his old in-
timates, they were so extremely worldly
and selfish. She knew of the affair between Myra and Falkiner—of her having
encouraged his addresses, contrary to what
was known to be the wishes of his parents,
and engaged herself to be his the moment
he was of age, consequently, that if she

married Delamere, it would be entirely
out of interested motives. How did she
wish that he might be timely apprized of
this! but with the pains that would be
taken to keep him in ignorance of all that
might frustrate the views of the family,
she conceived there was very little chance
of any thing of the kind, and sighed to
think of such a heart as his being thrown
away.

Strandmore, the place to which the St.
Doulagh's party, as already stated, was
going, was a romantically-situated village
on the coast, straggling over very high
hills, at the foot of which stretched a most
beautiful strand; the bay was formed by
two immense promontories, or headlands,
against the extreme points of which the
restless waves for ever dashed with fury,
while from every part of the village the eye
ranged over a vast expanse of Neptune's
dark domain. Of a fine summer morning, nothing could be more delightful than
to inhale the refreshing breezes from this,
or view the gentle swell of the rippling

waves, as they broke, with a kind of drowsy murmur, on the shore; but when this mighty mass of waters became agitated by a coming storm, while the cries of gulls, the sure precursors of one, assailed the ear in every direction, then indeed, from the images of dread with which it filled the fancy, was the sight of it appalling; more especially when, if a vessel got embayed in foul weather, destruction was all but inevitable.

The village consisted of a few pleasant private residences, several ranges of commodious lodging-houses, and an excellent hotel, the place in which our party proposed taking up their short residence. Delamere, whose guests they were given to understand they were to consider themselves, preceded them, to see that every thing was properly prepared for their reception, and about dinner-time, escorted by young Mayfield, they arrived, and found an elegant dinner awaiting them. Mrs. Mayfield was all delight; but inten

on losing no opportunity for forwarding
her plan, she chose to seem to consider
every thing as a compliment to her and
her daughters—" Really it was quite taking too much trouble for them, and she
didn't know how she and the girls could
ever be sufficiently obliged for all dear Mr.
Delamere had done to render them pleasant;" and without any hesitation, she
usurped the head of the table, to which it
certainly had been the intention of William to hand Mrs. Hamilton; while Myra
placed herself by him at one side, and one
of her sisters at the other; and in the same
way on their going out in the evening to
walk, each took an arm, to the utter precluding of any particular attention to
Grace.

Delamere felt vexed and disconcerted;
he had not by any means calculated on
being so entirely monopolized and engrossed; but in vain he sought to have a
little conversation now and then with
Grace: if for a moment he succeeded in
disengaging himself from the sisters, the

brother was sure to be on the alert, having received his cue, and instantly possessed himself of Grace, who, but for the object he had in view, that of aiding the designs of his sisters, would certainly not have been honoured with any attention from him, her well-known want of fortune rendering her of no consequence in his eyes, or rather a person it was a condescension to notice.

Mrs. Hamilton's having a number of old friends and acquaintances at the place, and in consequence being continually on the gad from one to the other, was the means of leaving her more at the mercy of the party than would otherwise have been the case. Still, while she felt herself evidently neglected, matters were so managed, that no one could have believed she had any grounds for complaint—the mother was all maternal solicitude, the sisters caressing, and the son entirely devoted to her; while Myra was so particularly fond of her, that she would share no other person's apartment, the hotel, from having other company in it, not being sufficiently large to accommodate so large a party with distinct chambers.

Grace, who by no means wanted self-possession, would certainly not have permitted the arts that were practised to keep her and William asunder to succeed, had she been aware how much it was his wish to have her a little more to himself; but prepossessed with the idea of having offended him in a way not to be forgiven, and with his really admiring Myra, she could not think of forcing herself more upon the party.

Left pretty much to herself, through the almost eternal gadding of Mrs. Hamilton at one side, and the manœuvring of the party at the other, Grace sought amusement in rambling about where she was least likely to meet with observation. In these moments, feeling indeed the want of a bosom friend, how continually did her thoughts revert to the idea of Rose!

how truly did she feel that her loss to her could never be supplied!

The shore, all along in this direction, was indented with a number of romantic coves, the little strands of which were completely strown over with a variety of beautiful shells and pebbles. Grace delighted to frequent these romantic places, attracted by the grandeur of the overhanging cliffs, perforated and shattered by the conflicting elements to which they were exposed, into a variety of fantastic forms, the resemblance of pyramids, arches, and ruinated fortresses, all begirt with the streaming weeds of decay and desolation, while seals, cormorants, and gulls, filled up every nook and crevice, mingling their plaintive and discordant cries, according to the variations of the weather, with the hoarse murmurs of the sounding deep.

After being near a week at Strandmore —" How does your friend Grace dispose of herself every day until dinner-time?" one morning inquired Delamere of Myra, knowing that she was not Mrs. Hamilton's

companion in her gaddings, and finding
she never walked out with the sisters.

"Really I don't know," said Myra—
"she has always made some excuse or
other for not walking out with the girls
and me, so I suppose she don't like it;
but perhaps," with something like a slight
sneer, "she may be writing a poem on
the beauties of the place, with which she
means to surprise us."

"Perhaps so," replied Delamere, gravely; "if she attempted the subject, I know
no one more calculated to do it justice."

"Oh yes, I know that," said Myra, in no
slight alarm at the idea of having a little
betrayed herself—"I know she has quite a
talent for writing; but," and her fair bosom heaved a gentle sigh, and with a look
of the most alluring softness, she cast her
blue eyes to the ground, "she is a talent-
ed being in every respect."

"Yes," said Delamere, with a smile,
and taking the hand of the little syren;
"but she has not engrossed every charm;"

and he kissed the white hand he had involuntarily taken.

All was safe then; and but a little more
management, and the field would be won.
—" Do you know," she said to Grace, as
they were dressing together for dinner,
" Delamere has been inquisitive about
the manner in which you pass the mornings; he is beginning to fear you may
feel yourself neglected, or—for to be sure
that could not be the case, as you know
it is our wish to have you always with us;
and indeed I wish you would begin to walk
out with us; for if you were with me, he
would not be able to draw me away by
myself, as he is continually trying to do;
and really he is getting so teasing. But
won't you walk with us for the future?
for, as I was going to say, he said——
but I really have quite confused myself."

" Oh, well; no matter," said Grace; " I
understand you sufficiently."

" And you will then," a little alarmed,
" walk out with us sometimes?"

" Oh yes, if you wish it so much," re-

plied Grace with a smile, the peculiar expression of which was not altogether lost
upon Miss Myra, and excited a degree of
confusion that made her avert her looks to
conceal it. But however Grace might
have doubted her truth in other respects,
she certainly did not discredit her insinuation with regard to Delamere; and the
result of which was, an involuntary air of
coldness towards him when they met at
dinner, and a studied avoidance of every
attention he wished to pay her.

Delamere was at first surprised, then
became piqued, and finally desisted from
any further attempts to attach himself particularly to her, as on this evening he had
been more than ever tempted to do.

But to detach William from Grace was
not sufficient for the furtherance of Miss
Myra's designs; in the walks which she
took with her sisters, who had themselves
to consider, and of course preferred the
direction in which they would have the
best chance of being seen, they were continually meeting with something or some

one to divert his attention from her, and
break in upon their conversation. Accordingly, with all the innocence of artless
simplicity, she said she had a great secret
to confide to him—namely, her wanting
to surprise mamma with a sketch of some
of the romantic scenery of the place; and
so proposed that he should secretly accompany her to the spot she had fixed on
for the purpose of taking it, either to
amuse her by reading, while she was employed with her pencil, or else assist her by
his advice. Of course, whatever were the
secret feelings or wishes of William, he
could not be so ungallant as to refuse her,
and accordingly to the place alluded to
they sped the next morning.

. Now it happened that this spot was the
very identical one fixed on by Grace for
really taking some views to surprise Mrs.
Hamilton with. The rocks were here
completely perpendicular, dented and
delved into a variety of fantastic forms,
pillars, caves, and arches, the entrance to

wild intricacies, within which all was
evening gloom and solemnity, while at
times a cabin child, or sportive kid, was
seen peeping over the very edge of the
cliffs, from which hung many a streaming
wreath of wild flowers, intermingled with
the sedge of the rock, a grey tint a little
further off betraying the hovel to which
they belonged; and all, in short, was wild,
romantic, picturesque, and well adapted
for the pencil. Completely engrossed by
hers, Grace heeded not the approach of
Delamore and his companion, till they
were almost close to her. That they had
not come to seek her, she was certain; and
perhaps the persuasion was the cause of
her not appearing any way discomposed
by their sudden appearance. But Delamore was taken by surprise; he had not
expected to find her there, and yielding
to a sudden sensation of delight at beholding her, he sprang over a few impediments in the way, and placing himself beside her, involuntarily passed one arm
round her waist, while with his other

hand he took hold of hers, to examine the sketch it contained.—" And so this is the way in which you are employing yourself every morning!" he said. " Why make such a secret of it? one or two of us could not have interrupted you, by being allowed to accompany you here."

" I made no secret of it," replied Grace.

" No!"

" No; for no one asked me a question on the subject."

" Now how can you say so, Miss O'Neil!" said the cruelly-mortified Myra, from the spot on which Delamere had left her, divided from the one where Grace was sitting by little pools of water and pieces of rock. " You know you never mentioned to any one what you were doing, so I am sure that was making a mystery of it.—But, dear me, I had no idea that this was such a nasty, plashy place," drawing her skirt tight round her; " do, Mr. Delamere, let us leave it for some other."

But Delamere could not attend to her; he was sitting close to Grace—he was holding her, unresistingly, to the heart that was so long panting to have her folded to it; and, in short, he could not bring himself to stir.—" Nay, I am sure," he said, " a more enchanting spot than this cannot be found. Besides, this is the very place, you know, you fixed on yourself for taking a sketch from."

" Yes; but that was before I knew what Miss O'Neil was about. You don't suppose, after her picking out the best of every thing, I shall employ myself in copying the fag end of cliffs, and all the rubbish she has chosen to reject."

Neither Grace nor Delamere could forbear laughing aloud at this remark. Miss Myra got quite affronted; the pretty pink colour of her cheeks became crimson, and her eyes sparkled with more than wonted animation.—" I seem to have amused you," she said ; " but I must confess, I don't think it over polite to laugh at one".

" Yet who, my dear girl," cried Grace, " could forbear laughing at your remark, as if I had absolutely made an end of the

cliffs as I sketched them? Come, skip
over these stones to me; and while we
are engaged, William (how pleased was
William to hear her call him William!)
will amuse us with the book I see peeping
out of his pocket."

Myra hesitated; but the danger of betraying any further petulance suddenly
occurring, she forced herself to accept the
invitation of Grace. Nothing, however,
was further from her thoughts than to
employ herself in the manner that was expected; indeed she could not, for having
no real taste or genius for drawing, to
sketch from nature was a stretch quite beyond her abilities: she affected, however,
to be very busy; and pretending to think
Delamere wanted to have a peep at what
she was doing, played off a thousand little
childishnesses, that she thought quite alluring.

Sick of her fooleries, Delamere at
length began to read; the subject was the
Bride of Abydos; from the perusal of this,
the other poems of the delightful author

came under discussion, and this discussion
naturally led to one on the respective productions of the other poets of the present
day. Myra got quite into an agony; having very little taste for any thing but
what was just calculated to render her
more alluring to the eye, she knew hardly
any thing of what her companions were
conversing about, and to have it discovered that she was the superficial little creature she was in reality, was absolute torture to her pride. Like all the rest of her
family, she made pretensions to superior
sense and accomplishments—pretensions
which the keenness and quickness of her
mother were no small means of having
supported; and to have these at length
detected to be false ones—the laugh—
the sneer, so often levelled at others, retorted upon her, was a thought that was
not endurable; but what was to be done?
She had no mother, no sister now at hand
to extricate her from the dilemma in which
she found herself; if she remained silent,
it would evince her stupidity, and if she

spoke, she would betray what she was so anxious to conceal. She tried a thousand ways to interrupt the conversation, or give a turn to it; but it was too interesting to those who were pursuing it to allow her petty little artifices to succeed; now she was frightened by the little crabs that were crawling about in the little pools of water—then she was sure the tide was coming in, and there was no knowing the danger that might ensue from their remaining longer where they were: at last she espied a tuft of weeds, or wild flowers, upon the point of one of the rocks, and she would get it for the examination of Charlotte, she was such a botanist. The rock was steep and slimy, and on turning to descend it, she either was, or pretended to be frightened, and called to Delamere to come to her assistance. He started up; but ere he had time to stretch out his hand to her, she made a sudden spring, and fell into his arms, or rather upon one of them, with such force, that he staggered back with the pain inflicted by the shock.

Grace started up.—" You are seriously hurt, I fear," she said to him.

William tried to make light of the matter; but it was evident to her his arm had sustained an injury, and she could not help being extremely provoked by the circumstance that had occasioned it.— " How could you be so ridiculous?" she demanded of Myra. " You really have been more like a restless child this half hour than a grown-up person."

" And I may ask, how can you be so ill-natured, as to seem to suppose that I would hurt any one intentionally, but more particularly dear Mr. Delamere!" cried Myra, hanging about him, and putting her handkerchief to her eyes.

" Come, come, our best plan now will be to hasten from this," said Grace, " that he may obtain the assistance I am sure he requires;" and they accordingly quitted the spot.

At the door of the hotel, Delamere parted from them, with an injunction that they should say nothing about what had

happened, as it really was not worth thinking about. Grace, however, was of a contrary opinion, and fearful he might not,
out of a false delicacy for the feelings of
Myra, do what was requisite for himself,
she had hardly been in her chamber.—to
which she repaired the moment she re-
entered the hotel, Miss Myra appearing
quite huffed with her—above a minute, ere
she decided on seeking him, to insist on
his having some surgical advice. As she
descended the stairs, she thought she heard
his voice in the sitting-room, and accordingly entered: but what words can give
an adequate idea of the confusion into
which she was thrown, or rather the shock
her feelings received, on beholding Myra,
the only person in the room with him, absolutely reclining against his bosom, with
her cheek apparently pressed to his!

Grace involuntarily started back, and
instantly retreated. She thought she
heard him calling after her; but she would
not wait to ascertain—the emotion she
was in would not permit her to delay

seeking refuge in her chamber; hopes had
begun to be conceived—expectations to
be experienced, that what was just
witnessed had completely destroyed.—
Well, well; who had she to blame for
this but herself? Had she not positively
declared to William, that in no other
light than that of a friend would she ever
more be induced to consider him, or allow him to consider her? And after this,
could she blame him for thinking no more
about her? Certainly not. But then if
he had really loved her as sincerely as he
pretended, would he so readily have taken
her at her word? And then to fix upon
a being so every way undeserving of his
affections—a heartless, selfish little co-
quette, who was actually jilting another
for him! in short, to form a connexion
that she well knew would be the means
of estranging him from all his old regards!
She could not help weeping in bitterness
over the thought, and wishing, that since
matters were likely to turn out in such a
way, she had never seen him again, feel-

ing that the William he was seven years ago, and the William he was now, were indeed very distinct beings.

END OF VOL. II.

Printed by J. Darling, Leadenhall-Street, London.

NEW PUBLICATIONS

PRINTED FOR

A. K. NEWMAN & CO.

LEADENHALL-STREET, LONDON.

———

	£.	s.	d.
Earl Osric, or the Legend of Rosamond, a romance, by Mrs. Isaacs, 4 vols	1	4	0
The Astrologer, or the Eve of St. Sebastian, a romance, by I. M. H. Hales, Esq. 3 vols.	0	18	0
The Contested Election, or a Courtier's Promise, by A. M. Ennis, Author of Ireland, or the Montague Family, &c. 3 vols.	0	18	0
Orientalist, or a Season in Ireland, 2 vols	0	15	0
Tales of Imagination, by the author of Bachelor and Married Man, 3 vols.	0	18	0
Farmer of Inglewood Forest, by Mrs. Helme, 3d edit. 4 vols.	1	0	0
Lovers and Friends, or Modern Attachments, by Ann of Swansea, Author of Chronicles of an Illustrious House, &c. 5 vols.	1	7	6
Eleanor, or the Spectre of St. Michael's, a Romance, by Miss C. D. Haynes, 5 vols	1	7	6
Very Strange, but very True, or the History of an old Man's Young Wife, by Francis Lathom, 2d edit. 4 vols.	1	0	0
Sir Francis Darell, by R. C. Dallas, Esq. 4 vols.	1	8	0
The Feuds of Luna and Perollo, a Romantic Tale of the Sixteenth Century, 4 vols.	1	2	0
The Midnight Wanderer, or a Legend of the Houses of Altenberg and Lindendorf, by Margaret Campbell, 4 vols.	1	2	0

[4c

THE CASTLE CHAPEL.

A ROMANTIC TALE.

Printed by J. Darling, Leadenhall-Street, London.

THE

CASTLE CHAPEL.

A Romantic Tale.

IN THREE VOLUMES.

BY

REGINA MARIA ROCHE,

AUTHOR OF THE

CHILDREN OF THE ABBEY; BRIDAL OF DUNAMORE; CLERMONT; DISCARDED
SON; HOUSES OF OSMA AND ALMERIA; MUNSTER COTTAGE BOY;
TRADITION OF THE CASTLE; TRECOTHICK BOWER; MAID
OF THE HAMLET; VICAR OF LANSDOWNE, &c.

VOL. III.

LONDON:

PRINTED FOR
A. K. NEWMAN AND CO. LEADENHALL-STREET.

1825.

THE

CASTLE CHAPEL.

A Romantic Tale.

———

IN THREE VOLUMES.

———

BY

REGINA MARIA ROCHE,

AUTHOR OF THE

CHILDREN OF THE ABBEY; BRIDAL OF DUNAMORE; CLERMONT; DISCARDED
SON; HOUSES OF OSMA AND ALMERIA; MUNSTER COTTAGE BOY;
TRADITION OF THE CASTLE; TRECOTHICK BOWER; MAID
OF THE HAMLET; VICAR OF LANSDOWNE, &c.

———

VOL. III.

———

LONDON:

PRINTED FOR

A. K. NEWMAN AND CO. LEADENHALL-STREET.

1825.

THE

CASTLE CHAPEL.

CHAPTER I.

"———————————————Sudden he starts,
Shook from his tender trance, and, restless, runs
To glimmering shades, and sympathetic glooms,
Where the dun umbrage o'er the falling stream
Romantic hangs; there, through the pensive dusk,
Strays, in heart-thrilling meditation lost:
                                Or on the bank
Thrown, amid drooping lilies, swells the breeze
With sighs unceasing, and the brook with tears.
Thus, in deep anguish, he consumes the day,
Nor quits his deep retirement till the moon
Peeps through the chambers of the fleecy east.
                        Then forth he walks,
Beneath the trembling languish of her beam;
                        Or while the world,
And all the sons of care, lie hush'd in sleep,
Associates with the midnight shadows drear."

WE left Eugene in a very awkward predicament in England. What his agitation was, on positively ascertaining the nature of the place into which he had been inveigled, may easily be conceived. Convinced, however, to give way to the feelings produced by the discovery, could answer no good end, but quite the reverse, he constrained himself to appear composed, and in the course of a few days reaped the benefit of the circumstance; it being deemed hardly probable that a person who appeared so collected, could be as described: the doubt led to a conversation, that developing the treachery that had been practised against him, he was forthwith released, with a firm conviction on his mind, that the person to whom he was indebted for what had lately happened, was the same through whose machinations he had already suffered so much, namely, Wilkinson. His impatience to return home was so great, that he did not write another letter, and accordingly arrived most unexpectedly at St. Doulagh's, just five days after the departure of Grace for Strandmore.

As previously settled, it was intended to have kept him in ignorance of what had happened till she was sent for; but through the blundering of one of the servants, this intention was defeated; and, on seeing the state to which Eugene was reduced by the disclosure, Mr. Hamilton opposed her being sent for, under the conviction that she could be of no immediate service to him, and the consequent cruelty therefore there would be in interrupting her present enjoyment; and accordingly, in pursuance of his advice and remonstrances, it was determined that she should know nothing of the arrival of Eugene till her return home.

From the absolute distraction of Eugene, on learning the untimely fate of her on whom his soul doated, it might well indeed be imagined that he was at present incapable in any way of being soothed or comforted—that, in short, till his grief had had time, in some degree, to spend or exhaust itself, it would not merely be

useless, but probably irritating, to attempt
to argue with or console him.   Thinking
in this manner, Mr. Hamilton did not attempt to unite with his family in opposing
his departure from St. Doulagh's, to the
place where Rose had died; more especially as Mrs. Brady would accompany
him, under the pretext of his not being
able to obtain access to her cottage, in
which he purposed taking refuge from all
who would be likely to intrude upon his
sorrow, without her being with him.

But little was Mr. Hamilton aware, in
advising him to be left for a time to the
unrestrained indulgence of his feelings,
what those feelings were; that it was not
simply grief he felt—natural grief, for the
death of one so young, so lovely, so fondly beloved—but grief heightened by remorse, by self-upbraidings, by the torturing thought of the grave having closed
over the beauteous form of her he had
wronged, without his having had the
power of speaking his compunction for
that wrong, or making any kind of repa-

ration for it. Oh, if any thing can allay the pangs of a self-accusing spirit, it is the idea of having made some atonement for that which it mourns! but without any hope of ever being able to do this, who can describe the acuteness of its anguish?

Mrs. Brady, in her indignant resentment at the conduct of Eugene, had fully determined on revealing to him every particular about Rose; but when she saw how completely he was overwhelmed by merely hearing of her death, without learning how she came by it, she began to feel a relenting towards him, that gradually induced her to give up this harsh intention; and well it was she did so, since, no doubt, madness would have followed the disclosure of the truth.

From what has been already stated of the habitation of Mrs. Brady, it must appear that no place could be better adapted for the indulgence of such feelings as Eugene's than it was. Here indeed was gloom and privacy, wildness and solitude—here he had no dread of intrusion, no fear of any observation that could occasion a restraint upon his grief. Mrs. Brady made a few ineffectual efforts to prevent its uninterrupted indulgence, and then following the advice of Mr. Hamilton, left him to himself—advice, as already hinted, owing to his utter ignorance of his real feelings.

All the favourite haunts of Rose were pointed out to him, for if any thing could impart a gleam of pleasure to his afflicted mind, it was the thought of threading in her footsteps, sighing where she had sighed, and breathing her name where his own had been so often uttered by her. Unable to taste the repose he was urged to seek, his restless pillow was often quitted for the monastery, where day's returning light frequently surprised him; here too evening often stole upon him unnoticed. But not to contemplate the remains of Gothic grandeur it exhibited, its clustering pillars, lessening in gradual perspective, or the pointed arches they supported, did Eugene frequent it. No—

seated on the fragment of some old tomb,
absorbed in one sorrowful contemplation,
his eye ran, unconsciously, along the vista
of the chancel, green with the ivy that
hung suspended from the arches, or were
mechanically fixed upon some lofty door-
way, or dilapidated window, through the
light tracery of which the distant mountains were beheld, now lit up with all the
magic of sunshine, now fading into the
cold purple hues of closing day, while
wild flowers and long grass hung streaming about it—no, he noticed not the
grandeur, the sublimity, by which he was
surrounded; he was alive only to one
idea, the idea of being in the place chosen
by her he lamented, for the indulgence of
that consuming anguish that had weighed
her to an untimely grave.

A mere worldling would have advised
his flying the dismal spot—would have
represented the folly of grieving so immo-
derately for what, sooner or later, must
have come to pass—would have recom-
mended change of scene, and gaiety, and

amusement, as a means of relieving his sorrow; but, alas! those who prescribe such remedies for the cure of grief know little of the real nature of it; that to a heart wounded like his, nothing that is not in unison with its feelings, that does not actually seem to feed its sorrow, can be of service; that there is an absolute indulgence in the enjoyment of these—an indulgence that can only be experienced in the stillness of solitude, amidst the quietude and loneliness of nature. But as it is only in the hour of affliction we view the world in the light it merits, so in that hour we naturally turn from it in disgust, to seek consolation whence alone it can be derived, in the hopes and promises held out by religion.

How awful indeed is the visitation of Heaven! and how vain for man to strive to argue with us while writhing under it! How mournful to the soul, to think that those we loved as life, shall no more return to dry our weeping eyes—that the voice that was music to our ears is silenced for ever—that the form it was rapture to gaze on is now cold, and shrouded, the prey of worms, and crumbling into dust! What could support or console us under these heart-rending reflections? not the forced condolence of pretended sympathies—not the bustle, and glare, and glitter of public assemblies!—no, the hopes alone held out by Revelation, of a happy reunion hereafter with those whom we here lament.

But at times, either the reflections of Eugene were so intolerable, or else the necessity of making a stand against his present feelings so evident, that he now and then was led to try and make an effort for diverting his thoughts, by exploring the romantic scenery that environed the monastery. Insensibly almost the contemplation of it would call his soul abroad, and by soothing him, in a degree, permit him to attend to what he saw. In pleasing admiration he would then dwell on the woods that clothed the steep sides

of the mountains, as their sea of leaves
waved in the breeze; hearken to the
cheerful sound of woodland harmony, that
seldom failed to fill the vale below—the
song of day's harbinger, its several divisions, far above art, as it, a little spot, floated
on the sunbeam; the restless pye, so pert
and garrulous; the cuckoo, mocking the vil-
lage-bells; the jay, a very termagant, that
seemed to scold all day; the glossy raven,
in the grass, making rude courtship to his
negro mate; the little goldfinch, plucking
the groundsel's feathered seed, or war-
bling, from some bough, its melodious
song; the swallow, skimming the glassy
pool, now dipping, then shooting, with
rapid speed, along; the rook, winging his
way to the high wood; the smoothly-sail-
ing owl, with his shrill *to-whit*, sending
the wanton mouse scouring home, from
his gambols round the primrose-head—
nothing escaped comment. Thus would
he wander, like the melancholy Jacques,
musing and moralizing on all he saw;

now lost amidst the gloom of woods, now seated beneath some social elm, or venerable oak; and such is the turn that violent grief and sorrow often take; the human mind must have something to occupy it, and incapable, while under the influence of these feelings, of any serious exertion, is led to dwell on what, in other moods, it might hardly have noticed.

His mind, on these occasions restored to a slight degree of composure, Eugene failed not to endeavour to argue himself into resignation, and call fortitude to his aid; but in a moment, how would all his efforts for this purpose be overthrown, by the sudden recurrence of his thoughts to the cause of Rose's death—the secret sorrow, the internal upbraidings which he was convinced had accelerated it! instantly would the vehemence of sorrow be renewed, and with precipitation he would fly to the dismal scene that was most congenial to it; not without keen reproaches for having tried, for having formed a wish to banish from his mind the idea of her

whose early death he was convinced was
imputable to him, and whose memory
therefore he was doubly bound to cherish.
—And was she really dead? he would
sometimes demand of himself, with a flood
of tears—she whom he had left so lovely,
with life just opening to her view—was
she already cut off, like a flower untimely
cropped? yes, like a dewdrop, as pure,
as bright, as transient, she had sparkled
for a minute, was exhaled, and gone to
heaven. Fain would he still have remained in ignorance of her, fain still have believed that they should meet again.

As he sat one evening within the ruined pile, dwelling, as usual, in bitter sad-
ness on the irreparable loss he had sustained, a rising moon, pouring a flood of
splendour through the eastern window,
and partially touching the surrounding objects, so as to produce an indescribably
beautiful scene of chequered light and
shadow, gave a heightening to the solemn
grandeur of the place, that almost imperceptibly drew his attention.—"And sure,"

he cried, with emotions of suddenly kindling awe and admiration, " if permitted
by Heaven to visit this nether scene, this
is the holy place the angelic spirit of my
Rose would choose to appear in. But no,
she will not return to bless my sight again—
she has reascended to her native skies, and
all that occupied her here on earth is now
forgotten. Since she will not come within the reach of my senses then again,
why, why should I not strive to banish
her my mind? but what base ingratitude,
to wish to detach my thoughts from her,
who, through my means, has been hurried into the oblivion of the tomb! No,
I would not, if I could, be guilty of such
ingratitude. The earth covers all that
my soul held dear—but whilst I live she
will still live too in my heart. Yet, oh
that I could behold her once more! could
catch a glimpse of her, as she now is, a
beatified spirit! But, no, no! vain is the
wish—she has passed the bourne whence
none return.—But, good God! what is
that I see? do my eyes deceive me? is

my fancy exercising itself to mock me?"
he exclaimed, as with the wildest emotion
he started up, at the sight of a figure,
standing motionless beside the mutilated
altar.

CHAPTER II.

" ——————Trúly I'll devise some slanders;
——————————one doth not know
How much an ill word may impoïson liking."

DELAMERE was heartily vexed by what
had occurred, the *mal-à-propos* entrance of
Grace into the drawing-room. He had
begun to see a dawning of hope, a gradually increasing kindliness of manner, a
something, in short, that almost tempted
or inclined him to think, had they met
before the writing of her renouncing letter, it would not perhaps have been couch-
ed in such decisive terms. Imagining this,
how provoking to think of any misappre-
hension being created at her side, that perhaps, from what she had seen, she might
be led to conceive he no longer had a
thought or wish about her, and according-

ly give up all further ones herself about
him!

Could he have explained what the real
fact was, that the young lady had actually
been on the watch to follow him into the
drawing-room, to express what she felt at
the accident that was attributable to her,
and that of her own accord she had, unconsciously of course he concluded, inclined against his bosom, and leant her fair
cheek, moist with tears of apprehension,
and regret, and anxiety, to his——but this
of course was quite out of the question, a
thing not to be thought of, or excused,
or in any way justified, but by there being
a positive claim to the disclosure of the
truth.

But Grace he well knew was not deficient in acute penetration, and by deter-
mining to be no longer foiled in his attempts to pay her those attentions his
heart dictated, he trusted he should be
able to make her quickly comprehend
what he wished, namely, that there was
at present nothing serious between him

and any other person, and which indeed he was now beginning to think there never would be, without coming to a full explanation with her, let that explanation be ever so long prevented.

With all her efforts to appear as usual, Grace still continued in a state of discomposure, or emotion, that kept her from making her appearance again amongst the party, till summoned to join them at dinner.

Light as Delamere made of what had happened at the cove, his arm had really sustained an injury, that rendered him unable to use it again immediately; in consequence his seat at the foot of the table was vacated to young Mayfield.

Mrs. Mayfield no sooner perceived this, than she motioned him to one next to her at the head of the table. William, however, feigning not to have noticed her invitation, hastened to place himself beside Grace.

Mrs. Mayfield and her daughters involuntarily exchanged looks; but they were

all adepts at self-command; so all was in an
instant smooth and smiling as ever: and
—" I should really like, dear Mr. Delamere," began the elder lady, affecting ignorance of the circumstance, for as usual,
the moment she returned from her walk,
Miss Myra had hastened to disclose all
that occurred in the course of it to her
mamma and sisters, " to know how you
came by that injury your arm has met
with—I hope through no inadvertence of
any one here?"

" My dear ma'am, 'tis really so insigni-
ficant a matter, 'tis quite ridiculous to
speak of it," said Delamere.

" Nay, I can't be persuaded 'tis of so
very little consequence; at all events, I
know some one," and she glanced signifi-
cantly at Myra, " that does not consider
it so; but then, to be sure, a very little
thing alarms and agitates her—she is so
gentle, so timid, or, in short, has so much
sensibility—too much, as I often think,
for her happiness; for if any thing hap-
pens to afflict any one she regards, she is

so miserable: but then real sensibility gives
so many charms to its possessor, and there
is withal something so very delightful in
it—for, as an elegant writer has observed,
' 'tis the source indeed of all that's precious
in our joys, as well as costly in our sorrows."

Delamere had never so great an inclination to laugh outright. There is such a
thing as a person's making themselves too
amiable; and this was the case with poor
Mrs. Mayfield at the instant. He had not
began absolutely to fathom the lady, but
still at times he was beginning to think
she was a little too sentimental, than
which nothing possibly can either be more
sickening or ludicrous.

Whether Mrs. Mayfield perceived any
slight working of the muscles, we cannot
pretend to say, but she gave a sudden, and
quite an adroit turn to the conversation;
proceeded, after a little general chitchat,
to express her hope that the accident of
the morning would not prevent his being
of Mrs. Benson's party that evening.

Delamere hesitated. Grace had decided against being of this party, owing to her dislike to mixing in any very large one, as she knew this would be, so immediately after the death of poor Rose; and William had heard her determination of remaining at home—and what might ensue from his doing the same, the opportunity it would afford for uninterrupted conversation, at once struck him; but then should she be disinclined to permit what he wished—should his seeking it be a means of putting her on her guard to prevent it? But the impulse of inclination was too powerful for resistance, and he accordingly replied to Mrs. Mayfield's question, by begging she would have the goodness, this one evening, to excuse his being her escort.

Mrs. Mayfield became still more alarmed—not from the idea of his being left *tête-à-tête* with Grace, for that she at once resolved should not be the case—but the wish she thought his choosing to remain at home seemed to intimate for it. However, as Mrs. Hamilton said, who was almost as great a quoter of proverbs as Sancho Panza himself—" Troy was not won in a day ;" it could not be expected that old impressions would be effaced in a moment, and so trying to keep up her hopes, and to flatter herself, that, by a little further management, all would yet turn out as she wished, she settled that Myra should not go to Mrs. Benson's, under the pretext of her nerves being so affected by what had occurred in the morning, as not to permit her, not choosing to give up going herself on account of the other girls.

The looks and manner of Delamere during dinner—his preference of a seat beside her, to the one to which he was invited by Mrs. Mayfield, at whose elbow Myra was always stationed at dinner, as a little young thing, still almost requiring to be under the paternal wing—above all, the earnestness with which he looked in her countenance, on her entering to dinner, had given to Grace a surmise of the truth, and in consequence she would per-

haps have been quite as well pleased with
a different arrangement about Myra. However, whatever she thought or felt on the
subject of this, she of course kept carefully locked up in her bosom, and made tea
for her companions, and laughed, and chatted, quite in her usual way, for somehow
she felt a heavy weight suddenly lifted off
her spirits.

Myra, as usual, did all in her power to
engross the attentions of Delamere exclu-
sively to herself, and for the purpose had
recourse to a thousand little artifices ; but
the gentleman was too polite, or too gallant, to permit her to succeed in these,
and their failure did not certainly tend to
render her smiles more natural.

At length, in hopes of making a diver-
sion in her favour by the circumstance, she
proposed a walk ; neither of her companions could make an objection to the proposal, the evening being delightful, and accordingly out they sallied, but in a different direction from the village, for, after
sending an excuse to Mrs. Benson, it

would not of course be the thing to have them seen parading about it.

The road they took was bordered at one side by the sea, and at the other by heathy fields, on which the evening sun was now shining with a placid lustre; the village murmur, intermingled at intervals with shouts of revelry and strains of music—for parties were continually taking place at Strandmore—followed them as they proceeded, gradually of course becoming still fainter and fainter, and all was calculated to attune the feelings to complacency, and revive agreeable recollections, if any were to be revived.

Whatever were the thoughts or recollections of Grace and William, there was an expression of serene pleasure in the countenance of one, of ineffable tenderness in the other, that certainly did not tend to heighten poor Myra's enjoyment of the walk.

They had proceeded some way, when a gentleman suddenly darted before them, from an adjacent field, and looking from one to the other, discovered to the alarmed Myra the features of her lover Falkiner, but wearing a very different expression to what they had heretofore done. Grace had a slight acquaintance with him, and distantly bowing to him, glanced at Myra. She saw her pale as death, nor did she wonder at it, for the looks of Falkiner indicated absolute fury. Myra returned her glance, with a look which seemed to say she implored her to try and extricate her from the predicament she was in. Grace took compassion on her, and as the only method she could devise for doing what she required, immediately led the way to a cabin hard by, under the pretext of wishing for a glass of water.

The cabin was empty, but voices were heard in the wild garden behind it, and thither Delamere went, to try if he could obtain for Grace what she pretended to require.

The moment he had left them—" Oh, if you have any pity on me," said the trembling Myra, " you'll go to that wretch without, and endeavour to prevail on him not to expose himself and me in the manner I see he meditates!"

" I should be very glad to oblige you," replied Grace; " but if you have given him any cause for reproach, is it probable that any thing I could say would have an effect upon him?"

" Oh, try! try!" cried Myra, in agony. " I am ruined and undone if he attempts entering into any explanation before Delamere! Say, if he'll only forbear speaking to me, he shall either see or hear from me in the course of a few hours."

Still Grace hesitated; it was a matter in which she did not by any means like to interfere. Why should she lend herself to the concealment of any thing that it was for the interest or happiness of another to have discovered?

Myra became almost convulsed with passion, or terror, perhaps both, at seeing her reluctance to oblige her.—" I see, I

see," she said, " what your good nature is!
but if not on my account, at least to prevent the risk of any unpleasant consequences, do not hesitate any longer to
comply with my entreaty. Should Falkiner address me in the manner I apprehend, 'tis not unnatural to suppose Delamere may resent the circumstance, and,
what then may not ensue!"

Startled by the suggestion, Grace instantly hurried from the cabin. She
found the incensed lover sullenly pacing
to and fro, as if positively decided on carrying into effect the purpose it was evident he had come for. Grace beckoned
him to a little distance from the cabin;
but it was many minutes ere, with all her
soft persuasiveness of manner, she could
accomplish her object in speaking to him,
that of trying to prevail on him to relinquish his intention of exposing his jilting
little mistress in the manner she merited;
nor could he finally be induced to do so
till she had given him Myra's assurance,

backed with her own, that she would see it kept.

While she was absent with him, William re-entered from the garden, and instantly missing her, inquired where she was? The looks of Falkiner had not been lost upon him, neither the glances exchanged between the ladies, and altogether there was a curiosity, an anxiety excited, that made him ask eagerly after Grace.

Myra hesitated: could she but induce him to believe that Falkiner was the lover of Grace, what a means might it not be of precipitating him into some overture to her! She saw that he suspected something, and that probably nothing but a falsehood would prevent inquiries that might be injurious to her. There certainly was a great risk of unpleasant consequences attached to the one she was considering about; but she felt persuaded something must be encountered to enable her to get over her present embarrassment; and accordingly, relying on her further invention, and the aid of her auxiliaries at home, to extricate her from any dilemma in which it might place her, she finally decided on venturing on it; and accordingly, in reply to Delamere's interrogation of where Grace was, told him, with a signifi- cant smile, not to ask her.

" But I must ask you," said Delamere, hastily setting down the cup of water he had procured, and making a step towards the door.

Myra caught hold of him—" Nay, I must beg you not to go out," she said; " I promised not to let you."

" Not let me!" exclaimed Delamere; " on what account, may I beg to know ?"

" Why, because—because Grace didn't like you should see her speaking to that gentleman we met just now—or rather that you should know she was acquainted with him."

" That gentleman ! who is he, pray ?"

" A—a Mr. Falkiner, I believe—do you know any thing of him ?"

" No, nothing—I know there is a family of that name living in some part of this county, but I know nothing particularly about any of them. But why should Grace dislike my knowing she is acquainted with this gentleman?"

" Why, because he is a lover she wants to get rid of."

" A lover—a lover of Grace's!" repeated Delamere, in a tone indicative of the most violent emotion.

" Yes, a lover of some standing."

" And why," asked Delamere, with a quivering lip, vainly trying to check the emotion he was in—" why try to get rid of him?"

" Indeed I don't know—because, as some people at least say, she thinks she might have a more advantageous offer.—But here you are making me tell things I know I shouldn't—indeed I wish you wouldn't ask me any more questions about the matter."

" But I must," cried Delamere, in agony; " if you wish to relieve me from downright——if you wish to oblige me," a little recollecting himself, "you'll tell me all you know of the affair."

"Well, I have gone so far, that I don't know how to draw back; but may I be sure that you'll not mention to any one what I tell you?"

"Assuredly—rely upon it that no unworthy use shall be made of any confidence reposed in me."

"Well, then, some people say——but the fact is, I suppose, not to fatigue you with repeating what people said, who perhaps knew nothing of the matter, Grace took some sudden whim into her head respecting him, for after encouraging him for months, and engaging herself to marry him, on his coming of age, before which he couldn't marry without the consent of his parents, just about the period that your return to St. Doulagh's was announced, she began to make an effort for breaking with him."

"And not before?"

"No, not before. And do you know

what the consequence of this has been?—
Falkiner has got jealous of you."

"Of me!" exclaimed Delamere again
with emotion.

"Yes, Grace told me so herself. He
accuses her, she says, of trying to break
with him, from a hope of your proposing
for her, through the intimacy or regard
that has always subsisted between you;
and that is the reason her apprehension of
his accusing her of this to you, and thus
injuring her perhaps in your esteem, that
she is so unwilling you should know any
thing about him. You must have seen
how pale she turned on meeting him just
now."

"No, I acknowledge I did not. If
either turned pale, I thought it was you
that did so."

"Me!—yes, I dare say I did; indeed I
felt myself turn pale, I was so agitated
by the fright I saw her in: but, silence,
here she comes! Don't stand so close to
me—there, do move away—lest she should
suspect we were talking of her."

Delamere did not require to be twice
urged to do this; he hastily turned towards the garden, as Grace entered, convinced, if their looks immediately encountered, some suspicion must be excited in
her mind of what he had been listening to.
But could he give credit to what he had
heard?—yet could he doubt it?—could he
give credit to what in a moment stripped
Grace of all her singleness of heart—her
sincerity—her beautiful ingenuousness—
of all that he had loved and delighted in
her for—that in a moment sunk her to the
low level of the artful and the selfish?
yet how could he imagine that a tale, so
well connected, was the invention of a moment? or, in short, that any one would
have dared to fabricate such a falsehood?
did not each circumstance tend to confirm
the truth of what he had heard? and indescribable was the agony of his soul at
the thought—the thought of being disappointed in the character of Grace—of her
nature being perverted from what nothing

could convince him it was not once; compared with this, the pain of thinking that in disposition she was indeed an altered being, slight would have been the pain of having her at once come forward to openly declare she was on the point of giving herself to another.

At length, making an effort to command himself, he inquired of Myra whether she felt herself yet inclined to return home? Again quite on the alert, Myra answered in the affirmative; convinced, from the looks of Grace, that if she encountered Falkiner again, there was no reason now to fear any thing unpleasant resulting from the circumstance.

The party accordingly left the cabin. Delamere had now but one arm at his command, the other being in a sling. On quitting the hotel, Myra had made an effort to seize it, but which he adroitly evaded, for the purpose of making Grace take it; but the case was now reversed—Myra had no occasion now to make an attempt to possess herself of it—it was voluntarily offered to her.

Grace was a little surprised; she saw there was something, but what, she could not possibly divine; for though she did not give Myra credit for all the virtues and amiable qualities she pretended to, she could not believe her capable of the baseness of insinuating any thing against her, at the very moment that she was trying to render her a service. Yet something certainly must have occurred, to occasion so great, so striking an alteration as was visible in the looks and manner of William. Could it be that there was any gentle reproach from Myra, for inattention to her during the preceding walk? in no other way could she account for what she noticed—no other cause could she assign for it; and if this were the case, there must be a more serious understanding between them than she had hitherto allowed herself to imagine. The incident of the morning recurred to her recollection; after what she had witnessed in the drawing-room, she now began to wonder how she could have doubted its being so; but she should not, she was sure, but for the manner in which William had conducted himself to her at dinner; well, that was owing to mere chance, she was now convinced, and she resolved not to let herself be deluded into a contrary belief, by any further attention she might accidentally receive from him. For those he had paid her, in the course of the day, he was now evidently trying to make amends to Myra. They laughed, and chatted, and whispered, and seemed totally to forget there was any other person of the party, they were so entirely engaged and engrossed by each other.

"How little one can make sure of any thing in life!" thought Grace, as she silently walked by them, or rather after them, her pace unconsciously slackening, as is the case when we fall into a meditative mood; "there was a time when I little thought I should ever have walked by the side of William, to be neglected for an-

other; and yet people are so attached to
this world, where such painful changes are
continually taking place—where the heart
is daily liable to be wounded by disappointments in friendship! As the poet
says—' the friend whose constancy we have
put to the test, we should grapple to our
heart with hoops of steel,' for how invaluable is such a one! I had such a one—so
tried, so approved—but she is gone, gone
to her native sphere!" and involuntarily
the humid eyes of Grace were raised to
the placid face of the evening sky. Delamere chanced to turn his head at the
moment; he started, at least Grace thought
so, and seemed on the point of speaking
to her, but suddenly checking himself, his
eyes reverted to his companion.

Well, this was a proof, a positive
proof, that there had been some little
pique between him and Myra on her account. Well, she should take care to prevent any thing of the kind again, for willingly she would not be the means of un-
easiness to William; and for the purpose,

her best plan would be, she thought, to return home without further delay; but there was a pang at the thought of thus entirely, unequivocally giving him up, that made her shrink a little from it; but she would consider about it, and by the morning, perhaps, see fully what was best to be done.

At the door of the hotel she parted from her companions, and repaired to her own room. She had hardly been here a moment, when she was followed by Myra, impatient to know what had passed between her and Falkiner.

Grace informed her; assuring her, that if the promise she gave him, by her desire, of hearing from her within an hour or two, was not kept, she might depend on seeing him at the hotel.

"The wretch!" exclaimed Myra, " I wish, with all my heart, he was in the Red Sea, with all the rest of the troubled and troublesome spirits one has heard of! But if I must write, what shall I say to him?"

"That's a curious question," said Grace. "After the long correspondence, by his account, you have had with him, I should suppose you could be at no loss to know how to address him now."

"How malicious!" muttered, or murmured, Myra between her white teeth; "but I shall have my revenge yet for all this.—But then you know," she said aloud, "this is to be a renouncing letter, and that is so very different."

"As you know what it is to be, I should presume," interrupted Grace, "you could be at no loss whatever about it; having read so much as you have done, I dare say you recollect the observation, ' that it is only when we are sitting down to write, *without being decided on our subject,* that we are perplexed about language."

Myra gave her another look, not quite so amiable a one as lady Pentweazle called up for the painter, and then turned to her rosewood writing-desk. Her letter was of the most deprecating kind; she assured Falkiner that her heart was still his

as much as ever; and in saying so probably
did not say what was untrue, and that of
course her promise of becoming his would
never have been revoked, but for the positive commands of her parents, who, persuaded that their union would never receive the sanction of his family, had insisted on her acceptance of the addresses
of Mr. Delamere; she therefore hoped,
that since it was not from any abatement
of affection, but absolute compulsion, she
broke with him, that he would not attempt to aggravate her unhappiness, by
unavailing reproaches or expostulations.

The moment she finished it, she sealed
it, lest Grace should ask to hear it; though
if she had, she was quite prepared to give
it a new reading. Having sealed, she applied to Grace to direct it.

"Excuse me," was the reply; "I cannot possibly do such a thing."

"Indeed but you must; for I have
burned my fingers in such a way with the
sealing-wax, that I can't do so myself."

Grace still hesitated; but a dread of

Falkiner's carrying his threat of coming to the hotel, if much longer delayed, and of what perhaps might be the result, at length induced her.

The moment Myra had succeeded in what she required, she ran off. She, at least, was a female that did not do things without having a reason for them; she had left Delamere in the drawing-room, and she now returned to him: in crossing the room, she dropped her letter, but without, of course, appearing conscious of having done so. Delamere, however, was not slow in noticing the circumstance. He hastened to take up the letter; the superscription caught his eye, and he became transfixed with agony, at the confirmation which all he had been trying to doubt received from seeing it. Yes, with a letter in his hand, directed in the well-known handwriting of Grace to Falkiner, it was absolutely impossible to any longer discredit the statement of Myra, as he had every instant felt himself becoming still more inclined, more tempted to do; not from conceiving it was a fabrication of hers, but merely the result of some misrepresentation of facts from others.

"Dear me, what are you looking at?" exclaimed Myra, suddenly turning round from a window, where something seemed to have attracted her regard for a minute; "Grace's letter to Falkiner, and which I promised to send for her directly! How could I be so careless as to drop it! but you won't tell;" and without waiting another instant, she snatched it out of his hand, and ran off to give it to a messenger.

"You know what that letter is about, no doubt?" said Delamere again, with rather a tremulous lip, on her return; "is— is it to appoint a meeting?"

"I am sure I can't tell. I have only the partial confidence of Grace; that is, I know nothing about her affairs but when she thinks I can serve her; but here she comes."

A little consideration had induced Grace indeed to descend to the drawing-room; by absenting herself from her companions,

she feared it might be supposed she was
offended by what had occurred in their
way back to the hotel, and not on any account now, from the persuasion she had
yielded to, would she have Delamere
imagine she thought any thing about
his attentions. The moment she entered,
Delamere hastily turned away to the
window at which Myra had again stationed herself. Not spoken to, Grace did
not speak; in silence she took up one of
the many books that were scattered about
the room, and sat quietly down to read.

"What a brilliant thought would it
not be," said Myra suddenly to Delamere,
"to surprise them at Mrs. Benson's! after
sending our excuses, our unexpected appearance there would quite excite a sensation."

"No doubt. But then with my arm
in a sling?"

"Oh, the very circumstance that should
make you anxious to go! for you don't
know the interest imparted to the appearance by the arm being in a sling."

"Indeed! Then since you assure me of this, of course I can't object to going."

"Very well then, if you don't, the sooner we set about preparing, you adonizing and I beautifying, the better, for quadrilles, I understand, will only be the order of the early part of the evening; and really one can't endure the bumkin country-dances now, with their up-and-down, cross over, and so forth."

"Why, no; they are not quite so well calculated for display as the others," said Delamere, laughing, perhaps a little sarcastically.

No notice whatever was taken of Grace; indeed it seemed to her as if they did not know she was in the apartment. Well, no matter; and she tried to fix her attention on her book. In a very short time they returned, equipped for the party, Myra being too fearful of Delamere's changing his mind, to permit herself to lose any time in dressing, as without him she would not go, for reasons, as her countryman says.

Lights were by this time brought in, and as Grace glanced at Myra, she certainly thought she looked very pretty.

Myra now chose to appear conscious that she was in the room.—" And what do you think of my dress?" she demanded, as she twirled herself round to let her view it. " This rose-coloured crape is certainly, I think, beauteous!—But, dear me! after all, what's the reason you are not coming with us? 'Tis really quite stupid your staying here by yourself," turning to Delamere to let him throw her shawl over her as she spoke, and then seizing his arm, without waiting for any reply from Grace, she vanished.

But all the gratification she anticipated to her vanity did not await her at Mrs. Benson's; lord Enniskerry, one of the most elegant Corinthians of the day, had put in the preceding one in his elegant yacht to Strandmore; and as he was loitering about the walk leading down immediately to the beach, the little Steyne of the place, he was attracted by our

party from St. Doulagh's; he inquired
who they were, and being told, in a general way, Mrs. Mayfield and her daughters,
of course concluded that Grace, who chanced this evening to join the set, and who
was the person indeed that had drawn his
attention to the party, was one of the family. He knew Mrs. Benson; and on
hearing of her party, put off his departure,
for the sake of obtaining an introduction
to the dark-eyed beauty that had so
charmed him. The moment he entered,
at his particular request he was introduced
to Mrs. Mayfield, and by her to her daughters; but in vain he looked about him for
the charmer of the preceding evening: at
length, unable to control his anxiety, to
know whether he should see her, any
longer, he inquired of Mrs. Mayfield whether her other lovely daughter was not
expected?

"My youngest girl?—my daughter
Myra?" said Mrs. Mayfield, every feature
beaming with delight, and casting her
eyes round her, to see whether any one was

sufficiently near to have heard the elating inquiry—" you compliment her, my lord; but I am sorry to say she will not be here to-night; she remains at home, out of kindness to a young friend, who was prevented by indisposition from coming."

" How amiable!" observed his lordship, but in a tone of evident chagrin; " but while we admire the motive that occasions her absence, we cannot but regret the circumstance."

Mrs. Mayfield bowed; she was all rapture to be so singled out—have such compliments paid: really it was enough to elevate her. But how unfortunate that Myra did not come, distinguished as she doubtless would have been, from what had occurred, by his lordship. She did not actually know whether he was a marrying man or no, but his evinced admiration, whether serious or not, could hardly have failed of leading to agreeable consequences —of making her more the fashion, and doubtless an object of still greater attraction to Delamere; and, in short, she be-

gan to think she would dispatch her
brother for her, with instructions to let
her know her reason for sending for her.
Having made up her mind to this, she
was in the act of holding up her fan to
beckon him to her, when there was a
slight bustle, or pressure, near the door,
and Miss Myra Mayfield and Mr. Delamere were announced. Was ever any
thing so delightful! Had Myra had
any secret intimation or whisper of being
so much wished for, that she came thus
unlooked for, and looking so beautiful?
She instantly hastened to meet her, lord
Enniskerry having that instant left her,
to pay his compliments to some one else
in the room, and proceeded to tell her of
all that had passed, namely, her own introduction to his lordship, and his particular
and flattering inquiries after her (Myra),
and the absolute agony into which he was
thrown on hearing she was not expected.

Myra listened to her with greedy ears.
—" And, dear me," she cried, with a sim-
per and side glance at Delamere, on whose

arm she continued leaning, to see how he was affected by hearing of the admiration she had excited, " I am sure I never thought," trying to look bashful, " that lord Enniskerry had noticed me in the least; or at least more particularly than ———"

" He's coming !" said her mother, touching her arm, and directly stepping forward to meet him.—" Well, my lord," she said, " I am happy to tell you I am able to introduce my daughter Myra to you, whom you were so good as to honour by your recent inquiries. She's just come in—most unexpectedly released from the restraint she had imposed upon herself.—Myra, my dear !" turning, to bring the young lady forward.

Lord Enniskerry stared for a minute, with a vacant look, as if she had been saying something he did not clearly comprehend; he then bowed, and expressed, or rather muttered, his happiness at the introduction, and, in short, did and said all that is usual on such occasions; but that

was all—there was no look of rapture, no
eager pressing forward to take the fair
hand of Myra; and both mother and
daughter were decidedly disappointed:
but after the manner in which he had
expressed himself about her, there could
be no doubt but that he must be delighted at the introduction; and under
the idea of this, and the attentions it led
her to expect from him, Myra began to
recover from the damping effect which his
little manifestation of emotion on her being presented to him, had had upon her
vanity.—" What an enviable being must
you be considered, my dear madam," said
his lordship, suddenly addressing himself
to 'Mrs. Mayfield, after a silence of a few
minutes on his part, " in being the mother
of so many lovely daughters!"

Mrs. Mayfield bowed, and smiled, and
fanned herself, and looked at Myra, and
from her to Delamere, and from him round
the circle, and then again turned to the
peer.

VOL. III.   D

" But won't your other beautiful daughter be here to-night?" his lordship proceeded to ask.

" My other daughter!" repeated Mrs. Mayfield—" I have no daughter at Strandmore but what is now present."

" Then of course I have been led into a mistake, and the beautiful creature that made one of your party last evening on the Steyne is not your daughter."

" Beautiful creature!" cried Mrs. Mayfield, again involuntarily repeating his words.

" Yes; the young lady I mean had a very large straw bonnet on, but which could not conceal, or rather prevent being discovered, one of the finest faces in the world; for a glimpse of it was sufficient to raise a curiosity that could not be satisfied without a complete view."

If any thing could add to the mortification of finding, that after all Grace was the real object of his admiration, it was the circumstance of Delamere also learning it. Mrs. Mayfield, with all her com-

mand of herself, trembled with passion,
and the rosy lips of Myra became for an
instant of a livid hue ; and well may we
here exclaim, speaking, as we are, of the
hideous effects of envy,

"Oh, blest indeed are they who can hear
Sighs for another with unwounded ear !"

Careless of the mortification he occasioned, lord Enniskerry quickly turned on
his heel ; he was one of those indeed who
had a most happy indifference about every
one's feelings but his own. Grace quite
occupied his fancy ; and having succeeded
in learning all that was requisite of her,
he made his exit from the assembly, to
try whether he could not obtain another
glimpse of her, or perhaps an opportunity
of introducing himself to her, to the no
small disappointment of many others there,
as well as of the Mayfield party. Of course
there was no counter attraction to detain
him; for as for the pretty little pink
and white girl, whom her mamma chose
to suppose he meant by what he had said,

he would as soon have made love to one of the wax dolls which she resembled, as to her. He had a delightful band on board his yacht. They were presently summoned, and took their station immediately opposite the windows of the apartment occupied at the instant by Grace at the hotel.

Grace almost directly threw aside the book with which she had been trying to divert her thoughts, and removing the lights to the back of the apartment, stepped out into the balcony, to enjoy the delicious strains that met her ear, little aware of their being solely intended for it, as a lure to bring her forward. The lights behind her would have been sufficient to have rendered her figure visible; but they were not required for the purpose, a full-orbed moon shining full upon the spot on which she stood, so that she was entirely revealed to the view; and as she stood motionless for a few minutes, entranced by the delightful melody she heard, with the silver light of the moon shed upon her dress, the ardent and romantic imagination of lord Enniskerry could almost have fancied she was a deity, to whom they were offering up the incense of adoration, in strains of heavenly harmony. Groups soon became collected about the hotel; but Grace hardly noticed any thing, so absorbed was she by the music—so perfectly in union; for, as may readily be imagined, the airs selected for her ear were those of the most seductive, the most impassioned description, with the hour, the scene—now dying away, at intervals, upon the enchanted ear, so as to permit the heaving sound of the billows breaking upon the shore to be distinctly heard—then swelling again into strains of grandeur, calculated to raise the soul to heaven. So engaged, so engrossed, she heeded not the approach of any one, and, of course, was somewhat surprised at suddenly hearing Delamere behind her.

He knew the character of lord Enniskerry, and on suddenly missing him from the party, instantly conceived a suspicion

of the truth; he tried to suppress the torture it excited, but in vain. Lord Enniskerry was young, gay, handsome, agreeable; and, in short, Delamere could not
rest without going to the hotel. What
he witnessed there was not calculated to
allay the agitation of the moment; he
rushed up to the apartment where Grace
was; the yellow-tinging plague was boiling
in his veins, and had he yielded to the
impulse of his feelings, he would instantly
have drawn her in from the balcony. Not
able, however, to entirely command himself—" You are kind to lord Enniskerry,"
he said, " by letting him see that his gallantry is not unnoticed."

" Kind!" said Grace, involuntarily repeating the expression, through her surprise at hearing him so suddenly, and half
turning in from the balcony—" I don't
understand you—who is lord Enniskerry?"

" You don't know!"

" No."

Delamere did not choose to explain.

" If," resumed Grace, after waiting a

minute for the reply she expected, " you mean to insinuate that the music here is intended as a compliment to me, whoever the person is that thought of such a one, they could not possibly have paid me a more agreeable one."

" Indeed!" said Delamere; but not in a tone quite as complacent as his usual one.

" Yes, I delight in music ; and from its effect upon my own feelings, can well give credit to all that has been ascribed to its wondrous power. But were the reverse the case, I should not like to acknowledge it, after what Shakespeare has said on the subject, of those who have no taste for harmony. But you too are fond of the ' concord of sweet sounds."

" Yes, very—I believe so."

" Believe so! you must be greatly, and very suddenly altered too, if you are not."

" Perhaps so——" but hardly knowing what he was saying, as he paced the room under the most violent agitation— " I hardly know what I am fond of—what I ought to be fond of! would that I did!

it would be well for me—well for us all, in a world where there is so much of deception, such constant deception, if we could at once ascertain what, or whom, were deserving of our regard and love! Why—why have we not the power of looking into the human breast? why of not detecting deception till the pangs it inflicts have fastened on the heart?"

" Rather say," cried Grace, who could not avoid thinking, from the manner in which it was uttered, that something more was meant by this speech than met the ear, " why should we be always in apprehension of it, as you seem to intimate we should? are we not instructed— is it not one of the most divine precepts of Christianity, to judge as we would be judged? and how, confident in our own integrity, should we like to be regarded with the scowling brow of distrust and constant misgiving? Besides, to yield to such feelings—is it not to impoison happiness, and make this world a still greater wilderness than sorrow teaches us to con-

sider it? A suspicious temper is an anti-
dote to all enjoyment, a blighting mildew,
that despoils every thing of its natural
beauty and fragrance, and then, so contrary to all that we conceive of real generosity. No, let not man,

' Who wears sweet smiles, and looks erect on heaven'—

let him not wrong the nobleness of his
nature, by giving way to so odious a feeling—a feeling calculated to deaden and
destroy every sympathy; in the consciousness of that nobleness, let him walk abroad
with caution, but not distrust."

Delamere had involuntarily stopped to
listen to her; and as he listened to her,
and gazed on her, she seemed to him, in
what she was saying, to be unconsciously
pleading her own cause.—" And sure," he
cried within himself, " something holy
must dwell within the breast from which
such sentiments emanate!" and again a
doubt of the truth, of the reality of all he
had recently heard and believed, began to

suggest itself; and yielding to its influence, he took her hand, and was gently
drawing her away, out of sight of those
who were still stationed outside the window, when in bolted young Mayfield, almost breathless, upon them, dispatched
by his alarmed mamma after Delamere,
on missing him from the room.—" Why,
what a deuced fright you have given
us all!" he exclaimed, addressing himself
to Delamere; " the moment my mother
missed you, she conceived you were taken
ill, and sent me off to learn."

" I am much obliged by her anxiety
about me," said Delamere; " but, no, I
was not ill."

" I am glad to hear it, both on your
account and my own; for you'll have no
objection then to return with me?"

" No, excuse me, I'd rather not."

" But I really can't—that is, if I do, it
must be at the expence of a most agreeable evening; for it. is the positive command of our lady governante that I do
not return without you," and he spoke

with almost a little degree of petulance; for amongst the beauty and fashion that night at Mrs. Benson's was a young lady, the heiress of a few thousands, who had smiled in such a way at his sweet nothings, as to induce him to think, if he did not neglect his chances, there might be hope for him.

Delamere hesitated, and looked anxiously in the eyes of Grace; but there was nothing in them to induce, or rather, invite him to stay; she did not understand the capricious kind of manner in which he had latterly seemed to treat her, and feeling hurt by it, could not avoid looking otherwise than cold at the moment.

"Very well," said Delamere to Mayfield, seeing there was no relenting in her looks, "rather than you should be disappointed through my means——" and they left the room together.—"And how well it was I was interrupted as I was!" thought Delamere, as they pursued their way back to Mrs. Benson's! "for, but for it, in what a dilemma might I have placed myself, from the feelings I should probably have given way to! Grace might, perhaps, have induced me to make some confession, that the reverting of my thoughts to Falkiner would not have permitted me to profit by. How could I forget—how could I suffer myself to be so agitated, as to forget him? how allow myself to give way to any jealous emotion, about a woman of whose indifference I was not only long since assured, but of her having now an encouraged lover? Well, we shall not be much longer domesticated together, and I shall take care, when we part, not to put myself again in the way of similar feelings."

The same was Grace's resolve, for a moment after his leaving the room, from conceiving, as was the case, that he had looked to her for some encouragement to remain. She regretted not having given it—but it was only for a moment: if he wished to converse with her, to have any private or particular conversation, he could easily obtain opportunities for the purpose,

she reflected, and therefore felt pleased
that she had acted as she had done: but
to shew him she was not to be treated
with this capriciousness was not sufficient,
his present manner of conducting himself
so agitated her nerves, as to make her
finally resolve upon no longer delaying
her return home.

CHAPTER III.

" ——————————Hear me a little,
For I have only been silent so long,
And given way unto this course of fortune,
By noting of the lady. I have mark'd
A thousand blushing apparitions
To start into her face ; a thousand innocent shames,
In angel whiteness, bear away those blushes ;
And in her eye there hath appear'd a fire,
To burn the errors that have been held
Against her truth."

DELAMERE was woke the next morning
to read a letter from Falkiner, requesting
a few minutes' conversation with him as
soon as he rose. The fact was, that completely imposed on by Myra's letter, Falkiner took it into his head to make an appeal to the generosity of Delamere, believing if he could be induced to give her
up, he need not fear every thing yet turning out according to his wishes.

Delamere immediately rose to receive

him. But what could be the object of the required interview? He began to suspect the truth, and could not avoid wishing, in consequence, that Falkiner had taken some other method of appealing to him, lest he should not be able to command himself sufficiently to avoid betraying the too great interest he felt for her he anticipated his being about implored to resign: but he had promised to see Falkiner, and an interview being inevitable, he endeavoured to collect himself accordingly for it.

Falkiner did not keep him long in suspense, as to the purpose for which he had solicited this interview; he was agitated and confused, but still too impatient to be relieved from the anxiety he was under, not to come quickly to the point. After a suitable compliment to Delamere, he frankly acknowledged his object in seeking him was, to endeavour to obtain his resignation of a lady to whom he had reason to believe they both aspired; but certainly he was warranted in saying, not with exactly equal pretensions, her affec-

tions having been long his, and the promise of her hand only revoked through
the authority of her family.

Delamere started. This was letting in
a new light on the subject. Was it really
true then that her connexions had interfered in the matter, and that to their persua-
sions, or rather, commands, it was, and not
to any lessening suggestion of her own, that
Grace had been led to endeavour to disentangle herself from the engagement she
had entered into with this young man?
Well, this certainly retrieved her completely in his estimation, and at the same
time accounted for all those changes of
manner that had alternately inspired him
with hope and depressed him with apprehension; yes, he could now account for
what appeared awaking tenderness over
confirmed indifference; love and duty had
created a conflict in her feelings, occasioned a struggle in her heart; and to this
was owing all that had so agitated him:
she wished to submit to the wishes of her
family, but her heart rebelled against their

authority. Yet, spite of her present involuntary opposition to it, might she not
yet be brought to acquiesce in it, if she
found nothing was done to render the further exertion of it useless, with regard to
Falkiner, by his refusing to attend to his
appeal? and could he think, could he prevail on himself to think of availing himself
of such a circumstance to possess himself
of a cold, lifeless, heartless form? could he,
who professed to love Grace so tenderly—
could he bear to think of being the means
of planting a thorn in her bosom, never
to be extracted? Yet, to give her up—
to resign her irrevocably to another—tear
from his heart the hope so long rooted
there, of yet calling her his—that hope,
that had so grown up, and entwined, and
intertwisted itself with every other, that
in tearing it up he should feel as if tearing
away every other!—but it must be done;
and after the pause of a minute, an unavailing pause, to try and subdue the agony
of his feelings, he gave Falkiner the required
assurance, namely, that he need be under

no farther apprehension of any disappointment to his happiness through his means.

Falkiner would have been profuse in his grateful acknowledgments, but Delamere, the tortured Delamere, could command himself no farther; and the air of impatience with which he hastily, as well as involuntarily, withdrew from these acknowledgments, was a hint to the other to retire.

Restless, and unhappy in her mind, Grace passed an uneasy night, and quitted her chamber in the morning with an intention of trying what a few turns on the beach would do for her. Just as she reached the hall, Delamere was coming out from the parlour where he had received Falkiner. On seeing her, he was instinctively drawing back, unable to endure encountering her looks till he had a little better recovered himself, when the voice of Myra was heard calling to him over the banisters, and glad of any pretext for avoiding Grace for the present, he

directly darted past her, and up the staircase.

Feelings of the most painful nature
transfixed Grace for a minute to the spot;
his attempt to draw back on seeing
her was not lost upon her; she might
not, however, have imputed it to any
positive wish to avoid her, but for his
subsequent conduct with regard to Myra;
his joining her the instant she called to
him, was a proof to Grace that his drawing back into the parlour at her sight
was not owing to any sudden recollection
of business within it, but entirely to a
wish to avoid her; and to speak the pang
inflicted by the thought would be impossible. The purpose for which she had descended to the hall was forgotten—she returned to her room in a state of confusion
and distress, that obliged her to sit down
for some minutes to try and recover herself.

How did she regret not having had resolution to leave Strandmore before! had
she done so, she should have saved herself

the recent shock; but she would not, by
lingering any longer where she was, expose herself to the recurrence of a similar
one. No matter through what motive
William wished to avoid her—whether for
the purpose of letting her understand
what his real sentiments for Myra were,
from a dawning suspicion of what hers
were becoming for him, or to humour
some jealous whim of Myra's—she would
not permit him again to let her see that
he wished to do so; she was decided on
her immediate departure—that very morning she would return home.

. Tears could not be suppressed; she was
weeping even bitterly, when she was surprised by Mrs. Hamilton, much alarmed
by her sending down to excuse herself
from appearing at breakfast.—" Why,
what's the matter, my dear?" she said;
" you are not ill, I hope?"

" No, not ill," trying to hide her tears
with her handkerchief, replied Grace,
" only a—a—slight headach; but I am
glad you have come up, for I wanted to

tell you I am going home this morning."

"This morning!" repeated Mrs. Hamilton in an accent of surprise; "why, what's the meaning of this? this is certainly a very sudden whim!"

"No whim," cried Grace; "I cannot think of being any longer absent from my father."

"Pooh! a few days more can be no great matter—we shall all be leaving this now in a few more; and your going away now will be quite a breaking up of the pleasure of the party."

"Oh, on that score we'll say nothing!" cried Grace, with a smile of bitterness.

"Well, at least," said Mrs. Hamilton, evincing by this expression that she perfectly understood her, "you won't pretend to doubt that your persisting in your resolution will be the occasion of pain to William?"

"To him! to William!" repeated Grace, in an emphatic tone; "oh no, not to him! to him perhaps least of any. No, no!" starting from her chair, and pacing the room in irrepressible emotion, "William no longer cares about me—no longer cares for any of his friends at the castle!"

"You think so? Well, did I ever hear the like of this!" exclaimed Mrs. Hamilton—"to tell me that William cares no longer for you, or any of his other friends at the castle! what on earth has put such a thing into your head?"

"No matter—don't ask me!" cried Grace, in a voice almost choked with emotion.

"But I must ask you, because I don't like to have injustice done to any one."

"Injustice!"

"Yes; for in doubting the regard of William you are guilty of the greatest. If I pleased, I could soon convince you of this: what would you say if I told you, that but for him you would not have had the happiness of embracing your brother so soon as you now expect?"

"What, is he the generous being to whom Eugene is indebted for his release from the horrors of perpetual imprisonment?"

"Troth is he—I was enjoined to secrecy, but the truth will out. The moment I found William had the power of doing what I wished, I wrote him the whole story, and, as I expected, he lost not a moment in hastening to release his friend; and if this is not a proof of regard——"

"A proof!" repeated Grace, with her clasped hands, and streaming eyes uplifted to heaven, as if calling down a blessing on him.—"But why, why allow me to remain so long in ignorance of this? Oh, had I sooner known it, what captiousness of feeling might have been prevented!—But my heart will burst if I longer delay to speak its grateful feelings to him!" and darting from the room, she flew down stairs, and meeting a waiter, sent a message to Delamere, requesting to speak to him for a few minutes.

She had seen Falkiner then, and wanted to express her acknowledgments to

him for the happiness he had afforded
her, was the thought that struck Delamere the moment he received her message. How could he bear these acknowledgments? but it was not to be avoided
what she desired; and he accordingly proceeded to the apartment where he understood she was expecting him.

" I have disturbed you at your breakfast," she said on his entering, " but I felt
it impossible to control the impulse that
has occasioned me to do so; but I cannot
give utterance to the feelings that urged
me to send for you; it is but this instant
I have learned what I am indebted to you
for—the happiness——but you may, you
must conceive what it is, and what my
gratitude must ever be to him who has
allowed me to experience such."

Delamere turned pale—he had not expected such an unequivocal acknowledgment of her attachment for Falkiner; for
still labouring under his mistake about
him, he referred all she said to him, and
his emotion at the circumstance was hard-

ly controllable. Something, however, it was necessary to say, and he accordingly forced himself to articulate, that being the means of happiness to her must be a source of happiness to him.

" Yes, I am convinced of that," said Grace; " but I will not detain you longer, only just to thank you for your kindnessess while here, for I am about returning home; my poor father can no longer spare me, I am sure. May I not," she added, a little anxiously, " give him the happiness of thinking he'll soon see you ?"

" I know not," said Delamere, his feelings, spite of all his efforts at resistance, overpowering him—" I am undecided, unsettled, about every thing; perhaps I shall never return to St. Doulagh's."

" Never !" echoed Grace, in a voice of dismay; " and——" but she checked the inquiry. He had made some discovery, she was sure, about Myra and Falkiner, and to this the pain, the shock, it occasioned, was owing the wretchedness he betrayed; and in her turn, she grew pale, and turned sick, at this evidence of strong attachment to another.—" That would be a terrible disappointment to many," after a long pause she added.

" It might be so; but with all my hopes, my plans of happiness, subverted, for what should I return to it? No—better for me to go to a place where nothing will remind me of the felicity I have been disappointed of.—Oh, Grace!" suddenly seizing her hand, " you are not to be blamed for it, for the affections are not at our command; but you have rendered me a miserable man."

" I!" exclaimed Grace, absolutely electrified—" I render you miserable!"

" You appear surprised—did you then imagine that my long-rooted feelings for you had undergone a change, so sudden a change, that I could bear the disappointment of the hopes, the wishes, they gave birth to, with composure? I tried, I resolved, to be silent on the subject, lest complaint should be construed into re-

proach; but the agitation of my mind has
borne down all before it."

"Oh! if indeed any unhappiness you
are suffering is owing to me," cried
Grace, in extreme emotion—"if to any
doubt of my regard it is owing, what is
there I would not do to convince you
that in doubting it you wrong me? can I
say more than that, if really essential to
your felicity to possess this——." She
paused, overpowered by her feelings, and
half averted her looks, while involuntarily
she stretched out her hand to him.

Instead however of having it caught
with the eagerness she expected, Delamere shrunk back—"What is it you
want me to imagine?" he demanded, in a
tone indicative of the agitation he was in;
"do you want me to imagine, that for
my sake you are ready to give up all your
own hopes and expectations of happiness?
No, Grace, no! if such is your meaning,
I have no claim to such a sacrifice; nor if
I had, would I accept it, after what has

E 2

occurred; with the knowledge I have of
your sentiments, the world could not now
induce me to accept your hand."

. The bright flush of joy, and surprise,
and reviving hopes, faded from the cheek
of Grace; she turned of a deadly paleness,
and her heart, at the same instant, of an
icy coldness. She had needlessly tormented
herself about him: his love, his affections,·
were still unalienated from her; but of
what use to find she had been labouring
under a mistake with regard to his sentiments, if he obstinately refused to be undeceived with regard to hers? were her
looks, her manner, so unintelligent as to
give no indication of what these really
were? or was it, that his pride had been
so seriously, so deeply wounded by the
indifference intimated by the manner in
which she had been led to express herself
in breaking with him, that no after relenting or retracting could be of any avail,
or, in short, avowal or acknowledgment
of reciprocal regard? What was to be
done? could she endure their both being

doomed to misery through this persistance
in error or pique? Yet, how could she
argue the point with him? how try to
reason him into the acceptance of her
hand? Impossible! such a thing was not
to be thought of; the delicacy of feminine
feeling, as well as manifold other considerations, revolted and militated against
it: yet, to see happiness within her reach,
and still unattainable, was a trial that indeed required all her philosophy, her firmness, her strength of mind, to enable her
to support with calmness.

Through the emotion she was in, her
hand got somehow entangled in the black
ribbon to which was appended the locket
containing the raven hair of William, and
drew it from its concealment. The quick
eye of William was instantly caught by
it—it was indeed well remembered by
him, being sent to her from Dublin, on
his going up there to embark for England, there being no place near St. Doulagh's to have the hair set at.—" Well,
this is kind, Grace," he said, taking hold

of it; " I see you did not then altogether
want to banish me your recollection. But
you would have been ungrateful had you
thrown this aside, for see how carefully I
have preserved and treasured this;" and
he shewed her her own long tress still
wound round his wrist.

Grace sighed involuntarily—" Ah, those
were happy, days in which that was
given!" she as involuntarily said.

" Yes," cried William, " for they were
days in which I indeed looked forward to
happy ones."

" Life was then just opening to our
view, in all its freshness," again sighed
Grace; " and, like children in a flower-
garden, little aware that all that is so delicious to their senses will yet fade and die
away: we looked round on its varied enjoyments with heightened delight, from
our ignorance of their unsubstantial and
illusive nature."

" Illusive indeed!" sighed Delamere.—
" But give me that locket, Grace; you'll
soon cease to value it any farther."

' If you think so," said Grace, " you
right in asking it back; and if you
lly wish to have it——" Her lip
;htly trembled as she applied her hand
the ribbon.

' Yet, no!" cried Delamere; " you'll
; throw it aside—you'll not possibly be
ed to throw it aside entirely, and it
l sometimes perhaps be the means of
ling a friend to your memory, who
ıld ill bear to think of being entirely
gotten by you."

' And yet you can talk of quitting us
!" said Grace, reproachfully; " well, no
tter. But whatever you may finally
ide on, you will not—you cannot be
unkind as to—to——" her agitation
ame every moment less controllable—
rithout letting my father have the hap-
ess of thanking you for what you have
ıe."

' Your father!" repeated Delamere,
:h a bewildered look; for still in his er-
about Falkiner, he knew not what it
s he had to thank him for, since he

could not suppose, from what he had heard, that his appearing to aid the wishes of Falkiner, by resigning any pretensions it might have been imagined he had to Grace, could have obliged him.

" Yes," replied Grace, with a look of surprise at his expression of perplexity; " it would be strange, I think, if he did not wish for a personal opportunity of expressing his gratitude for so great an obligation as that of the restoration of his son to him."

" His son! what, is it to Eugene you have been alluding all this time?"

" Yes; to whom else did you suppose?"

" I thought——but how, or rather, by what means, have you discovered that I was concerned in the enlargement of your brother? but I think I can guess."

" And I think I can guess what your surmise is," said Grace; " yes, it was through Mrs. Hamilton I discovered the circumstance—she was betrayed into the disclosure; and while I must admire, and

y appreciate, the feeling that enjoined
silence on the subject, I can hardly
bear being half angry with her for so
g keeping us in ignorance of the obli-
ion we owe you. Well," seeing him
k impatient, " I will not dwell further
it; I may as well indeed be silent, for
iat I feel I cannot do justice to.".

" And you really will leave us this
orning?" said Delamere.

" Yes," answered Grace, with a sigh,
i think I should not be any longer ab-
it from home."

" Of course you'll not depart without
st seeing——" He paused, unable to
ing himself immediately to articulate
e name.

" Who?" demanded Grace, after wait-
g a minute in expectation of his finish-
g the sentence—" without first seeing
hom?"

" Need I say? I thought you must in-
antly have surmised who I meant."

" No, really I have not the least idea."

" Then, of course, you have had no intimation of what occurred this morning;
if you had, you would have been at no
loss to conjecture; but I conclude you'll
not be allowed to depart without hearing
of it."

" You are speaking in riddles to me,"
said Grace; " do be more explicit—what
is it you seem to think I must hear before
I depart? or who the person I shall see?"

For a minute William turned away
impatiently from her—" Falkiner," he
then said; " with the communication he
has to make, of course he'll never let you
leave this without first seeing him."

" Indeed! then I should think it a most
extraordinary proceeding, his attempting
to detain me for the purpose; for he cannot possibly suppose that I can feel any
great interest in the concerns of so slight
an acquaintance."

" So slight an acquaintance!" repeated
Delamere, recoiling a few paces, as if to
have a better opportunity of gazing in her
countenance, to see whether she was jest-

ing in this assertion—" Falkiner a slight
acquaintance!"

" Yes; so slight a one as hardly to receive a recognising bow from me."

" Am I to believe you serious in what
you say?" cried Delamere, again approaching her; " yet no, I cannot."

" Yet I never was more serious in any
assertion," said Grace.

" May I really believe you?" again demanded Delamere, with increasing emotion; "yet, after what I have heard, what
I have seen—after holding in my hand a
letter directed to him, in yours—no!"
with a flush of indignant feeling colouring
his cheek—" no, it is impossible!"

" A letter directed by me to Falkiner!"
exclaimed Grace; " good Heavens! can
it be——" but checking herself—"let me
know how that letter fell into your hands
and I shall then be better able to judge
what I am to think."

Delamere informed her; and in utter
amazement at what she heard, Grace uplifted her hands and eyes—" Well," she

said, " this almost exceeds belief! that
any one, more especially one of my own
sex, my own age, could be capable of
such baseness, such deliberate treachery!"

" Then all I was led to give credit to
about Falkiner is false?". said Delamere.

" False!" repeated Grace, with almost
a look of indignant anger at his having a
doubt on the subject.

" How shall I command myself?" cried
the agitated William; "this is indeed——"

" The fact is simply this——." resumed
Grace.

" No, no!" interrupted Delamere, grasping her hand, " I can listen to no explanation; I must first be assured, beyond a
doubt, that I am under no mistake, no
delusion—that you are indeed free—at liberty to bestow your hand where you
please. Yet, of what consequence to me;
after all the assurance, after the avowal of
your cold, your icy indifference towards
me?. Oh, Grace! how could you write
me so mortifying a letter?"

Vexed at the sudden change in his

tone, his reverting to what she no longer
desired to remember, Grace, a little impatiently, tried to pull away her hand
from him, as she turned to a window.

"Yet, perhaps you did not mean I
should put the construction upon it I did,"
he proceeded—"did you, Grace—tell me?"
and he looked with the most anxious
fondness in her face; "or say, if all was
to do again, would you write me such a
letter?"

"What, a letter to give you up? to be
sure I would!" said Grace.

"You would!" cried William, dropping her hand, and again recoiling a few
paces from her.

"Assuredly, if matters were all now
exactly as they were then; for do you
think I would stand between you and fortune? the only difference is," slightly hesitating, "that now perhaps I might not
be so prompt or decisive," and she blushed, and smiled, and glanced half archly at
William, and half bent her eyes to the
ground, "in writing as I was then."

"Enough!" exclaimed the transported Delamere, catching her to his breast with sudden ecstacy—her on whom his heart had so long doated, to whom his soul had so long cleaved, for whom his love had grown with his growth, and strengthened with his strength, till it had become a feeling not to be subdued.

"What is the world to happy lovers?" demands the poet, and he might have added, "time;" for in vain Mrs. Mayfield sat, expecting William's return to breakfast, in vain Mrs. Hamilton Grace's to the chamber, from which she had fled so precipitately.

At length the patience of the latter exhausted, or rather, not being under the restraint which policy obliged the other to impose upon herself, she sallied forth in quest of the young lady: a waiter informed her where she might find her, and without ceremony she entered the apartment. But though she could not imagine that by either she would be considered as an intruder, yet there was a

something that convinced her she had
been an interruption to a most interesting
tête-à-tête. The persuasion naturally led
to the conclusion of an agreeable understanding having taken place between the
lady and gentleman, and the consequence
instantly anticipated from this filled her
with delight, there being hardly any thing
she had more at heart than a union between Grace and William, from the maternal affection she felt for both.—" So
here you are," she said, " quietly seated
together, while we have been all wonder
and astonishment to think what had become of you both! But come, I won't
set an example of scolding, for by this
time," glancing at William, " I suppose
there is a fine one in store for me, for the
discovery I made to Grace."

" No," replied William, " I am at this
instant in that complacent state of mind,
that I think it would be hardly possible
for any thing to provoke me to any thing
like ill-nature—just in that happy humour
with myself and all the world, that Yo-

rick describes himself to have been in
when he says, had he been king of France,
it would have been just the minute for an
orphan to have asked him for his father's
portmanteau."

· "Well, I am happy to hear this," said
Mrs. Hamilton; "it quite dissipates the
terror I was in of having incurred your
highness's displeasure; and Grace, I hope
she's in a not less agreeable mood; since,
if so, she'll not refuse staying the few days
longer we have to remain here."

William took Grace's hand.

· "Well, yes, perhaps I may be prevailed
on," she said, half laughing, and colouring,
and attempting to withdraw it; "but go,
it is really quite time for you to finish
your breakfast, or, at least, to allow poor
Mrs. Mayfield to finish hers, who all this
time has, I dare say, been waiting for you."

· "And you," cried William, "won't
you come too?"

"Oh no," said Mrs. Hamilton, interposing, too impatient to learn how matters
had been brought about again between

them, to let Grace join the party; "on her refusing to come down to breakfast, I ordered it above for her, and there it is now waiting."

"Very well, I must go then by myself; but remember, I give you timely notice, if you keep long away, you may expect to have me seeking you."

"Well, now tell me all about it," cried Mrs. Hamilton, as she hurried her up to the room where breakfast was waiting her.

"About what?" said Grace, with a sly smile, affecting not to understand her.

"About what!" repeated Mrs. Hamilton, her very cheeks colouring from impatience—"why, how this happy reconciliation has been brought about between you and William? But I see you knew well enough what I meant; it is only to amuse yourself you pretended ignorance."

"Well, you shall hear," replied Grace; "but you'll be surprised when you learn all I have to disclose."

"Not quite so much perhaps as you imagine, for I guess what you allude to.

I have latterly begun to suspect that——
but come, when I hear your story, you
shall hear my surmises."

Grace could not bring herself to trifle
any further with an impatience originating
in the most affectionate feelings.

When Mrs. Hamilton had heard her to
a close—" Well," she exclaimed, " I did
say I should not be quite as much surprised perhaps as you imagined, at the
explanation you had to give; but I confess myself infinitely more so than I conceived I should have been. There is an
old proverb——but 'tis vulgar to quote
such things; I shall therefore merely say,
that I certainly did latterly begin to think
that Mrs. Mayfield was not exactly what
at first might be imagined, and that
therefore it was not altogether impossible
that there might be a little underhand
work, or, to express myself in a more
modern and fashionable manner, *manœuvring*, to keep you and William asunder;
but any thing like the treachery practised
for the purpose I had no conception of.

However, since defeated, let us rest satisfied with that; since, to express the indignation it has excited, could answer no other end than to prevent one's living in that peace with one's neighbours that must naturally be wished."

"Assuredly," said Grace; "and not for any consideration would I have any notice taken of what I have revealed; the disappointment of such schemes as we have been speaking of must be a sufficient punishment, without the utterance of the contempt and indignation they excite; besides which, respect for the husband of Mrs. Mayfield, if no other motive, should prevent reproach to her."

"Still, however, it will be a difficult matter for me to keep up appearances towards her," rejoined Mrs. Hamilton; "though I know, to be sure, by doing so, I shall have a better opportunity of mortifying her than if I was to flame out at once."

"Mortifying her!" repeated Grace, in a tone of alarm.

"Oh, don't be alarmed," said Mrs. Ha-

milton, laughing, " I shall do no harm by
any thing I intend—only evince a little
malice.—But you have entirely given up
your foolish whim of going away this
morning?"

" Yes, I believe so."

" Oh, to be sure! I wouldn't for the
world you went, because it would be such
a triumph to the party below; for you
know, I conclude, that William, to please
them, has invited the whole set, lord Enniskerry, and all that he met at Mrs. Benson's last night, here this evening, and it
would be such a gratification to have you
fairly out of the way; but their being disappointed in their wish, or expectation,
of this, is not the only one they'll meet
with this evening, if I am not mistaken."

" Then you have some scheme in your
head," said Grace, shaking hers at her.

" No matter," laughing; " at least, let
me blab on whom I will, I won't blab on
myself—and there, I hear William's step,"
and jumping up, she ran to open the door
for him, and while he was in the act of
advancing to Grace, quitted the room.

CHAPTER IV.

" If you go on thus, you will kill yourself;
And 'tis not wisdom thus to second grief
Against yourself."

Bur though the figure he imagined he
had seen standing by the altar vanished
like a shadow at his approach, still Eugene
would not permit himself to think his
fancy had deceived him; and the excitement given to his feelings by this incident, hardly allowed him to pass a minute
out of the ruin. Again alarmed by what
seemed to her this pertinacious indulgence
of sorrow, Mrs. Brady remonstrated more
seriously than ever with him on the subject; but her counsel fell as profitless on
his ears as water on a sieve, and she was
induced again to leave him to himself, but
with a determination, if some speedy alteration did not take place in his manner

of conducting himself, to write to his friends on the subject.

A week elapsed without any thing again occurring like the recent incident, to revive the agitation it had occasioned him, when, one evening, just as he was beginning to admit an idea of having deceived himself by the belief he had yielded to, his eyes suddenly encountered again a figure standing on the selfsame spot on which he had before imagined he had seen one. He started up, but checked himself from springing forward, as his feelings nearly impelled his doing, lest the movement should occasion it, as before, to vanish from his sight. As eagerly he gazed on it, the features gradually became more revealed, and at length he beheld the perfect likeness of his Rose. At this sight there was an end of all further command over himself; with a cry that echoed through the vaulted arches of the building, he rushed forward; the phantom instantly shrunk back, but still not with such quickness as to prevent Eugene from perceiving

that it was into a narrow, dark passage,
contiguous to the altar, into which it
had retreated. Down this he pursued
it, now prevented seeing it by the pro-
jections in the walls, now again allowed
to catch a glimpse of it, still appearing to
glide, with shadowy lightness, before him.
At length he found himself beyond the
building, in a wild and solitary spot, overrun with briers and brambles, amongst the
hills. He looked round him with bewildering sensations, and at some distance
again espied the object of his pursuit; he
again rushed forward, the figure still keeping in sight, till it reached the desolate
court of an old ruined building on the
coast, about half a mile from the vale in
which stood the monastery, when it entirely disappeared.

Eugene knew not what to think; that
what had happened seemed for the purpose of alluring him to this dismal place,
he could not avoid thinking; yet for
what could he be enticed to it? If
any injury — any violence were medi-

tated, it could quite as well have been perpetrated in the place where the figure had appeared to him, as in the one to which it had been the means of drawing him. He drew back, to take a better survey of the building; it was one of considerable extent, and shattered and rifted as it was by the hand of time and the fury of the elements, to which it had been so long exposed, and streaming as it was with grass and weeds in every direction, presented a complete picture of desolation to the view. He listened, but heard nothing, save the hoarse murmur of the waves, as they broke upon the shore, the cries of the gulls that thronged the adjacent cliffs, and the rustling of the owl in her ivied lodgment on the battlements, welcoming the glad return of night, for by this time the last ray of sunset had faded from the hills.

Eugene felt himself strongly tempted to pursue the adventure, by entering the building: but if indeed he believed he was purposely allured to it, was there not

rashness in the thought? While he stood
hesitating, a light flashed on his eyes from
the loophole of a tower; he could no longer
command himself—he would endeavour
to solve what appeared so mysterious, and
accordingly rushed in: hardly had he done
so, when he heard some one behind him
softly bolting the door that had given him
admission to the place; he instantly turned,
and with a mingled sensation of surprise,
indignation, and alarm—for with all his
fancied loathing of life, the idea of murder,
which instantly occurred to him, was horrible to his imagination—beheld Wilkinson, his mysterious and, as it seemed to
him, implacable enemy, revealed to view
by a light in a contiguous apartment.

CHAPTER V.

" ⸻⸻I do beseech you,
Let me the knowledge of my fault bear with me :
If with myself I hold intelligence,
Or have acquaintance with my own desires—
If that I do not dream, or be not frantic
(As I do trust I am not), then,
Never so much as in a thought unborn
Did I offend you."

BUT though Rose, the beloved and lamented Rose, was torn from her friends,
it was not by the hand of death.   On regaining her senses, after fainting in the
monastery, some time elapsed ere she
could credit their evidence, on finding herself in a place utterly unknown to her, a
rude chamber, or cavern, reclined upon a
straw pallet, illumed by a dull lamp, stuck
against the wall, immediately opposite to
her.   When, at length, convinced that
she was under no illusion, it at once struck

her that she had been carried off by the contrivance of Mordaunt; she felt a persuasion of having seen him turning to catch her, at the moment she felt herself fainting away; and, in short, had not a doubt of being right in her conjecture. From the morning of their unfortunate recognition of each other in the castle of St. Doulagh's, she had experienced a foreboding dread of him. To the fears excited by this recognition she of course imputed what had now happened: but what did he intend to do with her? not destroy her certainly, else that would at once have been done. No—he had merely carried her off, she concluded, for the purpose of ascertaining whether, as yet, she had made any disclosure that could be injurious to him. This idea tended in a little degree to tranquillize her mind; but when minute after minute passed away, without bringing him to receive from her, as she fully expected, the satisfactory assurance he required, her heart again began to fail her, and quitting the couch, she took down the lamp, with a determination of exploring the place.

Aware of there being many secret vaults and passages belonging to, and connected with, the monastery, she would probably have imagined herself in one of these, but for the sound of dashing water, resembling that of the sea breaking on a rocky shore, and from which circumstance, be where she might, she was convinced it was not in any place connected with that build- ing. On looking about her, she soon per- ceived she was in a cavern, evidently con- structed by the hand of Nature, being en- tirely formed of immense rocks, that hung in huge masses, menacing from above; whilst those beneath, that composed the floor, rendered slimy to the foot by the distillations from the roof, caused her ad- vance to be both slow and dangerous, her feet continually slipping from beneath her; while, from the wavering light thrown upon the rocks, by the flickering blaze of the lamp, often made to fancy she saw

them trembling, she was continually starting back, with a scream, under the horrible idea of being crushed to death. At
length, after having got to some distance,
as she conceived, from the spot on which
she had found herself, she became thoroughly convinced, if indeed till then in
a doubt on the subject, of being removed
from the monastery, by plainly distin-
guishing the noise of the sea, and at the
same time the sound of various rivulets
dashing through the rocks at the bottom
of the cavern, and which, here and there,
as if in furious indignation of the impediments they met with, threw up a thick
spray around.

Dismal as was the place, yet nothing,
altogether, could be more romantic—fantastic as were the forms of the rocks, and
decorated as the cavern was with sparry
substances, that from their various curious
shapes, Rose could not but have admired,
and been infinitely amused with, at another time; but now the state of the unfortunate girl's mind was such as to ren-

der her but ill qualified to view any thing
with the eye of a naturalist. That the sea
made its way at times into this dark abode,
was evident from the quantity of sea-
weed and shells that were scattered about
—perhaps entirely filled it up; and as the
horrible thought occurred, Rose felt a
gasping sensation, uncertain as she was
whether she might not have been left
there to perish in this way. She knew—
she felt she merited punishment; she had
suffered herself to be led astray, and instead of endeavouring to expiate her error by penitence, had dared attempting to
brave the wrath of Heaven, for the purpose of saving herself from worldly shame;
but yet to meet with such a punishment
as this—to see the wave approaching that
was to overwhelm her—to recede but to
be overtaken by it—to die, in short, with
all the horrors of death before her, human
nature could not endure the thought, and
she shrieked aloud at the horrible ideas
conjured up by her disordered fancy.
There was now a new stimulant to make

her persevere in her efforts to get on; having succeeded in advancing a few yards further, she espied a small chasm, resembling a low arched door, at the side of the cavern; she directly crept through it, and ascending a few steps, found herself in a large chamber; she elevated the lamp, and as she stood looking about her, she fancied she saw something flitting across the further end of the room; she instinctively called out, and hurried forward—but no one replied to her call.

Seeing another door, she proceeded to explore; and advancing down a long passage, began to ascend the spiral stairs of an old tower, constructed within the thick walls, and with openings from the different landing-places into the successive chambers they wound round. They were so extremely steep, that Rose was often obliged to pause for breath, but was still encouraged to go on, from a hope, that if she once gained the summit of the building, she should be enabled, perhaps, to ascertain where she was.

At length she succeeded in her effort for this purpose, but not without the extinction of her lamp—a circumstance that would have filled her with horror, but for the clear bright sky she caught a glimpse of, as she approached the battlements. From these she had a full view of the ocean ; but though a full-orbed moon, rising over the restless waves, permitted her to see far around her, she could not discover any object that could give her an idea of where she was ; for more than once she had been prevailed upon by Mrs. Brady to take a drive towards the sea, so that, whether still in the vicinity of her late residence, or removed to a distance from it, was more than she could determine. A considerable part of what had been the main body of the building, she saw still remained attached to the tower ; could she make her way into this, it struck her she might perhaps be able to find an outlet from it ; but as she contemplated it, there was something so dismal, so desolate, in its appearance, that her very heart seemed to die within her at the thought of exploring it by herself.

As she stood leaning against the moss-clad battlements, undecided whether to continue where she was till daylight, in hopes of seeing some passing stranger, or endeavour at once to find her way to the other part of the building, she could not avoid contrasting the tranquillity of all around her, with the tumultuous state of her own feelings at the moment, or reflecting how much the passions, and follies, and errors of mankind, mar the benevolent intentions of the Deity. The night was bright and calm, so calm that there was hardly breath enough to stir the sedge of the rock—the glittering waves broke with a drowsy murmur amongst the pebbles on the shore—

> " ———————The floor of heaven
> Was thick inlaid with patens of bright gold,"

amidst which the moon was now seen walking in all her brightness; and all, in

F 3

short, was a scene of beauty and repose, well calculated to impart additional repose to a bosom previously at peace with itself.

The building stood upon a green cliff, in the indented part of a small bay, formed by far-projecting headlands, against the furthermost parts of which the waves continually broke in foam, that as it now caught the rays of the moon, had the appearance of so many broken masses of sparkling silver. " There is," says Rousseau, " extreme satisfaction when elevated on the highest point of the circumjacent country—the air is more pure, the body more active, and the mind more serene; lifted up above the dwellings of man, we discard all grovelling and earthly passions, the thoughts assume a character of sublimity, proportionate to the grandeur of the surrounding objects, and as the body approaches nearer to the ethereal regions, the soul imbibes a portion of their unalterable purity."

So Rose might have thought and felt in happier moments; but uncertain now what she had to fear, trembling at every sound, lest it might be the precursor of an approaching enemy, the present scene, with all its beauty, all its grandeur, was unable to fix her attention above a few minutes.

At length, summoning all her courage to her aid, she decided on endeavouring to make her way into the other part of the building, and accordingly began to descend the stairs. Having got half way, she turned from the landing-place into a small chamber, at the opposite side of which she observed a door. After some efforts, it gave way, and she beheld a spacious gallery before her.

With palpitating heart she ventured forward, but had not advanced far, when her further progress was obstructed by another door, which, like the one she had just passed through, was also fastened with a bolt. For a moment she again became irresolute how to act; then forcing back the bolt with a trembling hand, she found herself at the head of a broad staircase.

After listening a minute, she ventured
down, and entered a large dreary apartment, that, as well as she could see about
her, she judged to have been one of the
state rooms of the castle, in its pristine
days, a range of painted windows, lighting
it on either side, giving it the appearance
of a Gothic hall, and between which she
could perceive some pieces of old armour
gleaming in the twilight, while high folding-doors of carved oak shut it in at the
end, over which, in niches, were figures of
grim warriors cut in stone.

Rose made a useless effort to open these
doors; and was repeating the attempt,
when, with a sensation of terror that made
her fly from the place, she suddenly desisted, on fancying she discovered that
they were held by some one at the other
side. Having regained the stairs, she again
paused to listen, almost expecting to see
some one mounting them after her; but
she neither saw nor heard any one, and in
a few minutes became again a little recom-
posed in consequence. She had not cou-

rage, however, to venture down again; there was something in the depth and profundity of the gloom below that was appalling to her imagination, and accordingly giving up her intention of exploring any further for the present, she decided on returning to the tower, and watching there for day; but what was her consternation, when, on attempting to open the door leading into it, she found it fastened on the inside! Her blood ran cold, as if she had seen a ruffian stealing out upon her at the moment from some dark recess, through the apprehension inspired by the circumstance of there being some one invisibly watching her: but might not the closing of the door be owing to the wind? yet, in that case, would she not have heard the noise occasioned by its being forced back into its fastenings? Holding in her breath, she applied her ear to the crevice; but without being able to distinguish any sound that could justify the fear she was in. However, to repeat her efforts to force the door was more than she had courage to do, and accordingly she turned into an adjoining chamber, into which the moon was shining brightly at the moment, thus permitting her to satisfy herself that there was no one concealed within it.

The room was large, and in a few chairs and a bedstead still contained some articles of furniture; but that it had not been very recently inhabited, Rose was rather inclined to imagine, from the bedstead being destitute of every thing but curtains, of a dingy stuff, that gave to it something of a funereal appearance. She made her way to a chair by one of the windows, and in impatient longing for some indication of the dawn, raised her eyes to the sky, yet not without a shuddering sensation at the thought, that she perhaps might not be allowed to live to witness it. But the building might be a deserted one —under the persuasion that she might not, or rather could not be able to make her way out of the cavern, those who had carried her off might perhaps have quitted the place directly after securing her within it.

She tried to derive hope and confidence
from the thought; yet at the slightest
sound that met her ear she started and
trembled, lest of its being the announcement of approaching danger. But loathing
life as she did but a few days before, how
inconsistent, it may be remarked, was the
alarm now experienced with that feeling!
but in reply, we know not ourselves, till
actually put to the test, our real strength
or weakness; and, at all events, the most
despairing, the most indifferent about life,
would probably shrink at the thought of
encountering the actual glare of a murderer's eye. Worn out with agitation, a
kind of stupor was at last stealing over
her, when she was again completely roused by hearing the creak of an approaching
footstep; she started up, and looked wildly round the room for some way of hiding
herself. The bed was the only means of
concealment it afforded, and she accordingly darted to the other side of it; hardly had she done so, when she perceived,
through the curtains, an old hag-like look-

ing woman enter, who, after looking about her, with evident indications of surprise, began advancing towards the place where Rose had concealed herself, that is, between the bed and the wall.

Rose at this could no longer command herself; a shriek escaped her, and rushing out, she attempted to make her escape from the chamber; but was prevented by the old woman, who, notwithstanding her age, was quite as nimble, at least on this occasion, as she was.—" Ah! then what's the matter with you ?" she cried, holding her fast by the arm, by which she had seized her. " Sure then, my *jewel,* any how you don't take me for a witch, or a banshee, or a ghost—blessed Mary preserve us!" crossing herself, " or a fairy, that you look so scared ? Faith and troth gra, though there's plenty of them about this ould building, 'tis myself that's good flesh and blood, and has been so, any how, these seventy years !"

" Then I hope your age will induce you to act with honesty and humanity; if you have any Christian feelings, relieve me from the terror I am at present in; in a word, out of compassion to a miserable fellow-being, suffering under the most terrible apprehensions, let me know for what purpose I have been torn from my friends, and brought to this dismal place?"

" Ah then upon my conscience, and that's as good as if I had bibled it, 'tis the first time Kate Cavanagh's good nature was ever doubted! but dear, I don't wonder at your being in grief, for you'll never see the friends you have been taken from again."

" Never see my friends again! who has a right to detain me from them?"

" Troth *gra*, I know nothing more of the matter, than that *the* master means you sha'n't return to them."

" The master! and who do you mean by the master? is it Mr. Mordaunt?"

" Ah then see how 'cute you are!— troth, and it is himself, jewel."

" It is by his means, then, I have been kidnapped from my friends?"

" By who's else? sure, *honey*, this is his castle—one of the fine ould places his family got in this part of the kingdom, with many others, in the time of Cromwell; and a great and a rich man he is, who can do what he pleases."

" What, because he's rich?"

" Exactly so, *gra*."

" If he thinks so, he may find himself mistaken, however," said Rose—" find that his riches cannot set him above the laws of his country. I advise you therefore, for your own sake, as well as mine, not to lend yourself any longer to his villany; for, depend upon it, it will not escape punishment."

" Sure, *honey*, he says he has plenty of cause for keeping you here; so whether he can be punished or not for doing so, is more nor I know; but at all events, what need he care for the laws, when he has plenty of money to fee the lawyers if any one spakes against him? but be that as it may, troth, *jewel*, if I wished it never so much, I couldn't any how be after letting you go, for I have my husband here to watch over me; but all I can do for you I will, by making you snug and comfortable, if 'tis not your own fault; for our orders are, if you got obstropolous, to put you back again in the cavern, out of which you contrived to make your way so 'cutely."

" Then it was not intended I should be left there?"

" Left there!" repeated Kate, with a scream, as if horror-struck at the thought, " is it to be drowned alive! why, *jewel*, sure the tide flows in there at times. No, it was only intended you should be kept there till you got a little quiet, after finding yourself carried off from your friends."

" Quiet! and could it be thought I should readily become quiet, after finding myself torn away from my friends?"

" For all that, *jewel*, it will be the best thing you can do to try and become so, for sorrow *fut* of you, by hook or by crook, will be able to get out of this, as long as Darby and I live."

"And are you and Darby, by whom you mean your husband I suppose, the only inmates of the place?"

". The only living *sowls* here; 'tis many a long day since *the* master had any one but ourselves here."

"And are you not afraid obeying his orders about me, if I can prove that he has no right whatever to detain me here, and that I have friends who will not rest till I am discovered?"

"Troth, *gra*, there's no use in your preaching or coaxing; I as good as took my oath to *the* master, that hand or *fut* you shouldn't stir from this, without his lave; and any how it's not at this time of day I am going to perjure myself."

Rose's blood ran chill, her limbs trembled, and ere Kate could make an effort to catch her, she sunk at her feet.

On recovering her senses, she found herself on the chair by the window, with Kate hanging over her, chafing her temples, and Darby, as she at once conjectured the man to be she beheld, standing near, with a bottle and glass—a great, tall, gaunt-looking Irishman, with no other marks of age about him than those indicated by his deep wrinkles and changing hair; his athletic form still appearing to retain all its original muscular strength.

The moment Kate saw her unclose her eyes, she called to Darby for a drop of whiskey, which giving her, she offered to Rose, with an assurance that she would find it the right sort—the true *Inishone*, and the best thing in the world for warming and comforting her poor heart; but notwithstanding this assurance, and the preceding recommendation, the glass was pushed away, to the no small surprise of Kate, who, as she swallowed the " cordial drop" herself, exclaimed—" Well, to be sure, to see the difference there is betwixt people! but feel her hand, if she is not as cold as clay.—Ah then, Darby dear, since we can't get her to take a drop to warm her, blow up a sod or two, and put down the kittle, that I may get her a dish of tay. And, *jewel*," she proceeded, addressing herself to Rose, while Darby retired to obey her orders, " while I'm getting breakfast, wouldn't you be after trying to get a little rest? I'll get the bed ready in a minute for you, and a little rest will do you great good I think."

Exhausted by fatigue, anxious to be at liberty to try and collect her scattered, or rather bewildered thoughts, Rose made no objection; and with all the alacrity of a young person, Kate set about preparing the bed for her, continuing to assure her, while busied in doing so, that if not her own fault, she would be comfortable enough, as the best of every thing would be hers, and the range of the fine grand ould apartments of the castle, and plenty of good clothes, that had already been sent for her by *the* master.

Rose could not sleep, but felt it a refreshment to be able to recline her exhausted frame. After giving vent for some time in tears to the feelings of her surcharged heart, she began to recover some little degree of composure, through the arguments she made use of with herself; she saw there was no longer any cause for personal apprehension, and that even if her gaolers could not be won over to set her at liberty, there was still, from their manner, nothing particularly terrible to be dreaded from them. In addition to these sources of comfort, she deemed it hardly possible that the efforts she was well aware would be made to ascertain her fate, should not be successful; and, in short, hope, that springs eternal in the human mind, began again to exert its buoyant influence over hers. But whatever was the good nature of Kate, on which poor Rose built not a little, it certainly was not of a description that could induce her to do any thing likely to be injurious to her own interest; as far as words, and attentions to her comforts went, she was kind to Rose, but no further; to all she said or urged on the subject of letting her depart, she was as deaf or insensible as a post, neither entreaties, promises, or threats, having the slightest effect upon her; nor with all her address could Rose betray her into any

intimation of where she actually was; so
that whether removed to a distance from
her late residence, or still in its vicinity,
she remained as ignorant as ever.

Three days elapsed in this way, during
which she experienced all the agitations
of alternate hope and despair—now deeming it most unlikely that her friends
should not succeed in tracing her—now
fearing, from not already having heard
something of them, that their search would
prove fruitless, from the precautions taken
in carrying her away.

On the evening of the third day, as she
stood almost unconsciously gazing on the
rippling waves, from a window in her
chamber, she saw a small vessel standing
in for the bay, that from its gay streamers
she judged to be a pleasure-yacht. Her
heart throbbed tumultuously—could she
but attract the attention of those within
it! but even if they landed, she should be
at such a distance from them; and then
the windows of the room were so deep
sunk within the walls, that except she

could gain the summit of the tower, which from the precautions of Kate she now knew to be out of the question, she had but little hope of being able to obtain their notice; she remained, however, immovably watching the vessel. At last it cast anchor, and a gentleman, attended by a servant, landed, and began to ascend towards the castle; but whether with an intention of entering it, she could not ascertain, the court that gave immediate admission to the building being screened from her view by high masses of wall, overrun with weeds and brambles.

CHAPTER VI.

"Seems he a dove ! his feathers are but borrow'd ;
For he's disposed as the hateful raven.
Is he a lamb ? his skin is surely lent him ;
For he's inclin'd as is the ravenous wolf.
Who cannot steal a shape that means deceit ?"

IF Kate saw or knew any thing about the
strangers, Rose conceived it not unlikely
her being able to learn the circumstance
from her, and accordingly, under this idea,
waited with extreme impatience for the
hour that usually brought her with her
supper to her: with this Kate did not
make her appearance till considerably beyond the usual hour this night.

" Why, I thought," said Rose, fasten-
ing her eyes on her with intense anxiety,
" that I should not have seen you to-night,
Kate ;" but determined to try what the
effect of taking her by surprise might be,

"I accounted for your delay by your having visitors."

"Ay, visitors indeed—the de'il welcome them!" cried Kate, in a muttering voice; "their room would be more welcome than their company; not to be sure but that one must allow the son has a right to be welcome to his father's house."

"What, is young Mr. Mordaunt the person I saw landing from the vessel?" eagerly demanded Rose.

Kate raised her twinkling little eyes to her, with a scowling look—"Well, *musha*, and what then?" she said, in a tone evidently indicative of vexation at having betrayed so much.

"Oh, nothing!" replied Rose, endeavouring to still the perturbation of her heart; "only what brought him here, I wonder, as the place does not seem exactly in a state for visitors?"

"Old Nick, I suppose," cried Kate; "I'm sure it's myself that had a plague of him, two or three years ago, when he took it into his head to come over with a set like himself, turning every thing topsyturvy, till one didn't know whether they stood upon their head or their heels."

" Well, and is he now accompanied by any one?" asked Rose again, in spite of her wish to appear unconcerned, in an eager tone.

Kate looked at her for a moment without speaking, and then—" Well, what's the signification whether he is or not?" she said; " but anyhow I can tell you, Darby says, that if he finds you put hand or fut beyond the gallery whilst he is here, he'll make you go back to the cavern."

" Well, I am in your power," said Rose, " and must therefore submit to your tyranny; but I trust it will not be for a much longer time."

Policy prevented her saying more on the subject; if any benefit could be derived from what had occurred, it would probably be by her not seeming to be aware of the likelihood of any thing of the kind, and accordingly, influenced by this

idea, soon appeared to think no further
about it. That Mordaunt was not in the
confidence of his father was evident, else
would there have been no necessity for
concealing her from him; could she but
once make known to him the way in
which she was circumstanced, she hardly
permitted herself to doubt obtaining from
him the interference she required, more
especially if she did not permit herself to
disclose his father being the person she
had to complain of; but how to obtain an
opportunity for imparting to him what
she wished, she saw would perplex her
not a little.

Of Mordaunt's readiness to become her
champion, if acquainted with his character, she would not have entertained even
the shadow of a doubt, being exactly of a
description to render such an adventure
agreeable to him; but though he might
vie with the knights-errant of old in real
bravery and rashness, he assuredly could
not compete with them in real strictness
of principle, or, in other words, disinter-

estedness of motives for what he did—in
short, he was a gay, fashionable, dissipated
young man, brought up as the heir to an
immense fortune, in the lap of luxurious
indulgence, and allowed to become his
own master ere he knew what the government of passion was; his mother was a
beautiful Italian, of whom it was reported
his father had become enamoured ere his
first marriage, and with all her beauty, her
son seemed to inherit all her haughtiness
of character: he had, however, his redeem-
ing qualities—he was generous to what
the worldly-minded would have considered even a fault, kind in his feelings, and,
in all but affairs of gallantry, strictly honourable. His coming over to Ireland at
this period was unknown to all at home;
but he very seldom condescended, or rather took the trouble of making his movements known there; a friend of his had
become attached to a young heiress belonging to the Emerald Isle, at one of the
fashionable bathing-places in England; his
passion was not unpleasing to the lady:

but as soon as they saw she encouraged it,
her friends hurried her away, his fortune
not being exactly what they considered
they had a right to expect for her: but
the gentleman was not so easily to be disappointed, and on receiving a letter from her,
intimating that if on the spot, she thought
she might be able to manage an elopement
with him, Mordaunt, his confidant in the
affair, undertook conveying him over in
his yacht; and having landed him near
her residence, which happened to be in
this part of the kingdom, steered forthwith for the old castle of the cliff, there
to wait the issue of the adventure.

A day passed without Rose seeing, or
hearing any thing more about him, when,
on the decline of the second, as she was
standing at the window, now her almost
constant station, she suddenly observed
him loitering before it: she instantly attempted to raise the sash, but, to her utter
dismay, found, that while asleep in the adjoining chamber, to which, at her desire,
the bed had been removed, in order that

she might have the outer one for a sitting apartment, advantage had been taken of the circumstance to fasten both it and the other, in such a manner as to render impracticable any effort on her part to open it. Finding this the case, she would have forced out a pane, but at the instant she was muffling up her hand in her handkerchief for the purpose, she heard the step of Kate, and instantly retreated from the window, lest of exciting any suspicion or alarm in her mind.

Just as she was drawing back from it, Mordaunt, happening to turn, caught a glimpse, or rather fancied he caught a glimpse of her—for he was not quite certain whether what he saw was a shadow on the window, or in reality a human figure. A summons to dinner prevented his making an effort to satisfy himself on the point; but just as Kate was retiring from the room where he dined, after inquiring with all obsequiousness whether all was to his honour's liking, he carelessly demanded who she had got in the castle beside herself and her husband?

Kate was a little startled at the question, but concealing her emotion under a vacant look, with her usual cunning she inquired why he asked?

"Why, because I imagined," replied Mordaunt, in a still more careless tone, "that I saw some one at one of the windows."

"Oh, then the sorrow one your honour could have seen, for sorrow one but myself and the ould man live here; I got my niece, Biddy Connor, to come here last winter, but she thought she saw a ghost one night in the hall, and so off with her the next morning, in spite of all I could do to keep her, nor could all my coaxing ever get her back again."

Mordaunt's valet, who stood high in the confidence of his master, was in attendance on him at the moment. On Kate's retiring, he proceeded, evidently laughing, to satisfy himself that the door was closed.

" You seem amused, sir," said his master, happening to glance at him ; " pray
what has diverted you ?"

" Faith, sir, the ready invention of that
old hag,"

" What, is it a falsehood then she has
told me ?"

" As great a one as ever was invented—
there's some one here she wishes to remain undiscovered."

" Indeed ! and pray how may your sagacity have enabled you to find out that ?"

" You shall hear, sir—about three
hours ago, chancing to stroll into the kitchen, I saw a nice dinner there, consisting of a chicken, and vegetables, and
I don't know what, nicely dished out
on a tray, as if just about being served
up; upon which, of course concluding
it was for you, sir—' Pooh, pooh !' I
said, ' how stupid to get my master's
dinner ready so early, when he won't
dine these several hours !'—' Well, what
then ?' was the exclamation, in rather a
gruffish tone.—' What then !' I repeated ;

' why, of course, that dressed so long before he wants it, by the time he sits down to it, it won't be worth eating.'—' Ah! we'll see that,' said the old hag, ' for all that your master won't be finding fault with his dinner when he gets it;' and so saying she threw a cloth over the things, as if to hide them from my further inspection, and whipping up the tray, marched off with it. I couldn't help being curious to see what she was about, and accordingly stealing after her, followed her through two or three dark passages, to the entrance of one of the towers, whence about midway up the spiral stairs, she crossed one of the small apartments to a door communicating with the adjoining gallery, and disappeared: having taken the precaution of locking the door as she passed through, I, of course, could follow no further; but pausing to listen at it, I heard the voice of a lady, I'm certain."

" Young or old—couldst thou make out?" said his master.

" Young, I think."

"*Tant mieux!* I am the hero then for the adventure; but contrivance, I presume, will be requisite; for her priest alone, I conclude, could extort a confession of the truth from this Hecate."

" If even he could, if she deemed it her interest to conceal it."

Mordaunt, who was literally beginning not to know what to do with himself, was not a little pleased to meet with something to divert and occupy him; he had a lively imagination, that was easily excited, and became, in consequence, quite impatient to know more about the person of whom he had just heard. Kate was called back, for the purpose, as she was led to believe, of receiving some directions about supper; but just as she was again leaving the room, Mordaunt stopped her, to ask if there was not some part of the castle locked up that he had not yet seen.

" *Och*, no, your honour! that is, yes, to be sure there is, to keep in the rats; it's ourselves that would have been kilt long ago by them, they swarm so in these buld rooms, if we didn't keep the key turned upon them."

"Well, that's a good joke!" said Mordaunt; "as if the rats, if inclined to pay you a visit, would be kept away by a locked door! Despite of their inmates, I choose to see these apartments."

"Is it to be poisoned with dust, your honour? why, it's many a long day since any thing was done to these rooms; and then it's full of holes the floors are."

"No matter, see them I will; I don't know but I may have some part of the castle fitted up, and I choose to see the entire of it before I give any orders for the purpose."

"To be sure, your honour; but *musha* if I can tell, if I was hanged for it, where the key is; I never could make it out, high or low, since that jade, Biddy, was here; but I'll be sending to her to-morrow, and then I'll try if I can hear any thing about it."

"No, don't give yourself that trouble— I dare say we shall be able to manage without any thing of the kind.—So, do you hear, sir," turning to Johnson, " be in readiness to assist in forcing the door."

" Oh no, for the Lord's sake!" screamed the terribly-alarmed Kate; " for sure, if there's any mischief done, it's kilt myself will be by *the* master for it, for all the blame will be laid to my door. If your honour will have but a little patience, I'll try if I can't make out the key for you, without sending to Biddy for it."

" Well, away with you; but remember, if not back in a few minutes, I shall assuredly break open the door."

Kate withdrew, but in a state of perplexity that kept her for a few minutes motionless outside the door. She knew not but what Darby's assistance might be requisite in getting Rose out of the way; but then, she was equally uncertain that the determination of Mordaunt might not be imputed to some carelessness or inattention on her part, for Darby was not the most loving husband in the world; and accordingly she finally made up her mind to running all risks, rather than most likely incur abuse from him. Hastening to Rose the moment she had decided on this, she told her, in few words, that she must accompany her to another part of the castle, seizing her by the arm as she spoke, to conduct her to a room beneath the ones she occupied, and to which a flight of stone steps, concealed within the walls, and unknown to Rose till this instant, led from the chamber she slept in.

Convinced from this, and the perturbation of her manner, that some discovery relative to herself had taken place, Rose resolved not to let her succeed in her effort to get her out of the way; disengaging her arm from her, she peremptorily refused to stir from the apartment where she was. The eyes of Kate absolutely sparkled with rage at this declaration; after surveying her for a minute, with all the supposed malignancy of a witch, she again seized her arm, to try and force her away, but Rose resisted with all her might. She could not, however, immediately free herself from the grasp of the hag; while struggling for the purpose the door opening from the tower into the gallery was burst open, and the voice of Mordaunt, who, perfectly aware of what the intention of Kate was, had followed close on her steps, was heard.

Foiled in her plan of getting Rose out of the way, Kate no sooner distinguished the accents of Mordaunt than, with a loud scream, she rushed out of the apartment, and with outstretched arms opposing his immediate entrance into it, besought him to listen to her for a minute ere he proceeded.—" It's no use for to go to deny any longer," she said, " that there's some one here; and it's myself that never would have thought to deceive your honour about it, only for feard of *the* master."

" Why, you old witch!" exclaimed Mordaunt, " you don't want to insinuate that my father is in any way concerned in having a person confined here?"

" Is it myself," exclaimed Kate, with

a scream of well-counterfeited astonishment at the supposition—" is it myself say any thing disparaging of his honour? sure and that's the last thing I should be after thinking of!"

" Then why say it was out of fear of him you told me the falsehood you did?"

" Why, because the young lady that's here," replied Kate, determined to persevere in this story, let Rose say what she would in contradiction to it, under the hope, that if she concealed Mordaunt's being the person through whose means she was confined in the castle, he might be induced to forgive the discovery of the circumstance, " is the niece of an ould friend of his, who, to keep her out of the way of a scapegrace she wanted to run away with, asked the master's leave to lock her up here."

Mordaunt would not suffer himself to be detained another minute; a young lady locked up on the score of love was an object too interesting to his imagination not to render him impatient to see her. He rushed forward, Rose heard him ap-

proaching, and, as well as she could, tried
to collect herself to receive him, with a
determination not to attempt any contradiction to the statement of Kate, since she
felt indeed that it would be an awkward
and embarrassing thing to accuse the father to the son.

To a young lady so romantically circumstanced as she was, a romantic imagination always attaches the idea of beauty;
but for beauty such as met his eye on encountering Rose—beauty so replete with
all that grace and elegance that charms
and inspires love, that expression of sentiment that, at once affects the heart, and
seizes on the impassioned soul, he was not
by any means prepared: his start of surprise, his sudden stop, his eager gaze, all
proclaimed the feeling of the moment.
He was indeed transfixed for an instant,
so much was he taken by surprise. Quickly, however, recovering himself, he advanced towards the fair object of his admiration, and, with the elegance that was
so natural to him, apologized for the re-

cent disturbance, but which he expressed
his hope she would excuse, from the consideration of its being a means of introducing a person to her who only wanted
to know how he could serve her to devote
himself to the purpose.

Rose unhesitatingly informed him, from
the moment she knew of his being in the
castle, she had been on the watch to obtain his interposition, and now imploring
his protection, besought him not to let a
moment be lost in restoring her to her
friends.

This was a request, however, Mordaunt
could not think of complying with; what
he had heard of a lover entirely militated
against his acceding to it, so completely
was he charmed with her himself; but, of
course, his motive for not attending to it
was not to be suspected. After the hesitation of a moment, he assured her he
should instantly do as she required, had
he the power of seeing her himself from
the castle; but he was just then so peculiarly situated, that this was a happiness

he could not immediately give himself, and he much feared, from all he had heard and seen, there was no one else to whose care she could safely commit herself—a duel, which threatened to be attended with a fatal result, and in which he had unfortunately been a second, compelled him to a temporary concealment; but, one way or other, he should shortly, he was convinced, be out of suspense as to what he had to apprehend, and the moment he was, (till when he trusted she would remain satisfied in her present situation,) she might rely on his being her escort.

Upon hearing this, Rose immediately decided on writing to Mrs. Brady, as she could neither bring herself to think of remaining any longer in the castle, nor yet of leaving it without protection she could depend on. Having decided on this, she made known her intention to Mordaunt, in order to ascertain whether he would undertake having a letter conveyed for her, and where she actually was.

Happy at finding her still ignorant of

this, he had no hesitation in deceiving her on the subject, making her not only believe she was several miles distant from Mrs. Brady's, but in a part of the country so wild and dreary, as to render it unsafe for any one to travel who thought they had an enemy.

The moment the letter was finished, it was consigned to him. With eager impatience, the instant he received it from her fair hand, he withdrew, conceiving it might be a means of enabling him to judge how far matters had proceeded between her and the envied lover. Rose, however, lest of accidents, had worded her letter with such caution, as to prevent his deriving any kind of gratification from its perusal.

From the moment she believed it probable it might have been received, she became all restlessness and perturbation, from the hourly expectation she was in of seeing her friend; but when three days elapsed, without either seeing or hearing from her, hope and expectation began to.

give place to a misgiving of treachery, and
which she disclosed to Mordaunt.

With a well-dissembled look of regret,
since she had revealed her apprehension
about the fate of her letter, he would not
deny, he said, being under a similar one
himself, in consequence of having been
compelled to intrust it to a messenger of
Kate's recommending, adding, that since
it was very unlikely one to be depended
on could be procured, it was his advice,
to save herself needless trouble and anxiety, that for a few days longer, when he
fully expected he should be at liberty to
act as he pleased, she should endeavour to
make herself easy where she was.

Rose reluctantly consented, believing
it indeed useless to write again, and wanting courage, from what she had heard, to
depart from the castle by herself. Having
prevailed on herself to acquiesce in this
insidious advice, she set about endeavouring to calm her agitated spirits. This was
what Mordaunt wanted: so long as she
remained under her recent agitation, or

excitement of feeling, he knew it would
be useless hoping to engage or attract her
attention in the manner he wished; but
once sufficiently composed to permit of a
tranquil association, and he flattered himself his attentions would not be without
effect. Of his personal advantages he was
by no means ignorant—the success that
had hitherto marked his efforts to please
did not permit him to be so; and aided,
as his seductive arts would now be, by the
peculiar situation of the fair object against
whom they were directed, he entertained
but little doubt of ultimately triumphing
as he wished.

To the admiration she had inspired
Rose could not be blind, but she trusted
the statement of Kate would operate in
repressing any indications of this that
could be displeasing to her. But this was
a hope she soon saw was an idle one: Eugene had taught her the language of passion, and the feelings of Mordaunt were
but too soon understood, notwithstanding
the caution with which he wished to veil

them for the present, lest of prematurely alarming her. She tried to hope, however, that by not seeming to understand them, she might check them, and accordingly, forced herself to meet his burning glances, to hear his sighs, and feel the trembling pressure of his hand, without any apparent emotion, but at the same time, tried to gradually withdraw herself from his society.

With Kate for his friend, however, her efforts to absent herself from him proved ineffectual. Kate was one of those beings who made her own interest her paramount consideration; and finding it would be for this to please young Mordaunt, she soon became as completely subservient to him as she had ever been to his father.

Some books, that the yacht contained, were brought on shore, for the purpose of being read to Rose—works of some of the most celebrated poets of the day; they were well calculated to have a softening effect upon the feelings; and the justice that was done to them in reading by Mor-

daunt, was not of a description to lessen
this: his finely-modulated tones were the
very ones indeed for passion to breathe
itself in; and Rose found it difficult indeed, while listening to him, to maintain
the semblance of that cold composure she
had deemed it expedient to assume. If
for a moment, however, by a stealing tear,
a quivering lip, a sudden suspension of
the work she affected to be engaged on,
she forgot herself, it was only requisite for
Mordaunt to turn his penetrating eye on
her to see how she was affected, to recall
her to recollection. At length, his patience exhausted, his vanity mortified,
Mordaunt could not forbear, one evening,
on her complaining of her cruel detention
at the castle, from bitterly reproaching her
for the indifference which this complaint
was indicative of towards him—" Was
there any sympathy in our feelings," he
cried—" could you complain of what al-
lows us to enjoy the society of each other
without interruption ?"

VOL. III. H

" I don't comprehend you," replied
Rose, with cold gravity; " it would be
strange, I conceive, if I was not in some
degree impatient, under a circumstance
that keeps me away from my friends."

" Yes; but when you know your restoration to them will be a means——but
you say you do not understand me; can
I believe this?"

" At least believe," answered Rose,
" that I wish to understand nothing that
can make me regard you in any other
light than that of a person I can place confidence in. I hoped—I imagined, that
what the woman here gave you to understand, would have checked the expression
of any sentiment I should be disinclined
to listen to: let this however suffice, if
any further attempt be made to intrude
upon me subjects that are disagreeable, I
shall permit no consideration of danger to
detain me longer here,"

Mordaunt, not without a secret execra-
tion against himself for having betrayed
his feelings, till first assured of having ex-

cited some little interest in her heart, entreated forgiveness, assuring her if she
would but strive to forget what had displeased, he would not offend in this way
again.

On this condition, Rose promised what
he requested, feeling still fearful of departing without his protection.

From what had now occurred, Mordaunt saw clearly, that to hope to win her
so easily, or, in other words, supplant another in her affections, as from his high
opinion of himself he had conceived likely
to be the case, was out of the question; and
as remaining much longer where he was,
was, on many accounts, a thing not to be
thought of, he decided on a plan for taking her away with him; but which, for
fear of exciting suspicion, he determined
on not being precipitate in carrying into
effect.

CHAPTER VII.

> " Vice is a monster of such frightful mien,
> As to be hated, needs but to be seen;
> But seen too oft, familiar with her face,
> We first endure, then suffer her embrace."

WHILE young Mordaunt was revelling in the indulgence of guilty anticipations, his father was experiencing all the disquietudes of an alarmed spirit. On conveying Rose to the castle, he gave Kate to understand he was about returning to England; but such was not his intention, the intimation being merely given for the purpose of ascertaining how those in whom he was compelled to place confidence would act, if they thought him out of the way, and thus whether they were indeed to be depended on: that he previously had proof of this was certain; but then he knew not what alteration or change time might have effected in their principles or feelings; and, in short, felt all that fear and suspicion that still tortures the wicked. He soon contrived to learn the horrible surmise Rose's strange disappearance had given rise to in the mind of Mrs. Brady; but the assurance of all further inquiry after her being suspended for the present, in consequence of the belief of her having destroyed herself, afforded him but little relief, when he reflected how immediately in the vicinity of her late residence she was.

Aware of all the danger of allowing her to remain there, he would speedily have removed her from the castle, had he known how immediately afterwards to dispose of her. But this was not the case; his plan relative to her was a hasty and ill-digested one, and had consequently placed him in a dilemma respecting her, from which he knew not how to extricate himself. Unexpectedly, however, he was relieved from this by the information of one of his agents, that a vessel was about sailing from a neighbouring port for Portugal, the master of which, for a certain sum, undertook to take charge of, and place her in a convent there.

Something of this kind was what Mordaunt had had in contemplation; of course he received this intimation with no small pleasure, and all requisite matters being quickly arranged, proceeded to the castle for the purpose of giving up Rose to others.

On coming within sight of the building, he was somewhat startled by the sight of the vessel in the little bay before it; it struck him as bearing a strong resemblance to his son's yacht. But, no—surely no demon had driven him over at such a period!—In no slight agitation, however, at the bare surmise, he hurried forward, impatient to be out of doubt on the circumstance.

The actual appearance of one of those ghosts or banshees she so often pretended to see or hear, could hardly have startled Kate more than did his at the moment, so entirely unexpected was it, and so much was there to discover in the castle she wished to keep from his knowledge.

" Why, what the deuce, you have almost deafened me by your scream at seeing me!" he exclaimed, as he stole in upon her in the kitchen.

" Scream! ah, then, no wonder," cried Kate, making an effort to recover from the confusion into which he had thrown her, " when from thinking your honour was in England, I didn't know but that it was your honour's fetch I saw !"

" Well, you are now satisfied that it is not.—But whose vessel is that down in the bay ?"

" Vessel—vessel!" repeated Kate; " ah, then, isn't it lord Belturbert's ?" she added with ready quickness.

" His! And what brought it here?"

" Troth if myself knows: but it often puts in here."

" Oh, then there's nothing particular in the circumstance now ?".

" No, sorrow thing."

Satisfied by her answers that he had

alarmed himself without cause, Mordaunt presently became sufficiently composed to inquire about her charge.

Kate, in reply, with her usual cunning, to make the most of her own conduct, made the worst of Rose's; protesting there was no one knew the life she led with her, she was so violent at finding herself confined.

" You would be glad to get rid of her then ?"

" Troth and that's no lie, your honour."

" Then I am happy to tell you that will be the case to-night ;" and he proceeded to inform her, that about ten or eleven that night, a boat would be in the bay, to take Rose away.

Kate, after affecting great joy at hearing this, suddenly asked whether his honour wouldn't be pleased to take a seat by the fire, drawing forward one for him as she spoke, while she went to get a more *dacent* place ready for him.

Mordaunt did not refuse ; and having seen him seated, she hurried off to apprize young Mordaunt of what had happened. Little dreaming of any thing so *mal-à-propos,* he was sitting at tea with Rose, indulging himself in the dangerous contemplation of that loveliness that was every moment gaining still more upon him, insomuch as to confirm him in his determination of running all risks rather than resign her.

Kate having succeeded in giving him a wink, as she called it, unobserved by Rose, instantly after withdrew, and was quickly followed by him—" Well, what's the matter," he demanded, " that you gave me to understand you wanted to speak to me?"

" Matter !" she almost screamed—"*och !* and it's all over with us, that it is!"

" Why, what has happened—is captain Rock below?"

" Och! and I am sure, bad enough as myself would like to see the face of him, it's that I'd rather be after seeing than the face of him that's below now. *The* master is come."

"The devil he is!" exclaimed Mordaunt, starting.

"Oh! sorrow word of lie in it—he stole in upon me like a ghost, with a fine scheme in his head——that is, I mean," she added, recollecting herself, "acquainted with a fine scheme of the crature's uncle here, to have her carried off in a boat to-night, the Lord only knows where!"

"Indeed! then we must be beforehand with him; so send Johnson directly to me, that I may give orders for having every thing got ready for sailing as soon as it gets dusk."

Kate hastened away to obey him, and he returned to Rose, to acquaint her with what he had heard, and his determination to run all risks rather than let her be carried off in the way that was intended; he mentioned the orders he had given about getting the yacht ready directly; and Rose, dreadfully alarmed by the information she had received, believing, as she did, his father capable of any villany, rea-

dily assented to his proposition of availing
herself of it to effect her escape.

Kate, it must be allowed, had now a
busy time of it; from the son she returned to the father, to try and keep him in
play, till the other had got off with his
prize.

Mordaunt was in that kind of state,
that her fidgeting about, under the pretext of her getting supper ready for him,
was extremely troublesome. He did not
like, however, to affront her, by telling
her at once to quit the room, and had recourse therefore to the pretext of wanting
to write a letter, to get rid of her. She
no sooner left him, than he went out; he
had no doubt of the truth of her statement respecting the yacht; but own it
who might, it was a very awkward circumstance being stationed where it was,
just at this critical time, when any discovery relative to Rose might not only be
the means of defeating his present scheme
concerning her, but of involving him
in the most terrible predicament. After

much perplexity on the subject, the only
plan he could devise for relieving himself
from this, was to watch for the boat, and
see whether it could not move lower
down the beach, out of sight of the vessel,
to take Rose in; and in pursuance of which
plan it was he went out, on being left to
himself.

In order to avoid the chance of being
encountered by any one from the vessel,
he took a straggling path to the beach.
He had not advanced far down it, when
he heard himself followed; he turned with
quickness, and, to his utter amazement,
beheld his son, with Rose leaning on his
arm.

Rose, with a faint scream, attempted to
draw back, but was prevented by her con-
ductor, who knew there was nothing now
for it, but to brave out the matter.

" So, sir," said his father, first regaining
the power of speech, " this is a *rencontre*
I indeed little expected! How will you
account for all this?—But why allow myself to inquire of you," he added, with a

contemptuous expression of countenance, " after the shameful imposition you have allowed to be practised on me?".

Young Mordaunt was not of a disposition to bear scorn, even from a father, tamely; his dark eye kindled with answering scorn, and—" I shall not attempt to deny what I hold myself fully justified for," he said. " Whatever I may have to repent or regret in this life, it will not be any thing into which I have been led for this lady."

" That lady!" repeated his father, turning of a horrible paleness; and, " what— what"—with evident difficulty he articulated—" have you to say to that lady? what right, I say, sir, have you to interfere about her?"

" The right which her meeting with cruelty and injustice gave her. Every one has a right to interfere where these are practised. She required my protection, and she shall have it, in spite of all opposition."

" And in conveying her hence, is it

your intention to restore her to those from whom she pretends to be torn? No, no —I know you too well, to give you credit for such disinterestedness; you may have deceived her, but me you cannot deceive; and I swear you do not triumph in your duplicity!"

Young Mordaunt became terribly agitated—it was evident his utmost efforts were requisite to enable him to keep his struggling feelings under any control.— " I should be sorry, sir," he said, with forced calmness, " to seem to forget for a moment the respect you claim as a father, but what I promised this lady, I will fulfil at all hazards."

" Wretched young man!" exclaimed his father, " how can you persevere in this perfidy? Do I not know, that in what you are now doing, you are actuated by any thing but motives of purity? But to punish you for it—to put an end to the hopes in which you are now rioting—to stop the rovings of that licentious fancy— know," he paused for a minute, and then, not without difficulty, added, " that girl is your sister !"

Rose, with a shriek, involuntarily repeated the word. Young Mordaunt, evidently trembling, and with a countenance of dismay, looked at her.—" Oh no !" she cried, interpreting his look, " it is not—it cannot be so! Were I his child, could he have abandoned me to others—could he have treated me as he has done? no—I do not—I cannot credit the assertion."

" I breathe again," said young Mordaunt ; " yes, I see how it is ; and had any one but a father had recourse to so shallow an artifice, to try to prevent what I was determined on, I should have known how to resent the insult accordingly."

" By earth, by heaven, I have attempted no imposition on you !" exclaimed his father, rushing before him, as he attempted to move on, with Rose still supported by his arm, or rather clinging to it ; " as sure as you are my son, that girl is my daughter !"

Young Mordaunt involuntarily paused ;

the asseverations were too solemn for derision—" Why then this long concealment
about her?" he demanded; " why——"

" Ask me not," interrupted his father,
with a frantic look, and in a corresponding
tone, " ask me not, here at least—perhaps
you'll too soon hear all."

" No, impossible !" retorted young Mordaunt; " for I cannot hear too soon, as I
hope I shall, that you are able to vindicate
yourself of the cruelty of which you are
now suspected."

" Oh, let us return to the castle," said
Rose; " for I feel myself sinking under
the overwhelming effect of this discovery."

By the time she regained it, she had a
little recovered herself, and with intense
anxiety turned her eyes upon Mordaunt,
as did his son, for the promised, or at least
expected explanation of his motives for so
long disclaiming her; but this could not
immediately be given—it had never been
contemplated; and with so much to conceal as there was, so much to abridge or
gloss over, Mordaunt could not think of

venturing on it without some consideration—" No, no, not to-night," he cried,
in a hurried accent, as with feverish impatience he paced the room, distracted at
the dilemma in which he found himself,
" not to-night," fully understanding the
looks that were directed towards him;
" my feelings are too agitated to permit
what is desired immediately; but by to-
morrow I hope I shall be sufficiently composed to account for what now appears so
extraordinary—till when I wish to be left
to myself."

Rose, with a deep sigh, immediately
quitted her seat to withdraw; but too well
conjecturing his motive for not coming to
an immediate explanation of his conduct,
and from which she could not help feeling
a sensation of horror at the recent discovery, to find herself so closely connected
with a being of whom she had conceived
such terrible suspicions, was indeed a shock
she could scarcely support.

CHAPTER VIII.

"He that once sins, like him who slides on ice,
Goes swiftly down the slippery paths of vice;
Tho' conscience checks him, yet these rubs got o'er,
He sins securely, and looks back no more."

MORDAUNT could have gnashed his teeth
—could almost have torn the quivering
flesh from his bones, at the thought of the
disclosure into which he had been betrayed. Yet was it not one to which conscience had been long goading him? but
in reply, had not the danger which he
was aware must attend it, decided him
against it? He trembled—he shuddered
—his blood ran cold at the thought of
what he might perhaps have incurred by
it. Was there no way of relieving himself from the horrible apprehensions under
which he now laboured? could he not re-
tract what he had said? but, no—the use-

lessness, the folly of such an attempt, was
too evident to permit him to dwell on the
idea : he had betrayed himself to those
who were too much interested in ascertaining the truth, to allow any further effort, at deception to succeed, and by attempting which he should, in all probability, only add to his difficulties, and
finally provoke what he now might perhaps by a little address avert. Whatever
were the surmises or suspicions of Rose,
once positively acknowledged as his daughter, could he suppose she would give utterance to them—utterance to any thing
that could affect his safety or character?
but again disclaimed, what was there to
withhold or prevent her from publishing
them? and once published, what had he
not to dread? Besides, supposing he
could hope to succeed in inducing it to be
believed that his recent assertion was an
idle one, the mere suggestion of the moment, would it not be only to free himself
from one dilemma to plunge himself into
another? for how slight was the authority

he knew he possessed over his son! it was therefore absolutely expedient, his best and safest policy, that he should not attempt to contradict himself. But should he be mistaken in his opinion of Rose—should the name of father be no protection from the resentment he must have excited in her mind, or rather should she conceive it but a duty to the memory of her other parent, to inquire further into the particulars of what he told her—in short, resolve on what he would, he found himself tortured by apprehension; but it was right, it was proper it should be so; he knew, he felt he merited still greater sufferings than his alarmed conscience now inflicted on him—that he deserved to be dragged forward to condign punishment, an awful warning to mankind of the fallacy of hoping to elude the recompence due to sin—a terrible proof of the Divine vengeance, however long delayed, being yet sure to overtake us. Having finally decided on the confirmation of his assertion, he at length began to try and recall

his scattered thoughts, in order to consider what statement he should make: that
the correctness of it might be suspected by
Rose, he was not without an apprehension; but he relied on her natural feelings
for him for not revealing this.

His late wife's father was his uncle, and
the representative of the family. At an
early age Mordaunt was thrown, an un-
provided orphan, on his protection, his
own father, calculating upon a long life,
having made no effort to save any immediate provision out of the profits of a high
official situation, which he held under government, for a family. Mr. Mordaunt
was a man of an austere temper, who did
not confer kindnesses or obligations without making them felt; and while he gave
to his nephew all the advantages befitting
his rank, he made him perfectly understand, that the slightest provocation would
deprive him of his favour.

Impressed with this conviction, young
Mordaunt soon became anxious to render
himself in some degree independent; and

accordingly, at a very early period, expressed a wish to be allowed to enter the army; but this was at once negatived, nor would any other profession be heard of; and what he meant to do for him, or how dispose of him, he could not possibly conjecture; his having a daughter of course precluding all expectation of any considerable provision being intended for him.

After going through the routine of education usual for young men of rank, his uncle sent him to travel, under the care of the gentleman who had been his private tutor at the university.

To the lively and inquisitive mind of young Mordaunt, nothing could be more agreeable than was this. After visiting almost all the places of note on the Continent, he at length arrived at Venice, where, as usual, through the letters of introduction his uncle had procured him (anxious that by mixing in the first society of the respective places he visited, he should profit as much as possible by his tour), he soon became acquainted with the most distinguished families there.

It was just at this period that the young heiress of the ancient and illustrious house of Barberini had made her *début* in life. Previously to seing her, Mordaunt had heard a great deal about her; but all that he heard, or all that he in consequence imagined, fell far short of what he conceived her, when at last he actually beheld her. To all the natural loveliness of early youth, she united all those fascinating attractions for which the Italian females have been celebrated—the Juno-like air—the exquisite contour—the cheek of rich carnation tint—the sparkling eyes, saying perhaps too much—above all, the voice of siren sweetness, that, as a late elegant tourist has observed, would of itself alone be sufficient, without the aid of any other charm, to render a Venetian lady captivating. Mordaunt did not attempt, perhaps could not, to disguise the admiration he felt; he soon became the shadow of the enchanting Elenora; and to all, as well as to himself, it was evident that his homage at her shrine was neither unpleasing to herself or family.

Handsome, lively, and accomplished, as Mordaunt was, that to her it should not be unpleasing, could not possibly have excited surprise; but that her family, with their religious prejudices, should appear to encourage, or in any way sanction it, was a matter of some little remark; but in the apprehensions to which her father the duke had for some time been secretly giving way, these were now lost: the revolution was now at its height in France—he foresaw all that was likely to result from it—and to avoid the storm he believed impending, the outrages and ravages he anticipated on the Continent, and in the adjacent states, had had it for some time past in contemplation to transport himself and family, with all of his property that was transportable, to England, with no other hesitation on the subject than what resulted from the consideration of the insulated state in which he should find himself there. So painful was this idea to a person who had hitherto lived in the midst of a numerous connexion, that he could not help now and then experiencing something like a dawning wish for an alliance between his daughter and some one of the Englishmen of rank that still visited the place—a wish the reality of which he could no longer deny to himself, when from the assiduities of Mordaunt to his daughter he beheld a possibility of its attainment, and to his inability to repress which Mordaunt was indebted for the encouraging condescension of his manner towards him.

How Mordaunt was exactly circumstanced was not known; nothing had occurred to call for an explanation on the subject, and that there was any obstacle to his union with his daughter, from the want of an independent fortune, the duke therefore remained in ignorance of.

To exist without Elenora, Mordaunt soon began to think impossible; yet that he should ever possess her, he considered most doubtful, for except his uncle could be induced to sanction his addresses to her, by giving him an independence sufficient in some degree to entitle him to her hand, how could he possibly imagine, that her family, distinguished as they had ever been for pride and ambition, would bestow her on him? But, with his uncle's pride, the wish he had always evinced to aggrandize his family, would he not be delighted at the idea of his forming so illustrious an alliance? and under the persuasion, he was at length on the point of addressing him on the subject, when he received a letter from him, commanding him, in the most peremptory terms, to return to England, without a moment's delay after the receipt of it.

A little recovered from the shock attendant on the thought of so sudden a separation from his mistress, Mordaunt knew not how to regret a circumstance that would be the means of sooner termi-

nating his suspense about her, than a letter could possibly have been.

Immediate orders were given for his
departure; and in his farewell visit at the
Barberini palace, he informed them there,
that they might rely on either soon hearing from or seeing him again, an intimation which he trusted would make them
understand what he wished, namely, his
hope of being considered a pretender to
the hand of the lovely Elenora.

His uncle was by no means a man of
gracious habits; Mordaunt therefore could
not help being a little surprised, notwithstanding the prompt obedience he had
shewn to his commands—his consciousness,
indeed, that as yet he merited nothing unkind from him, at the reception he now
met from him; it was absolutely affectionate; and with the natural sanguineness of
youth, Mordaunt allowed himself to augur
from it every thing that was agreeable to
his wishes. But he was not long allowed
to remain in a state of delusion; the pe-

riod for understanding the real views and
intentions of his uncle respecting him had
now arrived, and with very little delay he
was given to understand, that for the sake
of aggrandizing his family, by keeping his
fortune entirely in it, his uncle had long
contemplated, and absolutely decided on, a
marriage between him and his cousin.

Mordaunt was thunderstruck; he could
not immediately speak, nor if he could
would he have done so—for how could he
express joy, express gratitude, at what his
very soul shrunk from? yet neither could
he his real feelings, convinced as he was, that
to disclose them would be his instant ruin.
But an answer must be given—there was
no alternative; he too well knew his uncle was a despot, who was not to be offended with impunity, and in faltering
accents he at length forced himself to express all he saw he expected him to say
on the occasion.

The die was cast: his mind was strong
and vigorous, and having acquiesced in
his uncle's plan, as soon as he had a little

got over its first overwhelming effect upon
him, he began to do what good sense dictated, by endeavouring to make exertions
to reconcile himself to it. As yet he had
not seen his destined bride, or at least
since they were both mere children, immediately after the death of her mother,
which happened when she was little more
than a mere infant, the young lady being
committed to the care of an aunt, at some
distance from her paternal home, by whom
she was brought up. But an introduction
between them was now no longer delayed;
and if Mordaunt had had a disengaged
heart, it is hardly possible but that it must
have been resigned to her; yet perhaps
there could not be a greater contrast than
she was to the enchanting being that had
already captivated it: the one was the
brilliant meteor, flashing upon the eye in
all the dazzling radiance of unrivalled
beauty—or rather the glowing rose, impossible to be overlooked; the other the meek
lily, liable to escape casual observation
from its concealing foliage, but when once

discovered, detaining the fascinated eye it
seemed anxious to avoid, from the charm
of its exquisite delicacy. Elegance was
indeed the charm of Miss Mordaunt, and
had Mordaunt been a painter, while the
enchanting Venetian would have been his
model for the queen of love, the other
would have been so for one of her attendant graces. Her manner corresponded
with her appearance—gentle, retiring, un-
assuming; Mordaunt could have fancied,
at times, there was an air of melancholy
in it—but what could have given rise to
such a feeling in her young bosom? and
as often as the thought occurred it was
dismissed, as a most improbable conjecture.

Preparations for their marriage immediately commenced. Proud, haughty, aspiring, fond of the glitter and parade that
the generality of mankind are attached to,
Mordaunt sought, in the splendour of these
preparations—in the idea of the affluence
that was about being secured to him, to
lose or stifle his regret for the loss of the

beautiful Venetian, but in vain—his heart
still clung to her idea with passionate regret; and at length yielding to the un-
pardonable, the cruel selfishness of that
heart that would be remembered by her,
though but too well aware to be so must
be at the expence of her tranquillity, he
addressed a letter to her, explanatory of
all that had occurred—his feelings, his sentiments, his disappointed wishes, his frus-
trated intentions, the cruel circumstances
that had compelled him to act so contrary
to the real dictates of his torn heart; and
which concluded by a passionate entreaty
to be allowed to retain a place in her memory, as a being that, whilst life remained, must continue to worship and idolize
her idea.

The marriage feast was hardly over
when the bridal festivities were exchanged
for lament and mourning; his uncle, in the
midst of his rejoicings at the completion
of his long-contemplated plan, suddenly
expiring in a fit. Had his marriage been
but a little longer delayed! was the invo-

luntary reflection of Mordaunt at the
moment; yet he had no right to complain of his destiny; he was united to a
lovely woman, whom every body admired
—he was possessed of a fortune that rendered him at once envied, caressed, and
followed—and he had a long perspective
of years before him for its enjoyment.

.. Domestic life was not the kind of life
that his proud and ostentatious spirit could
take pleasure in; yet he was not altogether inattentive to his wife, till by chance,
or at least seeming chance, he discovered
that she had been fondly, firmly, with the
sanction of her aunt, attached to another,
and that her acquiescence in her father's
plan for their union had been, like his, the
effect of fear, not choice. He immediately chose to imagine himself an injured
man from the circumstance, forgetting
that it was one he had no more right
to complain of, than he would have
permitted her to think she had of his
previous attachment to the Venetian;
but we are seldom as unjust to ourselves

as we are to others. Mordaunt was too selfish, had too much pride and vanity, not to make him wish to be the first in every one's regard and estimation; and from the moment he had reason to imagine, though certainly not from her demeanour or conduct, that he did not occupy the heart of his wife, from that moment he became utterly neglectful of her.

Just about this juncture the Barberini family arrived in England. Mordaunt could not resist the impetuous impulse that urged him immediately to throw himself in the way of lady Elenora; her manner soon reassured him, soon convinced him that he had not addressed himself to her feelings in vain. His handsome person, his animated and accomplished manners, the numerous advantages he was possessed of, had, in short, completely subdued her heart; and such, in short, was the force of her attachment for him, as to render it next to impossible that a letter, artfully worded as his was, should not have had the desired effect—that of quickly appeasing any indignation his relinquishment of her might have provoked, or, in other words, making her view him as a being more deserving of commiseration than of resentment.

But for what was he now pursuing her, bound, fettered, as he was? Supposing he were capable of the baseness of meditating to take advantage of the confidence she reposed in him, must not her rank, the powerful protection she enjoyed in her illustrious family, prove an insuperable obstacle to the atrocious design? But all was not vague—there was a glimmering of hope for him—the constitution of Mrs. Mordaunt was certainly delicate; she was in a situation too that was often attended with peril, particularly to a frame of delicacy; and should it be, as it seemed to be far from improbable, what then was to prevent his possession of the enchanting object of his adoration, except—except (what a check to the revellings of his fancy the possibility!) the unfortunate off-

spring should survive its mother, in which
case her fortune would immediately be
taken possession of by trustees, according
to the irrevocable settlement of his uncle,
leaving him what could scarcely be called
a slender independence.

With what intense anxiety was every
look of Mrs. Mordaunt's, now watched!
but through what different feelings and
motives than those to which they were
naturally imputed! Yet not without a
sensation of absolute abhorrence against
himself, did he at times think of the motive for this watchfulness—not without
shrinking within himself at the light in
which he should be regarded—the horror,
the detestation, were his heart now open
to the view of mankind.

In a word, he hated himself, yet he
made no effort to overcome the cause of
this hatred—instead of yielding to compunction, he rather sought to stifle it—instead of fleeing temptation, to court it;
and the punishment due to his obduracy
was yet his.

He gradually became moody and reserved—without allowing himself to define, or perhaps well knowing if he could define it, he felt as if there was something gloomy, something terrible, in contemplation; his musings were all to himself; suddenly he declared that the declining state of Mrs. Mordaunt's health was such, that it was absolutely requisite to convey her to a milder clime.

Some were surprised, and some attempted to oppose the measure; amongst the latter was Mrs. Mordaunt herself—but in vain. We shall not enter into the tedious details of his arrangements on this occasion; suffice it, that instead of taking her to the Continent, as he gave out, he conveyed her to St. Doulagh's—but with a silence, a secrecy, a caution, that prevented the circumstance from being known, or even, for a time at least, suspected, by any one but those whom he had found it requisite to take into his confidence. He had previously been over, in his boyish days, and had, at that period, formed an intimacy with our old friend, Barney O'Rooke, that he now turned to account: in short, he had a private conference with O'Rooke, with whom his intimacy had been kept up, by many subsequent favours conferred on him; and having proved to him that it would be for his interest to serve him in the present instance, informed him that a strong suspicion of Mrs. Mordaunt's fidelity had induced him to determine on secluding her for some time from her usual associates; and that on him he relied for managing matters in such a way, that no suspicion of her being at St. Doulagh's should be entertained. In doing this there was no great difficulty; Darby and Kate, afterwards transferred to the castle on the cliff, were then the persons in charge of St. Doulagh's, and, of course, it was their interest to remain silent on any thing the person in whose service they were chose to conceal; and he (O'Rooke) had a relation of his own, whose services he knew he could readily command in attending on the lady.

Whatever was the surprise of Mrs. Mordaunt at what her husband pretended to be the sudden change in his intentions, she gave no utterance to any displeasure on the subject. The victim of parental tyranny, torn from the object of her tenderest affections, she was in that frame of mind, in that state of feeling, that rendered all places almost alike to her, or if one preferable to another, that which was most retired, most secluded: but even if inclined to be angry at the apparent caprice of Mordaunt, the specious reason he assigned for it would perhaps have prevented any expressions of displeasure at the circumstance—"It suddenly occurred to him," he said, "that a journey to the Continent would be too much for her, and that his best plan would be to take her to St. Doulagh's, where she would be sure of all that quiet her present situation and delicate state of health required."

Meaning that their being in it should remain a profound secret, of course Mordaunt took care that neither should be seen

beyond the walls of St. Doulagh's. How
ill, from the horrible feelings that tormented him — that made him anxious
to fly from himself, could he bear the
gloom, the solitude, to which he had
now condemned himself! but they would
not be of long endurance: Mrs. Mordaunt
was near her confinement, and as there
must consequently be speedily an end to
all further irresolution about her, he
should not much longer be under a necessity of remaining where he was. With
what eager, what intense anxiety, was he
now continually demanding of Mrs. Cormack, the person procured by O'Rooke
to be her immediate attendant, what her
real opinion of her was — whether she indeed thought that the hour of danger that
was approaching would be one of more
than usual danger to her!

Of course, imputing this solicitude to
feelings very different to those to which
it was in reality owing, Mrs. Cormack could
hardly help wondering at what she was
told of the suspected inconstancy of Mrs.

Mordaunt towards a husband so affectionate, as well as handsome and engaging in
every respect. Yet notwithstanding the
opinion she was led to form of her, she
felt it impossible not to be interested for
her; there was an uncomplaining sweetness in her manner, an air of resignation
to every thing, that imperceptibly gained
upon, and attached her to her, rendering
her at times incredulous of what she heard
—since it seemed to her hardly possible that
a creature so apparently heavenly-minded,
looking, speaking, so like an angel, could
be guilty of what she was accused: once
she ventured to hint this belief to Mordaunt; but the reception it met with silenced her ever after on the subject.

CHAPTER IX.

"——— ——— ———Betake thee
To nothing but despair: a thousand knees,
Ten thousand years together, naked, fasting,
Upon a barren mountain, and still winter,
In storm perpetual, could not move the gods
To look that way thou went."

AT length the hour so anxiously, or rather perhaps fearfully, looked forward to by Mordaunt arrived: and after remaining some time after its announcement in a state of conflicting feelings, to which no language could do justice, Mrs. Cormack abruptly entered the chamber where he was shut up, to inform him that he was the father of a lovely girl, likely to do well, as she also trusted was the mother.

Mordaunt gnashed his teeth—"Both—both—likely to do well!" he cried, abruptly turning round on her, for he had involuntarily sought to avoid her looks on her entrance; " are you certain—are you positively sure—about the mother at least?"

No—she could not be positively certain of any thing of the kind, was the reply; but, with the blessing of Heaven, she hoped there was no danger.

Mordaunt waved her from the room. Should he then be forced——but the reflection was too terrible to be pursued. He positively refused seeing the infant; and, on being urged, sternly declared he never would, from his conviction (determined now on bringing matters to a close) of its not being his. Still, though he felt himself meditating some dire deed, he had not regularly planned, or decidedly settled, any thing in his own mind.

At length, one evening he cautiously placed a bottle of laudanum amongst the other things deposited for her use, in a closet adjoining the bedchamber of Mrs. Mordaunt, that with no self-deceiving persuasion that it was with no sinister-hope. He strove to forget, to divert his thoughts from what he had done, but in vain; and after a useless struggle with himself for some hours, he suddenly rushed out from the place where he had shut himself up, to remove the drug; but it was gone. His lifeblood seemed to curdle round his heart at the instant; but it might not be too late to prevent what he dreaded, and suddenly reviving at the thought, he was hastening to the chamber of his wife, when, wildly calling upon his name, he encountered Mrs. Cormack coming out of it.—Mrs. Mordaunt was dying; she was suddenly seized with convulsions, and nothing could save her!

Mordaunt rushed past the nearly-distracted woman into the chamber: the first thing that caught his eye was the fatal bottle; he snatched it up—it was empty of its contents, and the dreadful fact was evident. Oh, the horror of that moment! the horror of feeling we have commited a crime beyond recall! he shrieked in the frenzy of the thought—he rushed to the bedside.—Was there no way of saving her? But, no—no—that moment she expired, and he was, to all intents and purposes, a murderer in his own sight, and that of Heaven—stained indelibly, everlastingly, with human blood! the destroyer of the fragile flower, that had been intrusted to his care, in full security of its being ever fondly cherished by him! the murderer of his near kinswoman—the daughter of him to whom he was indebted for education and support—of his wife —the mother of his child! Oh! what was all that the world could now offer him, guilt-stained, loaded as he was with crime? But he was soon checked in giving utterance to his anguish by alarm for his safety: the change that took place, almost instantly after her death, in the aspect of Mrs. Mordaunt, led her attendants to suspect what had happened, and both, almost in the same breath, protested their belief of her being poisoned.

" Poisoned!" repeated Mordaunt, reeling back through terror; then, in a moment, through absolute desperation, recovering his self-possession, and seeing at once the course he must pursue—" Yet it must be so," he cried; " there is no other way of accounting for this frightful change. Unhappy being! she could not bear her own upbraidings, and so——But, my friends, this is a thing I must expect your inviolable secrecy about—the honour of our family is involved in it. Should it be disclosed, the cause of it must be also known; and, out of reverence to the memory of the good old man her father, not merely my relative, but benefactor, I would not, exclusive of every other consideration, have her descend into the grave with a stigma on her name."

It was an ugly affair—a very awkward one to be concerned in; and this conviction prevented there being any hesitation in his obtaining the promise he so artfully required.

The party having a little collected themselves, it was settled, that a convenient spot about the castle should be sought out for the interment of the body; immediately after which Mordaunt de-

cided on setting out for the Continent, and
thence dispatching an account of her death
and the infant's; for, since he had incurred
the horrors of guilt, it should not be for
nothing, he resolved.

Acquainted with every nook and corner
in and about the castle, Barney was not
long in discovering just such a spot as was
required; and, as soon as the night was
sufficiently advanced to prevent any danger of surprise or observation, it was settled that they should remove the remains

They were on the very point of doing
so, when the old building seemed shaken
to its very foundation by a loud thundering at the hall-door. A guilty conscience
is easily alarmed, and to describe the consternation of Mordaunt at this moment
would be impossible: nothing struck him
but that, in some way or other, some
matter had occurred to make something
wrong be suspected in the neighbourhood;
he could no otherwise account for what
at such an hour, appeared so extraordinary
a circumstance, as that of any one re-

quiring admission, and every limb shook
with terror at the thought, feeling, as he
did, convinced, that if any discovery took
place, he must be lost, so completely would
every thing make against him.

What was to be done?—if right in his
surmise, to refuse opening the door would
be of no avail. There was an immense
large old-fashioned chest in the room with
the deceased, and after a momentary hesitation, Barney proposed its being made
use of, in this emergency, to conceal the
body.

Mordaunt eagerly caught at the idea,
and what he suggested being done, the
chamber was promptly stripped of whatever could lead to a belief of its being recently occupied; and while they, that is,
Mordaunt and Barney, proceeded to conceal themselves, Darby proceeded to open
the door to its rude assailant. This was
a gentleman in the neighbourhood, who
having heard it was strongly suspected
that Mr. Mordaunt was then at St. Doulagh's, took upon himself endeavouring to

ascertain the truth of the conjecture, and for the purpose of being enabled to do which, decided on calling at an hour when, from not being expected, there would be no precaution, of course he concluded, to prevent his doing so.

Darby, however, was properly instructed in the part allotted to him ; and in reply to the blunt demand of—" Was not Mr. Mordaunt then in the castle ?" expressed his wonder, rubbing his eyes all the time, as if just roused from his bed, at what could have given rise to such a thought, *the* master being neither then at the castle, nor, for what he knew, ever expected to be at it again, but then far away with the poor dying mistress.

" Very extraordinary ! very extraordinary !" cried the disappointed Mr. Burke ; " very extraordinary then that such a rumour should have got afloat ! however, I suppose 'tis a lie !" and so saying, he sprung into his saddle, and galloped back with as much haste as he had galloped forward.

That a rumour had indeed got abroad, of his being at the castle, was now evident to Mordaunt; his consternation at the conviction was unutterable. His only plan, he saw, was to depart as speedily as possible; and Barney agreeing in the expediency of this, no time was lost in the final arrangement of all matters between them.

After some consultation, it was finally settled that, for the present, lest of any watch being set upon the present movements in the castle, a circumstance that Barney deemed by no means improbable, the body should be allowed to remain where it had been so hastily deposited; and in short, before daybreak, the party had dispersed: Mordaunt, so disguised as to have rendered it next to impossible for any one to recognise him, was miles off; Barney again in his own home, congratulating himself on having so far got out of the scrape, in which, to his great regret, he saw he had involved himself; and Mrs.

Cormack on her way back to hers with the deserted infant, whom pity was every moment more strongly attaching her to. She was a kind-hearted, excellent woman, incapable of voluntarily becoming subservient to any thing that was base or cruel. She wanted not discernment, and the result of her recent observations was, to excite the most fearful imaginings in her mind concerning Mordaunt, such as presently determined her on not giving up the poor babe to him, as he gave her to understand he should expect she would, as soon as he reached a place whence he might with safety send for it. No, both out of pity for it, as well as for the sake of its angelic mother, of whose purity she had by this time no more doubt than she had of that of the patron saint at whose shrine she knelt, she firmly resolved, let what would betide her for keeping it, not by giving it up to let it,

" With the innocent milk in its most innocent mouth,"

be haled out—she could make use of no

other expression—to murder; for the disposition old Mr. Mordaunt had made of his fortune was well known, and of course she was aware, that this poor infant was the only bar to its father's becoming sole possessor of the family property. But her husband was of a very different nature to hers; and to prevent any opposition to her plan, she was obliged to impose upon him the belief, of being assured of a handsome recompence for taking charge of the child, the real parentage of which she affected to be ignorant of; and taking an opportunity shortly after of having a private conference with Barney, she positively declared to him, that if he attempted to contradict the statement she meant to make of the child's death to its father, she would, without further hesitation, reveal all that had taken place at the castle; let the consequence of such a proceeding, and bad enough she had grounds for believing it would be, be what it might, to those concerned in the transactions there.

K 2

This threat was quite sufficient to induce the acquiescence she required from Barney—he took the solemn oath she demanded, to keep secret what she desired; and on receiving a letter from Mordaunt, instructing him to send her, with the infant, to him, returned for answer that the child was dead.

Whether Mrs. Cormack purposed to always deceive its father, as to its existence, we cannot pretend to say. She died in the course of a very short time after being at the castle, and on her death the child was consigned to the care of Mrs. Brady; and from her, as has been already stated, was taken under that of a lady, in the neighbourhood of its supposed father, the miller Cormack.

Although the intentions of Mordaunt were not quite so fell, perhaps, respecting it, as Mrs. Cormack allowed herself to imagine, yet he heard of its death with joy. There was now nothing to impede the accomplishment of his wishes, relative to the beautiful Venetian; and after bearing about for the usual time the mockery of wo, he made an open tender of his hand, and was accepted.

To judge from external circumstances, and what an object of envy was he now! and yet the poorest wretch that walked the earth was not more deserving of commiseration, for he had in his bosom "the worm that never dies." Go where he would, a pale and mournful image was ever present to his view. In the enjoyment of the pleasures, the luxuries, he had so amply the power of commanding, he strove to banish reflection, but in vain. From his outward show, however, none knew his inward torments—his personal safety demanded their strict concealment.

In due course of time a son was born to him, shortly after whose birth the whole of the Barberini property centred in lady Elenora, from the death of the duke her father; but all would not do—nothing could extract that from the overflowing cup of prosperity, which completely empoisoned it to him.

The stings of a guilty conscience were not, however, all he had to render him unhappy; he soon discovered that the real temper and disposition of lady Elenora were calculated for any thing but domestic bliss; that from her no soft compliances, no endearing attentions, were to be expected; that, in short, beauty—beauty that

> " ———— Soon grows familiar to the lover,
> Fades on his eye, and palls upon the sense,"

was her only recommendation and claim to love; and for her, a being with whom he now saw happiness was not to be enjoyed, he had sacrificed his soul's repose, the——but the reflection was one of too much horror to be pursued.

Contrary to the arrangement made with O'Rooke on quitting it, a feeling not to be subdued withheld him from returning to the castle, to remove from it the evidence he had left within it of his atrocious guilt; and to this feeling of invincible repugnance to entering it again, was owing his stipulating, on disposing of it to the O'Neil family, for permission to still retain a chamber or two locked up in it. It may seem extremely improbable, his acting in this manner, by his not doing all that lay in his power to prevent any risk of danger to himself; but what utterly inconsistent and improbable things are continually occurring in real life—and by what a strange infatuation is it, that we frequently hear of the guilty actually leading to their own betrayal! Be this as it may, whether what we have stated be declared beyond belief or not, yet so it was, a positive fact; and how much longer the castle might have remained the repository of the fearful secret that, in the alarm of fear, had been intrusted to its keeping, we know not, but for the circumstance that compelled Mordaunt to at length revisit it.

Guilt is generally over cautious; and so terrific to the imagination of Mordaunt was the thought of removing the chest by daylight, that, concealing his arrival in the neighbourhood, he entered the chamber where it lay in the dead of the night, and, with the assistance of Darby and O'Rooke, removed it to another place, there to remain till taken, the ensuing evening, to the place fixed on for finally depositing it in.

What occurred on that occasion is already known, as also the ensuing morning, when repairing at early dawn to the chamber, so long locked up, in order to carefully examine it, ere it was thrown open to every one who chose to enter it, Mordaunt encountered his daughter; but not entirely to the circumstance of encountering any one there prior to his own careful examination of it, though sufficient certainly to have excited no inconsiderable degree of alarm, was owing the agitation into which he was thrown at the instant, but by the belief, that in the figure before him he beheld the apparition of his murdered wife, so exact was the resemblance between her and the person whom he now saw.

Some minutes elapsed ere, notwithstand-

ing his natural strength of mind, and the
derision in which he had always uniformly
held every thing that bordered on superstition or credulity, he could not entirely
divest himself of the idea. Who it was
he actually saw—what their motive for visiting the chamber—or how they got admission to it, were, of course, all matters of
intense anxiety to him; but which, except
as far as it regarded the first, he was not
destined to be relieved from. His extreme
emotion, on again beholding Rose, from
the still more powerful likeness than even
before he conceived he traced in her to the
departed, is already known. Alive he
again beheld the every look and feature of
the latter; the only difference between
them, that one had looked the drooping
flower, the other the bright glowing one,
over whose young head no blighting mildew had yet shed its malignant influence:
in short, the resemblance was so strong,
as gradually to lead to an idea of some deception having been practised on him.

Barney was in consequence strictly interrogated, and the result was, a reluctant confession of the truth; for cunning as he was in his own way, yet for the deep, the wary, and penetrating Mordaunt, he was no more a match than a feather would be for a post.

Mordaunt was terribly agitated on discovering he had been deceived, involving, as did the existence of his daughter, so many consequenees of fearful import to himself: his first measure, on ascertaining it, however, was to assure Barney, whose first consideration he had by this time learned was for himself, that if, by any chance, directly or indirectly, he betrayed to any other the secret he had extorted from him, he might rely on being instantly deprived of the annuity that had hitherto been allowed him, to the exempting him from any anxiety relative to his means of living.

This threat would have induced O'Rooke to silence to the pope, had his holiness been his confessor. He readily promised not only the inviolable secrecy required

by Mordaunt, but to do all in his power
to aid him in getting Rose out of the way,
that is, away from St. Doulagh's; Mordaunt artfully pretending, that though,
from a conviction of her spurious birth,
he could not bring himself to own her
as his, yet, from the consideration of
her being still allied to him, he would
gladly rescue her from her present state of
dependence, and remove her to some place
abroad, where she might be introduced in
a different manner into life.

Finding that nothing could induce her
voluntarily to give up the protection she
enjoyed, he decided on having recourse to
stratagem, for the purpose of tearing her
away from it; for to let her remain quietly
undisturbed, now that he knew who she
was, was out of the question; but in the
furtherance of his plans, to prevent any
suspicion attaching to him, it was requisite that he should seem to depart from
the place: accordingly every thing necessary to induce belief of his positive depar-

ture was done, when in reality he was secreted in the house of Barney.

Continually hovering about the castle, in hopes by so doing of at length obtaining an opportunity of surprising Rose, he at length discovered the attachment between her and Eugene, a circumstance that threatened to render so still more difficult and perplexing his efforts to get her into his power, as to occasion him to have recourse to not merely dangerous, but even almost absurd measures to prevent a final engagement between them; but he was defeated in these; and at last convinced that for the present he could not succeed in his plan respecting her, without running a risk he shrunk from, he decided on its temporary relinquishment; and turning all his attention from her to Eugene, who, as a person but too much interested about her, if in existence, or at liberty, would suffer nothing to oppose his inquiries after her, if carried away from St. Doulagh's, he saw it was expedient to get out of the way. How, under

an assumed name, he introduced himself
to him, and obtained his confidence, is already known, as also the progressive steps
he took for involving him in destruction.
But his poisoned arrows fell short of their
mark; there was a shield interposed between him and the apparently undefended
bosom of innocence that he could not pe-
netrate; Eugene still escaped uninjured,
both out of the lion's den and from the
fiery furnace; and enraged as well as
alarmed at the circumstance, Mordaunt
believing, after his repeated disappointments concerning him, that it was useless
to attempt any thing further against Eugene, hastened to Ireland, with a determination of running all hazards to get
Rose into his power, persuaded, that if a
marriage once took place between her and
Eugene, O'Rooke, notwithstanding his
solemn oaths of secrecy, would, from the
regard he had for the O'Neil family, discover who she was: but the bird was
flown; he proceeded from St. Doulagh's
to the place to which it was supposed Mrs

Brady had taken her; but only to find there was some deception in the affair, and his rage at the circumstance was unutterable. Nothing could induce him to believe but that Mrs. Brady either suspected, or had discovered, her claim to fortune and right to another name, and that she had taken her off in the manner she had done, for the purpose of taking some advantage of the circumstance.

O'Rooke trembled for his annuity, which Mordaunt declared he would not continue to him if Rose was not speedily discovered. How she was, through means of the exulting O'Rooke, is already known; but notwithstanding the large portion of the leaven of selfishness that was mixed up in his nature, we must do him the justice to say, that if aware of what the real intentions of her father were respecting her, he would have kept the discovery that so delighted him to himself.

After all his turnings and windings, to find himself betrayed into a disclosure he had taken such pains, incurred such risks,

such danger, to avoid, was indeed a circumstance that required more command
over himself than he at present possessed,
to be able to think of with any thing like
calmness; yet when he reflected on the apprehension that had hurried him into it—
that but for it, nothing perhaps could have
prevented a crime, at the very thought
of which he involuntarily shuddered—he
could not accuse himself of folly. When
he thought of his own guilt, and reflected
on that which he had every reason to believe he had been so near betraying others
into, and for which, of course, he must
have been answerable—could there be any
mercy for such a wretch! he franticly exclaimed; could forgiveness be extended
to crimes like his? But he had involved
himself in a dilemma, from which no time
was to be lost in endeavouring to extricate
himself, if he valued his personal safety,
to say nothing of his name or character.
He was too much accustomed to contri-
vances, too keen and quick in seeing, in
all times of perplexity, what was best to

be done, not shortly to arrange within himself how he should act on this occasion. Accordingly, convinced that to attempt deceiving her with regard to the fact, that is, that she had a real right to his name, was useless, Rose was informed, after a night passed by him in intense deliberation on the subject, that a suspicion of her mother's fidelity had occasioned his unwillingness to acknowledge her for his daughter; but which suspicion having at length, by never-ceasing exertions to ascertain the truth, been discovered to be ill-founded, he had acted as he had done towards her, for the express purpose of revealing to her what had at last been so abruptly disclosed—as soon as the requisite arrangements for putting her into possession of the fortune to which, in right of her mother, she was entitled had taken place.

Whether his son had any doubt of the truth of this statement, we cannot pretend to say, but seeming credit was all that could be given to it by Rose; there

were too many circumstances to contradict it—to prove it the fabrication of the
moment, to permit it to have any weight
with her; but she would not—she dared
not give utterance to her real sentiments
respecting it; if they were known—if they
could be torn from her, oh, what might
not the fate of him be whom she was now
to consider her father! But regarding him
in the fearful light that she must ever do,
from the suspicions that had been excited
at St. Doulagh's—regarding him, in short,
as she was compelled to do, from what she
had been witness to, as a blood-stained
being—the destroyer of her mother, how
did she wish she had been allowed to remain in ignorance of the connexion between them! How did she feel that the
rank, the fortune, to which the discovery
of it was the means of raising her, would
be but a poor recompence for the constant
fears with which, knowing but too well
what he had to apprehend, she must be
tortured about him—the horror with
which his sight must ever inspire her! but

it was the will of Heaven, that through her, justice should at length be rendered to the injured dead; and while her heart was prostrated in gratitude to that divine Power which had guarded her from the evils to which the cruel abandonment of her natural protector had rendered her liable, she humbly implored that its mercy might be extended to the wretched sinner for whom she was so much interested; that at length repentance might touch his hitherto evidently obdurate nature, and that, awakened to a full conviction of his atrocities, he might throw himself upon him who died that he might be a ransom for many.

With the consciousness he had of what his real intentions respecting her had been, young Mordaunt could not bring himself to endure the idea of immediately encountering the looks of Rose again, and would, in consequence, have probably departed, as he decided on immediately doing, without seeing her, but for the consideration that she might impute the circumstance

to his regret and indignation at the diminution of fortune which the recent
discovery must occasion him. Accordingly he forced himself to send a message,
begging to be allowed to take leave of her
before his departure; and as he bade her
adieu, assured her, with a warmth that
permitted no doubt of his sincerity, that
to find she indeed regarded him as a brother, by applying to him if ever requiring
any service, would be a source of greater
happiness to him than he could express.

Acknowledged as his daughter, of
course his name would immediately be
assumed; and what strictures, what com-
ments, what dangerous inquiries, might
not the consequently from this circumstance, still greater publicity of the affair
occasion!

To prevent what he so greatly dreaded,
Mordaunt conceived the best and only
plan that could be thought of, would be
to promote an immediate marriage between her and Eugene. He wondered
that the thought did not immediately

suggest itself to him, more especially when on its occurring he reflected that probably nothing else could prevent the natural resentment of Eugene, at the sufferings to which, it could no longer be concealed, he had been the means of subjecting him, from leading to alarming consequences.

The torturing anxiety under which Rose naturally concluded her friends must be about her, induced an immediate wish for some communication with them; but this was opposed by Mordaunt, who wished, if possible, to prevent any thing of the kind, till her marriage had taken place, on the grounds, that in the first place there was an end to this imagined anxiety, in consequence of the belief occasioned by her sudden disappearance, and in the next, that till every step necessary for putting her in possession of her fortune was taken, he did not wish her to be known under her new name.

Rose did not oppose him; but her anxiety about Eugene was so great, from the terrible effect she feared her imagined death might have had upon him, that at length Mordaunt was induced to acknowledge his arrival at Mrs. Brady's, and the grief to which he had abandoned himself.

To know she might indulge herself with seeing, with hearing him again, and resist the impulse that urged her seeking the gratification, was impossible; and accordingly, unable to control herself in this instance, or rather feeling that she should hardly be able to persuade herself that she was not actually in a dream, till she had seen him again, she suffered herself to steal one evening, at dusk, to the monastery, the melancholy scene of her recent lamentations, and now the lonely haunt of Eugene, where, in the impassioned accents of despair, he now called upon her name.

With difficulty, as she listened to him, could she forbear revealing herself to him; but various considerations compelled her to let him remain yet a little longer under his cruel belief concerning her. On venturing again to the ruin, she did not escape however as she had done in the first instance, and finding she was followed, she deemed it expedient to acquaint her father with the circumstance, lest of any thing untoward happening, in consequence of trying to conceal it from him.

Mordaunt having by this time made all the arrangements he deemed requisite ere any disclosure to Eugene, or in other words, settled exactly how he would act, was not disconcerted by her information as he might otherwise have been. Till the explanation however, which on many accounts he still persevered in choosing to make himself, had taken place, he expressed a wish to Rose that she would not appear, and by himself repaired to meet Eugene.

" I cannot wonder," he cried, on seeing Eugene instinctively recoil at his sight, as already stated, " at the feelings your looks evince; but whatever cause there may be for indignation, there's none, I solemnly protest, for alarm in the present instance."

" What," exclaimed Eugene, with, a burst of indignation and scorn, " attempt to assert this, after having had recourse to stratagem to get me into your power!"

" To convince you then of the truth of the assertion, you are again free to depart the moment you please," said Mordaunt, unlocking the door behind him as he spoke.

Eugene hastily turned to it, but suddenly checking himself—" Can you deny," he demanded, " that you have been the means of inveigling me here?"

" No, I don't attempt it."

" And for what purpose?"

" For one that I mean to explain, if you will permit me."

" And can you, or rather will you," cried Eugene, with heightening indignation, as all he had suffered through means of this unprincipled man recurred to his thoughts, naturally recalled by his sight, " can you, or rather will you also, I repeat, account for your unprovoked enmity towards me—explain to me the cause of your seeking me out, as you did, like a persecuting fiend, to lead me to destruction?"

"Yes," replied Mordaunt, with all the coolness of a collected person.

"Good Heaven! and do you dare to tell me this?" exclaimed Eugene, with flashing eyes—"do you dare, with this coolness, to acknowledge yourself the villain I suspected—the villain through whose means I was near suffering all the horrors of an ignominious death—the almost equal horrors of lasting imprisonment—the villain through whose cruel machinations I was separated from my family, till the happiness that might have blessed my earlier return to them was lost for ever?"

"Yes—all this I dare confess: but is there not inconsistency in this conduct? you accuse me, with a full conviction on your mind of the fact, of my being a villain; and yet, because I do not deny the justice of the accusation, you burst into invective."

"No, no—you mistake—it is not that; but the coolness, the insulting coolness with which you acknowledge the fact, that works me up to this frenzy;" involuntarily applying his handkerchief to his brow as he spoke, rendered damp by the violence of his emotions.

"You can utter no reproach," said the other, "that can awaken resentment, because you can utter none that I am not conscious of meriting; but for all you have suffered through my means, I have the power of making reparation; had not this been the case, I never should have sought this meeting."

"You!" exclaimed Eugene, in a tone of scornful incredulity, and again recoiling—"you the power of making reparation for what you have made me suffer! no, mock not your guilty spirit with that hope—lay not that flattering unction to your heart. I know not your means, your fortune, your real rank in life—I am ignorant of all concerning you, but that you are a cool, deliberate, mysterious villain; but were the mines of eastern riches yours, and could

you turn out all their coveted contents be-
foreme, I would spurn them with contempt,
if offered by way of atonement for the injury you have done me! My mind's repose,
the quiet of my soul, is lost for ever,
through your means; but for you, I feel
a firm persuasion I should not have to deplore the loss of her on whom my soul
doted with all the fondness of early attachment; and yet you—you—the blaster of
my earthly happiness"—with a burst of
sorrow cried the anguished youth—" you
talk to me of reparation for the wrongs
you have done me, the sufferings you
have entailed upon me! To raise my
bride from her cold earthly bed—to give
her back, palpitating with life, to my eager arms—that, that could alone make
amends for your conduct."

" I know not how to attempt the explanation that will prove I have not mocked, I have not trifled with your feelings,
by the assertion I have made," cried Mordaunt, " while you thus continue agitated. Endeavour to compose, to collect

yourself—to prepare yourself for a surprise almost exceeding belief—in a word,
for a restoration to happiness, that will
have the semblance of a miracle."

Eugene started, and turned round with
quickness on the chair on which he had
thrown himself.—" Whither would you
lead my imagination?" he cried; " but,
no, no," again covering his face with his
hand, " have I not wept over her grave
—do I not know but too well that she is
gone for ever?"

" You are mistaken—you have been
led astray," said Mordaunt.

" How?" exclaimed Eugene, starting
on his feet, his eyes almost bursting from
their sockets.

" Yes—that is, I mean, in imagining
you wept over her grave—the rites of se-
pulture were never paid to Rose; but to
keep you in ignorance of this, Mrs. Brady
deemed it necessary to point out a particular spot to you as the one she was laid
in—there was no other way of avoiding a
dreadful story."

Eugene turned of an ashy whiteness—he gasped—" You do not mean," with difficulty he articulated, " to intimate——"

Mordaunt saw him staggering, and hastened to support him; but the horrible fear that was awakened—the dreadful thought that flashed across his mind, completely overcame him—his senses forsook him for a minute or two. On regaining them—" Have I been dreaming?" he cried, raising his head from the shoulder of Mordaunt, on which it had fallen; " but no—I see you still before you; but I thought—I fancied I had a glimpse of another—that I heard the murmur of another voice!"

Whilst speaking, his eyes roved round the room, and through a half-opened door in a distant part of it, he beheld another figure. He burst from the hold of Mordaunt, and rushed to the door; the figure attempted to recede from it, down the dusky passage beyond it; but this was prevented by Eugene——but to the imagination of the reader we must leave the

bsequent scene—all that followed—when,
the trembling form he caught hold of,
ugene discovered that it was his Rose,
is lamented Rose, he had caught to his
reast.

CHAPTER XI.

"Let there be a net spread for them; the sport will be, when they hold an opinion of one another's information, and no such matters; that's the scene that I would wish to see, which will be merely dumb show."

WE left Mrs. Hamilton busy in planning a little innocent scheme of mortification against the Mayfields, whose recent conduct merited some little punishment of the kind she conceived. Convinced, however, that Grace, notwithstanding the provocation she had received from them, would lend her no assistance in the affair, she took special care to keep her in ignorance on the subject; and the manner in which William contrived to keep Grace to himself during the morning, quite favoured her efforts for the purpose. Every one of fashion in the place was, as already stated, invited for the evening to the hotel, by Delamere, out of compliment to his fair friends; and amongst them lord Enniskerry, who had purposely delayed his departure, in hopes of again seeing, or obtaining an opportunity of being introduced to Grace.

Knowing how much the Mayfields depended on their advantages of dress for eclipsing Grace, she maliciously determined on letting them enjoy, and exult in the idea of doing so on the present occasion, till the last moment, in order that the disappointment and surprise she was preparing for them, might be heightened as much as possible.

For the purpose of completely deceiving them—of letting there be nothing to prevent their triumphing in the hope of completely outshining Grace that evening, she had recourse to a little artifice. By some means or other, she rummaged out an old yellow crape dress, and a large wreath of flaming poppies, and taking advantage of Grace's absence, laid them out upon her bed, as if intended for her dress that evening.

The trick took. Miss Myra, who with her sisters had been sitting in close divan in her mother's chamber, on their own costume for the evening, stole up to Grace's, to try if she could discover what she meant to wear. The wreath of poppies and the yellow dress instantly caught her eye, and she flew back in ecstacy, to tell them of the fright. Grace meant to make herself that evening.

" Such a hideous dress!" she said; " but I suppose she depends upon candlelight for making it appear new, for by daylight it is quite soiled; and then so old-fashioned in its make, with a waist, I believe, not two inches long. If she had any taste, plain as they are, she would prefer, I am sure, one of her white muslin frocks; but having worn nothing else since she came here, I suppose she wishes to appear in something else to-night; and fancies besides too, I suppose, from the ridiculous admiration Mrs. Hamilton is always expressing of her, even to her face, that let her wear what she will, she must look well."

" Well, love, you have no right, at all events, to be angry with her on this occasion," observed her mamma; " for it's not possible that she could have chosen any thing that could more set off the delicacy of your and your sister's beautiful dresses of lilach, than the one she has chosen to exhibit herself in. Poor thing! I suppose indeed she has no great choice; and really I cannot help thinking there is great unkindness in the friends of a girl, circumstanced as she is, without the power of procuring those adornments of dress that in a certain rank are now indispensable, in dragging her forward in the manner she has now been. However, I suppose they concluded it was only for her to be seen to be sought; but I rather imagine they may or will find themselves mistaken."

Mrs. Mayfield took upon herself giving

all the requisite orders for the entertainment of the evening; and, in short, from the manner in which she conducted herself, it was evident that she conceived, or at least chose to have it conceived, it given entirely out of compliment to her and her daughters.

At the usual hour the party began to assemble; but Grace was purposely prevented, by Mrs. Hamilton, making her appearance, till the arrival of all the expected guests. Just as she was about taking out one of those white frocks of which Miss Myra had spoken so contemptuously, Mrs. Hamilton informed her of having bespoke a dress for the evening for her, which she protested she would never forgive her if she did not wear, from the sweet little milliner from Dublin, and which, she pretended, would not be ready for her till rather a late hour.

At length, in the midst of Mrs. Mayfield's exultation at the admiration she conceived her daughters receiving—the complete triumph she anticipated their having that evening over every one else, the folding-doors of the apartment were thrown open, and—"Here come the poppies!" in a tittering whisper cried Miss Myra to her mamma, concluding it was Grace that was about entering, from knowing all the expected guests were by this time arrived : it was Grace indeed that entered, preceded by Mrs. Hamilton—but how different in her appearance from what was expected! instead of the yellow old-fashioned dress of crape, with a head making her look like a representation of Ceres, with its decorations of poppies, she wore one of white crape, tastefully decorated round the bottom with bunches of lily of the valley in white satin; while the pearl ornaments previously rejected from William, but which Mrs. Hamilton kept by her, in the hope of something like what had now actually taken place occurring, adorned her dark hair and white neck, that, without any hyperbole, might have been said to rival the pearls in whiteness. That a person must have been altogether destitute of, personal attractions who would not have looked well in a dress of this simple elegance, will readily be allowed; how then a person possessed of the advantages of Grace—that native elegance that nothing could disguise or conceal—appeared in it, with her beautiful cheek tinged with the bright glow of those delicious emotions that had been awakened in her bosom that day, may easily be imagined.

The Mayfields were absolutely petrified—they doubted the evidence of their eyes, or rather wished they could find they had deceived them; and their rage at the surprise occasioned them by Grace, was heightened by believing, judging of her by themselves, that they had been purposely led astray by her with regard to her appearance in the evening: but how little did they know Grace, when they imagined such a thing—how little the disdain she would have felt at the idea of what they imputed to her! The real contriver of the trick, however, quite enjoyed the sensation she saw it had occasioned, there being nothing that more delighted her than to see malice mortified, and the envious compelled to feel their own inferiority.

With that look of ineffable sweetness that was alone sufficient to render her enchanting, Grace advanced into the room. Every eye was turned in admiration on her, and all who had not previously seen her, were now eager in inquiring who she was. This was soon known. William, the enraptured William, involuntarily hastened to meet her, and leading her forward into the circle, introduced her to all those who were still strangers to her.

Of this number was lord Enniskerry, who the moment she was sufficiently disengaged to attend to him, requested her hand for the ensuing dance.

Grace hesitated — feelings already explained opposed her granting this request; but since she had been induced to mix in such a scene, the affectation she might render herself liable to be accused of, by declining to participate in its gaiety, occurring, finally induced her to accede to it.

Lord Enniskerry, who, previously to her entrance, had been amusing himself at the expence of Mrs. Mayfield, whose character he by this time perfectly comprehended, by paying attentions to Miss Myra, had no ears, no eyes, for any one but her, from the moment she made her appearance.

Grace could have excused this proof of his admiration, since the manner in which he strove to engross her attention entirely to himself, prevented her from having almost any opportunity of even conversing for a minute with William. But though William could have wished it otherwise, he was in too happy a frame of mind, his heart had its content too absolute to permit any thing like vexation or ill-temper. Assured of the affections of her on whom the recent struggle with his feelings had convinced him his own were unalterably fixed—secure of the hand of a woman calculated to shed lustre on any rank, and give happiness to any station, whose out-

ward graces, transcendent as they were,
were fully equalled by those placed

" About the thoughts and counsels of her heart,"

and possessed of an independence sufficient for all that wishes not unbounded could
desire, he conceived himself one of the
most enviable of mortals; and the gratitude and complacence natural to the
thought were fully experienced by him.

Nothing that could render the evening
agreeable to his guests was omitted by
him, and in addition to what he contrived
for their amusement, the gallantry of lord
Enniskerry led him to order a grand display of fireworks from his yacht in the
bay, while his delightful band took their
station opposite the hotel, filling up all
the intervals in the dancing, and playing
during the time the company were at supper: but envy and mortification took from
the Mayfields all power of enjoying the
evening; thus indeed proving, that the
hearts that admit the influence of malignant feelings, are as great enemies to their

own enjoyment as they wish to be to that of others.

But for what she suffered this evening, Mrs. Mayfield strove to console herself by the reflection, that she could speedily put an end to the triumph of Miss Grace, by returning to St. Doulagh's when she pleased; and on this she accordingly decided the ensuing morning, trusting that by hurrying Grace so precipitately away, ere it became absolutely the fashion to admire her, she might soon be forgotten. Her intention of quitting Strandmore that day, under the pretext of having received a letter from home, requiring her immediate presence there, was announced at breakfast, to the secret joy of Grace and William, from their impatience to rejoin the friends who would so sincerely participate in their present happiness.

Lord Enniskerry quickly heard of the intended departure of the party, and no sooner heard it, than, impetuous in all his feelings, he obtained a private conference with Grace; and having expressed to her

the sentiments she had inspired him with,
entreated to be allowed to wait upon her at
home, for the purpose of explaining them·
to her friends.

Grace thanked him for the honour done
her by those sentiments, but begged to be
excused granting the permission he required; and on being urged on the subject, candidly acknowledged herself already engaged.

She had none of that ridiculous and degrading pride and vanity that could urge
her to make a boast of any thing of the
kind; and accordingly made a request to
Mrs. Hamilton, who, from being in an
adjoining apartment, overheard the whole
of the conversation between her and lord
Enniskerry, to say nothing of the matter
to the Mayfields; for as to William, who
was present when his lordship's message,
requesting to see her alone, was delivered
to her, she neither could nor desired to
keep it a secret from him; perhaps pleased,
since an attachment so quickly formed
she could not but imagine would be as

readily got the better of, at the opportunity afforded her by the affair, of proving
to him the sincerity of her regard for him.

But the silence which she wished to
impose on Mrs. Hamilton relative to it, it
was impossible for Mrs. Hamilton to observe to the Mayfields, such an additional source of mortification was she convinced it would be to them. For a minute
they were indeed utterly astonished on
hearing of it, but it was only for a minute;
still ignorant of the explanation that had
taken place between Grace and William,
and disengaged as they consequently believed her, and destitute as they knew her
to be of fortune, that she should reject
such an offer, was a thing too incredible
for belief; and a smile, or rather sneer of
scornful incredulity, quickly testified to
Mrs. Hamilton that the only credit she
obtained from them in this instance, was
that of being the inventor of what she had
told them.

Still, however, notwithstanding what
they chose to doubt or disbelieve, there

was great secret dissatisfaction at the result of their visit to Strandmore not having been more satisfactory than it was
with regard to their views relative to Delamere, affording him, as it had done, such
facilities for paying court to Myra. They
strove, however, to believe that this was
entirely owing to the artful management
of Mrs. Hamilton, of whose wish for an
union between him and Grace they were
not ignorant; and accordingly decided, on
their return to St. Doulagh's, on endeavouring to disentangle him from her, or,
in other words, get him to themselves entirely.

On arriving at the rectory, Williams
having handed the ladies out, that is, Mrs.
Mayfield and her daughters, and received
the acknowledgments of the rector for his
polite and kind attentions to them at
Strandmore, was about making his parting bow, when Mrs. Mayfield, seeing what
his intention was, with a quivering lip,
interposing between him and the door,

protested they could not think of losing
him, as their guest, so immediately.

William expressed himself infinitely
obliged for the kindness that would have
detained him longer under her roof; but
his old room at Mr. Hamilton's being by
this time again ready for his reception, he
could not think, he added, of any longer
intruding on her.

In vain the lady protested it would be
a kindness, an absolute obligation, his
again becoming their inmate, they had so
many delightful schemes in contemplation
for the remainder of the summer, which
they wished him to be immediately at
hand, to consult him about.

William continued inflexible, and finally
made good his retreat to the carriage, in
which he had left Mrs. Hamilton and
Grace waiting for him. From the rectory
they drove straight to Mr. Hamilton's,
where, however, all that Mrs. Hamilton
did was to drop her trunk, and take up her
husband, so impatient was she to reach the
castle, from the joy she knew the commu-

nication of what had taken place at Strandmore would impart there.

Nothing indeed could exceed the delight occasioned by it to the anxious heart
of the poor lieutenant, sunk as he was in
absolute dejection, through the overthrow
of all his fond parental hopes and expectations respecting Eugene, and tortured as
he was with solicitude about Grace; for
worldly crosses had begun to force worldly
considerations upon his mind, and he was
beginning to see the evils attendant on
destitution. The happiness of his sister
on the occasion was not less, though perhaps not quite so vehemently expressed;
but it would not have been consistent
with her dignity to have appeared over-
joyed or much elated at any circumstance,
at least such a one as the present, lest it
should lead to the conclusion of her not
having expected such an alliance for Grace.

But the anxiety of Grace about Eugene
soon interrupted those feelings. His return could no longer be concealed, neither
the state of mind in which he had depart-

ed from the castle; and Grace instantly
decided on repairing to him, not without
being almost tempted to utter a gentle reproach at his arrival not having been immediately made known to her, conceiving,
as she did, that her sympathy in his deep
affliction, her soothing tendernesses, might,
ere this, have had a soothing effect upon
him.

Of course, that William could not be
induced to suffer her to depart without
him, may readily be believed; and accordingly, accompanied by him and Mrs.
Hamilton, prompt at every call, from
the real benevolence of her nature, to
weep with those that weep, and rejoice
with those that rejoice, it was finally settled that she should set off the next day,
to join the poor mourner; but a letter in
the course of the evening, by express from
Mrs. Brady, containing an explanation of
all that had occurred relative to Rose,
caused this intention to be a little longer
deferred, Grace no longer opposing the
entreaties of Delamere, backed as they

were by those of their mutual friends, to
permit the ceremony that was indeed to
unite their fates irrevocably, to take place
ere she proceeded on her short journey.

We slightly pass over the feelings occasioned by Mrs. Brady's letter, because a-
ware of our inability to do them justice;
but we have already mentioned the grief
excited by the supposed death of Rose, and
equal to what that grief was, it may readily
be supposed, was the joy of finding her still
alive. But this was not the only source
of gratulation—her marriage with Eugene
was of course considered as a certain matter, and in giving herself to him, she gave
back to the family the property they had
been so long deprived of.—" Wonderful,"
exclaimed Miss Agnes Flora Judith, "the
sudden turn matters sometimes take! to
think that at the very moment I gave up
all hope of our ancient house being restored to its original splendour, the cloud
that so long obscured it should be dis-
persing!"

"Yes," cried her brother, making an

effort to cough away the emotions that had nearly overpowered him, "'tis, as you say, Agnes, wonderful to see how suddenly the wind veers about, driving us at last into the very port we had long despaired of ever making."

That all was happiness in the breasts of those she expected so soon to join, Grace could not doubt, or if she did, it was through her knowledge of what the sentiments of Rose were, respecting Mordaunt, prior to the discovery of her relationship to him. Still, however, supposing her mind disturbed on this account, she could not bring herself to imagine, that with the prospect of an immediate restoration to the friends she so fondly loved, and with the power of rewarding the disinterested attachment of her lover, she could long remain completely unhappy; and perhaps she would have been correct in this conjecture, had Rose had nothing to reproach herself for; but that she had, she felt with all the bitterness of repentant anguish. Restored to all her natural correctness of judgment, from the effect which recent events had had in compelling her to recollect herself, she could no longer gloss over the conduct of which she had been guilty ; when she reflected on this, her utter forgetfulness of, and aberration from, all she ought to have held sacred, such were her overwhelming sensations of shame and remorse, that to fly to solitude became her fixed determination.

She was unworthy of associating with those she loved—sunk, abased, degraded, in her own eyes, how could she endure the thought of encountering theirs? No, the thing was impossible: it was only by withdrawing from them, by renouncing their kindness, their endearments, that she could obtain an uninterrupted opportunity of pouring out her tortured soul in penitence before her Creator, and expiating her transgressions in his sight. Could an error, that had been so nearly fatal in its results—an error that had tempted her to

think of rushing uncalled into His awful
presence, be ever sufficiently regretted or
atoned? Oh no, she felt not; and that,
from the horror with which she reviewed
the feelings it had led to, she must despair
of forgiveness for it, but for the gracious,
the benign, the blessed assurances of mercy held out by faith to the wretched sinner. The erring daughter of a guilty father, what indeed so fitting for her as seclusion from the world? Thinking as she
now did, how did she wonder that she
could ever have contemplated a union
with Eugene—could ever have permitted
her imagination to dwell upon the thought?
but it was entirely through the temporary
derangement of her mind; now that she had
regained all her wonted clearness of percep-
tion, how very different were her thoughts!
But would she have resolution to endure
the sight of the anguish which the overthrow of his fond hopes must occasion Eugene? to sustain the severe, the cruel trial
she had decreed for herself? Oh yes, she
would, she must—she would pray, fervent-

ly pray to Heaven, to be supported under it, as the only means of evincing the sincerity of her repentance.

She would explain her feelings to Eugene, and throw herself upon his love, not to add to their anguish by opposing her intentions. Ah! had she remained steady in the path of virtue—had she resisted the voice of the charmer, and the still more treacherous pleadings of her own heart, how different would have been her present sensations—her present prospects! she would not then have had to weep in unutterable anguish over the dreary thought of a lasting exile from those she loved, the dear, the domestic circle, where all her earthly happiness was centred—would not have had to deplore the thought of causing, perhaps, lasting misery to him who was dearer to her than life!—but she had erred without an excuse from ignorance of her duties for that error, and the only way to prove her contrition for her offence was, by voluntarily renouncing what she was

unworthy of enjoying; in short, she felt
that—

> " When lovely woman stoops to folly,
>   And finds too late that men betray,
> No grief can sooth her melancholy,
>   No tears can wash her guilt away."

But it was not through Eugene's means
alone that she expected her resolution to
be the occasion of the most arduous conflicts; her father had evidently decided on
their union, and it did not require much
penetration to see that he was not a person that could readily be induced to relinquish any thing he wished accomplished. Besides, what plea could she urge for
opposition to his wishes in this instance,
not merely surmised, but positively acknowledged as her attachment to Eugene
was? how could she account for her sudden determination respecting him? how
avoid incurring the imputation of the
most degrading fickleness and levity from
the circumstance? how prevent its being
ascribed to the sudden change in her fortune? and would not, must not this be the

conjecture of her friends at St. Doulagh's? and when she thought on this—of the light in which there was hardly a doubt she must be considered by them, from what she had decided on, when, after secretly permitting the addresses of Eugene, she, now that she had the power of amply rewarding his disinterested attachment, and by so doing, requiting her manifold obligations to his family, cast him off, refused, rejected him—her very soul sickened within her, and she felt almost tempted to give up her resolve; but the more severe the trial, the more she was bound to endure it, for her transgressions were not of a nature to be lightly expiated. Yet, to be accused of the odiousness of ingratitude—suspected of having been all the time she was in the castle an artful dissembler, feigning what she did not feel, insensible of the kindnesses conferred upon her—not even the apprehension of the sufferings of Eugene at the resolution she had taken, was so painful, so afflicting to her imagination, as the thought of this.

All that was requisite for him to know, or rather that could be explained to Eugene, being explained to him, Mordaunt intimated his wish for the marriage between him and his daughter immediately taking place, being impatient, on many accounts, to quit Ireland, yet convinced he could not with any propriety take his departure, till he had first seen all matters relative to his daughter finally concluded.

Since it was evident her father meant their marriage should be solemnized where they then were, would she not wish Grace immediately sent for? was the fond inquiry of Eugene, on the retiring of Mordaunt from the room, after the intimation of the wish just mentioned, to leave them at liberty to arrange all matters connected with the ceremony as they pleased.

Rose tried to answer, but could not immediately; the moment, the dreaded moment of explanation, was come, of opening her tortured heart to his view, and for an instant her feelings overpowered her.—" No," she at length said, in a voice

scarce articulate, " no, Grace must not be
sent for; already had she suffered too
much on her account, to voluntarily permit her to suffer more." Then, with a sudden burst of anguish, uncovering her face,
which her streaming tears had made her
bury for a minute in her handkerchief,
and turning her eyes full upon Eugene—
" Is it possible," she demanded, in accents
half reproachful, half tender, " oh, Eugene! is it possible that you have really
so mistaken my character and feelings, as
to permit yourself to imagine that I could
think of acceding, of consenting to what
is now proposed? No, Eugene, no! reflect on the past, and then tell me—is
there any thing for me but seclusion, utter
and eternal seclusion from the world?"

" I do not comprehend you," said Eugene, but with a degree of agitation that
appeared to contradict the assertion;
" what is it you would have me understand?—what is it you would intimate?"

" Must I then have the pain of being
more explicit? of plainly stating, that

from the light in which I consider my past conduct, I can in nowise be reconciled to myself, but by withdrawing from all that would have constituted my felicity here?"

"Am I to understand," exclaimed Eugene, with emotion no longer controllable, "that it is your intention to tear yourself from me? that the cup of felicity has only been raised to my lips, to be dashed away by the hand I thought least capable of such cruelty? Rose, you do not, you cannot intend what you have intimated! after being restored as it were by miracle to my arms—raised as it were from the very grave to bless me—you cannot have the barbarity to think of separating yourself from me—of making me suffer still greater anguish than that which has already rent my heart on your account, by making me, in addition to grief for your loss, endure the still more torturing pang of believing myself not dear to you?"

"Not dear!" repeated Rose, in anguished accents; "oh! of being but too dear to me, what fatal proof have I not already given! but, Eugene, on your pity—on the love you profess for me—on all that's generous, that's manly in your nature, I throw myself, not to aggravate the misery I am enduring by further reproaches or complaints! I have offended against virtue, against my own intuitive sense of right, and nothing can reconcile me to myself, nothing in any degree restore my lost peace, but the voluntary expiation of my offences."

"Rose, you drive me to distraction!" exclaimed the almost frenzied Eugene. " If such are your sentiments with regard to yourself, what must they be of me—of me, the cause of all you reproach yourself for—the villain who took advantage of your unsuspecting, your generous confidence in his honour, that holy innocence, incapable of a thought of harm, to lead you into error? Oh, richly do I deserve to meet the wretchedness with which you threaten me! to have my reviving hopes of earthly happiness for ever blasted! but

as mine's the fault, ' so well my life shall
pay,' for I swear, if you persevere in your
resolve, never to know a home again !"

" Unkind, inhuman Eugene, to torture
me in this manner! but you will not, you
dare not keep your rash vow ; it is not
possible you can forget that there are
others to live for, as well as me—friends,
connexions, who have claims upon all you
can do for their comfort, in requital for the
unhappiness they have suffered on your
account. You are not free from blame—
I would not, if I could, deceive you, by
asserting that I thought you undeserving
of censure ; for you could not have believed what you sought to induce me to
credit, that your family, regardless of our
then supposed disparity of rank, and my
want of fortune, would ever have sanctioned a union between us. But your offence is light, when compared with mine,
for to the violation of my sex's delicacy I
was guilty of in meeting you in the manner I did, I added the sin of ingratitude,
by encouraging a passion that I knew

but too well those to whom I was under countless obligations, the friends, the protectors of my youth, would never sanction; when I reflect on all this, I feel that I am unworthy of the title you would bestow on me—unworthy of being pressed to the pure bosom of my Grace as her sister—unworthy of being received into the family, whose confidence I so abused, as a daughter. You, Eugene, you, from the world's latitude, may be able to retrieve yourself in your own estimation; but never, never can this be the case with me!" and again gushing into tears, she hid her face in her handkerchief.

"And this is the happiness that, but a few short hours ago, I was so certain of!" cried Eugene, in a tone indicative of all the bitterness of his heart. "I will not torment you, Rose, by argument or entreaties; no, I will prove the truth of my love for you, by quietly consenting to become your victim—for as your resolve is taken, so is mine. With the consciousness of having driven you from life, could you possibly imagine I should continue in what is called the enjoyment of the world? The claims my family have upon me neither shall nor could be forgotten; but in dooming yourself to the relinquishment of domestic happiness, you doom me also to the renunciation of all that has hitherto been precious to my heart, or delightful to my imagination!"

Rose was about replying—was about remonstrating on the cruelty of such a declaration, when she was prevented by the abrupt entrance of Mordaunt, who, feeling as if he stood upon the edge of a yawning gulf, or tottering precipice, while he remained where he was, could not restrain his impatience for bringing whatever retarded his departure to a conclusion.

As he entered at one door, Eugene rushed out by another, unable, from the state of agitation he was in, to endure encountering him. His precipitate retreat struck Mordaunt as somewhat extraordinary, and he was on the point of inquiring into the cause of it from Rose, when his utter amazement at the state he saw her in, her quivering lip, her swoln eyes, for a moment checked his utterance. What was he to infer from what he witnessed? could it be that any misunderstanding had taken place between her and her lover? but no, he deemed this next to impossible, after their recent restoration to each other. Ever alive to his own safety, he became alarmed; could it be that Eugene, after all, notwithstanding all the advantages with which it teemed to him, had drawn back from the proposed alliance? if he had; to what could the circumstance be owing, but to some injurious suspicion, threatening perhaps his character, his safety? The idea no sooner occurred, than almost frantickly he demanded of Rose the cause of what appeared so strange?

Rose endeavoured to collect herself; she answered evasively, that an unwillingness, or rather determination, not to give her hand so immediately to Eugene as had been expected, had occasioned remonstrances from him her spirits were too weak to permit her to listen to with composure.

And was this all—was this really the truth? but no, Mordaunt did not, could not, bring himself directly to believe it was; her half-averted looks, her hesitating accents, led to a very opposite conclusion. Could it be that the sudden change in her fortune, her unexpected elevation to rank and consequence, had occasioned a revolution in her sentiments, awakened a vanity and ambition that rendered her unwilling to adhere to her engagement to Eugene? From the light in which he regarded her sex in general, the levity he ascribed to them, he did not deem the circumstance by any means an improbable one. Nor would he have cared about it, but that he conceived his safety involved in her final determination.

Should Eugene have heard any rumour to his prejudice—any hint or whisper of the dark transactions of other years, how could he hope that, already exasperated against him as he was, he would keep si-

lence on the subject, if any trifling on the
part of Rose towards him gave him cause
to consider himself still further injured
and aggrieved? and in a transport of mingled rage and alarm, at the thought of the
mischief she might be the means of drawing on him, if permitted to swerve from
her engagement, he sternly demanded
whether such was her intention—whether
indeed she had determined on giving up
her present lover—him for whose sake,
but a few hours back, she had averred
there was no privation she would not
cheerfully undergo?

Rose again hesitated to reply; resolved
as she was to give up Eugene, still she involuntarily recoiled from avowing this determination, as if in her inmost heart she
still entertained a hope that something
might occur to forbid such a sacrifice. Besides, what plausible reason had she to assign
for what must appear so sudden a resolve?
how avoid, by yet disclosing it, either being betrayed into a confession of the terrible truth, or else of exciting some pre-

judice against Eugene? At length she
falteringly said—" All she had at present
decided on was, to retire to some place
where she should be out of the way of
seeing any one, till she chose it herself;
the effect of recent circumstances upon
her health and spirits, rendering quiet absolutely indispensable to her."

Still Mordaunt looked incredulous—
still as if he doubted her sincerity to him;
but on his putting her truth to the test,
by saying, that if her wish was really for
retirement at present, he could, by her accompanying him from Ireland, introduce
her to a place where it would be gratified,
and finding that she did not shrink back
from the proposal, he became better satisfied, though not by any means so much
so as if she had consented at once to give
her hand to Eugene.

At length the unhappy Rose withdrew
to her chamber, where the feelings of her
anguished heart again burst forth with
violence.—" Had she then so far committed herself, as to render it next to impos-

sible that she could avoid immediately separating herself from Eugene? but for
what purpose should she linger longer in
his society? had she not solemnly decided
on an eternal separation between them?
and why then unnecessarily torture both,
by delaying it? Yet was there no way
of avoiding the dreadful sacrifice she meditated—the cutting herself off from the
happiness of belonging to Eugene, and incurring the hateful suspicions of baseness
and ingratitude from his family, which
she but too well knew her conduct in
giving him up would excite? If delicacy
and repentance on one hand demanded her
acting as she intended, on the other, did
not honour and justice require, that, possessed as she was of the power of making
restitution to his injured family for what
they had been so cruelly deprived of, she
should avail herself of it by giving him
her hand?"

She started—a sudden light seemed let
in upon her benighted soul—she wondered the reflection had not before occurred;
what tears, what anguish, would it have

saved her, by the pretext it afforded for
yielding to the wishes of her heart! in
pity to her anguish, it seemed to her as if
Heaven had now suggested the thought.
But short was the cessation of sorrow,
transient the relief from despair, when
inquiring from her father, she learned,
that her fortune was absolutely in her
power to do what she pleased with. There
was then no excuse for acting as she wished. Oh, the sinking of her heart at the
conviction, at finding that she must then,
after all, rend away the ties entwined
round it! since, without becoming the
wife of her beloved, it was in her power
to make restitution to his family of their
long-alienated property; and if she wished
to prove the sincerity of her repentance to
Heaven, she must part from him—but this
was not all—if she wished to save herself
from the torture of continued apprehension;
for should she not live, if she became his,
in constant dread of the discovery of that
secret, that must sink her for ever in the
estimation of those she loved—that must

convert all her delight in their society into shame, confusion, and terror?—yes, the die was cast; and to avoid the risk of what she could not support—to satisfy her own feelings, and reconcile her to herself, there was nothing for her but to withdraw from the world.

So great was the distraction of Eugene on learning her determination of departing with her father, that in order to sooth, and prevent any absolute resistance on his part to her intention, she was compelled to temporize with him, by leading him to believe that her object in quitting him at present, was to have an uninterrupted opportunity of deliberating on her future conduct, thus indirectly insinuating that her mind was not yet made up irrevocably on the subject.

But his importunities were not all the unhappy girl had to contend with, or distress her—Mrs. Brady, of whose being summoned to her the moment she was permitted to acknowledge herself still in existence, we have deemed it unnecessary to speak, ceased not pleading for Eugene. Her resentment against him long since subsided; and convinced of the sincerity of his attachment to Rose, by the manner in which he had mourned her supposed death, she could not endure the thought of his fond hopes of an union with her being disappointed. She was the last being in the world who could think of excusing error, or glossing over any thing that was wrong; but all circumstances taken into consideration, she could not avoid thinking the scruples of Rose in this instance too rigid: but in vain she represented this—in vain what the probable consequences of driving Eugene to despair might be—Rose was inflexible; there was but one way in which she could be retrieved in her own estimation, and considerations of higher import than those of mere worldly happiness decided her on being steady on the point.

Of course Mrs. Brady accompanied her; and could any thing have imparted a gleam of consolation to Eugene, it would have been the consideration of having such a friend with her as he knew this kind-hearted woman to be to him.

Rose knew not exactly the place to which her father purposed taking her. At first Eugene conceived her ignorance on the subject affected; but on receiving an assurance from her, that he should hear from her as soon as she had reached her destination, was induced to relinquish this belief. This promise, however, was not given without a previous stipulation, that, without her permission, he should not attempt to avail himself of her communication.

The presence of her father was, in some degree, a restraint on his feelings at the moment of parting; but when she was positively gone—when he could no longer discern the vessel that bore her from him, they burst forth with a violence that defied control. He became distracted—he raved with all the violence of despair—he had consented to his own misery, in letting her depart. Oh, why, why had he

acquiesced in such a cruel measure—why
had he not opposed, or rather steadily resisted it? Had he compelled her to remain, he should have succeeded in his expostulations with her; but by giving her
up to her own suggestions, he had sealed
his doom. But no, he would follow her—
he would assert, in the sight of the world,
his right to her hand, and force her to be
just to her vows to him. Force! how did
the expression grate upon his ear, coupled
with the name of Rose! Alas! let him
think or decide as he would, he felt himself miserable. He ranged through the
deserted apartments—how chilling the
sensations excited by their desolate appearance! it seemed to him as if it were
the silence of death that pervaded them.
He forgot every thing in his abstracting
wretchedness—his home—his expecting
friends—the letter, which, in the moment
of departing, Mrs. Brady had informed
him of her dispatching to St. Doulagh's,
till recalled to recollection by the absolute arrival of the bridal party from it.

Convinced of the conjectures, the torturing inquiries which the discovery of his anguish must occasion, he immediately forced himself to make an effort for dissembling it, pretending that the departure of Rose was in conformity to the wish of her father, for her passing a little time with him ere she gave herself up entirely to another.

Grace could not, of course, excluded as she had been from his and Rose's unreserved confidence, discredit this statement; but never, she conceived, were feelings and looks more at variance than his; for while his bosom, as she believed, was the seat of happiness, his countenance had all the haggardness of wo. For remaining in the dreary abode where they found him, there was no inducement now that Rose had left it; and accordingly, the morning after their arrival, accompanied by him, (but how reluctantly!) the party returned to St. Doulagh's.

Their return was the signal for the commencement of those festivities that are in

general the attendant on happy bridals.
Mrs. Hamilton, who took upon herself
the arrangement of every thing, was now
in her element, distributing gloves, &c.
The Mayfield family were not the last
who received the compliments usual on
such occasions. Till the absolute announcement of the event that had taken
place from Mrs. Hamilton, they were ignorant of it, owing to the marriage having been solemnized, at the express request of Grace, at a retired church, in the
way to Eugene. In the first transports of
her mortification, at the disappointment of
the hopes she had persisted in encouraging,
though certainly without any sufficient
reason, Mrs. Mayfield protested she would
never more notice any of the O'Neil family; but cooler thoughts soon prevailed—
the consideration of the conjectures which
an adherence to this resolve would probably occasion, united to the reflection of
the many pleasant opportunities it might
also be the means of losing her girls of
exhibiting themselves to advantage, now

that such a change had taken place in the affairs at the castle, soon succeeded in making her relinquish it, and gilding her face with artificial smiles, and crying content to that which grieved her heart, she proceeded in all due form, with the young ladies, to pay her compliments to the bride. Yet it was a most provoking thing, that the substance should be lost for the shadow, for no artifice could allure Falkiner back to the soft bondage of Miss Myra, for whom he would have been a most advantageous alliance. By some means or other he discovered the double part she had been playing: vain therefore were all her efforts to induce the renewal of his addresses; and now that the bandage of love had slipped from his eyes, he could not help wondering how he could ever have seriously admired such a trifling little butterfly of a thing as she was.

The Langrishes, about this time, joined the party at the castle; and soon after had the pleasure of meeting with a residence

every way desirable in the neighbourhood;
their regard for Delamere, and the pleasure they took in the society of the new
friends to whom he introduced them, being too great not to make them feel happy at the thought of settling at St. Doulagh's.

All about Eugene wore the smile of
content; but what they felt, he only feign-
ed. Benevolent and sympathizing as the
mind may be, still there are moments
when it cannot help being depressed at
the thought of only looking at happiness
through the medium of others. He rejoiced with all the warmth of friendship
and fraternal affection at the felicity of his
sister and Delamere; still there were times
when the sight of it, from the despair he
had yielded to, nearly overpowered him.
Nothing but a dread of exciting strange
speculations, could have detained him at
the castle, from the agony, too great almost for suppression, he felt at being dragged into scenes of festivity, in which he
could not participate—at his misery being

mocked by congratulations on happiness
that he felt not, that he dared not now
cherish a hope of ever experiencing. Oh!
this, this was indeed to drain to the very
dregs the baleful cup of misery, which he
had, by his own imprudence, prepared for
himself.

With difficulty could he retain the mask
of dissimulation he had assumed to deceive his friends, to prevent his operating
as a blighting mildew upon their enjoyments; there were moments when nothing but a precipitate retreat from the
beloved circle at St. Doulagh's could have
prevented the discovery he dreaded —
when nothing but the power of giving
utterance to the anguish of his o'er-fraught
heart could have saved him from madness;
of weeping unrestrained over his poisoned
bliss, amidst the softening scenes that
brought the image of his love to his view,
in all the angelic beauty of her happy
days of innocence. Could he have opened his wo-fraught bosom, he felt as if the

pressure on it would have been lightened; but he did not dare to touch upon, to hint at his wretchedness, lest of causing inquiries that must embarrass.

In the mean time the poor self-exile from all she loved had arrived at her destination—a ready-furnished cottage, that by chance her father had obtained a knowledge of, in one of the wildest and most romantic parts of North Wales, where environing mountains seemed completely to shut it in from an observing world. Could the quietude of nature have soothed the feelings of Rose, she would have been tranquillized; but the conflicts of her mind were too great, her wretchedness too intense, to permit of the effect of any external influence. Besides, considering herself but a transient tenant of the place, she did not allow herself to pay any particular attention to its situation, the moment she had executed the necessary deeds for securing her fortune to the family at St. Doulagh's, it being her intention to seek some solitude in Switzerland, where well her life should pay the forfeit of the error of her youth.

Hardly had her father seen her settled here, ere he took an abrupt leave of her, with something like a promise of shortly seeing her again, but which he never meant to keep. Full of fearful misgivings, from not being able to confide in the fidelity of those to whom he had been compelled to intrust the fatal secret of his life, he quitted his daughter, with a determination of immediately hastening to the Continent, there to remain under an assumed name; but hardly had he carried this intention into effect, ere he was seized with an illness, chiefly brought on by the dreadful agitation of mind he had lately gone through, that quickly threatened to have a fatal termination. That in the awful hour of approaching death he was awakened to a full sense of the enormities of his conduct, we must hope, and may believe, from the following lines, addressed to his daughter, in his almost expiring moments, and which, from the anxiety she had every way suffered on his account, were some relief to her feelings.

———

" Your mother was an angel, pure in thought and unsuspected by mortal—cherish her memory; and should you be tried with affliction, endeavour to imitate her example of patience under it, while you implore of Heaven the extension of its mercy for the wretched sinner who was

" YOUR FATHER."

———

But though it was some ease to the heart of Rose, to think that he had endeavoured to make his peace with his offended Creator, and was beyond the reach of those worldly inflictions she felt that, while he existed, she should have lived in constant apprehension of his being betrayed to, she still was miserable.

Immediately after his departure, Rose proceeded to take the necessary steps for the conveyance of her property. Some time necessarily elapsed in the execution of the deeds requisite for the purpose; and during this interval, what were not the mental struggles of the poor penitent! how often did she falter in her resolution! how often feel tempted to forego it, and seek refuge from further struggles in the fond arms of him she loved! But still was the impulse of affection checked, by the reflection of what she ought to suffer, of what she must suffer, if yielding to the weakness of her soul, she found herself yet an object of scorn, where scorn or slight could not be endured. Yet was this probable—was it probable that Grace, with her affection for her, her tenderness of nature, her benevolence, would ever treat her with scorn? Ah! let her not deceive herself on the subject—she was convinced she could not, would not; but yet, that with a knowledge of what had occurred, she could ever regard her as she had once done, she felt to be equally impossible. Or sup-

posing it were not, could she imagine that
Delamere would, in that case, ever permit
their intercourse to be what it was? No, no,
she felt assured he would not; and that to
save herself from pangs still more intolerable than those now endured, she must
be steady in her purpose. Yet to have
happiness within her grasp, as it were,
without being able to attain it—to behold herself, like a shipwrecked mariner,
within sight of the very haven, towards
which every fond wish had pointed, yet
without a hope of ever finding herself
within it—oh! was not the misery endured by this thought indeed an expiation of
her error!

Every day she became still more sunk
in wretchedness. The sweets of morning,
the balmy dews of evening, in vain shed
their influence around; she had no longer
eyes for the rich garniture of the fields—
no longer a spirit to be moved by the
kindling azure of the brightening sky, or
the soft shadows of the closing day; hope,

all hope of earthly happiness was relinquished; and who can speak the desolation of the heart from which this is banished?

Who that had beheld her, buried in profound solitude, shunning, as it seemed, the very light of day; could have imagined that she was in possession of all that could command what are called the enjoyments of life? Youth, beauty, fortune, talents, and accomplishments, were hers indeed; but a consciousness of error—a conviction that it is not an unaccompanied prayer for mercy will obtain it, rendered nugatory all those advantages, all those blessings.

At length Mrs. Brady became so alarmed, that she resolved on summoning Eugene over, still conceiving it next to impossible that he could persevere in imploring her to give up the resolution that was attended with such misery to both, without finally succeeding, and flattering herself that, with the removal of the regrets that now pressed upon Rose, would be removed every alarming symptom.

Hardly, however, had she carried her sudden determination into effect, ere she became so terrified at the thought of the mischief that might ensue from any sudden surprise to Rose, in the weak state to which she was then reduced, as to be induced to disclose to her what she had done.

The communication was a renewal of all those agonizing conflicts that had already so shattered the frame of the unhappy girl. For a minute she hesitated, whether she should not avail herself of the circumstance, to gratify herself with another meeting with Eugene; but no—for what purpose should she permit herself this indulgence, but to render still more insupportable the measure she had decided on? and accordingly she decided on flying him, by an immediate journey from the cottage; and from whatever place she stopped at, writing to him an explanation of her motives for this conduct.

Mrs. Brady saw her too much agitated to venture to oppose her; but still hoping that, as her emotion subsided, she would relent, and suffer herself to be prevailed on to turn back, she privately left a letter for Eugene, for whose reception instructions were left with those that remained behind; indicative of this hope, or rather completely deceiving him as to the cause of Rose's sudden departure, by an intimation of its being owing to a necessity for meeting the professional gentleman, to whose care the papers appertaining to her estate had been consigned.

Thus deceived; the first shock of the disappointment attendant on not finding Rose at home to receive him, Eugene quickly recovered the spirits to which the summons to Wales had restored him. It had indeed operated like magic upon him, rousing him from all the gloom and chillness of despair, to light and cheerfulness again. It could not be—he would not for a moment permit himself to imagine it had been without at least the indirect knowledge and approval of Rose; and the conclusion from this belief was of course that she had relented of her cruel resolve, and that, as he had long considered her his wife in the sight of Heaven, so she would soon become in the sight of man, and that in the smiling future there would be ample compensation for the distressing past.

Thus soothed into a persuasion of all he wished, with all his impatience for the return of Rose, his meditations were too delightful to permit the passing minutes appearing tedious; besides, there were many objects in the vicinity of the castle to interest and excite his curiosity; but after a casual survey of these, his favourite spot became the ruins of a lone dilapidated castle, on the very peak of the mountain that overhung the cottage. Hence the views were incomparably grand; the eye

took in successive ridges of those mountains that had been the fastnesses of ancient valour, interspersed with many a
smiling vale of pastoral beauty, and an extensive view of the Channel, with its romantic bays and bold headlands, which he
soon expected to recross, with his Rose in-
dissolubly united to him.

Here, on a fragment of the wall that
had enclosed the now silent and grass-
grown court of this mouldering edifice,
now abandoned to all the injuries of the
weather, the raving winds that moaned
mournfully through its melancholy chambers, or raged round its grassy battlements,
as if impatient to complete the work of
time, he was sitting one evening towards sunset, when from the waking
dream in which he was indulging, he was
suddenly roused by the rolling of carriage
wheels. The place was so completely
out of the beaten track, that this was a
sound rarely heard in it; and it instantly
struck him, that it was Rose that was ap-

proaching: his heart beat tumultuously—
but how great was his disappointment,
when, after straining his eyes for a few
minutes in the direction in which the
sound approached, he beheld, instead of
the carriage he expected to see, a hearse,
followed by a mourning coach, slowly
turning round the corner of the mountain that had previously impeded his view
of it.

Well, it could not be long now ere
Rose returned, for he had now been near
a week at the cottage, and trying to console himself by this hope for the disappointment just sustained, he resumed the
seat from which, in the agitation of expectation, he had started; but he did not
long retain it—the emotion just excited
had disarranged his thoughts, and he decided on a ramble.

Just as he entered the cottage at the
rear, he perceived the hearse drawing up
to the front door; he rushed forward—his
eyes darted into the mourning coach—

they were met by the streaming ones of
the wo-struck friend of his Rose. Question was unnecessary—the dreadful truth
at once flashed upon his mind, and all
was a chaos of darkness and distraction
for hours after to him.

The violent agitation occasioned by the
information of Mrs. Brady, the agonizing feelings excited by the thought of
what Eugene's would be, at finding she
had fled him, were too much for the previously exhausted frame of the unhappy
Rose. Ere she reached the place at
which she had given her companion to
understand it was her intention to stop, •
the fever of her mind had pervaded her
frame, and her senses wandered.

How, in this hour of heavy calamity,
did her afflicted nurse deplore what she
had done! Nothing probably saved her
from distraction, but the skilful aid she
had the power of immediately obtaining
for the poor sufferer. But all was unavailing—the disease of the patient was of a de-

scription to which no human skill could minister—a broken heart.

A few hours preceding her dissolution, the sufferer regained her senses; she was grateful to Heaven for their restoration, as enabling her to testify the holy faith in which she died, and impart consolation to the mourner that hung over her.

Oh, to what a blank, what a cheerless vacuity, did Eugene awake to, from his state of insensibility! and how did he shudder at the thought of the careless manner in which his eye had glanced at the hearse that contained the remains of her on whom his soul had so long dwelt for happiness!

Incapable of any exertion—widowed in every feeling—insensible to all but the greatness of his irreparable loss—what a shock would have been experienced by the family at St. Doulagh's, from the arrival of the remains of Rose, for interment there, being the first announcement of what had happened, but for the consideration of the gentleman she had appointed executor to her will, and who, at the first intimation of her danger, had been summoned by Mrs. Brady. Yet, with all the preparation for the melancholy circumstance, how nearly overwhelmed were they by the sight of the coffin of Rose, instead of Rose herself—beautiful, blooming, happy, as, but a few short days before, they fondly expected to have seen her! how overwhelming their sensations, that for her the bridal chamber had been decked in vain—the halls of her fathers, the followers of her family, prepared to receive her—that to the smile of welcome, the voice of friendship, she could no more respond—that a pillow of earth, a sod of the valley, was all she now required!

It was her dying wish that she should be conveyed to St. Doulagh's for interment; perhaps she may be condemned for the wish, aware, as she must have been, that obedience to it would be a means of keeping alive the grief her death occa-

signed; but perhaps few can so totally ab-
stract themselves from self, as not to wish
to be laid where their cold remains will be
venerated—for, as the poet says,

> " ——who to dumb forgetfulness a prey,
> This pleasing, anxious being ere resign'd,
> Left the warm precincts of the cheerful day,
> Nor cast one longing, ling'ring look behind?"

Incapable of consolation—of dissembling his wretchedness—of evincing any
present sympathy in the joys of others—
the bereaved Eugene was not long in deciding how he would act. Convinced of
the effect which the sight of his sorrow
must have upon the social enjoyments of
those he loved, he determined on bidding
farewell for a season to St. Doulagh's.

His friends rejoiced at his determination; and to render the change of scene
still more salutary, as they hoped, Delamere and Grace offered to accompany
him abroad; but he declined their offer,
from the unbearable restraint which their
company, with all his affection for them,

would have been upon his feelings. He passed to the Continent—nor did they hear more of him, till a letter was received, informing them of his having joined the patriot cause of Greece.

But for her sympathy in his sorrows, how pure would have been the happiness of Grace!—indeed, she often thought, almost too perfect, if every thing had turned out as she once fondly hoped and expected.

Two years have elapsed since the melancholy event that forced Eugene from his native country; yet still is the memory of the dear departed as fondly cherished as ever: but remaining in the place where they grew up together—where to look around without being reminded of her was impossible, it could not be otherwise; nor would Grace, if she could, have ceased to think of her—for the bitterness of grief assuaged, there is a pleasure in the tender regret with which we dwell on the recollection of those we have lost, that soothes the heart that cherishes it, in the idea that those we lament are now bright inhabitants of illimitable space, where, in the course of a few short years, the mourned and the mourners will be reunited, no more to be separated.

FINIS.

Printed by J. Darling, Leadenhall-street, London.

Lightning Source UK Ltd.
Milton Keynes UK
UKHW051847270520
363881UK00012B/195